JOURNEYS
COMMON CORE

Program Authors

James F. Baumann · David J. Chard · Jamal Cooks
J. David Cooper · Russell Gersten · Marjorie Lipson
Lesley Mandel Morrow · John J. Pikulski · Héctor H. Rivera
Mabel Rivera · Shane Templeton · Sheila W. Valencia
Catherine Valentino · MaryEllen Vogt

Consulting Author
Irene Fountas

Houghton
Mifflin
Harcourt

COMMON CORE

Unit 1

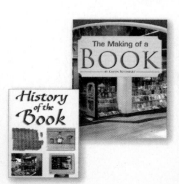

Unit 2

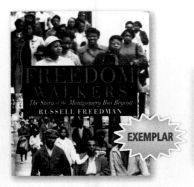

Freedom Walkers
INFORMATIONAL TEXT
by Russell Freedman

EXEMPLAR

Unit 3

Unit 4

Unit 5

Welcome, Reader!

You're about to set out on a reading journey that will take you from ancient Egypt to the modern world of robots. On the way, you'll learn amazing things as you become a better reader.

Your reading journey begins with a story about a young girl who is writing a book of her own.

Plenty of other reading adventures lie ahead. Just turn the page!

Sincerely,

The Authors

Unit 1

Vocabulary in Context

☑ TARGET VOCABULARY

publishing
manuscript
editorial
pressuring
disclose
maze
literary
revisions
wry
muted

Vocabulary Reader

Context Cards

 COMMON CORE **L.6.6** acquire and use general academic and domain-specific words and phrases/gather vocabulary knowledge for comprehension or expression

1 **publishing**

A publishing company prints millions of copies of books for people to buy and read.

2 **manuscript**

An author first writes a manuscript of a story. Later, those pages may become a book.

3 **editorial**

The editorial director is in charge of the department that corrects early versions of a book.

4 **pressuring**

Readers sometimes send letters pressuring, or urging, an author to bring back a favorite character.

Go Digital

▶ Study each Context Card.

▶ Use two Vocabulary words to tell about an experience you had.

5 disclose

The middle of a book might disclose, or reveal, a surprising event in the plot of the story.

6 maze

A writer's office may be a maze, a confusing path among books, papers, and computer equipment.

7 literary

A writer might need to hire a literary agent, someone whose business has to do with books.

8 revisions

An editor often asks the author to make revisions, or changes, to his or her writing.

9 wry

The author Studs Terkel wrote with a wry sense of humor, finding reasons to smile at the difficulties of life.

10 muted

A critic may include muted, or quiet, criticism in an otherwise favorable book review.

Read and Comprehend

Go Digital

☑ TARGET SKILL

Understanding Characters The **characters** in "The School Story" reveal a great deal about their personalities through such clues as their thoughts, words, and actions. As you read the story, use these clues, or text evidence, to help you understand how the characters respond to story events or change as a result. Use a graphic organizer like this one to help you.

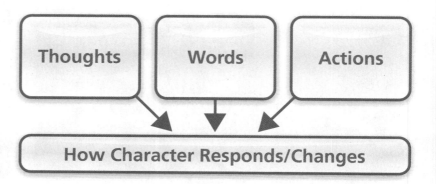

☑ TARGET STRATEGY

Question To deepen your understanding, ask **questions** before you read, as you read, and after you read.

COMMON CORE   **RL.6.3** describe how a story's or drama's plot unfolds and how characters respond or change

Personal Expression

People express who they are as individuals in many ways. Some people choose to express themselves through how they dress or wear their hair. People may even choose to write stories or create art as ways to express themselves.

How do you choose to express your talents and individuality? In "The School Story," Natalie is a talented writer. She wants to become a best-selling author, so she and her best friend, Zoe, come up with an unusual plan to get Natalie's first novel published.

ANCHOR TEXT

✓ TARGET SKILL

Understanding Characters

Use what the characters say, do, and think to explain how they respond and change in the story.

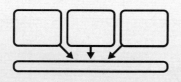

✓ GENRE

Realistic fiction has characters and events that are like people and events in real life. As you read, look for:

▸ realistic events
▸ characters who have feelings that real people have
▸ real-life challenges

COMMON CORE **RL.6.3** describe how a story's or drama's plot unfolds and how characters respond or change; **RL.6.4** determine the meaning of words and phrases, including figurative and connotative meanings/ analyze impact of word choice; **RL.6.10** read and comprehend literature

MEET THE AUTHOR

Andrew Clements

How has Andrew Clements written over fifty books, including such popular school stories as *Frindle*, *The Landry News*, and *Lunch Money*? He explains, "You don't have to do everything at once. You don't have to know how every story is going to end. You just have to take that next step, look for that next idea, write that next word."

MEET THE ILLUSTRATOR

C. F. Payne

C. F. Payne is known for his ability to make a picture look very real and very funny at the same time. In 1999, he completed a mural for Cincinnati Playhouse in the Park in his hometown of Cincinnati, Ohio. The mural depicts actors and playwrights whose work has been performed in that theater.

THE SCHOOL STORY

by Andrew Clements

selection illustrated by
C. F. Payne

ESSENTIAL QUESTION

How can the choices you make affect relationships with other people?

Natalie Nelson's widowed mother, Hannah, is a children's book editor at Shipley Junior Books. Hannah's boss, Letha, is pressuring her to find a "school story" that will become the company's next best-selling book. Natalie thinks "The Cheater," a novel she just wrote, could be that book— but she doesn't want to disclose her true identity. Natalie's friend, Zoe Reisman, comes up with a daring plan: turn Natalie into author Cassandra Day and Zoe into her agent, Zee Zee from the Sherry Clutch Agency! All Natalie has to do is make sure her story ends up with Hannah rather than with Hannah's coworker, Ella, keeper of unread manuscripts.

Natalie got off the elevator at Shipley Junior Books at 4:25. She walked to the desk and handed a thick brown envelope to the receptionist. Natalie smiled and said, "A messenger brought this— it's for my mom. Do you need to check it in, or can I take it right back to her?"

He looked at the address label and said, "All it needs is a date stamp and my initials." The stamp made a mechanical *ca-chonk* sound as he pressed it onto the front of the envelope, and then he scribbled his initials below the date. Now the package looked official. "Here you go." He handed the envelope back to Natalie, then pushed the security button to open the door for her.

Natalie wound her way through the maze to her mom's office. Her mouth was dry. Even though she'd been here a hundred times, she felt like a spy sneaking into a strange building.

"Hi, Mom."

As her mom swung her chair around and smiled, Natalie glanced at the phone console on the desk beside the computer screen. The Message Waiting light was dark. That meant her mom had already listened to Zee Zee's message.

"Here," Natalie said, and she handed the envelope to her mom. "This is for you."

ANALYZE THE TEXT

Simile The author says that Natalie "felt like a spy" in her mother's office. Why might Natalie feel this way about herself?

Hannah Nelson looked at the envelope. The large address label was printed in bright green ink. She read the return address aloud. "'The Sherry Clutch Literary Agency'? I just had a message from this agent, but I don't think I know her. . . . Oh, well." And she dropped the envelope onto the papers beside her computer. "Could you get me a juice or something, Natalie? I didn't even stop for lunch today."

Natalie returned with two bottles of apple juice and some shortbread cookies. Her mom held up her bottle for a toast, and when Natalie clinked it, her mom said, "Here's to our weekend!"

And at that moment Letha walked in. She stepped across the space carefully and leaned over to look at Hannah's computer screen. Natalie caught the sharp scent of Letha's perfume and took a step backward.

With a strained smile Letha said, "I love the weekend too, but I don't think it's quite here yet. Have you double-checked all those revisions, Hannah? The production manager is calling me for that text every half hour, and we can't get out of here until it's released."

Glancing around Hannah's workspace, she snatched up the new envelope and said, "What's this?"

Hannah said, "That? It's just a manuscript. Must be a new agency—Sherry something."

Letha read the label. "Sherry Clutch . . . oh, yes, I believe I've heard of her. She's supposed to be very bright. Listen—buzz me the second you're sure all those revisions check out, okay? And I want you to give this a look over the weekend." Letha dropped the envelope on Hannah's lap and swept out of the office.

Hannah shook her head and gave Natalie a wry smile. "So much for the weekend, eh? Listen, I've got to get back to work. Tim is probably gone by now, so you can hang out over there, okay?"

Natalie said, "Sure, Mom."

As she walked over to Tim's cubicle, Natalie tried not to smile. The editorial director of Shipley Junior Books had just pretended that she knew all about the Sherry Clutch Literary Agency. And then she had ordered her best editor to read a novel written by a twelve-year-old.

Alone in Tim's office, Natalie grinned. For the first time ever she was glad that her mom's boss was a fire-breathing, stuck-up know-it-all.

After Letha told her mom to read the manuscript, Cassandra Day couldn't wait to tell her agent about this unexpected development.

Natalie actually picked up the phone in Tim's office and dialed half of Zoe's number. Then she stopped and asked herself, *Do I really want Zoe calling me every five minutes all weekend long asking me, "Has she read it? Has she read it yet?"* Natalie hung up the phone.

Then she picked it up and dialed the number again. Zoe deserved some kind of progress report. *But she doesn't need to know everything—bad enough that one of us has to worry the whole weekend.*

"Zoe Reisman's room at the Reisman residence, Zoe Reisman speaking."

Natalie kept her voice low because her mom's office was only ten feet away. "Zoe? It's me. The manuscript is here. It's in my mom's office."

Zoe was excited. "Great! Is she going to read it? Did she listen to my message? Do you think she suspects anything?"

"I know she got your message, and she doesn't suspect a thing. And I'm pretty sure she's going to read it. So we'll just have to see what happens next."

"You know," said Zoe slowly, "you could maybe help things along. You know, like pick up the envelope and say, 'I wonder if this one's any good'—something like that."

Natalie smiled, but she talked in a serious voice. She wanted Zoe to calm down. "No, I think we better just let things move ahead on their own. If there's no action in a week or so, then maybe you can call her again."

Zoe did not like that idea. "A week? Are you crazy? A week is forever! If I don't hear from her in three days, then I'm going to turn the heat up—way up!"

"Look, Zee Zee, relax. I've got to get off the phone now, but I'll let you know if anything else happens, okay?"

Zoe said, "Hey! Maybe you could offer to read it for her—you know, help out around the office?"

"Zoe?" said Natalie. "No. No, no, no. Just be patient."

"Yeah," said Zoe, "easy for you to say."

"No, it isn't easy for me to say, Zoe. I want to know what she thinks about it as much as you do. But we're just going to have to let it move along one step at a time, okay?"

There was a pause, and then Zoe said, "Okay. You're right . . . I guess."

"I'll call you if there's any news, I promise."

"Okay," said Zoe. "Bye."

ANALYZE THE TEXT

Dialogue What does the exchange between Natalie and Zoe on pages 24–25 reveal about both their personalities?

When they finally left the office at seven-fifteen on Friday night, Natalie could see the envelope from the Sherry Clutch Literary Agency sticking up from the outside pocket of her mom's briefcase.

Natalie tried to think. She tried to decide what she was feeling. She couldn't figure out if she was happy or scared or numb or what. Because what Zoe had said at the very beginning was true now. All of a sudden her mom wasn't just her mom. She was her editor. Hannah Nelson would be the first person to read "The Cheater" in a professional way. Her own mom would be comparing Natalie's story to all the other manuscripts she had read during the past five years at Shipley Junior Books—manuscripts written by successful, established, professional authors. Part of Natalie wanted to snatch that envelope out of her mom's briefcase and toss it into a trash barrel. But it was too late for that. The day of judgment had arrived.

But that day wasn't Friday. Friday night when they got home, Natalie and her mom went right out again and ate at a Chinese restaurant and then caught a late movie at the local theater—one of those British movies where half the actors wear fancy clothes and the other half look like beggars. It was a lively story with plenty of action and a little bit of romance, but Natalie couldn't stay focused on it. Her mind kept wandering back to that envelope, still in the briefcase, sitting on a chair in the entryway of their loft.

And Saturday wasn't judgment day either. In the morning they went grocery shopping, and then there was the laundry, and then they both spent two hours cleaning the loft from one end to the other. And then it was dinner time.

Natalie went to her room to read after dinner, hoping that if she left her mom alone, she'd remember the manuscript. At about nine o'clock Natalie opened her bedroom door and walked softly toward the living-room area. Peeking from behind the big, leafy plants that framed the living room, she saw her mom. She was asleep on the couch, feet propped up on the coffee table, open magazine on her lap, bathed in flickering light from the muted TV.

Lying in bed later, Natalie tossed and turned. She thought about the heap of envelopes stacked up in Ella's darkened office. For every envelope there was a person somewhere, and Natalie knew how each of them felt. Those people were out there tonight, sleeping in hundreds of different beds in hundreds of different towns in dozens of different states. Every day each person woke up and thought, "Maybe the editor will read my story today," or "Maybe the editor will call me today." Every day each writer wondered if the mail would bring a letter, maybe good news from New York City.

And Natalie felt guilty. *Her* envelope wasn't in a heap somewhere in a dark office. Her story was in the editor's briefcase. The editor's boss had assigned *her* story as homework.

Natalie sat up in bed and looked at the clock. It was almost midnight. She groped for the phone on her bed stand and punched the glowing buttons.

Zoe answered on the third ring, groggy and grumpy. "Hello?"

"It's me, Zoe. I've got to tell you what happened."

It took Natalie about two minutes to tell Zoe how her story found its way home with the editor for the weekend.

Zoe was wide awake now. "So she read it? Did she like it? What did she say when she finished it? C'mon, tell me, tell me!"

"Well . . . she hasn't read it . . . not yet."

"She hasn't read it? So why did you call me in the middle of the night?"

Natalie hesitated. "Because . . . because I feel bad. I feel like the girl in my book. I feel like I'm a cheater too. All those other stories at my mom's office, stories that she'll never even look at? And here's my story, and it's all the way up at the head of the line. It just doesn't feel fair. That's all."

"Not fair? Who said things are fair? It's never fair, Natalie. You're a great writer, and someone like me isn't—is that fair? Is it?"

"Well . . . no. I guess not," said Natalie. "But you're great at things I stink at."

"Exactly," said Zoe. "It all evens out. It seems unfair, but it's not. Your mom is a good editor at a good publishing company, and someone else's mom isn't. Is that fair?"

"No . . . not really."

"Of course it's not fair. It's just the way it is. Didn't you have to work hard to write your book—just as hard as those other writers did?"

Natalie nodded as she answered. "Yeah, I did. I worked hard."

"So do you know why your book is going to get looked at and some of those other ones aren't? It's because you are who you are, and your mom is who she is, and you worked hard to write a great book."

Zoe paused to let that sink in. Then she said, "And there's another reason your book will get published and most of those others won't."

Natalie asked, "Why's that?"

In her best agent voice Zoe said, "Because you have a great agent, and those other schnooks don't! Now listen, Cassandra. I'm giving you good advice, you hear me? You hang up now and get a good night's sleep. And just stop thinking so much. You artists are all alike—thinking, thinking, thinking! Not to worry, darling. Zee Zee is going to take good care of you."

After hanging up, Natalie felt better, but it still took her another hour to get to sleep.

And even after her lecture to Cassandra, Zee Zee lay awake doing some thinking of her own.

> **ANALYZE THE TEXT**
>
> **Understanding Characters** How does Natalie feel now about what she did with "The Cheater" manuscript?

Then on Sunday it happened. It was late in the afternoon, and after finishing her math and English, Natalie settled into her beanbag chair to read about ancient Egypt in her social studies book. The chair was so comfortable, and she had stayed up too late the night before. The next thing Natalie knew, her mom was shaking her awake.

"Natalie, you won't believe this! You know this manuscript Letha made me bring home? Well, I opened it up, you know, just so I could tell her I looked at it? And I started reading it, and it's just . . . well, I couldn't stop reading! It's one of the best things I've read in a long time—and besides that, it's even a school story! Isn't that great?"

Natalie wanted to throw her arms around her mom's neck and burst into tears. She wanted to say, "It's mine, Mom! I wrote that! I wrote it for you, and I wrote it for Dad, and I'm so happy that you like it!"

But she couldn't, so she didn't. Instead Natalie gulped, and she smiled and said, "That's great, Mom. So, it's really good?"

Her mom nodded excitedly. "It's got such a wonderful feeling all through it . . . I mean, it needs some work here and there, but this Cassandra Day—that's the author—it's her first novel, and for a first novel it's terrific. I can't wait for you to read it."

And Natalie nodded and said, "I'd love to."

Dig Deeper

How to Analyze the Text

Use these pages to learn about Understanding Characters, Dialogue, and Similes. Then read "The School Story" again to apply what you learned.

Understanding Characters

Authors of realistic fiction create **characters** who are much like people in real life. They provide details, clues, and other text evidence to help readers figure out who the characters are and what they are like.

As you reread the realistic fiction selection "The School Story," think about the characters' thoughts, words, and actions. Use this text evidence to help you understand how the characters change or respond to story events as the plot moves toward a resolution.

Look back at page 31. How does Natalie's mom, Hannah, respond after she reads Natalie's manuscript? What do you learn about Hannah from this part of the story?

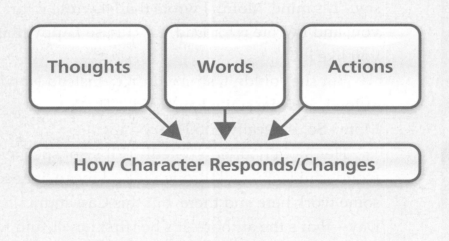

| Thoughts | Words | Actions |

How Character Responds/Changes

 RL.6.3 describe how a story's or drama's plot unfolds and how characters respond or change; **RL.6.4** determine the meaning of words and phrases, including figurative and connotative meanings/analyze impact of word choice

Dialogue

Written **dialogue** is a conversation between two or more characters in a story. Authors use dialogue to develop a story's plot and to reveal characters' personalities. For example, two characters discussing a topic or an issue they are dealing with can show how they think and feel about that topic or issue. As you reread "The School Story," think about what dialogue reveals about the characters' personalities.

Similes

Authors often use figures of speech to make interesting comparisons. A **simile** is a figure of speech that uses *like* or *as* to compare two very unlike things. A young man in a story who says "I felt like a turtle competing in the Kentucky Derby" is comparing himself to a turtle in order to say he felt slow as he ran a race. As you reread "The School Story," look for similes used to convey a character's thoughts and feelings and ask yourself why the character feels or thinks that way.

Your Turn

RETURN TO THE ESSENTIAL QUESTION

Turn and Talk

Review the selection with a partner to prepare to discuss this question: *How can the choices you make affect relationships with other people?* As you discuss, ask questions about your partner's answers. Cite text evidence to explain your own answers.

Classroom Conversation

Continue your discussion of "The School Story" by explaining your answers to these questions:

1. How do you think Natalie's mom would respond if she knew that Natalie was the author of the manuscript?

2. How might the story change if Natalie told her mom in the beginning that she wanted to publish a novel?

3. What are the good and bad points about Natalie and Zoe's plan?

DEVELOPING CHARACTERS

An Author's Creation Some authors create characters a little like themselves. Think about the characters Zoe and Natalie. Work with a partner to discuss what these characters might reveal about the author of "The School Story." Use stated details that show how the characters respond to story events, along with inferences about the characters, as evidence to support your ideas. Ask questions as needed to help you understand your partner's ideas.

WRITE ABOUT READING

Response Natalie uses a pen name (Cassandra Day), invents an agent (Zee Zee at the Sherry Clutch Literary Agency), and gives her manuscript directly to an editor (her mother). Do you agree or disagree that Natalie is "cheating" by using a pen name and delivering her manuscript to her mother? Does she take advantage of her mother's role at the publishing company? Write a paragraph to explain your opinion. Use reasons and evidence from the story to support your claims.

Writing Tip

State your opinion at the beginning of your response. Then organize reasons and evidence clearly to help readers understand your argument.

COMMON CORE **RL.6.1** cite textual evidence to support analysis of what the text says explicitly as well as inferences drawn; **W.6.1a** introduce claim(s) and organize reasons and evidence clearly; **W.6.1b** support claim(s) with reasons and evidence, using credible sources and demonstrating understanding of the topic or text; **W.6.9a** apply grade 6 Reading standards to literature **SL.6.1a** come to discussions prepared/explicitly draw on preparation to probe and reflect on ideas under discussion; **SL.6.1c** pose and respond to questions and make comments that contribute to the discussion

ELEVEN

by Sandra Cisneros

What they don't understand about birthdays and what they never tell you is that when you're eleven, you're also ten, and nine, and eight, and seven, and six, and five, and four, and three, and two, and one. And when you wake up on your eleventh birthday you expect to feel eleven, but you don't. You open your eyes and everything's just like yesterday, only it's today. And you don't feel eleven at all. You feel like you're still ten. And you are—underneath the year that makes you eleven.

Like some days you might say something stupid, and that's the part of you that's still ten. Or maybe some days you might need to sit on your mama's lap because you're scared, and that's the part of you that's five. And maybe one day when you're all grown up maybe you will need to cry like if you're three, and that's okay. That's what I tell Mama when she's sad and needs to cry. Maybe she's feeling three.

Because the way you grow old is kind of like an onion or like the rings inside a tree trunk or like my little wooden dolls that fit one inside the other, each year inside the next one. That's how being eleven years old is.

You don't feel eleven. Not right away. It takes a few days, weeks even, sometimes even months before you say Eleven when they ask you. And you don't feel smart eleven, not until you're almost twelve. That's the way it is.

Only today I wish I didn't have only eleven years rattling inside me like pennies in a tin Band-Aid box. Today I wish I was one hundred and two instead of eleven because if was one hundred and two I'd have known what to say when Mrs. Price put the red sweater on my desk. I would've known how to tell her it wasn't mine instead of just sitting there with that look on my face and nothing coming out of my mouth.

"Whose is this?" Mrs. Price says, and she holds the red sweater up in the air for all the class to see. "Whose? It's been sitting in the coatroom for a month."

"Not mine," says everybody. "Not me."

"It has to belong to somebody," Mrs. Price keeps saying, but nobody can remember. It's an ugly sweater with red plastic buttons and a collar and sleeves all stretched out like you could use it for a jump rope. It's maybe a thousand years old and even if it belonged to me I wouldn't say so.

Maybe because I'm skinny, maybe because she doesn't like me, that stupid Sylvia Saldívar says, "I think it belongs to Rachel." An ugly sweater like that, all raggedy and old, but Mrs. Price believes her. Mrs. Price takes the sweater and puts it right on my desk, but when I open my mouth nothing comes out.

"That's not, I don't, you're not… Not mine," I finally say in a little voice that was maybe me when I was four.

"Of course it's yours," Mrs. Price says. "I remember you wearing it once." Because she's older and the teacher, she's right and I'm not.

Not mine, not mine, not mine, but Mrs. Price is already turning to page thirty-two, and math problem number four. I don't know why but all of a sudden I'm feeling sick inside, like the part of me that's three wants to come out of my eyes, only I squeeze them shut tight and bite down on my teeth real hard and try to remember today I am eleven, eleven. Mama is making a cake for me tonight, and when Papa comes home everybody will sing Happy birthday, happy birthday to you.

But when the sick feeling goes away and I open my eyes, the red sweater's still sitting there like a big red mountain. I move the red sweater to the corner of my desk with my ruler. I move my pencil and books and eraser as far from it as possible. I even move my chair a little to the right. Not mine, not mine, not mine.

In my head I'm thinking how long till lunchtime, how long till I can take the red sweater and throw it over the school yard fence, or even leave it hanging on a parking meter, or bunch it up into a little ball and toss it in the alley. Except when math period ends Mrs. Price says loud and in front of everybody, "Now Rachel, that's enough," because she sees I've shoved the red sweater to the tippy-tip corner of my desk and it's hanging all over the edge like a waterfall, but I don't care.

"Rachel," Mrs. Price says. She says it like she's getting mad. "You put that sweater on right now and no more nonsense."

"But it's not—"

"Now!" Mrs. Price says.

This is when I wish I wasn't eleven, because all the years inside of me—ten, nine, eight, seven, six, five, four, three, two and one—are pushing at the back of my eyes when I put one arm through one sleeve of the sweater that smells like cottage cheese, and then the other arm through the other and stand there with my arms apart like if the sweater hurts me and it does, all itchy and full of germs that aren't even mine.

That's when everything I've been holding in since this morning, since when Mrs. Price put the sweater on my desk, finally lets go, and all of a sudden I'm crying in front of everybody. I wish I was invisible but I'm not. I'm eleven and it's my birthday today and I'm crying like I'm three in front of everybody. I put my head down on the desk and bury my face in my stupid clown-sweater arms. My face all hot and spit coming out of my mouth because I can't stop the little animal noises from coming out of me, until there aren't any more tears left in my eyes, and it's just my body shaking like when you have the hiccups, and my whole head hurts like when you drink milk too fast.

But the worst part is right before the bell rings for lunch. That stupid Phyllis Lopez, who is even dumber than Sylvia Saldívar, says she remembers the red sweater is hers! I take it off right away and give it to her, only Mrs. Price pretends like everything's okay.

Today I'm eleven. There's cake Mama's making for tonight, and when Papa comes home from work we'll eat it. There'll be candles and presents and everybody will sing Happy birthday, happy birthday to you, Rachel, only it's too late.

I'm eleven today. I'm eleven, ten, nine, eight, seven, six, five, four, three, two, and one, but I wish I was one hundred and two. I wish I was anything but eleven, because I want today to be far away already, far away like a runaway balloon, like a tiny *o* in the sky, so tiny-tiny you have to close your eyes to see it.

Compare Texts

TEXT TO TEXT

Compare Characters Work with a partner to talk about "The School Story" and "Eleven." Compare and contrast how both Natalie in "The School Story" and Rachel in "Eleven" respond to an uncomfortable situation. Work together to discuss your ideas and then write your answers. Use stated details from both stories as evidence to support your ideas.

TEXT TO SELF

Write a Character Sketch In "The School Story," Natalie writes a manuscript called "The Cheater." If you were to write a fiction story, who would your main character be? Write a description of the character. Include details about his or her personality, appearance, and background.

TEXT TO WORLD

Research Birthday Traditions People in different countries celebrate birthdays in different ways. Work with other members of a small group to research how different cultures around the world celebrate birthdays. Include a visual display, and present your research to the class.

RL.6.1 cite textual evidence to support analysis of what the text says explicitly as well as inferences drawn; **SL.6.1c** pose and respond to questions and make comments that contribute to the discussion; **SL.6.5** include multimedia components and visual displays in presentations

COMMON CORE

Grammar

What Is a Sentence? A **sentence** is a group of words that expresses a complete thought. A sentence must include a **complete subject**, all the words that tell whom or what the sentence is about, and a **complete predicate**, all the words that tell what the subject does, is, has, or feels. A **fragment** is missing one or both of these sentence parts.

	complete subject complete predicate
Complete Sentence	My friend writes books about her school.
Fragment (missing a subject)	Writes a chapter every week.
Fragment (missing a predicate)	A skillful and determined writer.

A **run-on sentence** is two or more sentences that are run together with commas or without any punctuation. It is hard to tell where one thought ends and the next one begins.

Run-On Sentence	I like mysteries I also like adventure stories.
Corrected Sentences	I like mysteries. I also like adventure stories.

Try This! The items below are sentence fragments and run-on sentences. On another sheet of paper, correct and rewrite them as complete sentences.

1. A career in writing.

2. The book has colorful characters its plot is fascinating.

3. Are often excellent writers.

4. Editors study a manuscript carefully, they look at every detail.

You can sometimes fix sentence errors in your writing by combining fragments with sentences or other fragments to make complete sentences.

Sentence and Fragment	Combined into One Sentence
Natalie trusted her mother's judgment. And hoped for a good reaction to the manuscript.	Natalie trusted her mother's judgment and hoped for a good reaction to the manuscript.

 Connect Grammar to Writing

As you revise your personal narrative paragraph, make sure you correct any run-on sentences. Rewrite fragments, or combine them with other sentences or fragments to make complete sentences.

Narrative Writing

✔ **Voice**   In a **personal narrative paragraph,** writers tell a true story about a personal experience. They write from the first-person point of view, and they use transition words and phrases to show the sequence of events. As you write your personal narrative paragraph, use precise words and descriptive details. Include dialogue to show your personality.

Isaiah drafted his personal narrative paragraph about buying a new pair of shoes. Later, he added precise words and descriptive details to share his thoughts about the experience.

Writing Traits Checklist

✔ **Ideas**
Did I describe events clearly?

✔ **Organization**
Did I arrange events in time order?

✔ **Sentence Fluency**
Did I combine sentence parts to avoid run-ons?

✔ **Word Choice**
Did I use precise words—strong verbs and adjectives?

✔ **Voice**
Did I show how I felt about the experience?

✔ **Conventions**
Did I use correct spelling, grammar, and punctuation?

Revised Draft

"These are the ~~perfect~~ shoes for you," said Mom.

"They're brown ∧and leather and very sturdy." My eyes

wandered over to the coolest ~~shoes~~ red canvas high-tops I'd ever

seen. You see, every year it's the same routine.

Before school starts, my mom tries to ~~tell~~ convince me

that I need a classic pair of brown shoes. But

not this year! This year is different because I'm

starting sixth grade. I'm leaving behind the

monkey bars and the dreaded boring brown

shoes. ∧I need clothes and shoes that shout, "I'm Isaiah!"

44

The Perfect Shoes

by Isaiah Jackson

."These are the perfect shoes for you," said Mom. "They're brown and leather and very sturdy." My eyes wandered over to the coolest red canvas high-tops I'd ever seen. You see, every year it's the same routine. Before school starts, my mom tries to convince me that I need a classic pair of brown shoes. But not this year! This year is different because I'm starting sixth grade. I'm leaving behind the monkey bars and the dreaded boring brown shoes. I need clothes and shoes that shout, "I'm Isaiah!" I glanced at the red high-tops again. My heart started to race. I wanted to tell Mom that I really, really liked the red high-tops, but I didn't want to sound ungrateful. Suddenly, I saw the wheels turning as Mom's eyes followed my gaze. Then a smile spread across her face. "OK, Isaiah," she said. "Maybe it is time for something different." Yes! Now I would have the perfect pair of shoes.

Reading as a Writer

How does Isaiah reveal his thoughts and feelings? What details can you add to describe your own thoughts and feelings about a personal experience?

In my final paper, I used descriptive words and details to show how I felt about my experience. I also used transition words and phrases to show the sequence of events.

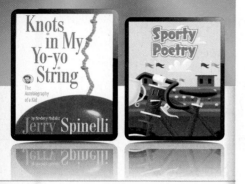

Vocabulary in Context

✓ **TARGET VOCABULARY**

mentor
employed
scholastic
grimly
contested
tumult
pursuit
culprit
deprived
miraculous

Vocabulary Reader   Context Cards

COMMON CORE L.6.6 acquire and use general academic and domain-specific words and phrases/gather vocabulary knowledge for comprehension or expression

46

1 mentor

The job of a mentor, or experienced teacher, is to guide and encourage a person who is learning.

2 employed

Men and women who have done well in sales jobs probably used, or employed, a friendly style.

3 scholastic

Employers look at the scholastic record of a person they might hire. Achievement in school is important.

4 grimly

People who work long hours for low pay often do their work grimly, with no satisfaction.

Go Digital

▶ Study each Context Card.

▶ Make up a new context sentence that uses two Vocabulary words.

5 **contested**

A referee makes many decisions in a game. Some are contested, or challenged, by players.

6 **tumult**

People preparing meals in the kitchen of a restaurant often work in a scene of tumult, or noisy confusion.

7 **pursuit**

A police officer might use flashing lights in pursuit of someone trying to get away after breaking a law.

8 **culprit**

A librarian may not always charge a fine when a culprit, or guilty person, brings back an overdue library book.

9 **deprived**

Workers who are deprived of sleep don't have the energy to do their jobs well.

10 **miraculous**

Scientists have discovered miraculous cures for diseases that were thought to be incurable.

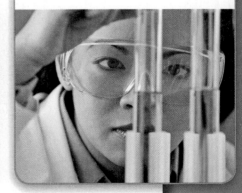

Read and Comprehend

☑ TARGET SKILL

Author's Purpose Every author has a reason, or **purpose**, for writing. Authors may write to give facts or information about a specific topic or to persuade their readers to believe something. Authors may also write to entertain an audience. As you read "Knots in My Yo-yo String," look for details and other text evidence to help you understand why the author wrote the selection. Record these details in a graphic organizer like the one below.

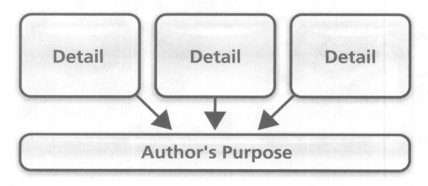

☑ TARGET STRATEGY

Infer/Predict Use text evidence and what you already know to help you **infer**, or figure out, what the author means as well as to **predict** what might happen in the future.

Sports

There is much more to sports than just winning. Physical activity, such as running or cycling, can help keep the body healthy. Learning the rules of a game and communicating with coaches and teammates can challenge an athlete's mind.

Individuals who play sports are not the only ones who benefit from a game. The people who gather to cheer their teams to victory are challenged and inspired, too. In "Knots in My Yo-yo String," you'll learn about how one sports game in particular inspired not only a school but an author as well.

ANCHOR TEXT

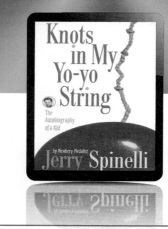

☑ TARGET SKILL

Author's Purpose Use details and other text clues to figure out the author's reason for writing.

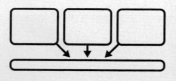

☑ GENRE

An **autobiography** is a true story, or account, of a person's life, written by that person. As you read, look for:

▶ first-person point of view
▶ the author's personal thoughts and feelings
▶ details about important events in the author's life

RI.6.4 determine the meaning of words and phrases, including figurative, connotative, and technical meanings; **RI.6.6** determine the author's point of view or purpose and explain how it is conveyed; **RI.6.10** read and comprehend literary nonfiction

MEET THE AUTHOR

Jerry Spinelli

Jerry Spinelli once wanted to be a cowboy and a baseball player, preferably for the New York Yankees. Then, in the eleventh grade, a football game which you'll read about in *Knots in My Yo-yo String* turned him into a writer. Spinelli says, "Writing is a way of completing my experience. It's like things that I see and feel have not totally happened to me until I write about them." Spinelli's book *Maniac Magee* won the 1991 Newbery Award. His wife, Eileen Spinelli, is also a writer and is the first person to read anything he writes.

Knots in My Yo-yo String

by Jerry Spinelli

ESSENTIAL QUESTION

Why is teamwork important?

On Friday evening, October 11, 1957, at Roosevelt Field, site of my fifty-yard-dash triumph five years before, Norristown High School played Lower Merion in a football game under the lights. Lower Merion was a powerhouse. Over the preceding three years they had won thirty-two games in a row. But Norristown was good, too. It figured to be a close, fiercely contested game, and it was. I was a junior now, sixteen years old, and my autumn sport had become soccer, but I still loved football. I was one of thousands in the grandstand.

As the teams changed field direction for the start of the fourth quarter, Norristown was leading, 7–6. Each team had scored a touchdown, but the Aces of Lower Merion had missed the extra point. But now a Lower Merion halfback was breaking free and racing downfield, blue-and-white-shirted Norristown Eagles in pursuit. The Eagles stopped him on the one-yard line, and the stage was set for one of the great moments in Norristown's scholastic sports history.

First down and goal to go on the one. One little yard. Thirty-six little inches. Lower Merion. Thirty-two straight victories. Who could stop them? In the bleachers across the field the Lower Merion fans celebrated. Norristown fans grimly awaited the inevitable.

The first Ace ball carrier plunged ahead helmet-first, the Lower Merion side erupted in a touchdown roar—but, strangely, no touchdown sign came from the referee. The ball carrier was crumpled in the rude arms of Eagle defender Mike Branca. The ball had advanced nary an inch.

Twice more the Aces ran the ball, attacking different points in the Eagle defense. The results were the same. The sound from the Lower Merion side was rising and falling as if directed by a choirmaster. But now, as the Ace quarterback bent over the center for the fourth time and barked out the count, Roosevelt Field fell silent. For the fourth time the Ace quarterback handed the ball to a running back—they refused to believe anyone could stop them from ramrodding the ball thirty-six little inches—and for the fourth time the ball failed to penetrate the end zone.

The impossible had been done.

Now it was the Norristown side that erupted, with a roar and a celebration that continued through the end of the game and burst from the stadium and spread out across the town and late into the night. I rode the tide. Lower Merion! We had beaten *Lower Merion!* I couldn't believe it. At home in my room I could hear the blaring horns, the shrieks of victory.

Again and again, following my old habit, I replayed the miraculous Eagle goal-line defense in my head. I went to sleep re-experiencing the event, re-feeling the thrill. In the morning I woke up and daydreamed on— and began to realize that I had a problem. For no matter how many times I replayed the goal-line stand in my head, I kept falling short of satisfaction. The scoreboard had said the game was over, but for me it wasn't, for me it was somehow frustratingly incomplete. I discovered that Roosevelt Field was not the only field that the game had been played on; the other was inside myself. The game kept happening and happening within me. I could not come to the end of it.

ANALYZE THE TEXT

Author's Purpose What clues on pages 52 and 53 hint at the author's purpose for writing this selection?

And then for no reason that I can recall, I sat down at my study desk and reached for a pencil and paper and wrote down a title. Then I began to write rhyming verse. And the verses became a poem:

Goal to Go

The score stood 7—6
With but five minutes to go.
The Ace attack employed all tricks
To settle down its stubborn foe.

It looked as though the game was done
When an Ace stepped wide 'round right.
An Eagle stopped him on the one
And tumult filled the night.

Thirty-two had come their way
And thirty-two had died.
Would number thirty-three this day
For one yard be denied?

Roy Kent, the Eagle mentor, said,
"I've waited for this game,
And now, defense, go, stop 'em dead,
And crash the Hall of Fame!"

The first Ace bolted for the goal
And nothing did he see
But Branca, swearing on his soul,
"You shall not pass by me."

The next two plays convinced all
The ref would make the touchdown sign,
But when the light shone on the ball
It still lay inches from the line.

Said Captain Eastwood to his gents,
"It's up to us to stop this drive."
Said Duckworth, Avery, Knerr, and Spence,
"Will do, as long as we're alive."

The halfback drove with all his might,
His legs were jet-propelled,
But when the dust had cleared the fight,
The Eagle line had held.

At last, for me, the game was over.

ANALYZE THE TEXT

Figurative Language What are some examples of figurative language in "Goal to Go" on pages 54-55?

On a September day in 1992, thirty-five years after Norristown High's historic goal-line stand, I stood before an audience of children and adults in Fargo, North Dakota. I was there in connection with my novel *Maniac Magee*, which had recently won the Newbery Medal for children's literature. The important award on this day, however, was the Flicker Tale, which had been voted to *Maniac Magee* as a favorite of North Dakota's young readers. A hundred elementary-school kids sat cross-legged on the floor as I accepted the plaque.

After giving a little talk, I invited the audience to ask questions. There were many. One of them stays with me still. It came from a boy, who said, "Do you think being a kid helped you to become a writer?"

Good question.

After writing "Goal to Go," I gave it to my father and forgot about it. Several days later I opened the *Times Herald* to the sports section, and there was my poem, printed in a box with the headline "Student Waxes Poetic." At school the next day everyone—kids, teachers, football coaches—told me how much they liked it.

That, I believe, was the beginning. By the time I went off to Gettysburg College two years later, I knew I wanted to be a writer.

I graduated from Gettysburg, attended the Writing Seminars at the Johns Hopkins University, spent six months on active duty with the Naval Air Reserve, got a job as a menswear editor for a department store magazine, and in my spare time began to write my first novel.

Three years later I finished it, but no one wanted to publish it. So I wrote another.

And another.

And another.

Wrote them on my lunch hours, after work, weekends. Four novels over thirteen years.

Nobody wanted them.

In the meantime I gained a wife, Eileen, also a writer, and six kids. One day for dinner we had fried chicken. There were leftovers. I packed the unclaimed pieces into a paper bag and put it in the refrigerator, intending to take it to work for lunch the following day. But when I opened the bag early the next morning, I found only chicken bones. The meat had been eaten away.

No doubt this was the work of one of the six little angels sleeping upstairs. Knowing no one would confess (I'm still waiting), I went to work that day lunchless and began to imagine how it might have gone had I known who the culprit was and confronted him or her in the kitchen. By noon I had decided to write down my imaginings. I was about to do so, intending to describe the scene from the point of view of the chicken-deprived father, when it suddenly occurred to me that there was a more interesting point of view here—namely, the kid's.

And so with ballpoint pen and yellow copy paper in a tiny windowless office on the fifth floor of the Chilton Company in Radnor, Pennsylvania, I wrote these words:

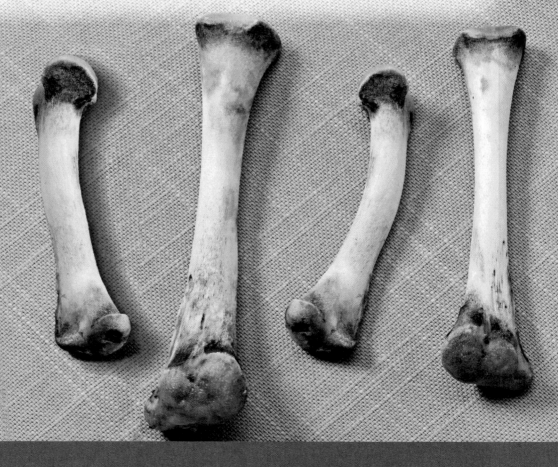

One by one my stepfather took the chicken bones out of the bag and laid them on the kitchen table. He laid them down real neat. In a row. Five of them. Two leg bones, two wing bones, one thigh bone.

And bones is all they were. There wasn't a speck of meat on them.

Was this really happening? Did my stepfather really drag me out of bed at seven o'clock in the morning on my summer vacation so I could stand in the kitchen in my underpants and stare down at a row of chicken bones?

ANALYZE THE TEXT

Point of View Why do you think Jerry Spinelli decided to tell the chicken-bone incident from a different point of view? How does this other point of view make the story more interesting?

That night at home I kept writing. I gave the chicken snatcher a name, Jason, and an age, twelve. And I started remembering. Remembering when I was twelve, when I lived in the West End, when I went to Stewart Junior High School, when I wanted to be a shortstop, when I rode a bike, when I marveled at the nighttime sky. In my head I replayed moments from my kidhood. I mixed my memories with imagination to make stories, to make fiction, and when I finished writing, I had a book, my fifth novel, my first about kids. I called it *Space Station Seventh Grade*.

It became my first published book.

In the years that followed, I continued to write stories about kids and to rummage through the attic of my memories. Norristown became Two Mills in my fiction, George Street became Oriole. There is a prom in one book and a girlfriend named Judy in another. There is a beautiful blonde who lives on an avenue called Haws and a mysterious man on whose front steps no kid dares sit. There is a zep and a mulberry tree, a Little League field, a park, a zoo, a band shell, a red hill, and a mother who whistles her kids home to dinner. There is a river called Schuylkill and a creek called Stony and a grocery store on a corner next to a house whose address is 802. And a brown finger in a white mouth. And a boy who is a wizard at untying knots in yo-yo strings.

Do you think being a kid helped you to become a writer?
I could have taken days to answer the boy's question, but neither he nor Fargo had that much time. So I simply nodded and smiled and said, "Yes, I believe it did."

A budding ballplayer (age 4, 1945)

Shortstop, Green Sox (age 12, 1953)

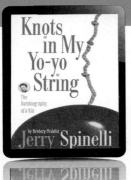

Dig Deeper

How to Analyze the Text

Use these pages to learn about Author's Purpose, Figurative Language, and Point of View. Then read "Knots in My Yo-yo String" again to apply what you learned.

Author's Purpose

Jerry Spinelli, the author of the autobiography "Knots in My Yo-yo String," had a reason, or purpose, for writing about a memorable high school football game. Although his reason for writing is not stated in the selection, he provides many clues that reveal his purpose.

To determine an **author's purpose**, use text evidence such as descriptive words and details about events. Figure out whether the author's purpose is to inform, persuade, or entertain the reader.

Look back at pages 54–55. What event does the author describe? What text evidence does the author give about his purpose for writing?

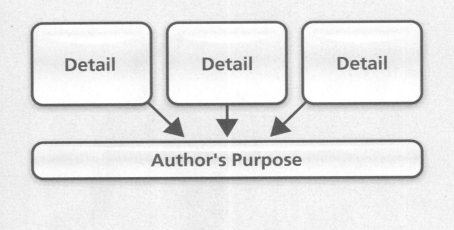

```
Detail        Detail        Detail
                 ↓
          Author's Purpose
```

RI.6.1 cite textual evidence to support analysis of what the text says explicitly as well as inferences drawn; **RI.6.4** determine the meaning of words and phrases, including figurative, connotative, and technical meanings; **RI.6.6** determine the author's point of view or purpose and explain how it is conveyed

Figurative Language

Authors often use **figurative language** to spark their readers' imaginations, but sometimes these words and phrases mean something different from what the words say. Look back at page 53. The author uses the phrase *rode the tide* to describe his excitement. The author did not actually ride the tide in the ocean. Instead, he joined the crowd in celebrating an important football victory.

Point of View

When authors write to inform, persuade, or entertain, they share their perspective, or **point of view**. The point of view lets readers share an experience as seen through an author's eyes. Sometimes authors write about experiences from a point of view that is different from their own. Then readers experience a story as if someone other than the author is telling it.

Your Turn

Turn and Talk Review the selection with a partner to prepare to discuss this question: *Why is teamwork important?* Find text evidence to support your ideas. Take turns explaining key ideas.

Classroom Conversation

Continue your discussion of "Knots in My Yo-yo String" by explaining your answers to these questions:

1. How does the author's choice of title help him make a point?

2. Why do you think Jerry Spinelli includes the description of a football game in his autobiography?

3. In what ways did feedback from kids, teachers, and coaches, as well as rejection by publishers, influence the author?

TWO VIEWS

Compare Descriptions Work with others to discuss why the author includes both the description of the football game on pages 52–53 and his poem about it on pages 54–55. Discuss these questions: *How is the description of the game different from the poem? How are the description and the poem alike? Why is it helpful to have two ways to look at the same football game?*

WRITE ABOUT READING

Response Author Jerry Spinelli says he uses his memories and imagination to write stories. Do you agree or disagree that it takes both to write a good story? Are both essential? Write a paragraph that states your opinion, and support it by sharing what helps you get ideas for stories. Then compare yourself to the author. Do you think alike? Include evidence that shows how Spinelli uses both memories and imagination in his writing.

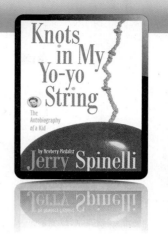

Writing Tip

State your opinion in a complete sentence. Use precise words and transition phrases to link your evidence with your opinion.

COMMON CORE **RI.6.1** cite textual evidence to support analysis of what the text says explicitly as well as inferences drawn; **RI.6.3** analyze in detail how a key individual, event, or idea is introduced, illustrated, and elaborated; **W.6.1a** introduce claim(s) and organize reasons and evidence clearly; **W.6.1c** use words, phrases, and clauses to clarify relationships; **W.6.9b** apply grade 6 Reading standards to literary nonfiction; **SL.6.1c** pose and respond to questions and make comments that contribute to the discussion; **SL.6.1d** review key ideas expressed and demonstrate understanding of multiple perspectives

Lesson 2

POETRY

Sporty
Poetry

✓ GENRE

Poetry uses the sound and rhythm of words in a variety of forms to suggest images and to express feelings.

✓ TEXT FOCUS

Line breaks vary the rhythm of a poem. A limerick has regular breaks after each rhyme. Other poems may break lines in unusual ways.

RL.6.10 read and comprehend literature

Go Digital

Sporty Poetry

A poem about sports, like Jerry Spinelli's "Goal to Go," can capture the tumult of an exciting game or a pursuit downfield. It can capture a miraculous victory or a contested call by an umpire who said a base-stealer was safe when the culprit seemed to be out! A sports poem can scold a mentor, as "Quitter" does. It can recall the good and bad times in many seasons, as "We Have Our Moments" does. Sports poems can also be funny, like the two limericks on page 68.

Quitter

Coach calls me a quitter
He mutters it under his breath
Loud enough for me to hear,
But quiet enough
So no one knows
When I prove him wrong.

Janet Wong

We Have Our Moments

Sometimes we leap and land.
Sometimes we trip and fall.
Sometimes we catch the other team before they score.
Sometimes we jump too soon and get faked out of our
socks.

We can be sharp on the pick-up play at third.
Or
we can have rocks in our heads and miss that
softly batted ball,
and miss that
one
sweet chance to
save
the
day.

I lose. I win. We lose. We win.
The team finishes in last place.
The team is
in the play-offs at last
and past defeats f a d e
fast.
We   have   our   moments.

Arnold Adoff

When I step on the basketball court,
They all jeer, "In your dreams! You're too short!"
Do I get in a funk?
Nope. I calmly slam dunk.
I would say I'm a pretty good sport.

Rob Hale

A bicycle racer named Raleigh
Told the cheering crowd, "Thanks! But, by golly,
I couldn't have done it—
I'd never have won it—
Without my dear passenger, Wally!"

Rob Hale

Write a Sports Poem

Write a poem about a sport you enjoy. Try a poem about a team deprived of a win, going grimly home. Write about a scholastic athlete who has employed a tricky move to score. Any idea will do!

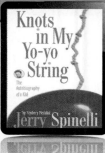

Compare Texts

Compare Poetry Choose a poem from "Sporty Poetry" and compare and contrast it with "Goal to Go." Discuss these questions with a partner: *Which poem is about not giving up? How does each poem tell about a game or sports event? How are the formats of each poem different?* After you have discussed your ideas, work together to write an answer to each question. Use text evidence from the poems to support your answers.

Write About Inspirations A football game and leftover chicken bones inspired Jerry Spinelli to write. Make a list of five things or events in your life that could inspire a poem or story. Explain why each is inspirational.

Guess the Famous Person Well-known authors are not the only people who write autobiographies. Use online or print resources to find an autobiography of a famous person. List the three most interesting facts you learn about the person. Share these facts with a partner, and have him or her guess the identity of your subject.

RL.6.9 compare and contrast texts in different forms or genres on their approaches to themes and topics; **W.6.7** conduct short research projects to answer a question, drawing on several sources and refocusing the inquiry when appropriate; **SL.6.1c** pose/respond to questions and make comments that contribute to the discussion; **SL.6.1d** review key ideas expressed and demonstrate understanding of multiple perspectives

COMMON CORE

Grammar

What Are the Four Kinds of Sentences? A **declarative sentence** makes a statement. It ends with a period. An **interrogative sentence** asks a question. It ends with a question mark. An **imperative sentence** gives a command. It ends with a period. An **exclamatory sentence** expresses strong feeling. It ends with an exclamation point.

Sentence	Kind of Sentence
Jerry Spinelli watched an exciting football game.	declarative
Did he write a poem about it?	interrogative
Turn to the sports section.	imperative
The paper has printed Jerry's poem!	exclamatory

Try This! **Work with a partner. Read each sentence below. Tell what kind of sentence it is.**

1 What is your favorite sport?

2 Think of a memorable game or match.

3 You can write a poem about it.

4 Create pictures with your words.

5 What an exciting match it must have been!

You can make your writing more interesting by varying the types of sentences and the ways the sentences begin. Writing that includes questions, exclamations, and commands, as well as declarative sentences, can help hold readers' attention.

Same Sentence Type

Some people thought Norristown could beat Lower Merion. Norristown won, and blaring horns and shrieks of victory announced the result.

Varied Sentence Types

Could Norristown actually beat Lower Merion? Blaring horns and shrieks of victory announced that Norristown had won!

Connect Grammar to Writing

As you revise your personal narrative, make sure you vary the types of sentences you use. Look for places where changing a sentence to a different type could add interest and variety to your writing.

W.6.3a engage and orient the reader by establishing a context and introducing a narrator or character/organize an event sequence; **W.6.3b** use narrative techniques to develop experiences, events, and characters; **W.6.3c** use transition words, phrases, and clauses to convey sequence or setting; **W.6.3d** use precise words and phrases, descriptive details, and sensory details; **W.6.3e** provide a conclusion

Narrative Writing

✔️ **Voice** In a **personal narrative,** writers tell a true story about something important to them. They write from the first-person point of view and use precise, vivid words to describe their thoughts, feelings, and reactions. Writing with voice helps readers connect with the writer in a personal way. As you revise your personal narrative, add sensory details that describe what you see, hear, smell, taste, or touch. Use transition words and phrases to show the sequence of events. End with a conclusion.

Willow wrote a first draft of her personal narrative about a soccer game. Later, she added precise words and sensory details to describe how she felt.

Writing Traits Checklist

✔️ **Ideas**
Did I make my ideas interesting?

✔️ **Organization**
Did I give my narrative a beginning, a middle, and an ending?

✔️ **Sentence Fluency**
Did I vary sentence types?

✔️ **Word Choice**
Did I use precise, vivid, sensory words?

✔️ **Voice**
Did I reveal my thoughts and feelings?

✔️ **Conventions**
Did I use correct spelling, grammar, and punctuation?

Revised Draft

Last Saturday was the day of our big soccer

game against the Sonics, our toughest rival.

All of us on the Rockets were very excited,

even though we'd lost our last two games.
                    nervous but eager
I felt ~~I wanted~~ to help my team win. It was the
     ∧

last four minutes of the game. The score was
        My stomach churned and my throat was dry
tied at 2-2. ~~I was scared~~, but the
            ∧
          ' cheers spurred me on
fans ~~helped me~~. We were running out of time
    ∧

and luck.

Lucky Enough

by Willow Tucker

Last Saturday was the day of our big soccer game against the Sonics, our toughest rival. All of us on the Rockets were very excited, even though we'd lost our last two games. I felt nervous but eager to help my team win. It was the last four minutes of the game. The score was tied at 2–2. My stomach churned and my throat was dry, but the fans' cheers spurred me on. We were running out of time and luck.

Marya kicked the ball to me, and I ran it toward the net to make the perfect goal. Suddenly, my neighbor's dog Lucky ran across the field and in front of me. His leash was dragging behind him, right into my path! Mr. Chin yelled, "Lucky, come back here!" but Lucky kept running. My foot got caught in his leash. I fell in a heap on the field. My perfect goal didn't happen, and I felt defeated. In a flash, though, my teammate Sophie took over, smacking the ball into the net to score the winning goal.

After the game, Mr. Chin apologized. He explained that Lucky had been chasing a squirrel. I patted Lucky on the head and said, "It's okay. You were just being a dog. We won anyway, so I guess it was our 'lucky' day after all."

Reading as a Writer

Which words did Willow add to make her writing more descriptive? How can you make your narrative more descriptive?

In my final paper, I made sure the description and dialogue revealed my thoughts and feelings. I also made sure I used vivid, sensory words to describe events and how I felt.

Vocabulary in Context

The Making of a BOOK
BY KAREN ROTHBART

History of the Book

☑ TARGET VOCABULARY

painstaking
exploded
submitted
negotiations
collaborate
repetitive
appealing
complement
appropriate
impaired

Vocabulary Reader

Context Cards

COMMON CORE **L.6.6** acquire and use general academic and domain-specific words and phrases/gather vocabulary knowledge for comprehension or expression

74

1 painstaking
Long ago, books were made through the painstaking process of copying by hand.

2 exploded
The number of digital books exploded once electronic readers became affordable.

3 submitted
These drawings have been submitted for judging in an art contest.

4 negotiations
The negotiations between the writer and publisher lasted for hours before they agreed.

Go Digital

▶ Study each Context Card.

▶ Discuss one picture. Use a different Vocabulary word from the one in the card.

---

5 collaborate

Architects and construction workers collaborate to make new buildings.

---

6 repetitive

The repetitive exercise of writing his name over and over caused his hand to hurt.

---

7 appealing

The library is an appealing place because of its calm and quiet atmosphere.

---

8 complement

The designers created stage props to complement the mood of the play.

---

9 appropriate

It was appropriate that he scored low on the test since he did not study for it.

---

10 impaired

This physically impaired athlete competes in wheelchair racing.

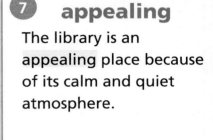

Read and Comprehend

☑ TARGET SKILL

Sequence of Events As you read "The Making of a Book," keep track of the **sequence,** or time order, of **events** in the history and development of books. Dates and signal words such as *first*, *after*, *next*, and *finally* can help you understand the sequence in which events happened and how they fit in the overall structure of the text. Authors also use chapters to organize sections of related events or information. Use a graphic organizer like this one to help you keep track of the sequence of events.

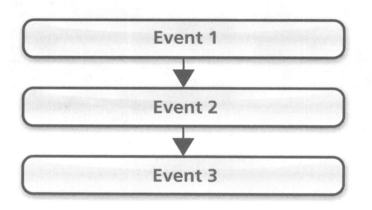

Event 1

↓

Event 2

↓

Event 3

☑ TARGET STRATEGY

Analyze/Evaluate Good readers **analyze,** or think carefully about, what they read. They also **evaluate,** or form conclusions about, facts and other text evidence presented to them.

Books

Creating books has changed much since the early days of writing with a sharp tool on a clay block. Throughout history, however, some things have remained the same. Every book begins with an idea and someone to put that idea into writing. Planning and producing a book, whether by printing it or preparing it as an eBook, requires the work of many talented individuals.

In "The Making of a Book," you'll learn part of the history of books. You'll also learn about the steps taken to turn an author's manuscript into a book.

ANCHOR TEXT

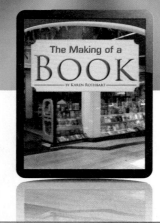

The Making of a
BOOK
BY KAREN ROTHBART

☑ TARGET SKILL

Sequence of Events
Identify the time order in which events take place.

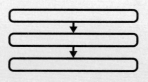

☑ GENRE

Informational text gives facts and other information about a topic. As you read, look for:

▶ headings that begin sections of related text

▶ photographs and graphics such as diagrams

▶ text structure—the way the information is organized

 COMMON CORE **RI.6.4** determine the meaning of words and phrases, including figurative, connotative, and technical meanings; **RI.6.5** analyze how a sentence, paragraph, chapter, or section fits in the overall structure; **RI.6.7** integrate information presented in different media or formats as well as in words; **RI.6.10** read and comprehend literary nonfiction

 Go Digital

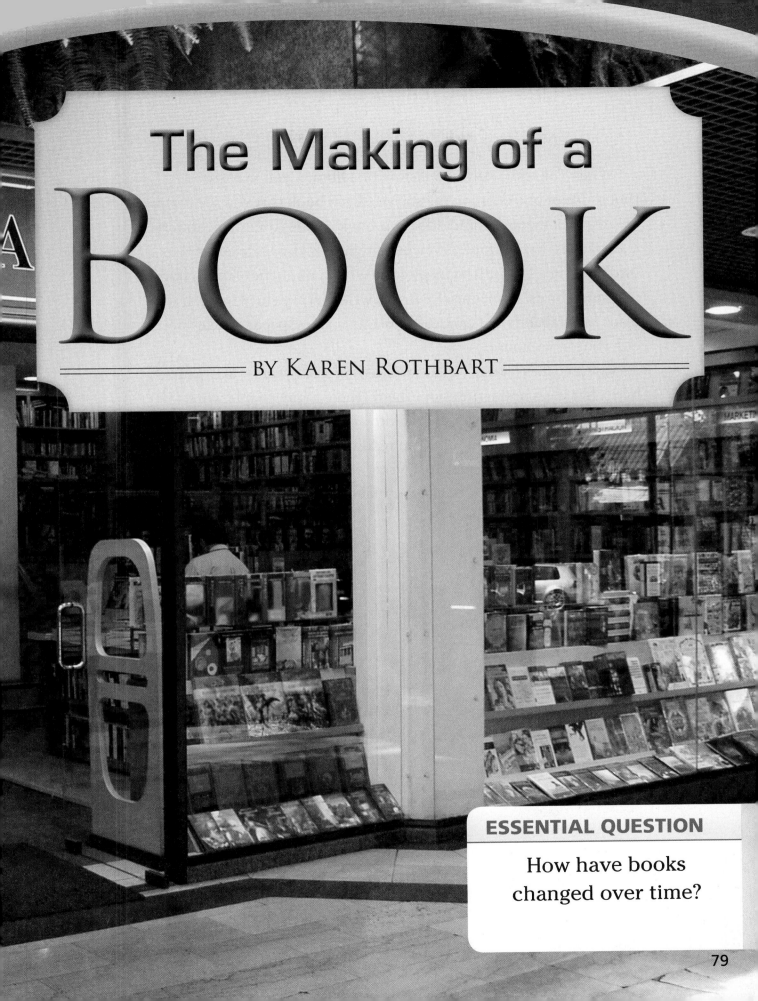

The Making of a

BOOK

BY KAREN ROTHBART

ESSENTIAL QUESTION

How have books changed over time?

CHAPTER 1

The Beginning

When you walk into a bookstore or a library, you may see thousands of books lining the shelves. Each book that you see began as an idea in someone's mind. Ideas for books come from many different experiences. For example, someone might notice a large empty bird's nest in a tree and be inspired to write a nonfiction book about migrating birds. Someone else might write a scary story that takes place in an abandoned cabin after reading a newspaper article about an old, run-down house.

It sometimes takes a writer months—or even years—to organize his or her ideas and write about them. Then, many people work together to turn the writer's work into an actual book. That is what book publishing is all about. Keep reading to learn about the history of publishing and how an idea in a writer's mind becomes a book you can borrow from the library, buy at your favorite store, or download as an eBook.

Early Books: From Clay to Paper

The oldest-known books were written in ancient Mesopotamia on clay blocks called *tablets*. While a tablet was wet, the writer would use a special tool called a *stylus* to write on it. He or she would press the point of the stylus into the clay to make marks. If the writing did not fit on one tablet, the writer would start a new one and give it a number. Put together, the tablets would be similar to a book with numbered pages. After the writer finished writing each tablet, he or she would place it in the sun or into a special oven called a *kiln* to harden. The dried tablets could last a long time; many of them have been discovered and are still readable today.

Clay tablet

Papyrus roll fragment

Later, the Egyptian papyrus roll came into use. The papyrus roll was a step closer to the modern printed book. Papyrus is a type of plant the ancient Egyptians used to make paper. Pieces of papyrus paper were pasted together, written on with a brush and colored inks, and then rolled up. The Greeks and Romans also used the papyrus roll.

After the papyrus roll came parchment. Parchment was made from stretched animal skin, which was better for writing because it had a smooth surface that absorbed ink well. It also could be scrubbed clean and reused.

Before 1450 there were only a few thousand books in Europe, because each one had to be handwritten by professionals called *scribes*. It was a painstaking process. By the late 1400s, however, the printing press had been invented in Germany, and the number of books had exploded. By 1500, about 9 million books had been printed.

ANALYZE THE TEXT

Domain–Specific Vocabulary
How can you determine the meanings of technical words such as *tablets*, *papyrus*, and *parchment*? What clues does the author provide?

An early printing press

From about 1550 until 1800, most publishers used the same method for printing books: a machine called a *printing press*. Each letter in a book was carved out of wood or metal and then set into a flat surface called a *platen*. This platen held all the words for one page of writing. The letters were then covered with ink and pressed against paper. The result was one printed page, but the page could be printed over and over to make many copies. To make the next page, however, the letters had to be removed and reset into new words.

Printers used a similar process to put illustrations in books. A picture was carved into a piece of wood called a *woodcut*. The woodcut was covered with a roller dipped in ink and then pressed against paper. A woodcut could be used over and over again.

With the invention of the printing press, printers could meet the public's demand for books. Books were mostly made with hard covers until the 1950s, when paper covers became popular. Paperback books were cheaper to make and to buy than hardcover books. They were also easier to carry. Most paperbacks were, and still are, reprints of books that were originally hardcover.

CHAPTER 2
Modern Publishing

Authors and Agents

Authors are people who write books; they begin the publishing process by creating manuscripts. A *manuscript* is a completed piece of writing. It may go through many drafts and revisions before it is ready to be submitted to a publisher who will buy it and turn it into a book.

Many authors hire literary agents to help them sell their work. Literary agents are helpful because they have contact with publishers and can determine the best way to present an author's work to them.

Part of an agent's job is to convince editors or publishers to buy an author's manuscript. An agent may send out a sample or an early draft to publishers to try to get them to offer a book contract, which is an agreement stating that the publisher will pay the author for his or her work. Sometimes when an author gets a book contract, the publisher will give him or her an advance—money paid to an author before the book is complete. An advance helps a writer finish a manuscript because it provides an income while the writer works through the writing process.

Agents may also represent the author in pay negotiations and meetings about how to package a book and promote it to the public. Finding the right agent is not always easy; the relationship between an agent and a writer is a special partnership. The agent has to be interested enough in the author's work to want to sell it, and the author has to trust the agent to represent him or her well.

Editors and Marketing People

Putting a book together is like putting together a puzzle. All of the pieces need to fit perfectly, and editors are the people who make sure that they do.

Editors work for publishers, and they perform many tasks. Some choose manuscripts or ideas to purchase, while others come up with ideas themselves and then search for the right authors to create manuscripts from scratch.

Most editors work with authors to make improvements to manuscripts by suggesting revisions, or changes. Even after a manuscript has been purchased, an editor may ask an author to delete some parts of it or expand others. Sometimes an editor will ask an author to rearrange—or even rewrite—the manuscript. An author and editor collaborate until both are happy with the end product.

The manuscript then goes to a copyeditor, who fine-tunes the writing by correcting problems such as grammatical errors and repetitive sentences. A copyeditor also will check facts so that faulty information does not end up in the final, printed book.

Editors aren't concerned only with the words on the page, however; they also think about how to persuade people to buy and read those words. They get help from the marketing department. People in marketing perform research and have a lot of interaction with customers, so they know how to make products appealing to buyers. Together, members of the editorial and marketing departments brainstorm ideas about how to make the book appealing to customers. Marketing people might make suggestions about cover art, pricing, and in-store shelf displays that will best showcase the book. They also might suggest when and where to set up events for the author, such as book signings.

Artists and Illustrators

Editors also team up with artists and illustrators. Together they decide which kinds of images should be on the cover and inside the book. They look for the right style that will complement the text and appeal to readers. Book cover images need to suggest what the book is about and catch the consumer's eye. Some books include photographs rather than illustrations. Editors find appropriate photographs for the book and get permission from the copyright owners to use copies of them, or they hire a photographer to take new ones.

Artists design how the print appears on the page. They decide which font, or type style, a book should have, because each font has a different personality. Artists also choose the size of the type and decide how to arrange words on the page. The words need to be easy and pleasant to read. Readers don't often notice good design, but a poor one can make a book difficult to enjoy.

Graphic Designers and Printers

Finally, the words and pictures are complete, and it is time to make the actual book. Graphic designers use computers to set the words into type, add the images, and make sure everything fits correctly. Because designers are able to do a lot of their work on computers now, changes are much easier to make than they were several years ago.

The graphic designer makes copies of the pages so the editor, author, and artist can check them. The team makes sure that all of the images and words are correct. Then the graphic designer prepares the book for the printer.

Printers produce the final books. Printers usually are separate businesses from publishers, but the two work together. The printer helps the publisher choose the right paper for the book.

Printers no longer use the printing presses from long ago. Today they use computers to print books. The printer uses computer files from the publisher to make metal printing plates. The plates are treated with chemicals so the ink sticks only to the words and pictures. Then a mechanical press puts the ink on the paper, making a printed page. Printers make as many copies as the publisher wants by using large printing presses. Presses may print on large sheets or huge rolls of paper. Presses are noisy, so workers must protect their ears so the constant whooshing and clanking sounds are muted.

The printer sets up the book's pages so they will be in the correct order after the paper is cut and folded. Special machines fold the pages in sections and glue them together, creating a book binding, while another machine adds a cover to the book. The book is ready to be shipped to bookstores, libraries, and schools. If a book is expected to be a best-seller, bookstores may ask the printer for thousands of copies before the book is officially released.

A modern printing press

Once the book is published, the selling process begins. Marketing people plan the book's publicity; they want as many people as possible to hear or read about the new book. They might publicize a book by sending advance copies of it to reviewers who will write about the book in newspapers, magazines, and on the Internet. For additional publicity, authors often travel to different places to give readings, sign their books, and talk with readers. Many authors also have their own websites or blogs. They give updates about their new books and share information about themselves. They hope that people will be interested enough to buy and read their books.

The publisher's salespeople speak with bookstores and libraries to convince them to buy copies of the book. Bookstores and libraries order the books they want from the publisher's warehouse, where the books are stored before shipping. Once the books are on shelves, readers can buy a copy at a store or borrow it from a local library.

> **ANALYZE THE TEXT**
>
> **Sequence of Events** The author has arranged the chapters in a certain order. How does Chapter 2 fit into the overall structure of the selection?

How Do Books Get Published?

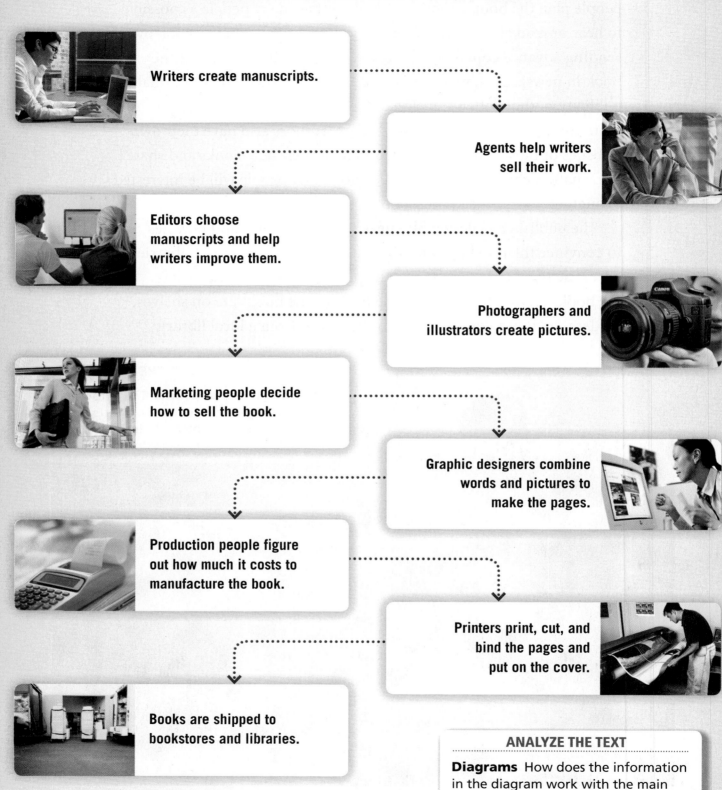

Writers create manuscripts.

Agents help writers sell their work.

Editors choose manuscripts and help writers improve them.

Photographers and illustrators create pictures.

Marketing people decide how to sell the book.

Graphic designers combine words and pictures to make the pages.

Production people figure out how much it costs to manufacture the book.

Printers print, cut, and bind the pages and put on the cover.

Books are shipped to bookstores and libraries.

ANALYZE THE TEXT

Diagrams How does the information in the diagram work with the main text to help you better understand the process of bookmaking?

CHAPTER 3
Beyond Hard Copies

Audio Books Many of the books you can read in hard copy are also available as audio books. An audio book is a recording of someone reading the text. With an audio book, people can "read" while riding a bus or train, exercising, or doing some other activity. Audio books also allow people who are visually impaired to enjoy texts and stories that are not available in large type or braille.

eBooks By 1999, many books were published both in print and as eBooks, available with the click of a computer mouse. In 2006, the eReader, a portable device that stores books and displays their text on a built-in screen, was introduced. Today people can read eBooks on eReaders, as well as on personal computers and smartphones. Creating eBooks has become a popular way for publishers to share content with readers.

The Future In the future, there could be even more ways to publish books. As the popularity of eBooks grows, publishers are changing their processes and even the ways in which they acquire and sell books. They also are seeing an increase in sales; people enjoy being able to have digital copies of their favorite books that they can take with them anywhere. Of course, there are others who will always be in love with the feel of a book in their hands as they turn paper pages. For now, readers and publishers have the best of both worlds.

Dig Deeper

How to Analyze the Text

Use these pages to learn about Sequence of Events, Domain-Specific Vocabulary, and Diagrams. Then read "The Making of a Book" again to apply what you learned.

Sequence of Events

In informational texts such as "The Making of a Book," authors may organize ideas according to the **sequence,** or time order, in which **events** happen. Authors often use dates and signal words such as *first*, *while*, *after*, and *finally* to help readers understand the sequence of events. Paying attention to the order in which events occur helps you understand where one event or a group of events fits in the overall structure of a section or text.

Look back at Chapter 1. In this chapter, the author describes the earliest forms of books. What text evidence helps you know how ideas in the chapter are organized? How does the chapter fit in the overall structure of the text?

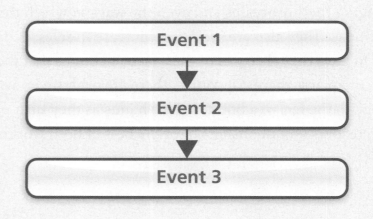

RI.6.4 determine the meaning of words and phrases, including figurative, connotative, and technical meanings; **RI.6.5** analyze how a sentence, paragraph, chapter, or section fits in the overall structure; **RI.6.7** integrate information presented in different media or formats as well as in words; **L.6.6** acquire and use general academic and domain-specific words and phrases/gather vocabulary knowledge for comprehension or expression

Domain-Specific Vocabulary

In informational text, authors often use **domain-specific vocabulary,** or technical words from a field of study, such as book publishing or computers. Authors may provide the meanings of the domain-specific vocabulary. If they don't, readers need to figure out the meanings of technical words in order to understand the text. As you reread "The Making of a Book," look for domain-specific vocabulary. Use clues in the text to figure out the meanings of words the author does not define.

Diagrams

Diagrams are graphic features that show the relationships between related things. They may show causes and effects or the sequence in which events or steps in a process take place. In a science text, an author might include a diagram to show the life cycle of an animal or to show the flow of energy in a food chain. Arrows in the diagram, rather than words, show how the elements are related. Understanding how to interpret a diagram helps you gain visual information that supports the text.

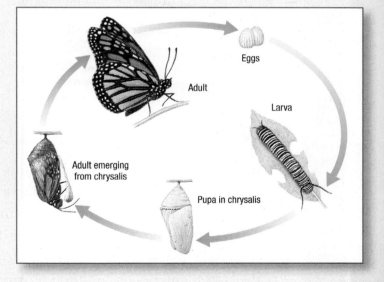

Your Turn

RETURN TO THE ESSENTIAL QUESTION

 Turn and Talk Review the selection with a partner to prepare to discuss this question: *How have books changed over time?* As you discuss, ask each other questions and use text evidence to explain your answers.

Classroom Conversation

Continue your discussion of "The Making of a Book" by explaining your answers to these questions:

1. Based on the selection, why do you think people save and collect old books?

2. It takes people, machines, and time to make books. How has the computer affected the book-publishing process?

3. In what ways must people collaborate, or work together, to make a book?

A PUZZLING QUESTION

Give Text Evidence In this selection, the author makes the following claim: "Putting a book together is like putting together a puzzle." Analyze the claim and state whether it is supported in the selection. Be sure to tell what the statement means and then provide examples that serve as evidence.

WRITE ABOUT READING

Response Which form of book do you prefer reading, printed or electronic? Why do you feel as you do? Write a paragraph in which you present and explain your opinion. Use your own knowledge as well as text evidence from "The Making of a Book." Organize your reasons and evidence clearly, and end with a conclusion that summarizes your ideas.

The Making of a
BOOK
BY KAREN ROTHBART

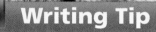

Writing Tip

Begin your paragraph by introducing your opinion. As you write, make sure you use complete sentences to explain your opinion and to provide reasons and evidence.

Go Digital

COMMON CORE **RI.6.1** cite textual evidence to support analysis of what the text says explicitly as well as inferences drawn; **RI.6.8** trace and evaluate the argument and specific claims in a text; **W.6.1a** introduce claim(s) and organize reasons and evidence clearly; **W.6.1b** support claim(s) with reasons and evidence, using credible sources and demonstrating understanding of the topic or text; **W.6.9b** apply grade 6 Reading standards to literary nonfiction

INFORMATIONAL TEXT

History
of the
Book

✓ GENRE

Informational text, such as this encyclopedia article, provides facts, illustrations, and examples about a topic.

✓ TEXT FOCUS

A **timeline** shows the sequence of important events over a particular span of time.

COMMON CORE — **RI.6.7** integrate information presented in different media or formats as well as in words; **RI.6.10** read and comprehend literary nonfiction

Go Digital

History of the Book

Throughout history, people have found ways to present their ideas. Writers have been recording their thoughts for thousands of years. These expressions from the past are not muted, but remain vibrant and meaningful.

Books have an important place in the timeline of recorded thought. This timeline runs from ancient symbols recorded on paper to the electronic books of our own time.

2300 B.C.E.
Babylonian clay tablets

3000 B.C.E.   **2000 B.C.E.**   **1000 B.C.E.**

3200 B.C.E.
Egyptian papyrus scrolls

From Papyrus to Print

People are always looking for better ways to record information and ideas. The ancient Egyptians used a form of paper called *papyrus*. Papyrus was made from a plant that grew along the Nile River.

The ancient Babylonians used clay tablets to record everything from goat sales to literary works. They even used clay tablets to record the first known map of the world. With this system, though, it was not easy to make revisions to a manuscript.

Parchment was a material made from the skin of sheep or goats. It was developed during the Roman Empire. Parchment lasted longer than papyrus.

Until the late 700s C.E., text had to be written and copied by hand. Book printing began in China around 868, but the type could be used only once. Around 1050, a Chinese printer named Bi Sheng invented movable type. Movable type could be used over and over.

Perhaps the biggest printing breakthrough came in Germany in the 1440s when Johannes Gutenberg developed a printing press. Movable type was set in a wooden form. The letters were coated with ink. Then a sheet of paper was laid on the letters and pressed with a wooden plate creating an entire printed page.

1440–1450 C.E.
The Gutenberg press

868 C.E.
Early printed book

100 B.C.E.   **500 C.E.**   **1500 C.E.**

190 B.C.E.
Parchment codex

1050 C.E.
Movable type

From Linotype to Online Type

In the 1880s, the publishing industry once again changed drastically. A man named Ottmar Mergenthaler invented the Linotype machine, which allowed its operator to use a keyboard to type the text. The Linotype machine created molds from lines of type (the process for which the machine was named). Text became cheaper to produce. The public began pressuring the industry to print more. People wanted both the wry humor of Mark Twain and the serious news of the day.

The first audio books were developed in 1931 by the American Foundation for the Blind. These books were known as "talking books." In the 1960s, talking books became popular with the public.

Today, the newest and fastest way to publish a book is electronically. An author can publish his or her own work on the Internet or as an eBook. The electronic process saves paper. However, an eBook may still go through several steps before publication. Many eBooks are available for free in electronic form on several websites, including one named Project Gutenberg in honor of one of the giants in the history of the book.

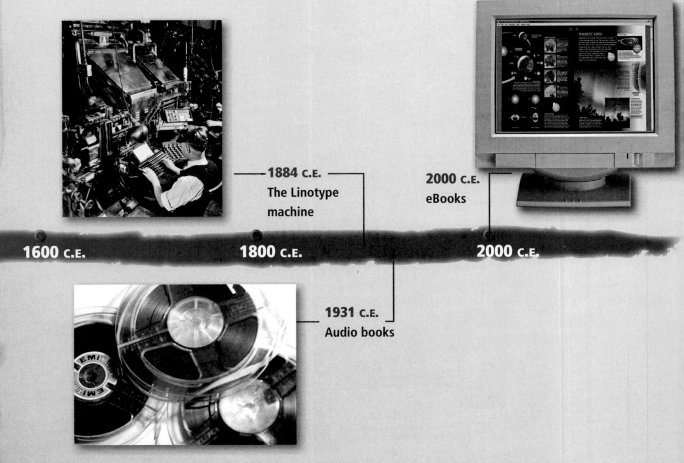

1884 C.E.
The Linotype machine

2000 C.E.
eBooks

1600 C.E.   **1800 C.E.**   **2000 C.E.**

1931 C.E.
Audio books

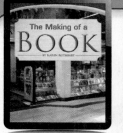

Compare Texts

TEXT TO TEXT

Compare Processes How were books produced before and after the invention of movable type? Write a paragraph that explains the differences in the processes. Also explain how movable type impacted book publishing. Use information from "The Making of a Book" and "History of the Book" to support your response.

TEXT TO SELF

Write About Expression Authors often work by themselves when they write. Artists often work alone, too. In some other forms of expression, such as music, people express themselves by working together in a band or choir. In what creative way do you most like to express yourself? Write about it and tell whether you prefer working with others or alone.

TEXT TO WORLD

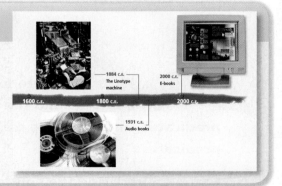

Compare Approaches Think about how "The Making of a Book" and "History of the Book" present information on bookmaking throughout history. How are the authors' presentations of events similar? How are they different?

Go Digital

COMMON CORE **RI.6.1** cite textual evidence to support analysis of what the text says explicitly as well as inferences drawn; **RI.6.9** compare and contrast one author's presentation of events with that of another

Grammar

Subjects and Predicates The **simple subject** is the main word or words in a complete subject. The **simple predicate** is the main word or words in a complete predicate. A **compound subject** contains two or more simple subjects joined by the conjunction *and* or *or*. A **compound predicate** contains two or more simple predicates joined by *and* or *or*.

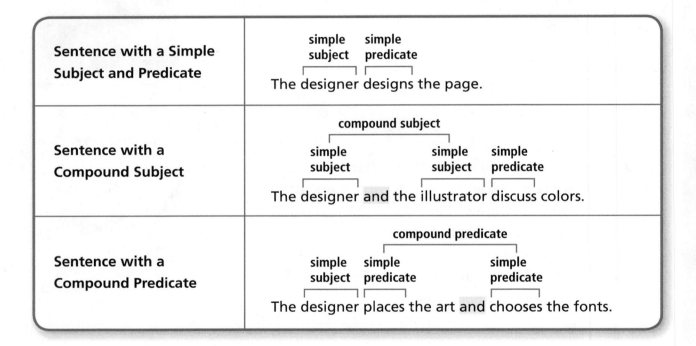

Sentence with a Simple Subject and Predicate	simple subject · simple predicate The designer designs the page.
Sentence with a Compound Subject	compound subject simple subject · simple subject · simple predicate The designer and the illustrator discuss colors.
Sentence with a Compound Predicate	compound predicate simple subject · simple predicate · simple predicate The designer places the art and chooses the fonts.

Try This! **Write the sentences below on a sheet of paper. Draw a box around the simple subjects, underline the simple predicates, and circle the compound subjects and compound predicates.**

1. The author and the editor discuss the manuscript.

2. An agent buys or rejects a manuscript.

3. I download eBooks and read them often.

4. The words and images work together to tell a story.

When you write, you can make your sentences less repetitive by leaving out extra words. Use a conjunction such as *and* to combine sentences that have the same subject but different predicates. You can also use *and* to combine sentences that have the same predicate but different subjects.

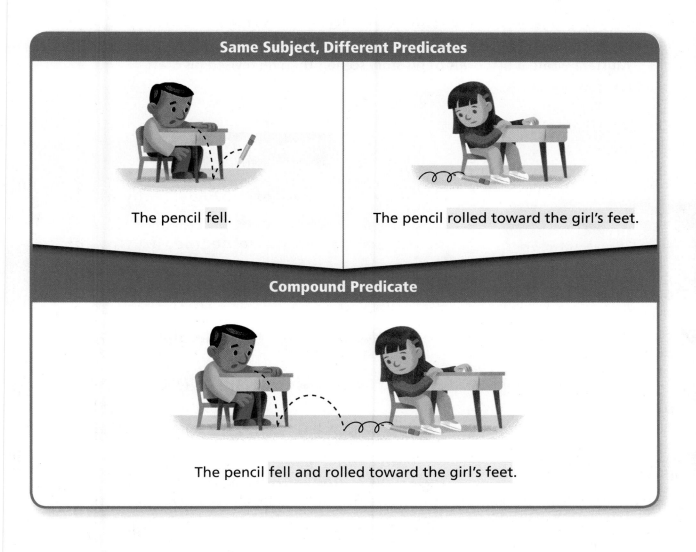

Same Subject, Different Predicates

The pencil fell.

The pencil rolled toward the girl's feet.

Compound Predicate

The pencil fell and rolled toward the girl's feet.

 Connect Grammar to Writing

As you revise your story scene, look at the subjects and the predicates of your sentences. If two sentences have the same subject but different predicates or the same predicate but different subjects, combine them with *and*. Combining subjects and predicates creates a variety of sentence types, which helps to hold your readers' interest.

W.6.3b use narrative techniques to develop experiences, events, and characters; **W.6.3d** use precise words and phrases, descriptive details, and sensory details

Narrative Writing

✅ **Word Choice**   In a **story scene,** authors present one episode within a longer narrative. The scene has characters, a setting, and plot events that may include a problem and its solution. Events are usually told in time order with a beginning, a middle, and an ending. Dialogue develops characters by showing what they think and feel. As you revise your scene, add sensory words to make the scene more descriptive.

   Mustafa wrote a first draft of his story scene. Then he revised his draft, adding sensory words.

Writing Traits Checklist

✅ **Ideas**
Did I include all story elements?

✅ **Organization**
Did I tell the events in correct time order?

✅ **Sentence Fluency**
Did I use compound subjects and predicates?

✅ **Word Choice**
Did I use sensory words?

✅ **Voice**
Did I reveal the characters' feelings?

✅ **Conventions**
Did I use correct spelling, grammar, and punctuation?

Revised Draft

   After two hours of staring silently at the
red-and-white checkered
   board, Jamal and Habib decided to stop for
                          sleek, black or white
   lunch. Each had moved his ∧ chess pieces

   across the board in strategic plays, trying to

   outfox the other. But now their growling

   stomachs were impatient, and it was time to
       hot roast beef
   eat. Over ∧ sandwiches, Jamal's mom asked,

   "How's the cover idea coming along, Jamal?"

Mystery Uncovered

by Mustafa Barifi

Jamal and his mom welcomed Habib into their apartment. "It's a day off from school," Jamal lamented, "but I still need to do the cover artwork for our class's book by Monday."

Ever confident, Habib replied, "You'll have time this afternoon to figure that out. Let's play some chess."

After two hours of staring silently at the red-and-white checkered board, Jamal and Habib decided to stop for lunch. Each had moved his sleek, black or white chess pieces across the squares on the board in strategic plays, trying to outfox the other. But now their growling stomachs were impatient, and it was time to eat. Over hot roast beef sandwiches, Jamal's mom asked, "How's the cover idea coming along, Jamal?"

Jamal looked at Habib and paused, thinking. Then he answered, "This morning, I didn't know what it should look like, Mom, but now I think I do. I'll make a red cover with a big white square in the middle. Inside the square frame, I'll paint a beautiful black horse leaping out of the center."

"Sounds perfect," said Habib. Then he chomped on a carrot and smiled.

Vocabulary in Context

☑ **TARGET VOCABULARY**

torrent
accustomed
void
swiveled
clustered
transmissions
doleful
clamor
urgent
coaxed

Vocabulary Reader   Context Cards

COMMON CORE **L.6.6** acquire and use general academic and domain-specific words and phrases/gather vocabulary knowledge for comprehension or expression

102

1 torrent
Like a torrent, or a rushing stream, people pour out of the subway on their way to work.

2 accustomed
City pigeons are accustomed to sharing their home with humans. They are used to people.

3 void
A vacant lot is a void among city buildings. Most big cities have these empty spaces.

4 swiveled
This revolving door has swiveled, or turned, to let people in and out of the building.

Go Digital

▶ Study each Context Card.

▶ Use a dictionary to confirm the meanings of these words.

 **clustered**

At lunchtime, hungry customers can be found clustered around street vendors selling food.

6 transmissions

Police officers in the city communicate by sending and receiving radio transmissions.

 doleful

An abandoned building can be a doleful sight. It may give a sad look to a neighborhood.

8 clamor

A crowd in a city stadium might make a deafening clamor after an exciting victory.

9 urgent

This ambulance answers an urgent call. Cars move aside so it can rush to an emergency.

10 coaxed

Many store owners have easily coaxed, or persuaded, customers to come in for big sale events.

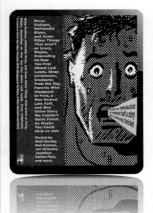

Read and Comprehend

☑ TARGET SKILL

Story Structure All stories have the same basic elements. Story elements include the **setting**, the **characters**, and the **plot**, which is a sequence of **episodes** or events. As the episodes unfold, characters respond to a problem until they find a solution to it. All of the story elements work together, so if any were to change, the story would probably be very different. As you read "The ACES Phone," look for text evidence that helps you recognize the story elements. Record them in a graphic organizer like this one.

Setting	Characters
Plot	

☑ TARGET STRATEGY

Monitor/Clarify As you read "The ACES Phone," **monitor**, or pay attention to, your understanding of the text. When something does not make sense, stop to **clarify**, or make clear, the parts that are confusing.

 RL.6.3 describe how a story's or drama's plot unfolds and how characters respond and change

Animal Signals

Humans and animals alike have developed different ways to communicate. Humans are able to communicate verbally by using sounds to form words. Animals cannot use words, but they do use sounds to communicate. They also use body movements and signals. A dog wagging its tail, for example, may be sending a signal that it wants to play.

Have you ever wondered what it would be like to understand animal signals and sounds? In "The ACES Phone," a boy finds a mysterious phone that allows him to listen in a way that no other human can.

ANCHOR TEXT

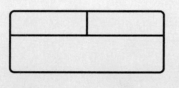

Story Structure Examine details about characters, setting, and plot. Notice how the sequence of episodes relates to changes in the story characters.

Science fiction is a fantasy story that is based on science ideas and technology. As you read, look for:

▶ technology of the future
▶ events that could not happen in real life
▶ ideas that are based on science or technology

COMMON CORE **RL.6.3** describe how a story's or drama's plot unfolds and how characters respond and change; **RL.6.10** read and comprehend literature; **L.6.3b** maintain consistency in style and tone

MEET THE AUTHOR

Jeanne DuPrau

At the tender age of five, precocious young author-to-be Jeanne DuPrau crayoned her first major literary endeavor, in red and green, depicting a fantastical creature made of snow, whom she called Frosty. Since then DuPrau has crafted and published several novels, including *The New York Times* bestseller *The City of Ember*, as well as *The People of Sparks*, *The Prophet of Yonwood*, *The Diamond of Darkhold*, *The Earth House*, and *Car Trouble*. *The City of Ember* garnered several book awards and was recognized as an American Library Association Notable Book. In addition, *The City of Ember*, cornerstone of the Books of Ember science-fiction–fantasy series, is available as a graphic novel illustrated by Niklas Asker. A film adaptation directed by Gil Kenan, called *City of Ember*, was filmed in Belfast, Northern Ireland, where part of a former shipyard was converted into a post-apocalyptic metropolis to serve as the film's setting.

When queried about how young people can replicate her success, DePrau urges aspiring scribes to read and write voraciously and to be insatiably curious about and intrigued by the world around them. DePrau herself, when she is not writing, spends her time in a wide variety of leisure pursuits: ice skating, bird watching, piano playing, gourmet cooking, and puttering in her garden with her canine companion, a Norfolk terrier named Jockey. DePrau, who was born in San Francisco, California, currently resides in Menlo Park, California. Over the years, she has earned her living not only as a writer of young-adult fiction but also as an English teacher, a technical writer for a multinational computer company, and an editor for educational publishing companies.

MEET THE ILLUSTRATOR

Suling Wang

Suling Wang is an accomplished artist and multimedia designer whose education includes a Bachelor of Fine Arts Illustration degree from the Academy of Art in San Francisco, California, and a Bachelor of Science degree in mechanical engineering from Stanford University in Palo Alto, California. Among the books for children and preteens that Wang has illustrated in her evocative, detailed style are two renowned publications by Laurence Yep: *The Magic Paintbrush* and *When the Circus Came to Town*. She also created the illustrations to accompany *Raymond's Perfect Present*, written by Therese On Louie. Wang, who currently resides in San Francisco, California, also devises interactive computer animations and innovative electronic designs for a plethora of multimedia applications.

THE ACES PHONE

from **NOISY OUTLAWS, UNFRIENDLY BLOBS, AND SOME OTHER THINGS...**

by Jeanne DuPrau
selection illustrated by Suling Wang

ESSENTIAL QUESTION

What is the difference
between hearing
and listening?

Martin loves his big family, but there's barely enough room for him in his crowded
urban apartment. He spends a lot of time skating outdoors, feeling that there is
a void in his life he ought to fill. When he finds a cell phone in the park one day,
Martin presses the speed-dial numbers to see if he can identify its owner. He gets
nowhere until he presses the number 5....

The phone rang only once. Then there was a click and a brief silence. And then came a sound unlike anything he'd heard before. It seemed to come from both far away and near, a clamor made up of a thousand thread-like voices—and along with the noise came a blast of feeling so strong it nearly knocked him off the bench. He pitched forward, as if he'd gotten a sudden terrible cramp. The feeling poured into his ear and flooded down through his chest and into his blood and raced like fire all through his body. It wasn't rage or fear or joy or love but a mixture of all of them, so strong that he cried out and dropped the phone on the ground.

The pigeons, thinking it might be something to eat, flocked around it. He bent down to pick it up, shaking. Cautiously, he put the phone near his ear—not right against it this time—and listened. The strange, immense chorus of sound still poured out, and the feeling jolted him again. It was so strong that he couldn't stay sitting on the bench. He had to get up and move.

He paced furiously around the playground, under the swings, over to the slide, around the jungle gym. It was a good thing no one was there—he knew he looked very odd, as if the wind was blowing him this way and that. After a long time, he began to notice something.

The feeling that shot through him changed slightly as he changed his direction. When he walked toward the baseball diamond, his heart beat harder, as if he were afraid. When he walked toward Avenue B, he grew calmer. When he went out of the park and down 14th Street, he felt weighed down by sadness.

It was like that game where you're looking for something and the other person says, "You're hot! No, you're getting colder! No, *really* cold! Now you're hot again!" But what was he looking for? He had no idea.

The next day he had a terrible time concentrating at school. He was wildly impatient to try out the phone again. It wasn't quite as cold, so a few people were in the park when he got there—a mother pushing her toddler on a swing, a couple of kids going backward down the slide, and an old woman in a knit hat and a lumpy purplish coat trudging along the path by the baseball diamond.

ANALYZE THE TEXT

Alliteration On page 108 the author uses alliteration, repeating a beginning consonant sound in a series of words to emphasize important ideas or to create a mood. Where does the author use alliteration on page 110? How does it affect the mood of the scene?

Martin stood within a clump of trees at the corner of the park, turned on the phone, and pressed 5. Once again, the torrent of sound-feeling rushed through him and forced him to start walking. He went toward Avenue B, since that had made the feeling calmer yesterday. But it didn't work today. Everything was different. He felt a pang of fear as he went toward the jungle gym, and a jolt of joy as he neared the picnic tables. Finally, when he got back to the park bench, he just stopped. He turned off the phone and sat down, completely confused.

That was when he felt a poke in his back, and a voice said, "That phone you got. That's mine."

He whirled around. Behind him stood the old woman he'd seen before. She was glaring at him from under the rim of her knit hat, which looked like a purple pancake drooping just above her eyes. She pointed to the phone in his hand and said again, "That's mine. I musta dropped it yesterday."

Martin held onto it tighter. "Prove it," he said.

The old woman laughed. "Easy. I bet you called my number 5. Right?"

He just stared at her. All of a sudden he recognized her—Mrs. DeSalvio was her name, though she was usually called just Mrs. D. He'd seen her for years around the neighborhood, always tramping along with a phone held to her ear. People joked about her. They said she must have the most long-winded family in the world, because she always seemed to be listening, hardly ever talking.

"Ever heard anything like that before?" she said.

He shook his head. "What is it?"

She came around to his side of the bench and sat down beside him with a thump, wafting out a smell that reminded Martin of a pastrami sandwich. "Why should I tell *you*?" she said.

"Because you want your phone back," said Martin, edging away and putting the phone in his pocket.

She pinned him with her eyes. They were clear eyes, Martin saw. "First," she said, "you tell me about you. Who are you? Talk to me."

He could have just stood up and walked away. Or run. She could never have caught him. But he thought the phone probably *was* hers, which meant she knew what was going on with it. And he wanted to know, too. So he talked.

She listened. She said, "Good, good," when he told her about skating. She frowned and bunched her lips up when he told her about where he lived, the too-small, too-crowded, too-noisy apartment that he didn't want to go home to after school. "You should have a job after school," she said.

"Yeah," said Martin. "But I don't know how to do anything."

She leaned close to him and spoke in a low voice. "Do you like animals?"

"Animals? Sure."

"What kind?"

"All kinds, I guess."

"You like dogs?"

"Yeah. Wish I had one."

"Why don't you, then?"

"No dogs allowed in the building."

"Awright," said the old woman. She took some crumbs out of her pocket and tossed them to the pigeons who clustered around her feet. "Now. Can you handle the strange?"

"What?"

"The strange," she said irritably. "You know, the strange, the unusual, the slightly weird. Can you handle that?"

"Sure," said Martin. He *liked* the strange and unusual.

"I wouldn't tell you this if I thought you were going to laugh," she said. "Or spread it around to your friends."

"I wouldn't," said Martin, which was the truth.

"I have this hunch you might be the one, that's why I'm telling you," she said.

"The one?" said Martin. "What one?"

But she didn't answer. She just studied his face, as if his brown eyes, his wavy black hair, and his chipped front tooth were giving her some kind of clue about him. "Awright, then," she said finally. "That number you called—" she paused. She squinched up her eyes. She lowered her voice to a hoarse whisper. "That number taps you into the dogs."

Martin stared at her. He didn't get it. "What?" he said.

A gust of wind blew some crumpled food wrappers across the playground. The pigeons rose into the air and settled again.

"Let's walk around," the old woman said. "I'm freezing to death, sitting here like this."

So they walked around the path that circled the playground, around and around, and she explained. "You know, dogs," she said, "they don't talk. They don't have the words, just the feelings. They got feelings so strong they fill up the air, like . . . like . . ." She waved her hands around. "Like a big network of radio waves. This phone taps into the network. If you're not used to it, you call that number and the feelings come roaring through and knock you down."

"That's what happened to me," Martin said. "But what's the point of a phone like that? And where did you get it?"

"An old guy in my building gave it to me," she said, "a long time ago. And the point of it is: ACES."

"What's that?"

"Assistance for Canines in Emergency Situations. ACES."

"I don't understand," said Martin.

"Let's sit down," she said. "My feet hurt, walking around like this."

So they sat down again. "You figured out that the feeling changes when you change direction," she said. "I saw you doing it."

"Yeah," Martin said. "But I don't know why."

"Let me have the phone," she said, holding out her hand. Martin gave it to her. She punched in the number. She frowned, clenched her jaw, and put the phone to her ear. For a few seconds she listened; then she nodded and handed the phone to Martin. "Hold yourself strong," she said, "and you can take it."

He tightened all his muscles and listened. Again the feelings rampaged through him, but they didn't strike him down.

"Okay," said Mrs. D. "That's good." She took the phone back and turned it off. "Now, here's what you're hearing. This network here covers about twenty blocks. There's others, all over the city— you don't have to worry about them. For this one, the park is the center. We're getting the vibes of all the dogs in that twenty-block area, pets and strays both. What you're hearing is like hundreds of little streams all running together in one huge river. You listen real hard and careful, and you can hear the different—well, not *voices*, exactly, more like transmissions."

"I figured that out," said Martin. "If you keep trying, you can find the way that feels better."

"That," said the old woman, "is exactly what you *don't* want to do. You gotta go the way that feels *worst*, that's the whole point." She fastened the top button of her coat and turned the collar up. "Come on," she said. "I'll show you."

She made the call again. She stood up, listening. She took a few steps, changed direction, took a few more steps, and kept doing this for a minute or so. Then she handed the phone to him. "Okay," she said. "Listen hard, and you'll hear a sort of wail, and you'll feel something kind of heavy and sad. Walk this way"—she pointed toward Avenue B—"and the sadness will get worse. What you want is to find where it's coming from. So you keep going toward it. It's hard, but the more you do it, the stronger you get."

So Martin walked. He set out up Avenue B, gritting his teeth because the sad feeling was indeed getting worse. The wail was thin and far away, like a needle of sound, and the sadness was like a stone in his chest. Every time the stone grew lighter, he knew he was going the wrong way. He had to pick out the faint wail from the chorus and turn toward it, again and again.

The whole time, Mrs. DeSalvio kept talking. "Last week, out near Anderson Avenue, I found a little mutt that got the worst of a dogfight. One side of him all bloody." She stamped along beside him, shaking her head. "We got an arrangement with the animal shelter, by the way," she said. "They fix up ACES dogs for free."

ANALYZE THE TEXT

Style and Tone How does the author maintain a consistent tone of sadness as Martin follows the signals to the dog in distress?

They were in Martin's neighborhood now. "That's where I live," he said, pointing at his building. "On the third floor. There's seven of us." He would have told her more—about how his father wanted to look for a better place but never had time, about how he had to share his room with a four-year-old and a five-year-old—but the stone in his chest was dragging on his words, making them heavy and hard to say. He fought against the desire to sit down on the sidewalk and curl up into a ball.

"Then there's the worst ones," said Mrs. D after a quick glance at his building. They turned the corner onto 18th Street. "That's when you find people being cruel to their dogs. Now this I can't stand."

Martin put his free hand over his other ear. He didn't want to hear about it. The sadness coming at him over the phone was almost more than he could stand. The stone in his chest felt like a load of bricks now, attached by a chain to his heart.

They turned up Carter Street, and went by the Chinese grocery and the noodle shop and the dry cleaners. Every now and then, Mrs. D took the phone from him and listened herself to make sure he was doing it right. "This is a real heavy one for your first time," she said. "Sorry about that."

Past the used bookstore they went, past the ice cream place. Martin's knees wanted to crumple. His feet weighed ten pounds apiece.

"But it isn't all bad, I want you to know," Mrs. D went on. "I can't tell you how many lost dogs I've returned to their families."

Martin wasn't listening. He was afraid he couldn't stand it any more. He thought he might collapse onto the curb and start sobbing. "I can't do this." He gasped out the words, and at first she didn't hear him. "I can't—" he said again, but he kept going anyhow, and in a minute he realized something odd. He'd come to a spot where, no matter what direction he took, the feeling grew just a tiny bit weaker. If he stood still, it was horribly strong. He told her so.

"Then we're here," she said. "This is it."

They'd come to a big apartment building—350 Lincoln Avenue—with wide steps leading up to a double door. The door was open, because two men carrying a table between them were coming out.

"Grab the door," Mrs. D whispered to Martin. He did, and they slipped inside.

"Awright. Now listen again. You should hear that one voice all by itself now."

He listened. The doleful feeling led him up the first flight of stairs and down a hall. At the end was an open door. It was clear that whoever lived here had moved out. Big taped-up cardboard boxes stood in the hall.

"You want me to take over now?" said Mrs. D.

Martin shook his head. He wasn't going to go through all this just to quit at the end.

"Then go in there and find out what's going on," she said. "I'll wait for you out here."

Martin turned off the phone and handed it to Mrs. D. He stepped into the apartment. It was nearly empty, except for a rolled-up carpet. He smelled paint. The only noise was a faint scraping sound coming from another room. He followed the sound.

In the living room, which overlooked the street, stood a man facing the windows, with his back to Martin. He was taping a piece of paper to the glass.

"Excuse me," Martin said.

The man turned around. "Who are you, kid?"

Martin said his name. "Is there a dog here?" he asked.

"Sure is," said the man. "In there, in the kitchen." He pointed across the hall. "People left him behind, can you believe it? Just left him, without a word." He turned back to his taping. "So I gotta take him to the pound, unless you want him."

Martin went into the kitchen. There, under the kitchen table, tied to a table leg with a piece of rope, was a curled-up heap of sorrow—a small dog, white with brown patches and triangle ears. Without raising his head, he swiveled his eyes to look up at Martin. His tail was tucked down around his rump. He was trembling.

Martin squatted down and put his hand on the dog's back. "Hey, dog," he said quietly. "Hey, good dog, I'm here now." He untied the rope from the table leg and coaxed the dog to his feet. Slowly, he led him out of the kitchen.

The man was sweeping the floor of the living room now. Martin looked at the piece of paper taped to the window. It said: FOR RENT.

"How much?" he asked.

The man told him. Martin's heart sped up. "How many bedrooms?"

"Four," the man said.

Martin's heart beat so hard it made his voice shake. "I know a family that might like it," he said. "Nice people. *My* family. Will you hold it till I can get my father to come look?"

"Okay," said the man. "But you better get him right now. This place is going to go fast."

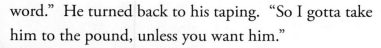

ANALYZE THE TEXT

Story Structure What episodes in the story had to take place in order for Martin to find out about the apartment for rent?

When Martin came out, Mrs. D (who'd been listening by the door) cast a glance at the little dog and told Martin her hunch had been right: she was turning over the ACES job to him. "Meant to be," she said. "Meant to be, no doubt about it. Just in time, too, my feet are too old for this." She frowned at him, and her purple hat fell down over her eyebrows. "Now, you won't get sick of this and quit, will you?"

"No," said Martin.

"And if you do ever want to quit, you'll find someone to take over, won't you?"

"Yes," said Martin.

She nodded once and handed him the phone. Then she reached out and snatched it back again. She hit the 5 button and held the phone to her ear. "Just want to listen one more time," she said. She stood there for a minute or so. Then she turned and stumped away.

And in the months and years that followed, people in the neighborhoods around the 14th Street Park became accustomed to seeing a tall boy on his inline skates every afternoon, gliding along the streets with a cell phone pressed to his ear. They figured he was a delivery boy of some kind. He never told anyone what his job really was. To his family and friends, he said he was out practicing his skating. It was true that he got a lot of practice. Some days he skated for miles, answering dozens of urgent calls. Other days there might be only two calls, or only one. And now and then came a day when the feelings pouring through the phone contained not a single thread of distress, when all the dogs in all the twenty blocks were well-fed and contented, either safe at home or romping happily with their people. On those afternoons, Martin left his skates in the apartment (at 350 Lincoln Avenue), went to the 14th Street Park, and played ball with his own dog, who was no longer sad.

118

COMMUNICATIONS Among Creatures

Like other works in the genre of science fiction, Jeanne DuPrau's "The ACES Phone" is predicated upon ideas about science and technology: imaginative extrapolations drawing upon the author's love of science and her ideas about a possible future for technological innovation. Sometime in the not-too-distant future, perhaps, humans and other creatures could, conceivably, communicate with each other using powerful new technological innovations—even using special cell phones that could intercept "feeling waves" from dogs! However, though such advances might be at least remotely plausible, this "Assistance for Canines in Emergency Situations" cell-phone technology does not currently exist.

Even without ACES cell phones, however, we humans are learning to comprehend some facets of other animals' emotional states and to interpret some of the information they communicate, either directly to us or among themselves. Animal communication, much like human communication, uses the powers of the sensory organs (eyes, ears, noses, mouths, skin) to transmit and receive messages: animals signal each other and intercept each other's signals via visual communication (sight), acoustical communication (hearing), chemical communication (smell and taste), and tactile communication (touch).

Visual messages from animals are signals that other animals, and sometimes people, can see; one example is canine "play-bowing." A dog or other canine (such as a wolf) will bow to another to signal a willingness to play and an absence of aggression. When a dog bows to another dog, lowering its chest toward the ground and crouching down on its front legs while wagging its tail, it is inviting the other dog to romp, to play, to have fun. The bowing dog is also signaling an absence of aggression; saying, in essence, "I won't try to hurt you—this is all just for fun!" You may have observed enthusiastic pet dogs making this gesture toward their human companions, too; they are communicating "Let's play!" with canine body language.

Acoustical, or sound-based, signals are messages transmitted via soundwaves to other animals, which perceive the messages and interpret the information conveyed in them—sometimes as warnings or threats, sometimes as "words of welcome." Some species of animals emit quite specific sounds to communicate specific information to other animals—either members of the animals' own social network or outsiders. The vervet monkey, for example, a creature that lives in complex social groups in parts of eastern Africa, uses distinct calls to warn the other members of its troop of different types of dangerous predators; one vervet call might indicate that a hungry leopard is approaching the troop, and another might warn of a poisonous snake entering the troop's vicinity.

Zoologists are still unraveling many mysteries of animal sensory communication; for example, chemical messages, called pheromones, which involve smell and taste, are difficult for humans to perceive and study. Tactile communications, involving touch, are often easier to understand; anyone who has had a cat rub up against his or her leg can at least guess at the ideas being expressed: "I like you," or perhaps, "I'm here; notice me."

The multifaceted, sometimes surprising domain of sensory communication among animals can be fascinating to explore; there is still a great deal for us humans to attempt to understand. As far as we know, our closest friends, the canines, are not yet capable of communicating with us or with each other by cellular telephone; that capability still lies squarely within the realm of literature and, in particular, science fiction. However, dogs and other animals most certainly do communicate, in myriad ways, both with others of their species and, on occasion, with people. With what you have already learned, you can now interpret at least one sensory message that a creature in your neighborhood might send: the next time a dog bows to you, he or she is not trying to be formal; it's playtime!

Dig Deeper

How to Analyze the Text

Use these pages to learn about Story Structure, Alliteration, and Style and Tone. Then read "The ACES Phone" again to apply what you learned.

Story Structure

The science fiction story "The ACES Phone" contains characters, setting, and plot, which are all important **story elements**. These story elements work together to make up the **story structure**.

The plot includes **episodes,** or events, that happen in a certain sequence. Pay attention to how the episodes unfold to understand how the characters respond or change as the plot moves toward a resolution.

Look back at pages 110–118. Why does Mrs. DeSalvio change her mind and allow Martin to keep the ACES phone? What are the episodes that lead her to change her mind?

Setting	Characters
Plot	

RL.6.3 describe how a story's or drama's plot unfolds and how characters respond or change; **RL.6.4** determine the meaning of words and phrases, including figurative and connotative meanings/analyze impact of word choice; **L.6.3b** maintain consistency in style and tone

COMMON CORE

Alliteration

When authors use **alliteration**, they repeat a beginning consonant sound in a series of two or more words: for example, *the deep, dark depths.* Authors may use alliteration to emphasize important words or to create a mood, which is the emotion readers experience when reading a selection.

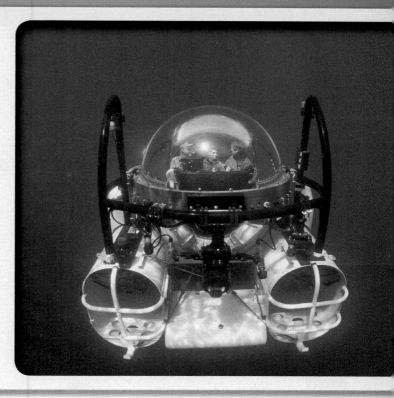

Style and Tone

The way in which an author tells a story allows for his or her own voice to be heard. Authors often maintain a consistent **tone** throughout a scene in a story to create a specific mood. For example, an author who writes *The icy wind swirled and howled around me as I sat shivering alone in the dark* wants to create a fearful tone.

Your Turn

RETURN TO THE ESSENTIAL QUESTION

 Turn and Talk Review the selection with a partner to prepare to discuss this question: *What is the difference between hearing and listening?* As you discuss, take turns reviewing and explaining the key ideas in your discussion.

Classroom Conversation

Continue your discussion of "The ACES Phone" by explaining your answers to these questions:

1 What do you learn about Martin from the way he reacts to the strange sounds on the ACES phone?

2 What do you think the author wants the reader to learn about communication and listening to others?

3 Why does Mrs. DeSalvio decide that Martin is the right person to rescue dogs?

WHAT DID YOU HEAR?

Listen with a Purpose Work with a partner to find examples in the text of Martin and Mrs. DeSalvio listening. What do they hear? What happens to them when they listen? Discuss how listening helps them solve at least three problems. Cite text evidence to support your ideas.

Response At the end of "The ACES Phone," Mrs. DeSalvio gives Martin the ACES phone to keep. Do you think Martin should be given the phone? Write a paragraph that explains whether Martin is the right person to rescue dogs. Use story details and what you have inferred, or figured out, from the text as evidence to support your argument.

Writing Tip

As you write your response, make sure that each sentence includes a simple subject and a simple predicate. Remember to use transition words and phrases to link the evidence for your argument.

COMMON CORE **RL.6.1** cite textual evidence to support analysis of what the text says explicitly as well as inferences drawn; **RL.6.3** describe how a story's or drama's plot unfolds and how characters respond or change; **W.6.9a** apply grade 6 Reading standards to literature; **SL.6.1c** pose and respond to questions and make comments that contribute to the discussion; **SL.6.1d** review key ideas expressed and demonstrate understanding of multiple perspectives

✓ **GENRE**

Informational text, such as this science article, gives facts and examples about a topic.

✓ **TEXT FOCUS**

Graph Informational text may include a graph, a diagram that shows how different facts and numbers relate to one other. A graph may present information that is the same as or enhances the text.

COMMON CORE **RL.6.7** compare and contrast the experience of reading to listening or viewing; **RI.6.10** read and comprehend literary nonfiction

Silent Noise

by Jacqueline Adams

Dog owners are accustomed to seeing their pets prick their ears when everything seems silent. Like many animals, dogs hear sounds that are beyond human reach.

Biologist Katy Payne listened to elephants communicate at a zoo in Portland, Oregon. Even when the elephants seemed to be silent, she felt the air throb. It reminded her of the throbbing from a pipe organ's low, doleful tones.

Payne began to wonder if elephants made noises not heard by humans. She recorded the elephants with devices that pick up sounds below the range of human hearing. She discovered a torrent of rumbling. "There was a whole communication system down there that people hadn't known about," she said. This would help solve an elephant mystery that had puzzled biologists for years.

Elephants pick up frequencies too low for humans to hear.

How Low Can You Go?

Biologists have heard a wide range of elephant sounds, from mothers' gentle rumblings as they coaxed their calves along to urgent trumpeting that warned of danger. But how elephants kept track of each other in the wild remained a mystery. Elephants lived clustered in groups that stayed a couple miles apart but traveled in the same direction. When one group changed direction, other groups swiveled to follow. How did the elephants know what faraway groups were doing?

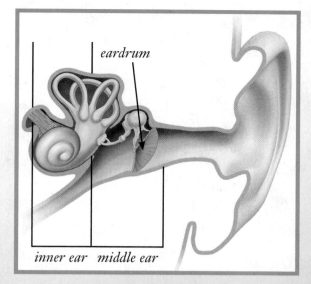

eardrum

inner ear middle ear

The mystery was solved when Payne discovered that elephants communicate with infrasonic sound. Because low-pitched transmissions travel farther, elephants can communicate over long distances.

Catch the Wave

Sound energy travels in waves. When sound waves reach the outer ear, they are funneled inside, starting a chain reaction. The eardrum vibrates, moving tiny bones in the middle ear and passing the waves to the inner ear.

The number of waves that travel each second is a sound's frequency, measured in hertz (Hz). The human ear is tuned to hear frequencies between 20 and 20,000 Hz.

Squeaks and Chirps

Animals such as dogs, dolphins, and bats go to the opposite extreme. They pick up supersonic, or ultrasonic, sound frequencies. These sounds are above the range of human hearing.

Even though bats can see, sight isn't enough for finding insects at night. Bats send out a clamor of supersonic chirps into what looks like a dark void. These high-frequency waves bounce off insects and come back to tell the bat where the insects are. To humans, what seems like a quiet night is filled with "silent" noise!

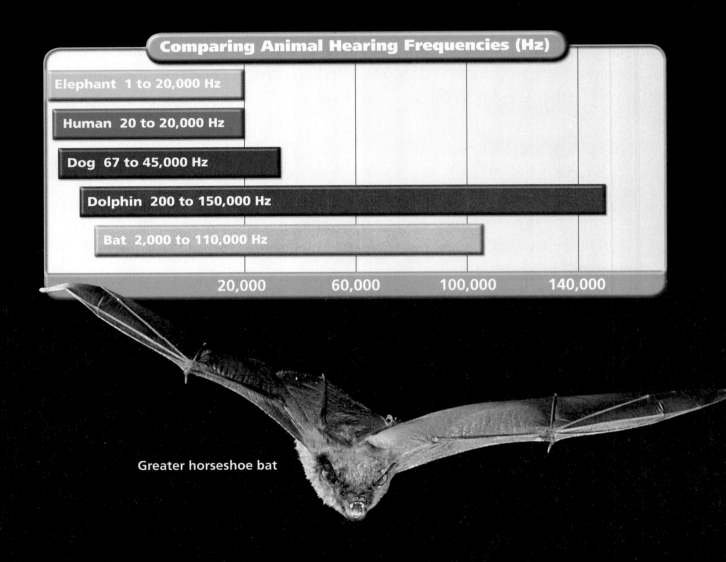

Comparing Animal Hearing Frequencies (Hz)

Elephant 1 to 20,000 Hz

Human 20 to 20,000 Hz

Dog 67 to 45,000 Hz

Dolphin 200 to 150,000 Hz

Bat 2,000 to 110,000 Hz

20,000   60,000   100,000   140,000

Greater horseshoe bat

Compare Texts

Compare Signals "The ACES Phone" and "Silent Noise" are about animal sounds and communication. Use the following questions to compare and contrast the selections: *In what ways are the ACES phone and the sound device used by scientists similar? How are the animal signals coming from the ACES phone different from the animal signals heard by scientists?* Use text evidence from both selections to support your answers.

TEXT TO SELF

Translate a Message In "The ACES Phone," Martin hears dogs in distress. Think about a time when you could tell what an animal was trying to communicate. Write a brief explanation of how the animal's noises, behaviors, or movements sent a message. Include an illustration and a speech balloon to show what the message was.

TEXT TO WORLD

Learn About Animal Rescue "The ACES Phone" is a science fiction story that features a way of rescuing dogs in distress. Find out about animal-rescue organizations that exist to help animals in need. Use a local telephone book or online resources to help you locate information.

COMMON CORE **RL.6.1** cite textual evidence to support analysis of what the text says explicitly as well as inferences drawn; **RL.6.9** compare and contrast texts in different forms or genres on their approaches to themes and topics; **RI.6.1** cite textual evidence to support analysis of what the text says explicitly as well as inferences drawn

Grammar

What Is a Common Noun? What Is a Proper Noun? When you talk or write about a general person, place, thing, or idea, you use a **common noun**. When you talk or write about a particular person, place, thing, or idea, you use a **proper noun**. Names of people, places, and organizations are proper nouns. In a proper noun with more than one word, such as the name of an organization, capitalize the first word, the last word, and all other important words.

Common Nouns	Proper Nouns
woman	Mrs. DeSalvio
street	Avenue B
organization	Assistance for Canines in Emergency Situations

An **appositive** is a word or group of words that comes right after the noun that it explains.

The flier is from Friends of the Park, a community organization.

Try This! **With a partner, read aloud each sentence below. Identify common and proper nouns. Then find the two appositives. Identify the noun that each appositive explains.**

1. Pilar Burgos, my best friend, loves animals.

2. She volunteers at the Oceanside Aquarium.

3. The aquarium is located at the intersection of Beach Road and Railroad Street.

4. Pilar is a member of Cat and Dog Companions, a group of volunteers.

You can make your writing clearer by adding appositives after proper nouns. Using precise common nouns instead of general ones will make your writing more interesting.

Proper Noun without Appositive, General Noun	Proper Noun with Appositive, Precise Noun

Mrs. DeSalvio asked Martin to give her the device.	Mrs. DeSalvio, an older woman wearing a knit hat and purple coat, asked Martin to give her the cell phone.

 **Connect Grammar to Writing**

As you revise your fictional narrative next week, think about replacing general nouns with proper nouns or precise common nouns. Also, remember that some nouns can be explained by adding appositives.

COMMON CORE **W.6.4** produce writing in which development, organization, and style are appropriate to task, purpose, and audience; **W.6.5** develop and strengthen writing by planning, revising, editing, rewriting, or trying a new approach

Narrative Writing

Reading-Writing Workshop: Prewrite

✓ **Organization** Every **fictional narrative** needs an interesting conflict, or problem, involving its characters. As you explore the topic for your story, think about different kinds of conflicts you might choose. Develop a plot with a conflict your readers will find interesting.

Antoine made a chart to generate story conflicts for his main character. Then he chose his favorite idea and created a story map to organize his narrative.

Writing Process Checklist

▶ **Prewrite**

✓ Will the setting, characters, and plot interest my readers?

✓ Will I enjoy writing about this story idea?

✓ Does my plot have a conflict and resolution?

✓ Have I planned a dramatic, exciting climax?

✓ Do I know how I will develop my characters?

Draft

Revise

Edit

Publish and Share

Exploring a Topic

Person Against Person	Person Against Supernatural Forces	Person Against Self
A boy can communicate with birds & tries to stop the town millionaire from cutting down the town forest.	A boy finds markers that make drawings come to life, but *his brother* ∧accidentally creates monsters that chase the boys.	A boy superhero develops a fear of heights & has trouble rescuing people.

130

Story Map

Setting	Characters
Place: Jake's home, a two-story house in a quiet suburban neighborhood Time: the present	Jake: ordinary kid, likes to draw, brave Ralph: Jake's younger brother, causes trouble, easily frightened

Conflict: Jake has special markers, but his brother finds them and creates monsters.

Event 1: At a flea market, Jake finds markers that make drawings come to life.

Event 2: Jake sets up a booth where he draws anything people request.

Event 3: Ralph finds the markers and draws monsters.

Climax: The monsters come to life and chase Jake and Ralph.

Resolution: Jake erases the drawings, and the monsters disappear.

Reading as a Writer

What elements of Antoine's plan will make the conflict interesting? What can you do to your story's conflict to make the plot more interesting?

When I organized my fictional narrative, I included interesting events that show how the conflict unfolds.

Vocabulary in Context

TARGET VOCABULARY

aspect
tendency
aptly
genuinely
tension
parallel
welfare
credit
predominantly
innovation

Vocabulary Reader

Context Cards

**L.6.6** acquire and use general academic and domain-specific words and phrases/gather vocabulary knowledge for comprehension or expression

1 aspect

Being in a family has many sides to it. One aspect is doing things together.

2 tendency

Some family members have a tendency, or are likely, to enjoy the same kinds of food.

3 aptly

The composer J. S. Bach had twenty children. Aptly, or fittingly, seven of them also became famous musicians.

4 genuinely

Even though brothers and sisters may fight, they genuinely, or truly, care about each other.

Go Digital

▶ Study each Context Card.

▶ Tell a story about two or more pictures, using Vocabulary words of your choice.

5 tension

Disagreements about chores can cause tension, or stress, among family members.

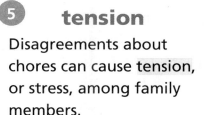

6 parallel

This father and son have parallel interests. They both enjoy cooking the family meal.

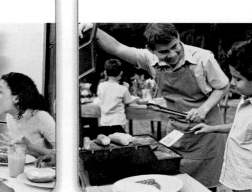

7 welfare

Parents are often concerned for their children's welfare—their health and safety.

8 credit

An author's family members often receive credit, or recognition, on a page of a book.

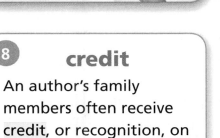

This book is dedicated to my parents, with gratitude.

9 predominantly

Going to the movies is what this family predominantly, or mostly, does for entertainment.

10 innovation

Children often teach their grandparents how to use a new gadget, or technological innovation.

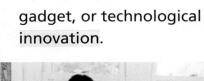

Read and Comprehend

Go Digital

☑ TARGET SKILL

Fact and Opinion As you read "The Myers Family," look for **facts** which give evidence that can be proved, and **opinions** or claims which give personal views and beliefs. Look for words that can signal opinions, such as *thinks, wants, believes*, and *feels*. Note how the facts and opinions the author includes tell about the Myers family. Use a graphic organizer like this one to help you.

Fact	Opinion

☑ TARGET STRATEGY

Summarize As you read "The Myers Family," briefly **summarize**, or retell, the important parts of the text in your own words.

COMMON CORE

RI.6.2 determine a central idea of a text/provide a summary; **RI.6.8** trace and evaluate the argument and specific claims in a text

134

Performance and Visual Arts

The arts provide forms for expressing yourself in creative ways. Performance arts include dancing, singing, playing music, and acting. Visual arts include painting, drawing, and sculpting.

Creating a book that people will want to look at, read, and enjoy takes planning and hard work. In "The Myers Family," you will learn how a family works together to create both a literary and a visual experience for readers.

ANCHOR TEXT

Pass It Down
*Five Picture-Book Families
Make Their Mark*

LEONARD S. MARCUS

✓ TARGET SKILL

Fact and Opinion Decide whether an idea can be proved or if it is a feeling or belief.

✓ GENRE

A **biography** tells about one person's life or several people's lives and is written by another person. As you read, look for:

- ▶ information about why the person or people are important
- ▶ opinions and personal judgments based on facts
- ▶ events in time order

 COMMON CORE **RI.6.3** analyze how a key individual, event, or idea is introduced, illustrated, and elaborated; **RI.6.6** determine the author's point of view or purpose and explain how it is conveyed; **RI.6.8** trace and evaluate the argument and specific claims in a text; **RI.6.10** read and comprehend literary nonfiction

MEET THE AUTHOR

Leonard S. Marcus

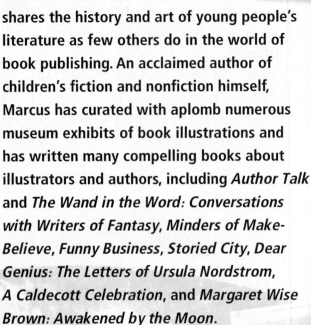

As a renowned historian, versatile writer, and incisive book critic, Leonard S. Marcus knows and shares the history and art of young people's literature as few others do in the world of book publishing. An acclaimed author of children's fiction and nonfiction himself, Marcus has curated with aplomb numerous museum exhibits of book illustrations and has written many compelling books about illustrators and authors, including *Author Talk* and *The Wand in the Word: Conversations with Writers of Fantasy*, *Minders of Make-Believe*, *Funny Business*, *Storied City*, *Dear Genius: The Letters of Ursula Nordstrom*, *A Caldecott Celebration*, and *Margaret Wise Brown: Awakened by the Moon*.

Marcus has curated children's book exhibitions at the Eric Carle Museum of Picture Book Art, the New York Public Library, the Boston Athenaeum, the Enoch Pratt Free Library in Baltimore, the Joslyn Art Museum in Omaha, and the Meridian International Center in Washington, D.C., among others. He also reviews books qualitatively for magazines such as *Horn Book*, judges contests for literary awards such as The Ezra Jack Keats New Writer Award, and has received accolades for his participation as literary director of The Night Kitchen Radio Theater on satellite radio. Marcus was born and raised in Mount Vernon, New York, and later matriculated at and graduated from Yale University and the University of Iowa Graduate Writers' Workshop.

The Myers Family
from Pass It Down

by Leonard S. Marcus

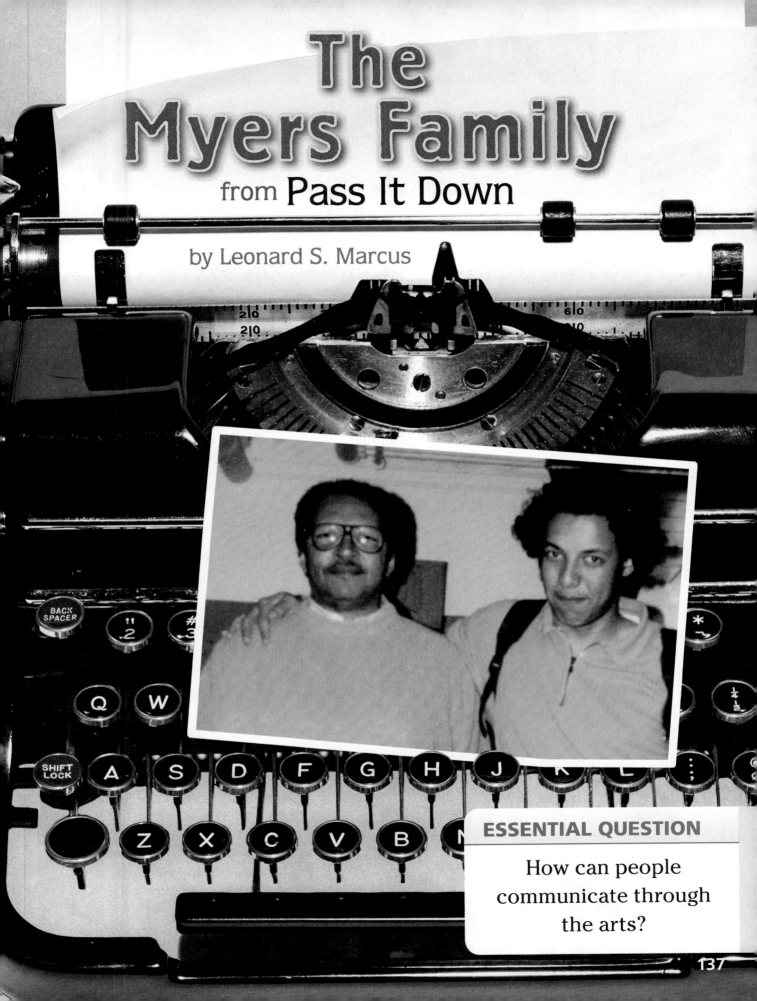

ESSENTIAL QUESTION

How can people communicate through the arts?

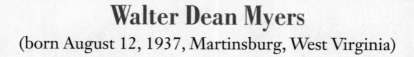

Walter Dean Myers
(born August 12, 1937, Martinsburg, West Virginia)

Christopher Myers
(born October 17, 1974, Astoria, New York)

"We lived on the cusp," Walter Dean Myers says of the Jersey City home where his son, Christopher, grew up during the 1970s. "On one side of our house, the neighborhood was all white. On the other side it was predominantly black. Christopher was a mixed-race kid. Because he could read at four, he started school early. His classmates were all two years older than him. He was not a good athlete. So he was pushed around a bit in school."

"Classmates looked at me," Christopher Myers recalls, "as if I had three heads."

Walter, the author of *Bad Boy* (Amistad/HarperCollins, 2001), grew up knowing a lot about not getting along well at school. Raised by foster parents in the economically depressed Harlem of the 1940s, he was a restless, inward-looking, overtall boy with a lisp and a serious tendency to take a fist to anyone who made fun of him. His foster parents worked long hours to make ends meet. Although genuinely concerned about his welfare, they were often unaware when their son skipped entire weeks of school.

Walter was lucky enough to have a few teachers who, despite his record as a troublemaker, wanted to help him. Some gave him books that made him hungry for more books. Reading—and by middle school, writing—became his life preservers.

Walter Dean Myers and Christopher Myers

As a teenager, as Walter became more aware that "blacks did not have the same chances as whites," his doubts about the future multiplied. It never occurred to him that he might one day write a book. Even as a first-time author, as a man in his thirties, Walter says, "I didn't think I was going to have a career. I thought that maybe I would get published occasionally." After years of earning his living as an editor, Walter became a full-time writer in 1977. He was forty. Christopher was three.

"I'm an early riser, and when Christopher was going to day care," Walter recalls of that time, "I'd finish work in the late morning and pick him up, and we would hang out together in the afternoon, which was very cool. We talked, very often solving the world's problems. I enjoyed his company.

"We read together: first comics, which had been forbidden to me as a child, and *Reader's Digest*, because we both loved jokes. Later, we read poetry." On weekends, father and son took the train into Manhattan and headed for their "Golden Triangle"—their three favorite bookstores, including one called Forbidden Planet—from which they always returned with armloads of books.

Walter, as his foster father had done with him, often told Christopher farfetched stories that he presented as true. Christopher remembers: "I wouldn't eat Brussels sprouts for years because of a story he told me. I had asked him, 'What *are* they? They're so odd-looking.' He responded with a long, involved story about a war we had fought in the sixties with a race of very small aliens. Brussels sprouts were the aliens' leftover heads. I was glad to find this out because now I knew why I was *never* going to eat Brussels sprouts again."

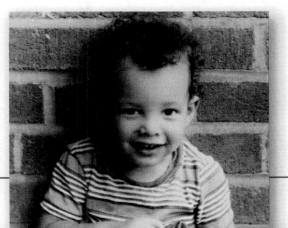

Christopher, age two

ANALYZE THE TEXT

Fact and Opinion The author argues that reading and writing became Walter Dean Myers's lifesavers. How do the facts in the selection support the author's claim?

This was not the only way that Walter taught his son not to believe everything he heard or read. "Pop," Christopher says, "would go through my school history texts and write corrections in them. When a book referred to 'bringing the slaves from Africa,' he would cross that out, wanting to be sure I understood that African *people* had been *enslaved*. I was a good student, but I learned early on that education didn't necessarily happen in school. And I learned from Pop that books did not come down from on high: that people wrote them, and that there was work for me to do."

Christopher was drawing two hours a day by the time he was nine. Walter takes no credit for this. "His mom, who paints, must have noticed he had talent, because I didn't! Connie would put his drawings up on the refrigerator or the wall. At about ten, he won some contests, but I still wasn't paying much attention. Then he had a picture published in a children's magazine. I saw it—a drawing of an antelope or something—and said, 'That's really *good*.'"

Connie took Christopher to museums and comic book fairs and once, on his birthday, on a tour of Marvel Comics. Walter, meanwhile, involved his wife and their son in every aspect of his work.

Christopher remembers: "My father wrote ten pages a day. When he was done, he would come down and have me read it out loud so that my mother and he could talk about it."

As a teenager, Christopher accompanied his mother to the library to help research Walter's books. "Digging up information about African-American history strengthened my link to my cultural background," Christopher says. "I also realized that there were true stories worth finding, and that it was possible to unearth them."

Christopher and Walter at an event celebrating the publication of Harlem, *Stapleton Branch Library (Staten Island), New York Public Library, May 1998.*

Collage self-portrait made by Christopher, age fourteen.

When Walter discussed a new publishing contract with his wife, he encouraged Christopher to join in the discussion. "He wanted me even at nine and ten to see," Christopher says, "that a contract is part of the process by which books are made."

What Christopher most wanted, however, was to draw the pictures for his father's books. He recalls the first time he and his father talked about this: "I was ten and reading fantasy novels when Pop said one day, 'Let's do a fantasy together. What would you like to see in it?'

'How about a black unicorn?' I said.

'That's cool,' he said. 'What's his problem? We need to give him a problem.'" Years passed before Walter was able to answer his own question and finish *Shadow of the Red Moon* (Scholastic, 1995). Christopher, then a college student, illustrated the book, finally getting his wish.

ANALYZE THE TEXT

Analyze Events What anecdotes in the selection explain the events that lead to Walter Dean Myers and Christopher collaborating on their first book?

In all, Christopher illustrated two of his father's books while still at college: *Shadow of the Red Moon* and a picture book called *Harlem* (Scholastic, 1997). Both times, Walter suggested the idea and both times, Walter says, "the publisher was not happy about it. It gets too personal. They did not want to have to turn down my son. So Christopher did sample illustrations and had them accepted. When *Harlem* won a Caldecott Honor, everyone began saying, 'Father, son; father, son!' It's been much easier since then."

In 1999, Christopher launched his solo career with *Black Cat* (Scholastic, 1999), a haunting picture book that, aptly, traces the wanderings of a stray cat as he makes a place for himself in a big and not always welcoming city.

The next picture book Walter wrote for Christopher to illustrate was about the blues. As in the past, Christopher showed his father the artwork for *Blues Journey* (Holiday House, 2003) only after he had finished it.

Walter says, "I think he's still afraid of that father-and-son thing, the father as judge." Christopher agrees. "If we talked about it sooner, he might make some comment that would 'get into my head.'" But Christopher is not alone in his worries. Walter adds, "We're both nervous because we both want to hold up our end. We feed on the tension."

"Writing *Blues Journey*," Walter recalls, "was easy for me. I am comfortable with the blues lyric form." For Christopher, however, illustrating his father's poems was anything but easy. "I wanted the images to tell a parallel story, not just link one-to-one to the poems."

Walter admired his son's artwork but was puzzled by "a picture with a fisherman and his net. It didn't seem to go with any of the poems. So I wrote another poem to go with the image.

"Years earlier," Walter says, "I learned about the power of images from Christopher. My wife and I collect photographs. We have about ten thousand, most of black life between 1855 and 1940. I began collecting them when I was teaching a writing workshop for middle-school kids in Jersey City. Christopher, who was thirteen, was there too, drawing the illustrations for their yearbook. The kids were so into the images Christopher was making, I thought, let's bring in some photographs. That experience also led to *Brown Angels*" (HarperCollins, 1993).

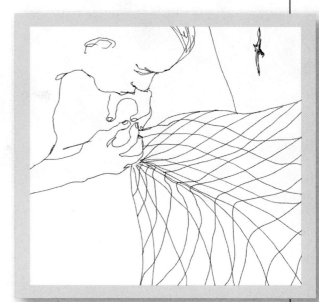

Pencil study by Christopher for Blues Journey.

Finished art in mixed media on brown-bag paper for the fisherman poem in Blues Journey.

Looking back, Walter says, "I think that probably I have gained more from Christopher than he has from me. I've published more than eighty books. After a while you repeat yourself. But with Christopher's constant push toward innovation, I feel refreshed."

When Walter first saw the art for *Blues Journey*, he paid Christopher his version of a high compliment: "If I'd known you were going to do something that good," he told his son, "I would have written it better."

By now, Christopher usually knows when his father is teasing. "Oftentimes," he says, "he'll call me. I'll pick up the phone and he'll say, 'Why you talking on the phone?' And I'll say, 'Because you called me.' 'Well, I'm working,' he'll say. 'I can't talk to people like you!' Then he'll hang up the phone. In that joking way of his there's also a seriousness—the idea that he's always working, and that my life has to be about always working too."

> **ANALYZE THE TEXT**
>
> **Author's Purpose** What words and phrases in the text let you know the author's perspective on Walter Dean Myers and his son?

blues journey

by Walter Dean Myers
illustrated by Christopher Myers

Blues Journey *(mixed media on brown-bag paper, Holiday House, 2003).*

Dig Deeper

How to Analyze the Text

Use these pages to learn about Fact and Opinion, Author's Purpose, and how to Analyze Events. Then read "The Myers Family" again to apply what you learned.

Fact and Opinion

Biographies such as "The Myers Family" contain facts about real people, along with some of their opinions. A **fact** is a statement that can be proved to be true. An author includes facts in order to give information. An **opinion** tells a thought, feeling, or belief. It cannot be proved. However, by including reasons and evidence for opinions, an author can build a strong **argument** for his or her **claims.**

Look back at page 139 in "The Myers Family." In this section, readers learn that when Walter Dean Myers and his son "would hang out together," Walter Dean Myers thought it was "cool." Which sentences support Myers's opinion? Has the author built a strong argument?

Fact	Opinion

RI.6.3 analyze how a key individual, event, or idea is introduced, illustrated, and elaborated; **RI.6.6** determine the author's point of view or purpose and explain how it is conveyed; **RI.6.8** trace and evaluate the argument and specific claims in a text

Author's Purpose

Part of an **author's purpose** for writing a biography may be to show his or her point of view, or perspective, on the subject. Author Leonard Marcus shares information that tells about three members of the Myers family. From this information, readers get to know what the Myers family is really like and how they learn from each other. An author may give positive or negative information about a subject based on his or her point of view.

Analyze Events

Authors of biographies must choose which **events** to include when writing about a subject's life. Events in a sequence often lead up to an important milestone in a life. The author writes about several events in the lives of Walter Dean Myers and his son. Analyzing how these events are introduced and illustrated throughout a text can give readers a better understanding of the Myers family.

Your Turn

RETURN TO THE ESSENTIAL QUESTION

 Review the selection with a partner to prepare to discuss this question: *How can people communicate through the arts?* Ask questions of your partner to clarify his or her answer. Ask your partner for text evidence that supports the answer.

 **Classroom Conversation**

Continue your discussion of "The Myers Family" by explaining your answers to these questions:

1. What early impact did a few teachers have on Walter Dean Myers's life as an adult?

2. In what ways did Christopher's mother help teach him?

3. Name two ways that Christopher's parents showed their strong interest in visual images? What text evidence supports your answer?

FATHER, SON

Find Facts Walter Dean Myers didn't pay a lot of attention to his son's artwork until Christopher's drawing was published in a magazine. With a partner, discuss what Walter Dean Myers then did for and with his son that helped lead Christopher to become an artist. Find evidence in the biography that supports your answers.

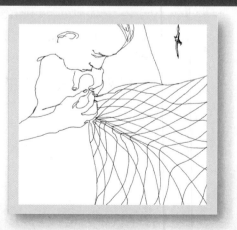

WRITE ABOUT READING

Response Walter Dean Myers believes that he has gained much from working with Christopher. In what ways do you think Walter Dean Myers was influenced by his son? Write a paragraph explaining your opinion. Use facts and events from the biography as evidence to support your opinion.

Writing Tip

State your opinion at the beginning of your response. Use words and phrases to link the different reasons and evidence for your opinion.

RI.6.1 cite textual evidence to support analysis of what the text says explicitly as well as inferences drawn; **RI.6.3** analyze how a key individual, event, or idea is introduced, illustrated, and elaborated; **W.6.9b** apply grade 6 Reading standards to literary nonfiction; **SL.6.1a** come to discussions prepared/explicitly draw on preparation to probe and reflect on ideas under discussion; **SL.6.1c** pose and respond to questions and make comments that contribute to the discussion

Sound Check

Sound Check

by Joel Mallery

CAST OF CHARACTERS

Elisa Santos, age 12

Manny Santos, age 15

Anna Santos, age 10

Pedro Santos (Dad)

Elena Santos (Mom)

Setting: Elisa's middle school, Portland, Oregon.

Elisa: Hurry up, Manny! We still have tons to do.

Manny: Elisa, relax. You have this annoying tendency to get worked up before a show. I don't need the tension.

Elisa: Aren't you concerned about my welfare? We're singing in front of *my* school and *my* friends.

Manny: You should give your family a little more credit. We're professionals. Dad knows every aspect of the music business.

Elisa: I know, but what if I hit a wrong note?

☑ GENRE

Readers' theater is a text that has been formatted for characters to read aloud.

☑ TEXT FOCUS

Directions A text may include a set of instructions telling how to do something, often by guiding readers to follow a series of steps.

 RL.6.10 read and comprehend literature

150

 Go Digital

Anna: La-la-la-la-la . . . What? I'm just doing my scales.

Manny: I think we should all focus predominantly on setting up the sound system. Read me the directions, Elisa.

Elisa: Okay. I'm sure I did the first one.

1. Plug in the amplifier.
2. Put the instruments and the microphones where they belong on the stage.

Anna: I'm on it!

Elisa: Shh! Where was I?

3. Connect the correct cords to the guitar, keyboard, and microphones.
4. Plug all cords into the amplifier.
5. Connect the speaker cords to the amplifier and then to the speakers.

Manny: Nothing is happening. Hmm, I think we may genuinely have a problem.

Mom: Is everything ready for the performance?

Elisa: Mom, Dad, thank goodness you're here. We don't have any sound!

Dad: Really? I can hear you just fine.

Elisa: Dad! This is my worst nightmare and you're making jokes!

Mom: Did you check that the correct cords are connected?

Manny: Yes. See where they're running parallel to the stage?

Mom: The speakers are plugged in to the amplifier.

Anna: Hey, did we try this plug?

Manny: Wow! Plugging in the amp! What an innovation!

Elisa: I guess I forgot to do Step 1.

Dad: That's okay. Luckily, Anna was here.

Anna: I guess I supply the power in this family.

Mom: Aptly put, Anna!

Dad: Great idea for a new song! Here's to Anna, the hero of the hour! Just plug her in and she'll supply the power!

Compare Texts

TEXT TO TEXT

Compare Text Forms Talk with a partner about "The Myers Family" and "Sound Check." Discuss how the Myers family and the family in "Sound Check" express their creativity. How are both texts about working together? After you discuss your ideas, work together to write your answers, using evidence from the text as support.

TEXT TO SELF

Write a Story Walter Dean Myers told his son that Brussels sprouts were "aliens' leftover heads." Draw a picture of a food you don't like. Write an imaginative story that explains what it "really" is.

TEXT TO WORLD

Explore Careers Writing, making music, and creating art are valuable talents. With a partner, brainstorm a list of careers that use these talents. Choose one from your list and research the education and training needed to work in that career. Then give a brief explanation that summarizes what you learned.

COMMON CORE **RL.6.1** cite textual evidence to support analysis of what the text says explicitly as well as inferences drawn; **RI.6.1** cite textual evidence to support analysis of what the text says explicitly as well as inferences drawn; **SL.6.1c** pose and respond to questions and make comments that contribute to the discussion

Grammar

How Are Plural and Possessive Nouns Formed? A **singular noun** names one person, place, thing, or idea. A **plural noun** names more than one. To form most plural nouns, add **-s** or **-es** to the end of the noun. A **possessive noun** names who or what owns or has something. To form a singular possessive noun, add an **apostrophe** (') and **-s**. Also add an apostrophe and **-s** to form the possessive when a person's name ends in **-s.** When a plural noun ends with **-s**, add only an apostrophe to form the possessive. When a plural noun, such as *men,* does not end with **-s**, add **'s**.

Nouns			
Singular	**Plural**	**Singular Possessive**	**Plural Possessive**
museum	museums	museum's	museums'
process	processes	process's	processes'
story	stories	story's	stories'
shelf	shelves	shelf's	shelves'
woman	women	woman's	women's

Try This! Copy the chart of nouns below onto another sheet of paper. Write the missing forms of each singular noun.

Singular	Plural	Singular Possessive	Plural Possessive
1 contest	_____	contest's	_____
2 child	_____	child's	_____
3 class	classes	_____	_____
4 library	_____	_____	libraries'

When you write possessive nouns, make sure you use the correct noun form and put the apostrophe in the correct place.

Incorrect	Correct
Blues Journey contains Walter Dean Myers' poems and his sons illustrations. This book can be found on many library's shelves.	*Blues Journey* contains Walter Dean Myers's poems and his son's illustrations. This book can be found on many libraries' shelves.

Connect Grammar to Writing

As you edit your fictional narrative, check each possessive noun to make sure it is written correctly.

Narrative Writing

Reading-Writing Workshop: Revise

✔ **Word Choice**   In "The Myers Family," the author chooses words and phrases carefully, thinking about the feelings and images his language will communicate. As you revise your **fictional narrative**, think about what details will create a vivid picture for your readers. Add precise words and phrases to create those details. Words that appeal to the senses can help your readers "see" and "hear" the story events.

Antoine drafted his story about a boy whose drawings come to life. Later, he added descriptive details and sensory language to make his writing vivid and to make his readers curious about what will happen.

Writing Process Checklist

Prewrite

Draft

▶ **Revise**

☑ **Does my beginning introduce the characters and setting?**

☑ **Does my plot contain a conflict, climax, and resolution?**

☑ **Did I include descriptive details and sensory language?**

☑ **Does my ending resolve the conflict?**

☑ **Did I combine sentences correctly?**

Edit

Publish and Share

Revised Draft

Everything he drew came to life! Next to his drawing of a ^tropical^ bird, a real bird suddenly appeared^, singing and chirping^. Next to his drawing of a motorcycle, a real motorcycle appeared^, crushing his desk^!

Much more excitement was yet to come.

Jake^'s^ ~~had a secret~~ (When) it got out, people everywhere wanted him to draw something for them. So he started ~~to draw for customers~~ ^his own booth at the flea market^.

Jake and the Remarkable Markers

by Antoine James

Jake Morris was an ordinary boy until he discovered some remarkable markers at a flea market. There were many bright colors in the set, plus one marker that didn't seem to have any color at all. When Jake took them up to his room and started drawing, he soon discovered that these were no ordinary art supplies. Everything he drew came to life! Next to his drawing of a tropical bird, a real bird suddenly appeared, singing and chirping. Next to his drawing of a motorcycle, a real motorcycle appeared, crushing his desk! Much more excitement was yet to come.

When Jake's secret got out, people everywhere wanted him to draw something for them. So he started his own booth at the flea market. People stood in line for an hour just to have Jake draw something. They didn't even care what he drew! Everyone seemed delighted.

Everyone, that is, except Ralph, Jake's younger brother. Ralph stood off to the side of the line, scowling. Ralph didn't like art or drawing. The only thing Ralph really liked was causing trouble.

Reading as a Writer

Where did Antoine use details to make his writing vivid? Where can you add descriptive details to your own story?

In my final story, I added descriptive details and sensory language to give readers a more vivid picture. I also used possessive nouns correctly.

Test
POWER

Read the passage "Maddie's Changing Ways." As you read, stop and answer each question using text evidence.

Maddie's Changing Ways

When the alarm clock buzzed for the second time, eleven-year-old Maddie dragged herself out of bed. As usual, she was tired from staying up late to watch a movie on TV. She hurriedly got ready for school and stuffed her notebook into her backpack on the way out. She had a feeling she had forgotten something, as she often did, but there was no time to worry about it.

In class, Maddie had a hard time concentrating. During a complicated math lesson, her mind began to wander. She was gazing out the window when her teacher, Ms. Lorenz, gently tapped her shoulder and said, "Maddie, unless I'm mistaken, you've forgotten your homework again. I'm sorry, but you'll have to stay after school today."

"I had a feeling I had forgotten something," Maddie mumbled.

---

1 How would you describe the character of Maddie from the episodes in the passage so far? Use examples from the text to support your response.

After school, Ms. Lorenz asked Maddie to choose a book from the classroom library and read quietly. Maddie picked up the nearest book on the shelf and yawned as she began to read. The book was about a girl who won a trumpet in a contest but didn't know how to play it. The girl then met a famous musician who invited her to a movie set. An illustration of the movie set sparked Maddie's interest. The picture made the character and plot come alive. Maddie became so involved in reading that at first she didn't hear Ms. Lorenz tell her she could go home. Maddie asked Ms. Lorenz if she could borrow the book.

RL.6.3 describe how a story's or drama's plot unfolds and how characters respond or change; **RL.6.4** determine the meaning of words and phrases, including figurative and connotative meanings/analyze impact of word choice; **RL.6.5** analyze how a sentence, chapter, scene, or stanza fits in the overall structure; **L.6.5a** interpret figures of speech in context

"Yes, of course," Ms. Lorenz replied. "I'm glad you're enjoying it, but please remember to write a story for your homework assignment tonight. I think you have the ability to write a very interesting story if you just keep your nose to the grindstone."

Maddie wasn't sure what a grindstone was, but she thought it would be pretty difficult to write anything with your nose pressed up against a stone. She tried to imagine doing that and laughed to herself at the picture in her mind.

> **2** What does the phrase *keep your nose to the grindstone* mean? Tell how the use of this phrase affects the tone of the passage.

That evening Maddie finished the book she had borrowed. She got so caught up in that story, though, that she completely forgot she was supposed to write a story of her own. As a result, she had to stay after school again the next day.

Ms. Lorenz told Maddie to use the time to write the story that she was supposed to have written the night before. After thinking about the assignment for a while, Maddie decided to write about a girl who loved movies. To make the story more exciting, she decided the girl should possess the power to jump into movies and become part of the action. Maddie's imagination began to soar as she began writing. Ideas just seemed to tumble out of her mind onto the paper.

> **3** How does the scene in which Maddie writes her story contribute to the development of the plot?

When Ms. Lorenz returned the story to Maddie the next day, there seemed to be green ink everywhere. (Ms. Lorenz used green ink to make comments and corrections because she believed students associated red ink with negative feelings.) Most of Maddie's papers came back sprinkled with green ink highlighting careless spelling and grammar errors. Maddie thanked Ms. Lorenz and tucked the story into her backpack to look at later.

That night, Maddie smiled as she read the comments Ms. Lorenz had written, beginning with "Nice job, Maddie! I like the way you included vivid details that make the characters seem real. Your plot is full of exciting events. I wish *I* could jump into movies! Write another draft to correct your errors, and turn it in next week."

Ms. Lorenz was a hard grader, but her helpful comments made Maddie want to do better. Maddie began to write a new version immediately, taking care to correct her previous errors. However, she got so caught up in rewriting and correcting her story that, once again, she forgot all about her other homework.

When Maddie put her story into the homework box the next morning, Ms. Lorenz said, "I find it delightful that you are returning *anything* to the homework box, Maddie, but you still owe me your other homework. I'm afraid you'll have to stay after school again today to do it." So that's what Maddie did. It's really not that hard to get the homework done, she thought, if you keep your nose to the grindstone and don't get distracted. Again, she pictured herself trying to write while keeping her nose pressed to a stone. She chuckled, and Ms. Lorenz looked up from correcting papers to smile at her.

That night, Maddie flipped through the television channels, looking for a movie to watch, but she found nothing that caught her interest. The idea popped into her head that the book she'd read about the girl with the trumpet would make a great movie. What if she wrote a *treatment* for the book, the way professional writers do to suggest ideas for movies? The treatment Maddie wrote identified which scenes and characters from the book to use in a movie.

When Ms. Lorenz returned Maddie's movie treatment, there were many corrections in green ink, but Maddie was pleased to see many positive comments. Ms. Lorenz had even included information about how to turn a treatment into a movie script.

With encouragement from Ms. Lorenz, Maddie began to get better about remembering to complete her homework assignments on time. She also found herself spending less time in the evenings watching movies and more time working and reworking new movie ideas.

As the weeks went by, Maddie noticed that her writing and her grades were steadily improving. When Ms. Lorenz suggested that she share some of her work with the class, the other students liked Maddie's ideas.

In fact, they liked them so much that they decided to work as a class to make their own movie from one of her scripts!

---

4 In what ways did Maddie change from the beginning to the ending of this story?

Unit 2

Vocabulary in Context

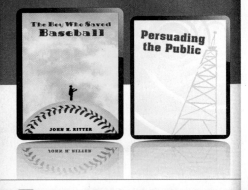

The Boy Who Saved Baseball
JOHN H. RITTER

Persuading the Public

✓ TARGET VOCABULARY

phenomenal
showdown
fundamental
flair
lingered
savor
gloat
berate
reserve
brainwashed

Vocabulary Reader

Are You a Team Player?

Context Cards

COMMON CORE **L.6.6** acquire and use general academic and domain-specific words and phrases/gather vocabulary knowledge for comprehension or expression

---

1 phenomenal

Winning a baseball game with a home run does not happen often. It is a phenomenal event.

2 showdown

Two rival football teams often meet each other in a showdown, or decisive contest.

3 fundamental

A glove is the fundamental, or basic, tool of an outfielder in a baseball game.

4 flair

A professional soccer player may display a lot of flair, or showy skill, during a game.

Go Digital

▶ Study each Context Card.

▶ Use two Vocabulary words to tell about an experience you had.

5 lingered

These fans have lingered on the field after the game. They are in no hurry to go home.

6 savor

This athlete takes a moment to savor, or enjoy, his feeling of accomplishment.

7 gloat

It is bad sportsmanship to gloat when you win, or to jeer about being better than another player.

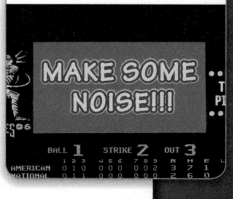

8 berate

A coach might berate, or angrily scold, players for not trying hard enough during a game.

9 reserve

Reserve players don't start in a game, but they may be called upon to play at any moment.

10 brainwashed

This sign urges people to cheer. Are they being brainwashed, or can they decide for themselves?

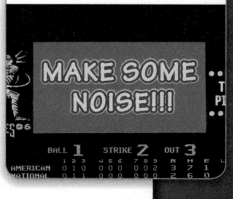

MAKE SOME NOISE!!!

BALL 1 STRIKE 2 OUT 3

AMERICAN
NATIONAL

Read and Comprehend

 Go Digital

☑ TARGET SKILL

Theme The **theme** of a fiction story is the central idea or message about life that the author wants readers to understand and remember. Readers must usually infer, or figure out, the theme from details such as the plot, setting, dialogue, and character changes. As you read "The Boy Who Saved Baseball," look for details that are clues to the theme. Use a graphic organizer like this one to record details and infer the theme.

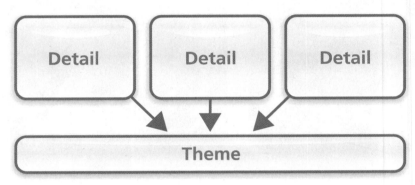

| Detail | Detail | Detail |

Theme

☑ TARGET STRATEGY

Analyze/Evaluate Study carefully, or **analyze**, the text in order to **evaluate** it, or form an opinion or judgment about it.

 COMMON CORE

RL.6.2 determine a theme or central idea of a text/provide a summary

The Media

Magazines, newspapers, the Internet, television, radio, blogs—what do these things have in common? Each is one type of medium within the larger group that we call the *media*. The media communicate information and keep people informed.

The media also have the power to influence people. When you listen to the media's points of view, you should also consider your own thoughts and feelings. In "The Boy Who Saved Baseball," you'll learn about media attention surrounding a small-town baseball game and about one boy's thoughts and feelings about that game.

ANCHOR TEXT

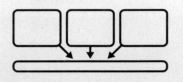

The Boy Who Saved **Baseball**

JOHN H. RITTER

☑ TARGET SKILL

Theme Think about details such as the characters' actions to determine the selection's theme, or central idea.

☑ GENRE

Realistic fiction has characters and events that are like people and events in real life. As you read, look for:

▸ characters who behave just as people do in real life
▸ a main character who overcomes a challenge
▸ real-life challenges

COMMON CORE **RL.6.2** determine a theme or central idea of a text/provide a summary; **RL.6.3** describe how a story's or drama's plot unfolds and how characters respond and change; **RL.6.4** determine the meaning of words or phrases, including figurative and connotative meanings/analyze impact of word choice; **RL.6.10** read and comprehend literature

MEET THE AUTHOR

John H. Ritter

"The driving force behind all my stories comes primarily from finding something that really bugs me," explains young-adult baseball novelist John H. Ritter. Influenced by his mother's songs and his father's sportswriting career, as well as by legendary groundbreaking figures as diverse as baseball icon Roberto Clemente and singer-songwriter Bob Dylan, Ritter developed an enduring love for both baseball and creative writing as he grew up. In addition to playing ball and playing music, Ritter was both a successful student and a notorious prankster in school, earning him recognition in high school as both Senior Class President and Senior Class Clown. In 2009, he wrote and published a prequel to *The Boy Who Saved Baseball* entitled *The Desperado Who Stole Baseball*.

MEET THE ILLUSTRATOR

Robin Eley

Robin Eley's work has garnered several awards and has been featured in an array of books, magazines, and newspapers. Eley was born in London, grew up in Australia, and attended the Illustration Academy in Sarasota, Florida. He earned his Bachelor's Degree in Fine Arts from Westmont College in Santa Barbara, California, where he also captained the basketball team. Eley now resides in Adelaide, South Australia, where he pursues his artistic visions, teaches illustration, and plays basketball.

The Boy Who Saved Baseball

by John H. Ritter   selection illustrated by Robin Eley

ESSENTIAL QUESTION

How do the media influence how people feel about events?

167

Local landowner Doc Altenheimer has promised his neighbors in Dillontown that he won't sell his land to a group of developers headed by Alabaster Jones, on one condition. Young Tom Gallagher's baseball team, the Dillontown Wildcats, will have to do what they've never done before—beat the all-star team from the camp down in Lake View Mesa. The task seems impossible until two things happen: a multitalented player, Cruz de la Cruz, joins the Wildcats' camp; and Cruz and Tom manage to persuade the gruff former star major-leaguer Dante Del Gato to be their coach. Over just a week, the team has grown in confidence and ability. Tom has even developed a computerized batting practice program called HitSim to help the team get ready for the big game. First the town, and now much of the country, is rooting for the Dillontown Wildcats.

By now, droves of reporters and photographers and television crews roamed the grounds. The dirt roadway cutting through Doc's land and heading to the ballpark was jammed, both sides, with satellite trucks, microwave trucks, radio vans, and SUVs.

All around the ball field, news crews set up lawn chairs, coolers, tripods, and umbrellas.

Some of the townspeople showed up with cookies and ice-cold lemonadeberry tea for the press, serving a few opinions to them as well. After he'd finished hitting, Tom heard one Los Angeles newscaster begin his interview with Mrs. Gleason by saying, "Folks, something phenomenal is happening in America today. There are more baseball games across the nation tonight than people have seen

in years. From little hamlets like this one to the last weed-filled vacant lots in cities everywhere, the Wild West showdown flavor of this Big Game has fired up interest and imaginations all over this land."

"Just focus on your hitting and fielding," Del Gato reminded everyone as the team finished its second round of batting practice. "Hitting, fielding."

Then came the sports network truck, and the players stopped what they were doing and stared as it all sank in. The Dillontown Wildcats were going *national*.

"Don't pay any attention," Del Gato called from the pitcher's mound. "Crying out loud, they got nothing better to do than hound a bunch of kids?"

Tom hustled out and sat atop the old stone wall in right field, pretending to be taking a break, while he spied on the guy from the sports network.

"How long's he going to pitch, fella?" he asked Tom.

"One more hitter, then we're done."

The reporter turned to a man with a camera on his shoulder, stepping out of the huge white truck. "Roy! Only one more batter. Get down there!" Then he slapped at his shirt pocket, retrieving a notebook and a pen. "What's your name, partner? How old are you? What's it like to have a legend like 'El Gato Loco' coaching your squad?"

Tom wanted to answer every question, but the last one reminded him that he needed to stay focused. "Sorry, I can't talk now." Then he couldn't help himself. He had to know. "Is that why you're here? All because of him?"

"Oh, no. Don't you see, kid? This Big Game, your whole situation here, has caught the attention of the entire nation. It's David versus Goliath! It's loyalty versus the big bucks. The small-market team fighting for its life against the big-money boys who want to come in and bulldoze right over them. It's a metaphor for the entire game of baseball."

"It is?"

"I'm telling you, buddy. It's *more* than a metaphor. This could be a meta*five*!"

With that, he stabbed the pen back into his pocket, folded the notebook, and ran toward the cameraman, followed by another guy wrapped in headgear and holding a furry microphone on a pole.

Luckily for the reporter, and for everyone in the stands, the last batter was Cruz. Because he put on a show.

"Ramón," he called out. "This one's for you." On the next pitch, he served up a low line into left field, two steps to the right of Ramón.

"María, get ready," he yelled, and the next one, a sharp ground ball, sizzled down the first-base line. María snagged it on the short hop.

The crowd *woo*ed at how easily she made the play.

By the time Cruz called Tom's name and sent him deep against the right-field wall, hoots and whistles ripped out of the stands for both hitter *and* fielder. More than that. Between pitches, Tom now heard a definite buzz of surprise, of discovery and awe.

"What're you feeding 'em for breakfast, Gallagher? A box of Wheaties and a pound of nails?"

Every hitter had done well that day, better than usual. The fielders had all displayed fundamental improvement, even over yesterday. But Cruz's show was full of flair and finesse. He could not miss. Like a pool player, he called his shots, hitting any pitch, high or low, toward any player. Hitting the ball as if it were standing still.

Finally, the awesome display seemed to be sinking into the minds of the fans in the stands, particularly those, like Doc, who'd been there since Monday.

The ballpark became a canyon of quiet, save for Cruz's roll call and the slap of the ball on his maplewood bat. "Frankie, turn two!"

Frankie charged the hot grounder, stabbed it, tossed it to Tara at second, who relayed it to María at first. Smooth as *mole de chocolate* (MOH leh deh choh koh LAH teh). Again the crowd called out its admiration.

Tom felt a giddy light-headedness as he watched. For the first time, he felt happy to be here. Tara, running back to second, smiled and gave him thumbs-up.

At the end of practice, the low voices in the dugout and the serious looks of quiet confidence on the faces of the other players only convinced Tom's suspicions that they felt it, too.

"We got half a chance," said Ramón.

"Yeah," added Rachel.

There it was. The team's two quietest players had spoken the words no one else had dared to say.

172

"Grab all your stuff," Del Gato growled, bringing a bucket of balls in from the mound. "We're going to jog out of here. And if those reporters come swarming around—well, you know the drill."

The players rose and filed out of the dugout. They started through the crowd and back to camp. Except for one. Tom lingered behind, sitting alone on the old pine bench. He wanted to savor the thrill of this moment. He wanted to allow everything that had happened to sink in. He let his thoughts fly loose, like leaves in the wind, like sagebrush whizzing past his face as he ran through the hillside chaparral. Then he reached for the sports bag next to his feet, pulled out his Dreamsketcher, and began to write.

Images of newscasters, landowners, outsiders, and locals who came to root or gloat, hate or berate, filled the movie screen of his mind. He painted the scenes in drawings and word pictures as fast as he could scratch. This awkward, ten-membered, twenty-legged caterpillar of a team, cocooned for days in the school library and on a sunken baseball field, was now breaking out into butterfly beauty, putting on a show, catching everyone's eye.

Tom pushed his pen along the paper, capturing the moment. He could still hear the roar, the drumbeats. He could hear footsteps. He looked up.

There stood Alabaster Jones.

ANALYZE THE TEXT

Metaphor A metaphor shows how two very unlike things are similar. How does the author use this figure of speech to describe the team on this page?

"Well, Tom Gallagher," he said. "Just the man I'm looking for." He descended the dugout steps. "You boys must think you're pretty smart."

Tom only stared, afraid even to blink or breathe.

"Yes, sir," Mr. Jones continued, "I heard all about what you and that Mexican boy did. Think you're some clever *muchachos* (moo CHAH chohs), don't you?"

Tom managed a slight shrug.

Mr. Jones stepped closer, lowering his face into Tom's, and grabbed the neck of his T-shirt. "You ride off and bring back that no-good disgrace of a human being to coach this team of miserable misfits. Get him to show you a little something about hitting. Huh? Speak up!"

"Mr. Del Gato is not a disgrace. He has a lot of grace."

The man twisted his fists, tightening Tom's shirt around his neck.

"Shut up. Now, I'm only saying this once, so listen good. If by hocus or by pocus you happen to win tomorrow and this land deal falls through, you will sincerely regret it. I have associates in this town who promised me that they will personally shut down Scrub Oak Community School, fire the staff, and make all you kids hike down and back each day to that Lake View Mesa school if things don't go as planned. And why would we all do that? Simple lack of funds, my boy. It's big tax dollars you kids are playing with. Big money all around. Do you understand?"

He did. Instantly, Tom could see a whole chain of events, like dominoes falling whap-slap into each other. Either the Wildcats lose tomorrow, or Tom's parents lose their jobs. Then maybe even their home.

Compared to that, a few houses up on the hill didn't seem so bad.

Mr. Jones must've read the understanding on Tom's face. He let go of his shirt and smiled.

"Good," he said. "Because I can cause you more hurt than a heart attack." He grinned so wide, his sunburned lips turned white.

Tom stared back, blinking hard. But if Tom had learned anything during the past week, he'd learned when he had to speak up and when it was better to be silent.

And now was a time to speak.

"We're not trying to hurt you," said Tom. "We don't have anything against you at all. Why are you trying to hurt us?"

"Oh, you poor, poor boy. Listen, if you win that game, you'll be hurting me far more than what I could ever do to you. And I mean right here." He tapped his white sports jacket on the left side of his chest. "In my wallet."

Then Mr. Jones's face seemed to change, turning softer. Worry rose in his eyes. "You see, son, I was once a lot like you. I was young. I had stars in my eyes. But what you don't understand is that in the game of life, money wins. Brains can only take you so far. Talent barely gets you in the door these days. But this"—he held up his hand and rubbed his thumb against his first two fingers—"this opens more doors than dynamite. With this, you have instant respect, instant power."

Mr. Jones turned, but he did not leave. He looked off toward Rattlesnake Ridge as if imagining what all this land would be like after he was done with it.

"Remember," he said, "without money and the wish for even more money, Columbus never would've sailed to America. Then where would we all be today? Think about that."

ANALYZE THE TEXT

Understanding Characters How do Tom's feelings about winning the game change after he talks to Alabaster Jones? Why do they change?

Under the stars that Friday night, all of the players joined in the wheel-spoke circle, and all eyes were wide open. Who could sleep with the weight of the fate of the town squeezing down on them?

Okay, Wil could. But he'd had three *burritos grandes*, four slices of watermelon, and a mango after catching batting practice all afternoon.

"No one expects us to win," said Clifford, lying with his knees up and hands behind his back. "I think somebody's going to be real surprised."

Ramón agreed. "My dad came by this morning saying, 'Don't worry. This game doesn't even matter. Sooner or later this whole place will be houses and eight-lane freeways.' I just smiled and said, 'Yeah, Dad, we know.'"

"That's what the mayor said, too," Frankie added. "But when he was watching batting practice today, he was white as a tortilla."

"Yeah," Cruz agreed. "But I think his true color was *alabaster*. Right, María? What are you going to say to him after we ruin his plans?"

Tom's gut clenched.

"Hey, look, you guys," María answered. "Don't get overconfident. Remember, batting practice is one thing. But in a game—especially this one—it's different. There's a lot of pressure."

"She's right," said Ramón. "But I think Cruz and Clifford are, too. The way I see it, as long as we think we have a chance, we have a chance."

Tom kept silent. His mind was still frozen under the snake eyes of a man named Jones who loomed above him like a viper over a rat. What did he expect Tom to do? Tell Cruz and everyone to throw the game? Tom was just the bench guy, the reserve player. Even if he got into the game, which would only happen if one team was way ahead of the other, he could strike out and make an error or two, but big deal. It would hardly affect the game.

Maybe, he thought, he could coach first and trip everyone as they ran the bases. Or maybe he could go out to the scoreboard with a mirror and shine sunlight into all the batters' eyes. But he hated these thoughts. In fact, he was tired of thinking.

"Tom," said Cruz. "What do you think?"

Boom went his heartbeat.

"About what?"

"About the neural receptors inside our brains."

"*What?*"

"Okay, then. Are we going to win tomorrow?"

"Oh, I don't know. It's up to you guys."

"*Aaapp!*" said Frankie. "Wrong answer."

"Well, he *doesn't* know." It was María coming to Tom's defense. "No one does. We spent three days swinging at the same stupid pitch a million times. But it was in the *library*. What about real life?"

"What about it?" asked Clifford. "You saw us today. We smashed the chips-and-dip out of the ball."

"So?" Rachel rustled inside her bag as she flipped over to her stomach. "I mean, I don't know what happened to us in the library. If we got hypnotized or reprogrammed or brainwashed or what. All I know is, we can't forget we're human beings. And human beings have control over their thoughts. And as long as we concentrate on doing our best, we shouldn't worry about winning or losing."

She paused, her voice lowered to a whisper. "I just believe that when people do things with good intentions, good things happen. Like when Tom and Cruz rode off to see Del Gato. But when we do stuff out of fear, bad things happen." She looked around. "A lot of people are afraid of what might happen tomorrow. But *we* can't be. Then, whatever happens will turn out okay."

"Even if we lose?" asked Frankie.

"Even if we lose. I mean, from where we are, losing may look like a total disaster. Like we just accidentally busted down someone's wall." Though he couldn't see her, Tom could hear the smile in her voice. "But you know, we only see it from here. How does it look from the hawk's nest? Or from the stars?"

No one said a word. Everyone, even Tom, searched the night sky, roamed the ether, bouncing around between the moon, the stars, and the eucalyptus trees.

From treetop, from the hawk's perch, Tom thought about the game, the town, the hillsides. In a million years—a short time, really, in space years—would it even matter whether they won or lost? In a thousand? What about a hundred?

Who could say? But he knew one thing. Rachel was right. He'd seen it too many times. When he froze up from fear, he did stupid things— like never talking to Doc about the ball field. And when he let his mind fly above the fear, he saw hitting a baseball as just another form of GPS tracking.

No matter if his parents got fired and his family had to move. No matter what trouble Alabaster Jones might cause. Tom determined that tomorrow he would play to win. And now he wondered how he could've considered doing anything else.

ANALYZE THE TEXT

Theme What is the theme the author is trying to convey to readers? How do you know?

JOURNALISM, LITERACY, AND LIBERTY

In "The Boy Who Saved Baseball," some of the locals preparing for the big game were doubtless impressed by the arrival of national newscasters. Others, including Mr. Del Gato, were distressed: how dare those crass journalists and photographers descend *en masse* like that, pestering the players and fans for the sake of a few lines of copy? It takes more than a little grouchiness from the public, however, to keep the press from its appointed rounds—whether the journalists involved are delivering news of critical importance to the nation or just providing a little entertainment through anecdotes of human interest.

For hundreds of years, humankind has read about the recent past in the words of journalists: reporters, columnists, essayists, bloggers, social-media gurus, and others. However common such writing and reading may seem today, one needn't travel too far into the past to find a time when the news, and indeed the written word itself, was available only to the elite, to the very few—for the simple reason that most people, for most of history, could not read at all. Even if they had been literate, the masses of people could hardly have found a word to read, for the huge quantity of text we now see every day is a relatively recent phenomenon. And if they had found a word or two to read, they might not have been free to read them.

Precursors to the modern newspaper, the epitome of journalism and the most accessible form of news for generations, appeared about two millennia ago, in ancient Rome. During the same time period, Chinese emperors, empresses, and other government officials were being briefed on current happenings via regularly published reports. However, both the Chinese and the Roman reports had to be copied by hand; therefore their circulation was severely limited—not just by the low literacy level of the populace but also by the labor required to make multiple copies. Government censorship, too, played a major role in limiting the spread of the printed word; rulers were reluctant to allow their subjects access to information that might make them rebellious.

About five hundred years ago, literacy levels among the general populace, in many parts of the world, began to rise dramatically. The invention of the printing press by Johannes Gutenberg in fifteenth-century Germany sparked a revolution in publishing, or the making public of information and ideas; by 1500, several thousand printing presses were operating in Europe. As printed language spread, so did literacy; and as literacy spread, so did the desire for liberty—including the freedom to print and read as one chose, without censorship.

Gutenberg's press was swiftly replicated and improved upon, and European publishers began distributing books by the millions. Then, approximately four centuries ago, newspapers for the general public began proliferating in many European cities, including London, where one of the first daily newspapers emerged in the early 1700s under the masthead *The Daily Courant.*

In the same period, journalism began to establish itself in the American Colonies, where at first most news items focused on information about London and the rest of Europe. Gradually, as independence-minded thought began to flourish in the Colonies, newspapers became more local, less European in content—they began to focus on ideas and issues in the Colonies themselves. Journalists and publishers such as Benjamin Franklin began using the press as a vehicle for not only news but also witty commentary on issues of the day.

The rest, as they say, was history; journalistic freedom and relatively widespread literacy helped to fuel the flames of the American revolutionary spirit and, ultimately, lead to the founding of the most freedom-loving nation in the history of the world. In the words of America's most revered publisher,

"Without freedom of thought, there can be no such thing as wisdom; and no such thing as public liberty, without freedom of speech."

—Benjamin Franklin,
The New England Courant, July 9, 1722

Dig Deeper

How to Analyze the Text

Use these pages to learn about Theme, Metaphor, and Understanding Characters. Then read "The Boy Who Saved Baseball" again to apply what you learned.

Theme

The author of the realistic fiction story "The Boy Who Saved Baseball" wrote it with a message about life for readers to understand and remember. This message is the **theme**, or central idea, of the story.

Authors do not always state the theme of a story directly. Think of details in the story that show the characters' feelings and actions. Then think about real people's feelings and actions. Look back at the first paragraph on page 178. What does Rachel tell her teammates? Use Rachel's message and other text evidence in the story to infer the theme of "The Boy Who Saved Baseball."

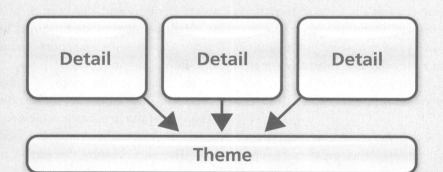

RL.6.1 cite textual evidence to support analysis of what the text says explicitly as well as inferences drawn; **RL.6.2** determine a theme or central idea of a text/provide a summary; **RL.6.3** describe how a story's or drama's plot unfolds and how characters respond and change; **RL.6.4** determine the meaning of words or phrases, including figurative and connotative meanings/analyze impact of word choice

Metaphor

A **metaphor** is a figure of speech that compares two things that are very different. In many metaphors, one thing is called something else. For example, in the metaphor *the sun was a jewel shining in the sky*, the sun is compared to a shining jewel. Authors use metaphors to help create images in their readers' minds and to appeal to the readers' five senses.

Understanding Characters

Characters in realistic fiction are much like people in real life. They experience real problems and try to find solutions to them. As the characters respond to challenges, their thoughts and beliefs may change. Recognizing these changes helps readers better understand the characters. As you read the selection again, note Tom's feelings about the game at different points in the story. How does Tom's response to different plot events show how he grows and changes as the plot unfolds?

Your Turn

Turn and Talk Review the selection with a partner to prepare to discuss this question: *How do the media influence how people feel about events?* As you discuss key ideas, listen carefully and contribute to your partner's ideas. Use text evidence to support your ideas.

Classroom Conversation

Continue your discussion of "The Boy Who Saved Baseball" by explaining your answers to these questions:

1. How might the story have changed if Tom had not spoken to Alabaster Jones?

2. How does the media's presence at the field affect Tom and his teammates?

3. In what way do you think Tom is responsible for saving the game of baseball? What text evidence helped you form your opinion?

NO FEAR

Analyze Details Work with a partner to discuss the players' conversation the night before the game. Discuss these questions: *In what way do Tom's friends help him overcome his fear of Alabaster Jones and what might happen in Tom's community? Why is this an important event in the story? How does this part of the story help develop the theme?* Describe how this event or scene fits in the overall structure of the story.

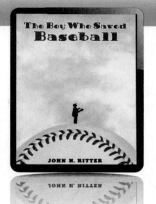

Response Tom Gallagher decides that he will play to win. What will happen if his team wins? What will happen if his team loses? Write a paragraph to explain whether you agree or disagree with Tom's decision. Use evidence from the text to support your opinion.

Writing Tip

State your opinion in the first sentence of your paragraph. Then organize your reasons and evidence in a logical order.

COMMON CORE **RL.6.1** cite textual evidence to support analysis of what the text says explicitly as well as inferences drawn; **RL.6.5** analyze how a sentence, chapter, scene, or stanza fits in the overall structure; **W.6.1a** introduce claim(s) and organize reasons and evidence clearly; **W.6.9a** apply grade 6 Reading standards to literature; **SL.6.1c** pose and respond to questions and make comments that contribute to the discussion

Persuading the Public

by Cecelia Munzenmaier

Most Americans see or hear more than two hundred advertisements each day. They read them in magazines, newspapers, mail, and e-mail. They hear them on the radio. They see them on television, on billboards, and in skywriting.

The goal of commercial advertising is to persuade people to buy things. Other forms of persuasion try to influence how people think. Editorials or letters to the editor, for example, express an opinion. They present an arument and give reasons why people should agree with that particular point of view.

✓ GENRE

Informational text, such as this article, gives facts and examples about a topic.

✓ TEXT FOCUS

Arguments are often made in advertisements or letters to the editor in an attempt to convince a reader to think or act in a certain way.

COMMON CORE **RI.6.8** trace and evaluate the argument and specific claims in a text; **RI.6.10** read and comprehend literary nonfiction

Persuade

Save 50 percent when you subscribe to *Persuade*, the opinion magazine!

Ads Attract Attention!

Advertisements use pictures, slogans, and celebrities to get people's attention. Ads often include a call to action. That message tells people how to improve their lives, usually by buying a certain product. Public service advertising campaigns also seek to persuade people. They do not promote a product. Instead, they give people information about how to make better choices. A public service announcement (PSA) might urge people to exercise, be tolerant of others, or recycle.

Chef Joe's Choice—
SOUPS TO SAVOR!

Chef Joe's Tomato & Red Pepper Soup

Chef Joe selects only the finest vegetables, bursting with garden-fresh flavor.
For your health, choose Chef Joe's soups!

Keep It Clean!

This commercial ad (left) uses marketing flair—a slogan and a company celebrity—to promote a brand of soup. This public-service ad (right) uses a catchy slogan and effective pictures to persuade people not to litter.

Letters Express Opinions

Billions of dollars are spent on advertising each year, but mailing a letter to the editor of a local newspaper may be just as powerful. It can be an effective way to persuade people and change minds.

Letters to the editor are among the most popular features of newspapers and magazines. Radio and television stations also may share opinions and comments from listeners and viewers.

Whether in print or on the air, the most effective letters focus on one main argument and present facts and reasons to support it. Readers or listeners are invited to consider, and perhaps share, a point of view. Here is an example.

Letters to the Editor

To the Editor of the *Sentinel*:

I believe our new gym should be named for Coach Len Burns.

Coach made all kids feel a part of the team, whether they were stars or reserve players. He taught us not to gloat when we won. He taught us not to give up when we lost. He gave us the confidence to face any showdown.

For thirty years, he has been a phenomenal coach. His lessons have lingered for many athletes. That's why the new gymnasium should be named for Len Burns. He is the man who taught us how to be good players and good sports.

Sincerely,
Alex Sims, basketball player
Hoyt Middle School

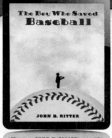

Compare Texts

Compare the Power of Persuasion With a partner, compare "The Boy Who Saved Baseball" to "Persuading the Public." Discuss these questions: *In what ways do advertisements persuade people? How are these ways similar to the way the media, Alabaster Jones, and Tom's friends use persuasion?* Use text evidence to support your answers.

TEXT TO SELF

Write a Dialogue Alabaster Jones tries to persuade Tom to lose the big game. How would you react in a similar situation? Imagine that you are talking to a friend who is being pressured to do something. Write a short dialogue that shows what you and your friend might say to each other.

TEXT TO WORLD

Summarize an Argument Read an editorial or a letter to the editor in a newspaper or digital publication. Summarize the argument used to support a claim. Tell whether the writer's argument is persuasive. Include examples to support your opinion.

COMMON CORE **RL.6.1** cite textual evidence to support analysis of what the text says explicitly as well as inferences drawn; **RI.6.1** cite textual evidence to support analysis of what the text says explicitly as well as inferences drawn; **RI.6.8** trace and evaluate the argument and specific claims in a text; **SL.6.1c** pose and respond to questions and make comments that contribute to the discussion

Grammar

What Is a Verb? A **verb** is a word that shows an action or a state of being. When a verb tells what the subject does, it is an **action verb**. When a verb tells what the subject is or is like, it is a **being verb**. Some being verbs are called **linking verbs** because they link the subject to a word in the predicate. Most linking verbs are forms of the verb *be*.

Action Verb	Linking Verb
Tom opened his sports bag.	He was alone in the dugout.
He grabbed his Dreamsketcher.	The stands were empty.

A verb may be more than one word. The **main verb** expresses action or a state of being. The **helping verb** works with the main verb but does not show action.

helping verb   main verb
Tom's teammates are talking.

helping verb   main verb
Rachel has shared her thoughts.

Try This! With a partner, read aloud each sentence below. Find one sentence with a linking verb and three with action verbs. Which sentences have a main verb and a helping verb?

1 Tom and the others searched the night sky.

2 The moon was large and bright.

3 Tom was thinking about the threats from Mr. Jones.

4 He will play without fear tomorrow.

You can make your writing clearer and more vivid by replacing vague verbs with exact verbs.

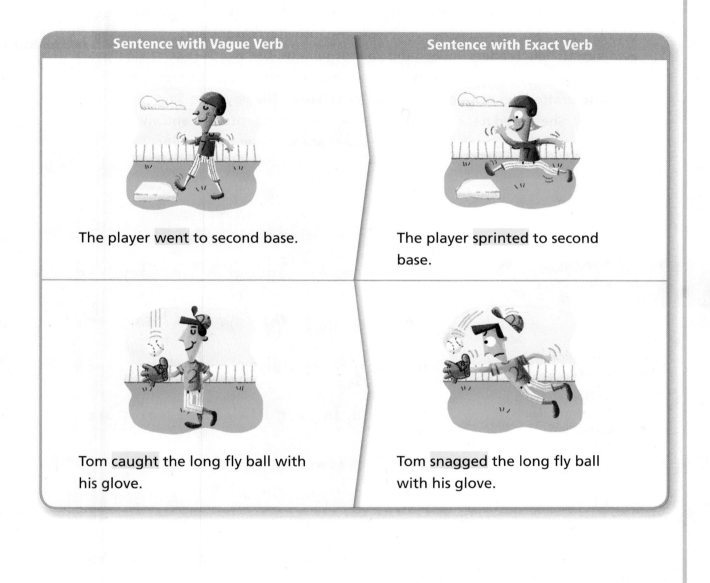

Sentence with Vague Verb	Sentence with Exact Verb
The player went to second base.	The player sprinted to second base.
Tom caught the long fly ball with his glove.	Tom snagged the long fly ball with his glove.

Connect Grammar to Writing

As you revise your response paragraph, replace vague verbs with exact verbs.

Argument Writing

✔ **Voice** In a **response paragraph**, writers state opinions, or claims, about selections they have read. They form opinions from the conclusions they have drawn. As you revise your response, provide reasons and evidence to help readers understand your argument. Use words that clearly connect your opinion with the reasons and evidence that support it.

Jesse drafted her response about a character in "The Boy Who Saved Baseball." She stated her opinion first. Then she added sentences and vivid words to draw her readers in, using a voice that shows her personality.

Writing Traits Checklist

✔ **Ideas**
Did I draw logical conclusions?

✔ **Organization**
Did I support my claims with reasons and evidence?

✔ **Sentence Fluency**
Did I use a variety of sentence types?

✔ **Word Choice**
Did I use vivid and specific words?

✔ **Voice**
Does my writing show my personality?

✔ **Conventions**
Did I use correct spelling, grammar, and punctuation?

Revised Draft

I agree with Rachel in "The Boy Who Saved Baseball" when she says that losing feels worse up close; from a distance, it doesn't seem that bad. In fact, I think her words are very wise. The reason why I believe this is that I experienced a ∧bittersweet loss. My soccer team lost a home game to our biggest rival, the Westside Wolverines.∧ Imagine how awful we felt! Plus, our legs ~~really hurt~~ were limp spaghetti by the time we finished. The next day, our team ∧studied ~~watched~~ a video of the game.

Lose Some, Win Some

by Jesse Ureste

I agree with Rachel in "The Boy Who Saved Baseball" when she says that losing feels worse up close; from a distance, it doesn't seem that bad. In fact, I think her words are very wise. The reason why I believe this is that I experienced a bittersweet loss. My soccer team lost a home game to our biggest rival, the Westside Wolverines. Imagine how awful we felt! Plus, our legs were limp spaghetti by the time we finished. The next day, our team studied a video of the game. We identified our weak spots and improved our defense. I had a week to think about how to improve my game. During that time, I didn't feel so bad about my team's loss because I had the distance to see that losing isn't the end of the world. As a result of this, our team won an important victory the next week. We crushed the Oaktown Titans, 3–0! Now our loss is ancient history. Time gave us the distance we needed to see that losing is not so bad after all—as long as you win some, too!

Reading as a Writer

How does Jesse draw readers into her writing and show her personality? How can you make your own writing voice stronger?

In my final paper, I added sentences to draw readers into my writing and to show my personality. I used a variety of sentence types. I also used vivid and specific words.

Vocabulary in Context

1 observe

If you **observe** the Ferris wheel carefully, you can see the people who are riding on it.

2 raucous

The **raucous** cymbals of the marching band were so noisy, we had to cover our ears.

3 looms

As soon as you pass the carousel, the roller coaster **looms** in front of you. It seems so huge!

4 zany

This **zany** clown figure doesn't just look funny; it is a bank in which you can save money.

Vocabulary Reader

Context Cards

COMMON CORE **L.6.6** acquire and use general academic and domain-specific words and phrases/gather vocabulary knowledge for comprehension or expression

► Study each Context Card.

► Use a dictionary to confirm the meanings of these words.

 **gigantic**

The cyclists used a gigantic rope to pull themselves across the river.

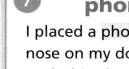 **impressive**

This outdoor sculpture of a needle and yarn in Milan, Italy, is very impressive. We all stopped to stare at it.

7 phony

I placed a phony, or fake, nose on my dog and took this photo. Then he pawed it off.

8 distinguish

Knots can be hard to distinguish. It can be difficult to tell one from another.

9 intriguing

Watching someone juggle five rings at once is intriguing.

10 correspond

The four strings of a ukulele correspond to four different musical notes.

Read and Comprehend

Go Digital

☑ TARGET SKILL

Text and Graphic Features Informational texts like "Do Knot Enter" often provide graphic features that represent and support the information found in the text. As you read the selection, use the illustrations along with the information in the text to help you understand the topic of knots. Use a graphic organizer like this one to show how the illustrations and text work together to give you a better understanding of the topic.

Graphic Feature	Text	How They Go Together

☑ TARGET STRATEGY

Summarize As you read "Do Knot Enter," stop occasionally to briefly retell, or **summarize,** the most important ideas in your own words.

COMMON CORE

RI.6.2 determine a central idea of a text/provide a summary; **RI.6.7** integrate information presented in different media or formats as well as in words

Critical Thinking

What do people do when they solve a complex puzzle? First they analyze, or examine carefully and in detail, the shape of each puzzle piece. Then they determine how the pieces should be combined. This process of solving the puzzle does not involve memorizing something; it involves using critical thinking skills.

You use critical thinking skills every day. When you conduct science experiments, read texts, or solve math problems, you use critical thinking skills to help you learn. In "Do Knot Enter," you will learn about a math problem that involves knots. You will also use critical thinking to figure out how knots and unknots work.

DO KNOT ENTER

by Ivars Peterson and Nancy Henderson
Illustration by Remy Simard

☑ TARGET SKILL

Text and Graphic Features
Examine how the text and its illustrations work together to provide information about knots.

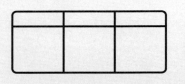

☑ GENRE

Informational text gives facts and other information about a topic. As you read, look for:

▶ graphics that help explain the topic

▶ facts about a subject or topic

COMMON CORE

RI.6.3 analyze how a key individual, event, or idea is introduced, illustrated, and elaborated; **RI.6.4** determine the meaning of words and phrases, including figurative, connotative, and technical meanings; **RI.6.5** analyze how a sentence, paragraph, chapter, or section fits in the overall structure; **RI.6.7** integrate information presented in different media or formats as well as in words; **L.6.5a** interpret figures of speech in context

MEET THE AUTHORS

Ivars Peterson and Nancy Henderson

Ivars Peterson has served as the editor of *Science Magazine for Kids* and written a weekly online column to help young people understand and enjoy mathematics. He and his wife, freelance writer Nancy Henderson, have collaborated on two books for middle-school students: *Math Trek: Adventures in the MathZone* and *Math Trek 2: A Mathematical Space Odyssey*.

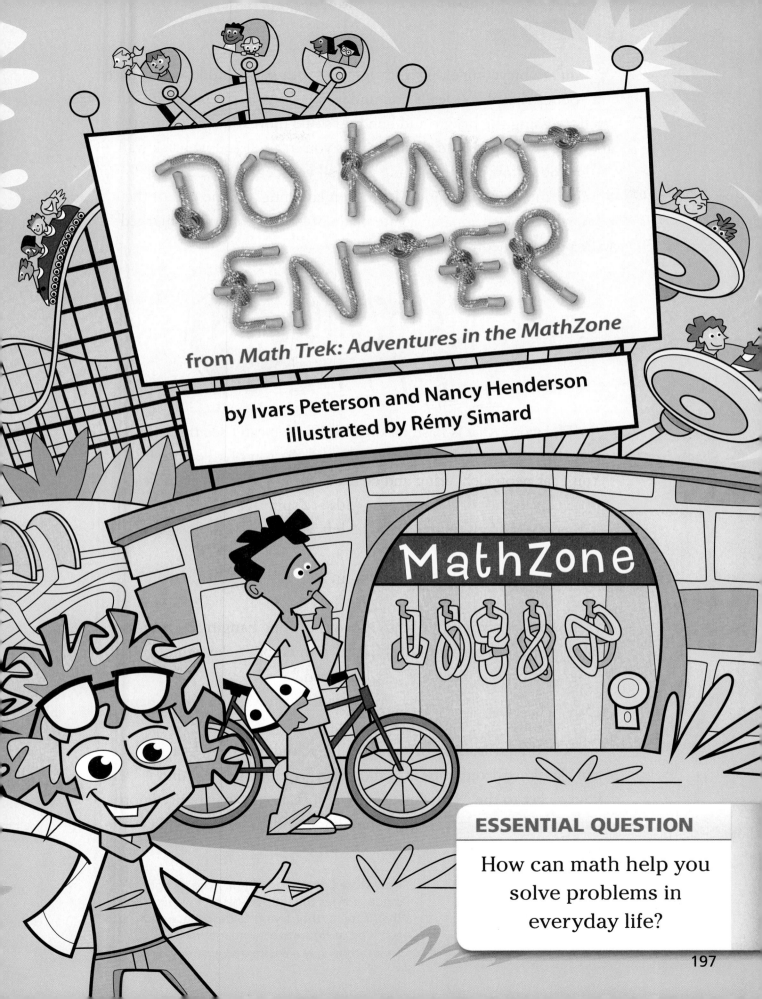

DO KNOT ENTER

from *Math Trek: Adventures in the MathZone*

by Ivars Peterson and Nancy Henderson
illustrated by Rémy Simard

MathZone

ESSENTIAL QUESTION

How can math help you solve problems in everyday life?

You are bicycling along a straight, smooth path. Suddenly the path bends sharply. It leads you under a bridge then loops back over itself, crossing the bridge and bending some more. It twists under and over itself again and finally brings you to a tall yellow brick wall.

As you follow the path along the wall you begin to hear bells dinging, motors whirring, and children laughing. At the end of the path, you come to a massive gate made of knotty pinewood, marked with a glaring neon sign.

The word *Knot* is flashing on and off. You can't see through the gate, but when you look up, you observe the top of a Ferris wheel. You hear people cheering and chattering. Raucous music blares in the background. To the right, kids are spinning around on a crazy-looking flying saucer. To the left, a roller coaster looms above the wall.

MathZone? It looks more like an amusement park than a study hall!

Your eyes turn to five tangled loops of rope hanging from hooks on the gate. To the right of the gate is an empty ticket window with a sign that says, "Tickets Knot Required."

Puzzled, you lock your bike to a lamppost, walk up to the gate, and tug on one of the knotted loops.

"Hold your horses," says a metallic-sounding voice, as a zany-looking droid pops into the ticket window. "Your mind is your ticket to the MathZone," it says. "To open the naughty knotty gate, just find the knot that is not a knot. When you untangle it, the gate will unlock."

ANALYZE THE TEXT

Figurative Language What types of figurative language does the author use on this page? What is the author trying to describe and say in each type of figurative language used?

Knot A

Knot B

Knot C

Knot D

Knot E

Which of these tangles is not a true knot?

You study the five knotted loops, wondering which one you ought to try to untangle. Can you figure out which loop is not a knot?

Try it

Use your own loop of string to copy the five knots on the gate and figure out which one you can untangle.

What to do:

1. Loop the string around, following the pattern in the diagram of Knot A. Be sure to cross under or over exactly as shown. Then tape the ends together.

2. Try to untangle the string so that you can form a plain circle or loop in which no part of the string crosses any other part. If it can be untangled completely, then it's not a knot, even though it may have looked like a knot when you started.

3. Follow the same steps for Knots B, C, D, and E to figure out which four are knots and which is not.

You Will Need:

- piece of string or rope about 3 feet (1 m) in length (a long shoelace works well)
- masking tape

Knot C is the unknot.

Knots and Unknots

Have you ever watched a magician tie a gigantic knot then magically make it fall apart? Sometimes what looks like a very impressive knot isn't a knot at all. Magicians and escape artists are experts at tying phony knots.

Mathematicians are especially interested in knots that can never be undone. Mathematically, a knot is a one-dimensional curve that winds through itself in three-dimensional space and catches its own tail to form a loop. You can untie a shoelace and untangle a fishing line, but you can't untie or get rid of the knot in a mathematician's knotted loop. To turn a tangled shoelace into a mathematical knot you would have to tape the shoelace's ends together. Then you wouldn't be able to untie the knot.

If a loop has no knot in it and can be made tangle free to look like a circle, mathematicians call it an *unknot*. Only one of the tangled loops on the MathZone gate is an unknot.

To Be or Knot to Be

Knot theorists are mathematicians who look for patterns that distinguish true knots from messy tangles called *unknots*, which can come apart when shaken. Knot theorists also look for ways to classify different types of knots.

How many different knots can you make? To tell one from another, you can start putting them into groups by counting how many times the rope or cord crosses itself. To make it easier to count, lay each knotted loop down on a table.

A trefoil knot has three crossings. The trefoil knot on the right is the mirror image of the trefoil knot on the left.

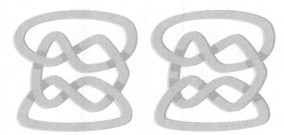

Both the granny knot (left) and the square knot (right) have six crossings. The two knots are not the same, however, because their crossing patterns differ.

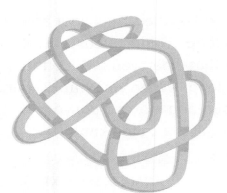

Here's an example of a loop that looks knotted but really isn't. Magicians sometimes use loops like this one in their tricks.

Knot A on the MathZone gate is called a *trefoil knot*. With only three crossings, it's the simplest type of knot there is. In the top left diagram, the trefoil knot on the right is a mirror image of the trefoil knot on the left. Are they both the same knot? No. There's nothing you can do to make one knot exactly like the other without cutting the loop, rearranging the strand, and joining the ends again (unless you look at it in a mirror).

Knot B on the MathZone gate is the only type of knot that crosses itself four times. Mathematicians call it the "figure-8" knot. Knot D has six crossings. Most people know it as the familiar "granny knot." A square knot also has six crossings. Are a square knot and a granny knot the same knot? Look at the crossing pattern for each knot to the left. Do you see the two places where the knots differ?

Mathematicians have identified 1,701,936 different knots with 16 or fewer crossings. It was very tricky for them to come up with the list because sometimes two knots can look different but really be the same. At other times, a tangle that looks like a knot is really an unknot.

To keep from getting fooled, mathematicians have worked out some formulas that can serve as shortcuts for telling a knot from an unknot and one knot from another. They're still searching for a single formula that identifies all possible knots.

ANALYZE THE TEXT

Text and Graphic Features How do the illustrations and the text work together to describe knots and unknots?

Here is a knotty trick to try with your arms.

What to do:

1. Place the string on a table in a straight line, with one end near your left hand and the other end by your right hand.

2. Without touching the string, fold your arms like this: With your left hand, grab your right arm above the elbow. Bring your right forearm over your left forearm and tuck your right hand under your left armpit.

3. Bend over and pick up the left end of the string with your right hand, and the right end with your left hand. Keep your arms folded as you do this.

4. Unfold your arms while holding the ends of the string. You should end up with a knot in the string.

How it works:

When you are holding each end of the string, your arms and the string form a closed loop. Folding your arms is like tying them in a knot, so that when you pick up the string, you create a knotted loop. When you unfold your arms, the knotted part of your loop moves from your body onto the string! The result is a trefoil knot.

You Will Need:

- piece of string, anywhere from 8 inches (20 cm) to 3 feet (1 m) in length

---

ANALYZE THE TEXT

Text Structure How does the author's choice of text structure help explain the knot trick?

Cat's Cradle

Have you ever played cat's cradle? You can use a loop made from about 6 feet (2 m) of nylon cord or other smooth string. Hang the loop on your thumbs, and pick up the loop with your little fingers, so that the string goes across the palms of your hands.

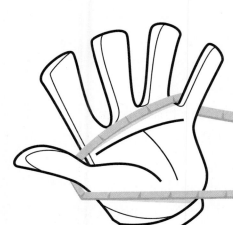

Then slip each index finger under the string on the opposite palm and pull your hands apart. You can loop your fingers in and out of the string in different ways to form various knotlike designs. No matter how much you cross the string to form different designs, however, you can always untangle it into the unknotted loop you started with. Every cat's cradle creation, including "Jacob's ladder," is an unknot.

A complex sequence of cat's cradle moves leads to this **intriguing** unknot known as "Jacob's ladder," or the "Indian diamonds."

Lord Kelvin's Knots

Mathematicians originally got the idea of studying knots from William Thomson, known as Lord Kelvin. Lord Kelvin was a famous physicist who lived more than 100 years ago in England. At that time, scientists didn't know that atoms consisted of particles called *electrons*, *protons*, and *neutrons*. They did, however, suspect that atoms of oxygen, hydrogen, iron, sulfur, and other elements were not exactly alike because of their different chemical behavior.

Lord Kelvin suggested that atoms might be like little whirlpools in an invisible fluid that fills all space. He proposed that different elements would correspond to different knotted tubes of fluid whirling in closed loops. For example, atoms of the simplest element, hydrogen, might look like a trefoil knot, and those of other elements might look like other knots. Inspired by that theory, mathematicians started to make tables of all possible types of knots.

Mathematicians continue to study knots, although Lord Kelvin's theory turned out to be wrong. We now know that there is no invisible fluid filling all space and that the number of protons in the nucleus of an atom is what decides which element it is. Lord Kelvin still made a name for himself in science for several discoveries and inventions, including the Kelvin temperature scale, which was later named for him.

Knots in Your Body

Would you believe that when you catch a cold or the flu, your body could be getting tied up in knots?

Scientists are using the mathematical study of knots to help understand the long, skinny, twisted loops and links of DNA, or deoxyribonucleic acid—the molecules that determine the genetic code for every living thing. If a single DNA strand were magnified to become as wide as a telephone wire, it would be more than a mile (more than a kilometer) long. Heaps of DNA strands sit like microscopic spaghetti inside plant and animal cells. Those strands may be twisted around one another, joined together to form loops, or tied in knots.

Molecular biologists have discovered that when a virus attacks living cells, it can break up unknotted loops of DNA, then rejoin the strands to form knots. Biologists and mathematicians are now working together to use knot theory as a way to figure out how viruses work. That could lead to a cure for certain diseases—maybe even a cure for the common cold!

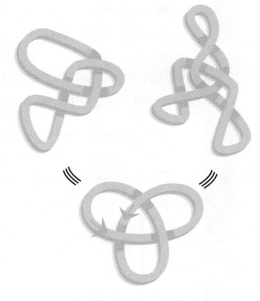

The two tangled loops of DNA, as seen under an electron microscope (top), both turn out to be trefoil knots (bottom).

Dig Deeper

How to Analyze the Text

Use these pages to learn about Text and Graphic Features, Text Structure, and Figurative Language. Then read "Do Knot Enter" again to apply what you learned.

Text and Graphic Features

Informational texts provide facts and other information about a specific topic. They also provide **graphic features,** such as diagrams, to support the information that is provided in the text.

As you reread "Do Knot Enter," think about how the graphic features work with the text to provide you with a deeper understanding of knots and unknots. What information would you be missing without one or the other?

Look back at pages 199 and 201. How do the diagrams of Knot A and the text contribute to your understanding of knots?

Graphic Feature	Text	How They Go Together

COMMON CORE

RI.6.3 analyze how a key individual, event, or idea is introduced, illustrated, and elaborated; **RI.6.4** determine the meaning of words and phrases, including figurative, connotative, and technical meanings; **RI.6.5** analyze how a sentence, paragraph, chapter, or section fits in the overall structure; **RI.6.7** integrate information presented in different media or formats as well as in words; **L.6.5a** interpret figures of speech in context

Text Structure

Text structure is the way in which an author organizes the information in a piece of writing. Some informational texts explain how to do or how to make something. As you reread "Do Knot Enter," pay attention to how the authors introduce, illustrate, and develop an idea. Look for headings that signal sections of related information. Ask yourself how each section of information fits in the overall structure of the selection.

Figurative Language

Authors sometimes use **figurative language** to make a text more interesting and to help readers understand what they read. As you reread the selection, pay attention to the author's use of figurative language. See if you can find **onomatopoeia**, or a word that imitates a sound. Examples of onomatopoeia are *hiss*, *buzz*, and *squish*. Look for **figures of speech** such as *raining cats and dogs*, in which the phrase means something different from what the individual words mean. What effect do words and phrases like these have on the meaning of the text?

Your Turn

RETURN TO THE ESSENTIAL QUESTION

Turn and Talk

Review the selection with a partner to prepare to discuss this question: *How can math help you solve problems in everyday life?* Contribute to the discussion by reviewing and explaining key ideas in the selection that support your answer.

Classroom Conversation

Continue your discussion of "Do Knot Enter" by explaining your answers to these questions using text evidence:

1. Why might two knots look different but really be the same kind of knot?

2. Why do you think knot theorists use models, like the string models in the selection, to study knots?

3. How is the mathematician's knotted loop important to the study of DNA?

DETERMINE MEANING

Use Reference Sources "Do Knot Enter" contains words specific to the study of knots. Choose three of the following words and find them in the selection: *theory, atom, formula, mathematicians, particles, molecules.* Look up each word in a print or digital dictionary to find its meaning, pronunciation, and part of speech. Write a new sentence for each that includes a definition. Share your sentences with a partner.

Response The last section of "Do Knot Enter" explains the connection between the mathematical study of knots and the study of DNA. What are the most important ideas in this section? Write a summary of how molecular biologists are using the study of knots to help them better understand DNA.

Writing Tip

Include only the most important ideas from the last section of the text. Use your own words to tell the main ideas.

INFORMATIONAL TEXT

☑ GENRE

Informational Text
Writers sometimes provide information in the form of a step-by-step activity that you can do yourself.

☑ TEXT FOCUS

A **diagram** is a type of graphic feature that provides a clear visual of what is being described in the text.

RL.6.7 integrate information presented in different media or formats as well as in words; **RL.6.10** read and comprehend literary nonfiction

THE KNOT THAT IS NOT

A trick with knots that will dazzle your friends and family!

illustrated by Michael Garland

STEP 1

loose
single knot

Take one thick shoelace and tie a loose knot in the center. Keep that knot loose so your audience can see a little daylight through it. Hold the shoelace and knot up to your audience and say: "See that I have made a knot in this shoelace!"

STEP 2

Let the audience examine it. Then take the two ends of the shoelace and cross them, a few inches from the top. Tell the audience: "I will now trap this bottom knot in its place with a series of tight, locking knots at the top."

STEP 3

tight
knots

Tie the crossed ends into a knot, leaving some extra shoelace to work with. Then tie a second knot on top of the first. Then tie a third knot on top of that. You should now have three tight "locking" knots at the top and still one loose knot at the bottom.

STEP 4

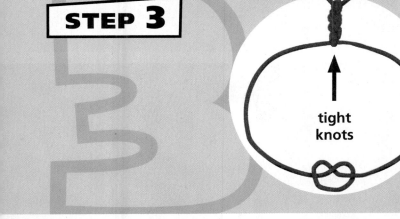

Announce: "I will now try to untie the bottom knot while keeping all the other knots locked securely in place." Add: "Even though that seems physically impossible to do!"

STEP 5

Now place the knotted shoelace behind your back where the audience cannot see it. Struggle mightily with your hands, arms, and torso.

STEP 6

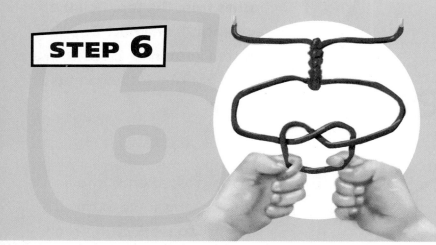

Pretend you are trying to untie the knot while you are really doing the following:
- Feel for the loose knot.
- Open it up.
- Spread the knot out with both hands until it rises to the top and joins the other three knots.

With a great flourish, return the shoelace to the front where the audience can see it. Hold it up and announce: "The bottom knot, as you can see, has now disappeared!"

Take a bow.

Only you know that the bottom knot has not disappeared. You simply moved it to the top!

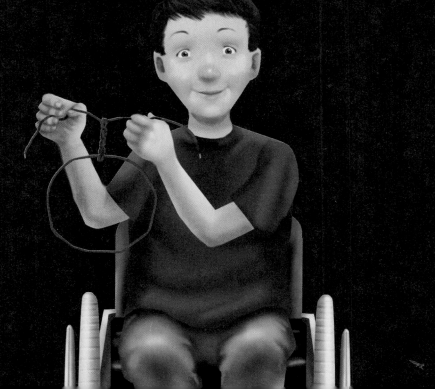

Compare Texts

Compare Activities "Do Knot Enter" and "The Knot That Is Not" teach readers how to tie different knots. Use the following questions to help you compare and contrast the texts: *How does each selection present the subject of knots? How does each selection use text and graphic features?* Write an answer to each question. Use evidence from the texts to support your answers.

TEXT TO SELF

Write a Paragraph The selection "Do Knot Enter" provides a riddle for you to solve. Think of another time when you used critical thinking to solve a problem. Write a paragraph explaining the problem and the steps you took to solve it.

TEXT TO WORLD

Reveal Magic Tricks Magicians around the world perform tricks that involve tying fake knots. With a partner, research another common trick that magicians perform. Use print or online resources to find out how the trick is done. Share your findings with the rest of the class.

RI.6.1 cite textual evidence to support analysis of what the text says explicitly as well as inferences drawn; **RI.6.7** integrate information presented in different media or formats as well as in words; **W.6.10** write routinely over extended time frames and shorter time frames

Grammar

What Are Transitive and Intransitive Verbs? A **transitive verb** is an action verb that "sends" its action to a noun or pronoun called the **direct object.** Two or more direct objects make up a **compound direct object.** An **intransitive verb** has no direct object. The same verb can be transitive in one sentence and intransitive in another.

Transitive and Intransitive Verbs	
Transitive Verb	direct object Some math theorists study knots. *Knots* receives the action of *study.*
Intransitive Verb	The magician's knot untangled magically. *Untangled* has no direct object.

An **indirect object** usually tells *whom* or *what* was affected by the action. The indirect object comes between the transitive verb and the direct object.

transitive verb   indirect object   direct object

The magician teaches the children a new knot trick.

Try This! **Read the sentences below. On another sheet of paper, write the verb in each sentence and label it *transitive* or *intransitive*. If it is transitive, write the direct object. Also write the indirect object, if the sentence contains one.**

1. The mathematicians identified over a million knots.

2. My fake knot fooled everyone.

3. The scientist showed the research team the results.

4. DNA exists in every living thing.

You can vary sentence structure and make your writing easier to read by combining direct objects from different sentences.

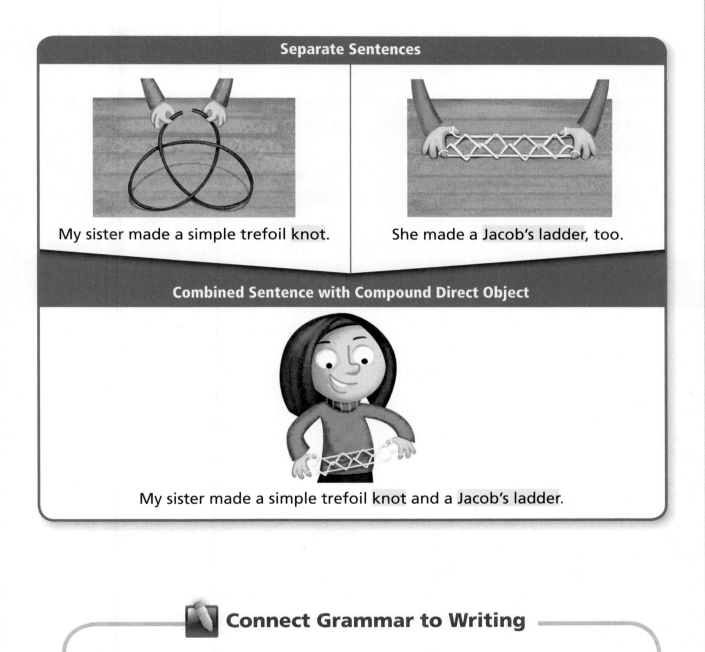

Separate Sentences

My sister made a simple trefoil knot.

She made a Jacob's ladder, too.

Combined Sentence with Compound Direct Object

My sister made a simple trefoil knot and a Jacob's ladder.

Connect Grammar to Writing

As you revise your argument paragraph, look for sentences that you can combine. Join direct objects from related sentences into a single sentence with a compound direct object.

W.6.1a introduce claim(s) and organize reasons and evidence clearly; **W.6.1b** support claim(s) with reasons and evidence, using credible sources and demonstrating understanding of the topic or text; **W.6.1c** use words, phrases, and clauses to clarify relationships; **W.6.4** produce writing in which development, organization, and style are appropriate to task, purpose, and audience

Argument Writing

✔ Organization In an **argument paragraph,** writers introduce a strong claim about a topic. They show their understanding of the topic by presenting relevant reasons supported by evidence. As you revise your argument paragraph, think about how best to influence the reader. Organize reasons and evidence in logical order. Use words and phrases that show how the claim, reasons, and evidence are related.

Tristan drafted his argument about the importance of using math to solve a baking problem. Later, he revised his paragraph so that his ideas were organized in a clear way.

Writing Traits Checklist

✔ **Ideas**
Did I state my claim at the beginning?

✔ **Organization**
Did I put my reasons and evidence in a logical order?

✔ **Sentence Fluency**
Did I use verbs and objects correctly?

✔ **Word Choice**
Did I use specific words and phrases to link ideas?

✔ **Voice**
Did I use a formal writing style?

✔ **Conventions**
Did I use correct spelling, grammar, and punctuation?

Revised Draft

I had always thought that math was a school subject. I added and multiplied fractions on math tests; I didn't do it anywhere else. ~~But~~ However, last month I decided that math is a valuable tool that can be used anytime, anywhere. The reason I changed my mind is that I used math to solve a chocolate chip cookie catastrophe. It began when my mom asked me to help her bake cookies. I measured out three cups of flour and added two eggs. Since the cookies were for a big party, my mom asked me to make six dozen.

Math to the Rescue

by Tristan Marlborough

I had always thought that math was a school subject. I added and multiplied fractions on math tests; I didn't do it anywhere else. However, last month I decided that math is a valuable tool that can be used anytime, anywhere. The reason I changed my mind is that I used math to solve a chocolate chip cookie catastrophe. It began when my mom asked me to help her bake cookies. Since the cookies were for a big party, my mom asked me to make six dozen. I measured out three cups of flour and added two eggs. As I mixed in other ingredients, I noticed that the dough was very dry. Not a problem—or so I thought. When the oven buzzer went off, I inspected my work. All of the cookies were as hard as rocks. Even worse, they tasted awful. Suddenly, I realized that I had not calculated my ratios for measurements correctly! I knew I had to make another batch. Before I started baking, I wrote out ratio equations to help me figure out the right amount of ingredients. As a result, math helped me bake the perfect chocolate chip cookies.

Reading as a Writer

What changes did Tristan make to improve his organization? In your argument paragraph, are the ideas told in logical order? Can you add any words or phrases to link ideas?

In my final paragraph, I moved one sentence that was out of order and added specific words and phrases to connect ideas. I also made sure that I used verbs and objects correctly.

Go Digital

Vocabulary in Context

✓ **TARGET VOCABULARY**

principle
elegant
equations
reluctant
detached
decomposition
specimens
complex
compromise
shriveled

Vocabulary Reader

Context Cards

COMMON CORE **L.6.6** acquire and use general academic and domain-specific words and phrases/gather vocabulary knowledge for comprehension or expression

218

1 principle
A scientific principle, such as Isaac Newton's law of gravity, is an important rule that can guide future research.

2 elegant
This computer processor is an elegant solution to a scientific problem, resolving it in a simple, ingenious way.

3 equations
Much of math and science is working with equations, in which one thing is equal to another.

$$\frac{5}{8} \div \frac{15}{16} =$$

$$\frac{5}{8} \times \frac{16}{15} = \frac{2}{3}$$

4 reluctant
A scientist would be reluctant, or unwilling, to handle chemicals without taking safety precautions.

▶ Study each Context Card.

▶ Discuss one picture. Use a different Vocabulary word from the one on the card.

---

5 detached

A scientist may try to be detached, like an outside observer, in order to keep an open mind.

---

6 decomposition

The decomposition, or rotting, of dead plants returns essential nutrients to the soil.

---

7 specimens

Geologists collect specimens of rocks and minerals. They carefully study the samples.

---

8 complex

The science of weather covers both simple and complex ideas that explain natural phenomena.

---

9 compromise

Lab partners may need to compromise to get along. They may settle on an idea both can agree on.

---

10 shriveled

Science can explain how a plump grape changes into a shriveled, dried-up raisin.

Read and Comprehend

✓ TARGET SKILL

Conclusions and Generalizations As you read "Science Friction," use text evidence, along with your own experiences, to draw conclusions and make generalizations. A **conclusion** is a judgment drawn from ideas in a text. These ideas may not be stated directly. A **generalization** is a broad statement that is true most of the time. Use a graphic organizer like this one to help you combine your own experience with text evidence to draw conclusions and make generalizations.

My Experience	Text Evidence	Conclusion or Generalization

✓ TARGET STRATEGY

Infer/Predict Use text evidence to figure out, or **infer**, what the author means, and **predict** what might happen in the future.

RL.6.1 cite textual evidence to support analysis of what the text says explicitly as well as inferences drawn

Experiments

In science, researchers often do experiments to learn why things happen. Experiments are tests or trials. When scientists conduct experiments, they want to discover or prove scientific facts or laws.

When students conduct experiments, they may want to find out what happens to things over time, or what results occur when different elements are combined. In "Science Friction," you'll learn how one team's plan for a science experiment produces some unexpected results.

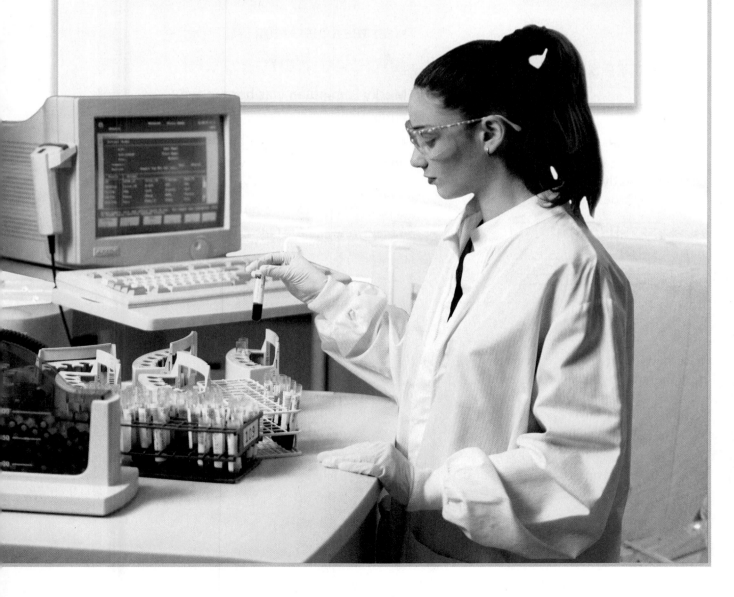

ANCHOR TEXT

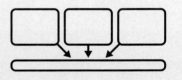

✓ TARGET SKILL

Conclusions and Generalizations Use text evidence and your experience to figure out ideas that aren't stated directly and ideas that are generally true.

✓ GENRE

Realistic fiction has characters and events that are like people and events in real life. As you read, look for:

▶ characters who have feelings that real people have
▶ realistic settings and events

 COMMON CORE **RL.6.3** describe how a story's or drama's plot unfolds and how characters respond or change; **RL.6.4** determine the meaning of words and phrases, including figurative and connotative meanings/analyze impact of word choice; **L.6.5c** distinguish among connotations of words with similar denotations

MEET THE AUTHOR
David Lubar

David Lubar originally aspired to be a comedian. He sold a joke for seventy-five cents and still has the check. He also loves pinball and even created an Atari pinball game. With thirteen books (including *Dog Days* and *Flip*) and many video games to his credit, Lubar has a remaining goal: to write a movie or a cartoon show.

MEET THE ILLUSTRATOR
Macky Pamintuan

Macky Pamintuan was born in the Philippines. His parents found that keeping Macky busy with pencils and paper was the best way to keep him happy. As an adult, Pamintuan moved to California. He is the illustrator for the book series *Weird Planet* and *Nancy Drew and the Clue Crew*.

Science Friction

from Tripping Over the Lunch Lady and Other School Stories

by David Lubar
selection illustrated by Macky Pamintuan

ESSENTIAL QUESTION

How can mistakes turn into answers to problems?

When Ms. Adler assigns groups for projects in her sixth-grade science class, she has one team member draw names from a box. That's how science geek Amanda finds herself in a group with class clown Benji, Ms. Perfect Ellen, and the mysteriously silent George.

Unlike oxygen and hydrogen, some things didn't combine very easily. For example argon, neon, and the other inert gases. Or the four of us. Ellen and George didn't move. Ellen obviously wanted everyone to come to her. George didn't seem to care who went where, so I walked over to his desk. So did Benji. Ellen had no choice except to join us.

"Hey," Benji said, spreading his arms wide, "group hug."

Ellen and I both went, "Ewww." Some things were too gross even for calm, detached scientists.

"Just kidding," Benji said.

"Knock it off," I said. "We need to get organized."

"Who said you were in charge?" Ellen asked.

"I'm good at science," I said.

"So am I," Ellen said. "And I'm organized." She held up her notebook, which was disgustingly neat. My notebook looked like the wrapper of an exploded firecracker—which didn't mean I wasn't a good scientist. I'd just been too busy to straighten it out. Though I'm sure I could never get Ellen to believe that I knew what I was doing.

I tried to think of a scientific approach to picking a leader. Meanwhile, George reached into his pocket and pulled out a quarter. He flipped it into the back of his left hand, covered it with his right hand, and looked at Ellen.

"That's no way to pick," she said.

He looked at me.

"Heads," I said.

Heads it was.

"So, when shall we meet?" I asked.

It turned out that they had stuff going on all week except for today right after school. Three coin tosses and a short argument later, we agreed to meet at my place.

"My room's a little messy," I warned everyone.

"Messy room, messy mind," Ellen said.

"Empty room, empty head," Benji said.

Much as I hated to admit it, I was starting to like him.

We met outside after school and walked to my house. On the way, Ellen mentioned thirty-seven reasons why she was so great and wonderful and perfect, Benji made nineteen jokes, and George kicked a rock.

When we went inside, my mom got all excited. "Oh, you brought friends, Amanda. How nice. I'll make snacks." She seemed to think I spent too much time by myself.

"Watch your step," I warned everyone as we approached my room. I pushed against the door. It didn't move. I leaned into it and gave a hard shove.

"Eeew. You want us to go in there?" Ellen scrunched up her face.

"Hey—it's not dirty. It's just messy." I walked over various piles of clothes, books, magazines, and other essentials, then plopped down on my bed. Okay—actually, I plopped down on the clothes that were on my bed.

Ellen tiptoed in, followed by Benji and George. George sat on my hamper. Ellen perched on the edge of a chair. "You should fire your maid," she said. "Ours would never leave a room like this."

I ignored her.

"Wow. It's sort of like you live inside a laundry basket." Benji walked over to the highest mound of clothes, right near my bookcase, and reached up. "Hey, I can touch the ceiling." He thumped his chest and shouted, "I'm king of the laundry!"

ANALYZE THE TEXT

Conclusions and Generalizations What conclusions can be drawn about Amanda based on text evidence?

225

"Cut that out," I said. "We have work to do."

"Knock, knock." My mom appeared with a tray stacked full of goodies. Before anyone could speak, she'd handed each of us a plate. Turkey sandwiches, and baby carrots with little dishes of ranch dip. Mom made great sandwiches.

"Okay—back to the project," I said. "What about chemistry?"

"Boring," Benji said.

George nodded.

I took a bite of my sandwich. I really loved chemistry, but I was willing to compromise. "Biology?" I asked.

"Not interesting," Benji said.

George curled his lip.

I took another bite, and tried another field. After getting similar responses from them for everything I could think of, I looked over at Ellen, who'd been sitting quietly, eating her snack. Even there, she was disgustingly neat. I didn't see a crumb on her plate. She'd finished her sandwich and started on the carrot sticks.

"You like chemistry?" I asked her.

"Astronomy," she said, dabbing a speck of mayonnaise from the corner of her lip with her napkin.

That figured. I bet if I'd mentioned astronomy, she'd say she liked chemistry. We kept talking, but got absolutely nowhere. Ellen didn't like any of my ideas. I didn't like any of hers. Benji seemed more interested in touching the ceiling.

And George just sat there. Though, compared to the noise everyone else was making, I had to admit I was beginning to appreciate the value of silence. We only had an hour because Ellen needed to leave for a piano lesson. When it was time to go, we agreed that everyone would think about stuff for a week. Then we'd get back together.

"Nice friends," my mom said after they'd left. "Wouldn't you like to have a neat and tidy room where all of you could hang out?"

"It's fine the way it is," I said. I'd rather spend my time trying to understand the universe than straightening out one little unimportant part of it.

We met the next week. Mom brought snacks again. And once again, we couldn't agree on anything. Finally, I said, "Look, we can't keep going like this. If we don't pick a project now, we're toast."

"Planning is important," Ellen said.

"So is toast," Benji said.

"But we aren't planning, we're arguing," I said.

"We are not," Ellen said.

"We are too," I said.

"Are not."

"Are too."

"R2-D2!" Benji shouted.

"You're the only one who's arguing," Ellen said.

We argued about that until it was time for her to go.

Third week—third meeting. We might as well have been in third grade. Ellen and I argued. Benji seemed fascinated by his ability to touch the ceiling near my bookcase. I actually thought about moving that pile of clothes, but I sort of hated to spoil his fun. George kept his thoughts to himself, though he did seem interested in checking out some of the books I'd stacked up next to the hamper, which surprised me.

We finally agreed that since we couldn't agree on a project, everyone would bring an idea next week and we'd vote for the best one.

Week four. I voted for my project. Ellen voted for hers. Benji voted for Albert Einstein. George didn't vote, but he did offer the use of his quarter.

"Look," I said. "It's obvious we can't agree. So let's each start an actual project. Next week, we'll pick the best one, and everyone will work on it."

ANALYZE THE TEXT

Connotation/Denotation Amanda describes Ellen as "disgustingly neat." Does that phrase have a positive or negative connotation? How can you tell?

Week five. We each decided we needed another week. Everyone left right after our snack. When Mom came back for the dishes, she sniffed, looked at my piles of clothes, and said, "You really need to think about picking up."

She was right. It was getting a little stuffy. But I couldn't pick things up just then. I needed to think about my project. So I found a more elegant solution. I opened a window.

Week six.

"What's that supposed to be?" I asked Benji when he lugged his project into my room.

He looked down at the pile of ice-cream sticks and coat-hanger wires attached to a board with bits of duct tape, bent nails, and large globs of glue. "It's a roller coaster."

"You're kidding."

He shrugged. "It sort of fell apart. I'm not great with tools."

I figured he'd make a joke about the project, but he just sighed and said, "Sorry I let the group down."

I looked over at Ellen, who hadn't brought anything. "Did you start a project?" I'd expected her to drag in a display charting the life cycle of designer handbags.

"I tried to spot comets," she said. "It would be so great to discover a new one. Dad bought me this excellent telescope last month. But it's been cloudy every night."

I waited for her to say she was sorry, but she didn't. I guess the word wasn't in her vocabulary. I glanced at George. He shook his head and spread his empty hands. Then I looked at my desk, where I'd balanced a large board that contained my experiments. I'd grown crystals in various solutions. "I guess we'll have to use mine," I said. "Notice how the copper sulfate produces a—"

Just then, Mom appeared in the hallway with a tray. She pushed at the door. Then she pushed harder. There still wasn't enough space for her to get in. She gave the door a good, hard shove. I could feel the floor shake.

On my desk, the whole display started to slide. I tried to dash across the room, but I tripped on a pair of jeans. All of my hard work crashed to the floor.

I lay on my stomach, staring at the icky mess. Mom put the tray down in the hall and squeezed through the doorway. "That's it. I've had it. This room is a disgrace." She grabbed a handful of clothes from the floor. I expected her to drop them somewhere, or toss them. Instead, her eyes opened wide. Then she went, "Eeewww."

I looked over. Under the clothes was . . . something. It was dark green and shriveled. *What in the world is that?* I leaned closer. It was some kind of food.

"That does it!" Mom yelled. "You are grounded until this room is clean."

"But—"

"Disgusting." She shook her head and walked out.

I stood there, staring at the *thing*. Whatever it was, I hadn't put it there. I was a slob, but I wasn't a pig.

Behind me, Ellen whispered something.

I spun toward her. "If you mention your maid one more time, I'm going to scream."

Ellen flinched and backed away from me. I realized I was already screaming.

"I just wanted to tell you I was sorry," she said.

"What?"

"I'm sorry. It's my fault."

"Your fault?"

She shrugged. "I'm allergic to wheat."

I let her words roll around in my brain for a second, hoping I'd somehow misunderstood what she meant. But the equations only seemed to have one solution. Ellen didn't eat bread. Ellen's plate was always empty. Ellen had just apologized. "Are you telling me you've been stashing sandwiches in my room?"

"Not sandwiches. Just the bread. The turkey was delicious."

"Why?"

"I didn't want your mom to think I didn't like her food. And I felt kind of funny about mentioning my allergy. I try so hard to fit in, but it's not easy sometimes. I'm not good at it like you are. You're just so comfortable with stuff."

"What?"

"You don't worry about what people think," she said. "I worry so much that I always end up saying the wrong thing. And you're so smart. I have to study so hard. I have to keep everything so carefully organized, or I get lost. But you—you're so good at science."

"Oh." I'd definitely need to think about what she'd just said. I guess I'd been making a lot of assumptions. But at the moment, I had a more urgent issue to deal with. I looked at the moldy slab. "How many?"

"Every week," she said.

"Where?"

She went to various clothes heaps in my room and revealed the slices of bread, which ranged from slightly moldy to totally overgrown.

Benji picked up the pieces and laid them out on my desk. If the bread hadn't been buried in my wardrobe like some sort of ancient Egyptian funeral offering, I probably would have found it pretty fascinating.

"I'm sorry," Ellen said again. "I'll explain to your mom that this was my fault. And I'll help you clean your room. Okay? If there's one thing I'm really good at, it's straightening up." She looked at me like she expected me to turn her down.

ANALYZE THE TEXT

Characters' Motivations What were Ellen's motivations for acting the way she did? Why does this surprise Amanda?

230

She seemed really sorry. "Sure. You can help. That would be wonderful."

"I'll help too," Benji said.

George nodded.

"Thanks," I said as we tackled the top layer. "This is great. But we still don't have a project."

"Sure we do."

I was so shocked by the voice, I just stared at George.

"We do?" Benji asked.

George nodded and pointed at the bread.

"Mold!" Ellen said. "We have a whole display of the stages of mold growth."

"Yeah," I said. George was right. We had pieces of bread for each week. "But is that enough?" It was hard to imagine a whole project from some slices of moldy bread. Then I realized it wasn't just about mold growth.

"Look," I said, flipping a piece over.

Ellen nodded. "Mayonnaise. It's acidic."

"Yup. We have an example of mold inhibition too. We just have to figure out a way to display it so you can see both sides."

"Great," Ellen said. "But what if it's still not enough?"

"Oh, there might be some more . . ." Benji said.

"What do you mean?" I asked.

"Promise you won't kill me?"

"No."

"Promise you won't make it slow and painful?"

"No."

He shrugged. "I sorta don't like turkey a whole lot."

"Oh, please don't tell me you've been stashing meat in my room."

He nodded.

"Where?" I sniffed and looked around.

Benji pointed at the top of my bookcase.

"You slimeball," I said as I climbed a chair to take a look. Oh, yuck. There were five piles of turkey in various stages of decomposition, neatly laid out from left to right. It was absolutely disgusting. It was also pretty fascinating. And I guess I was relieved to know the smell wasn't coming from my clothes.

I looked over at George. "What about you? Is there anything you don't like?"

He lifted a stack of books to reveal baby carrots.

"Good grief. How could all of you just hide food away like that?"

"Well," Ellen said, "the place is kind of a dump. If you don't care, why should we?"

"When in Slobovia," Benji said, "do as the Slobs do."

I couldn't argue with them. All they'd done was sink to my level. Maybe this was one area where it wouldn't hurt for me to try to be a bit more like Ellen. But just a bit. No way would my pens ever match my wardrobe.

We got back to work At five, I asked Ellen, "Don't you have a piano lesson?"

"It won't hurt me to miss one." She flipped open her cell phone and made a call.

Right after that, George left. I figured he had some sort of appointment he couldn't cancel. But I was grateful he'd helped for as long as he could.

There was still plenty to do. The rest of us kept working.

"I found it!" Benji screamed a couple minutes later.

"What?" I asked.

"The floor!"

I stared down at the spot where he pointed. "So that's what it looks like."

"Nice rug," Ellen said.

"Thanks. I forgot I had one."

Just as we were finishing, George returned, holding a beautiful display case with sections for the bread, turkey, and carrots. It even had mirrors in it to show both sides of the specimens.

"Wow," I said, "that's perfect. Did you build it?"

He nodded.

"You're a genius with your hands," I said.

He smiled.

Ellen patted him on the shoulder. "And you don't waste time talking unless you have something to say."

"I'll do the captions," Benji said. He started coming up with these awful puns that made everyone groan, like, "Spore score and seven weeks ago," "Rot and roll," and "Bacterial Girl." But we laughed too. And I knew Ms. Adler had a great sense of humor, so I figured it wouldn't hurt to use Benji's titles.

Ellen, who had beautiful handwriting, lettered the signs. I typed a report to go along with the display. As we all finished up the project together, I realized I'd discovered an important scientific principle. It had nothing to do with mold, but everything to do with chemistry. Some elements combined quickly. Others combined slowly. And some didn't combine at all unless you mixed them together under high heat and intense pressure.

We got an A. Ms. Adler complimented us on our planning. "I'm impressed," she wrote, "that you worked so nicely as a group and immediately got started on a well-planned and complex project. Your use of familiar food items was especially clever."

That afternoon, as I was leaving school, I found Ellen, Benji, and George waiting for me.

"Want to hang out?" Ellen asked.

"Do you?" I asked back.

All three of them nodded. I thought about those reluctant elements again—the ones that didn't want to combine. When you finally got them together, they usually formed incredibly strong bonds.

"Seems a shame not to take advantage of all our work cleaning your room," Ellen said.

"Good point." I didn't have the heart to tell them that

half the floor had vanished again. They'd find out for themselves soon enough. On the other hand, it would give us something to do. There was one other thing I had to tell them, though. "This time, I think we should make our own snacks."

They all agreed about that too.

Dig Deeper

How to Analyze the Text

Use these pages to learn about Conclusions and Generalizations, Connotation/Denotation, and Characters' Motivations. Then read "Science Friction" again to apply what you learned.

Conclusions and Generalizations

In "Science Friction," author David Lubar includes many details about characters and events in the plot. Sometimes he does not tell readers everything. Readers must use text evidence and their own experience to draw a **conclusion**, or make a logical guess about what is happening.

Readers can also make a **generalization**, or a broad statement that is true most of the time. Look back at page 226 in "Science Friction." Here, Amanda's mom asks her nicely if she would prefer a neat room for the kids to be in. You can draw the conclusion that Amanda's mom isn't happy and wants Amanda to clean her room. Then later, after the project, Amanda's room is messy again. What generalization can you make about Amanda?

My Experience	Text Evidence	Conclusion or Generalization

COMMON CORE **RL.6.1** cite textual evidence to support analysis of what the text says explicitly as well as inferences drawn; **RL.6.3** describe how a story's plot unfolds and how characters respond or change; **RL.6.4** determine the meaning of words and phrases, including figurative and connotative meanings/analyze impact of word choice; **SL.6.1c** pose and respond to questions and make comments that contribute to the discussion; **L.6.5c** distinguish among connotations of words with similar denotations

Connotation/Denotation

Authors choose words carefully to help readers understand characters. Look back at page 225. Amanda describes her room as *messy*. The dictionary, or **denotative,** meaning of *messy* is "disorganized." One additional, or **connotative,** meaning of *messy* is "dirty." A connotation can be negative or positive. For example, people who are careful about their spending can be described as "thrifty" (positive connotation) or "miserly" (negative connotation).

Characters' Motivations

Authors often use **characters' motivations** to move the events of a story along. In "Science Friction," Amanda says she is "good at science." She also probably wants to get a good grade on her science project. Amanda is unhappy with her team's lack of progress for three weeks. Finally, in the fourth week, she takes charge. She tells everyone to start a project and bring it the next week; then they will choose the best one. What is Amanda's motivation for doing this?

Your Turn

my WriteSmart

Turn and Talk

Review the selection with a partner to prepare to discuss this question: *How can mistakes turn into answers to problems?* As you discuss, ask each other questions and reflect on the ideas presented. Use examples from "Science Friction" to explain your response.

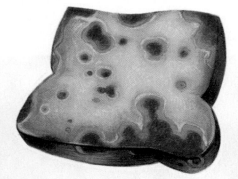

Classroom Conversation

Continue your discussion of "Science Friction" by explaining your answers to these questions:

1. In what ways do Amanda's feelings about each team member change by the end of the story?

2. Ms. Adler calls the project "well-planned," "complex," and "clever." Why does she choose those words?

3. What would Amanda say if her mother asked how she felt about the team and the way the project turned out?

ONE MORE TIME?

Think Again Will Amanda and her teammates ever work on a project together again? Write a paragraph that explains your prediction, and include text evidence from the story as support. Tell what the team members might do differently in the future. Base your prediction on events in the story. Share your paragraph with a partner.

Response Write a summary of "Science Friction." Identify the setting, the characters, and the problem. Include only the most important episodes that lead to the completed science project. Tell how the characters solve their problem and what they learn. Remember that a summary uses only details from the story and contains no opinions.

Writing Tip

Remember that an action verb tells what the subject of a sentence does. Use action verbs such as *hide*, *clean*, and *build* to retell the story's episodes in your own words.

COMMON CORE **RL.6.1** cite textual evidence to support analysis of what the text says explicitly as well as inferences drawn; **RL.6.2** determine a theme or central idea of a text/provide a summary; **RL.6.3** describe how a story's or drama's plot unfolds and how characters respond or change; **W.6.9a** apply grade 6 Reading standards to literature; **SL.6.1a** come to discussions prepared/explicitly draw on preparation to probe and reflect on ideas under discussion; **SL.6.1c** pose and respond to questions and make comments that contribute to the discussion

INFORMATIONAL TEXT

GROWING MOLD

by Ed Schuler

You're hungry. You grab some bread. Ewwww! It's moldy. This may be a question you're reluctant to ask, but what is mold, anyway?

Mold is a type of fungus, a microscopic organism that grows on organic matter such as food. Mold eats bacteria, which, as you'll read, can sometimes be a good thing!

As a detached observer, you can see for yourself how mold grows under different conditions. You might even learn a scientific principle or two while you're at it!

A 300x magnification of the mold fungus Epicoccum purpurascens, *often found in decomposing foods*

COMMON CORE **RI.6.3** analyze how a key individual, event, or idea is introduced, illustrated, and elaborated; **RI.6.10** read and comprehend literary nonfiction

A MOLDY EXPERIMENT

What You Need
- bread (three dry slices)
- cheese (three medium-hard slices)
- tomato (three slices)
- plastic wrap
- plastic knife
- small paper plates

STEP 2

What To Do
1. Make three separate groups, each with a slice of bread, cheese, and tomato. Cut each slice in half. If using three foods is too complex, you can compromise and use one.
2. In Group A, wrap a half-slice of each food in plastic. Leave the rest unwrapped.
3. In Group B, put one set of halves in a dark cupboard. Put the others in an indoor location that has constant light.
4. In Group C, put one set in a warm, dark place. Put the others in a refrigerator.
5. Check your samples daily for a week. Notice how mold forms as food changes (becomes shriveled or fuzzy) through decomposition.

STEP 3

What To Look For
- Which foods grow mold first? Which foods grow the most mold?
- Which food has more mold on it, the wrapped food or the unwrapped food?
- What equations can you make between mold growth and location? Does mold grow better in light or dark? in warm or cool places?

STEP 4

FLEMING'S MIRACLE MOLD

Mold once helped scientists find an elegant solution to a big problem.

In 1928 a Scottish scientist named Alexander Fleming was working in a hospital lab, hoping to find a way to fight bacterial infection. To study bacteria, Fleming grew specimens in dishes. One day, he noticed that a mold had grown on one specimen. Then he discovered that around the mold, bacteria had died.

What had killed them? It was a chemical in the mold!

After years of further research, scientists used the mold, *Penicillium notatum*, to make a drug called penicillin. At first, penicillin was hard to make in large batches. Then scientists found that it grew fast on corn and rotting melon.

By the mid-1940s, the United States was making 650 billion doses of penicillin per month. Infections that once were deadly could now be cured with an antibiotic drug made from a mold!

Alexander Fleming, 1952. The background photo on this page shows spores of the mold used to make penicillin.

Compare Texts

TEXT TO TEXT

Compare "Mold" Texts Talk with a partner about "Science Friction" and "Growing Mold." Discuss these questions: *In what way does each text tell about mold growth? How are the two texts different?* After you discuss your ideas, work together to write an answer to each question. Include evidence from the texts.

TEXT TO SELF

Write About Groups "Science Friction" shows how a diverse group can work together. Think of a time when you were part of a group or a team. What were some of the challenges of working together? What were the benefits? What was the result? Write a paragraph that answers these questions.

TEXT TO WORLD

Explain Fungi Mold is a type of fungus. Mushrooms and yeast are fungi, too. Look up *fungus* in a dictionary. What do you think is the value of studying fungi such as mushrooms and yeast? Share your thoughts with a partner.

COMMON CORE **RL.6.1** cite textual evidence to support analysis of what the text says explicitly as well as inferences drawn; **RI.6.1** cite textual evidence to support analysis of what the text says explicitly as well as inferences drawn; **W.6.10** write routinely over extended time frames and shorter time frames; **SL.6.1c** pose and respond to questions and make comments that contribute to the discussion

Grammar

What Is a Coordinating Conjunction? The connecting words *and, or,* and *but* are called **coordinating conjunctions**. You can use these conjunctions to join two simple sentences into a **compound sentence**.

Coordinating Conjunctions in Compound Sentences
The group had its first meeting, and Amanda became the leader.
Would the group cooperate, or would it waste time on squabbles?
Amanda liked chemistry, but Ellen was more interested in astronomy.

In each part of a compound sentence, the subject and verb must agree.

singular subject   singular verb   coordinating conjunction   plural subject   plural verb

Mold grows on bread, and meat and vegetables rot.

Try This! **Work with a partner. Identify the conjunction in each sentence below. Then explain the subject-verb agreement in both parts of the sentence.**

1 Ellen puts her clothes away, but other students toss their clothes anywhere.

2 Students pick topics for projects, or teachers assign topics.

3 George says very little, but Ellen and Benji talk a lot.

4 Ellen has the moldy bread, and Benji has the rotting meat.

Choppy writing does not flow smoothly. It contains too many short sentences, one after the other. You can avoid choppy writing by combining separate sentences that have related ideas into a compound sentence. Remember to use a comma before the conjunction in a compound sentence.

Separate Sentences

Ellen hid her wheat bread.

Benji hid his turkey slices.

Compound Sentence

Ellen hid her wheat bread, and Benji hid his turkey slices.

Connect Grammar to Writing

As you revise your book review, look for short sentences with related ideas that you can combine into compound sentences. You should also look for long sentences that you can turn into compound sentences.

W.6.1a introduce claims and organize reasons and evidence clearly; **W.6.1b** support claims with reasons and evidence, using credible sources and demonstrating understanding of the topic or text; **W.6.4** produce writing in which development, organization, and style are appropriate to task, purpose, and audience; **W.6.9a** apply grade 6 Reading standards to literature

COMMON CORE

Argument Writing

✔ **Ideas**   To write a **book review**, writers analyze and evaluate a book and then give an opinion about it. To analyze and evaluate a fiction book, ask yourself these questions: *Are the setting and characters well developed? Is the plot interesting? Is the story enjoyable to read?* To create a good **argument** to support your opinion, give the **reasons** you believe as you do. Your reasons should include **evidence** from the story.

Amy wrote a book review in which she stated her opinion about the setting of "Science Friction." Later, she added evidence from the story to support her reasons clearly.

Writing Traits Checklist

✔ **Ideas**
Did I state my opinion clearly and support it?

✔ **Organization**
Did I arrange ideas in a logical order?

✔ **Sentence Fluency**
Did I include compound sentences?

✔ **Word Choice**
Did I use proper nouns and coordinating conjunctions correctly?

✔ **Voice**
Did I express my argument in my own unique way?

✔ **Conventions**
Did I use correct spelling, grammar, and punctuation?

Revised Draft

"Science Friction" is an entertaining story to read. The characters are funny. ~~The~~ , and t The conflict leads to a surprising ending. The most important element of the story, though, is its setting. Most of the story happens in Amanda's room. What makes her room interesting is that it is like many real teenagers' rooms. ∧ It is messy, piled high with clothes, books, and magazines.

The Importance of Setting

by Amy Nukaya

"Science Friction" is an entertaining story to read. The characters are funny, and the conflict leads to a surprising ending. The most important element of the story, though, is its setting. Most of the story happens in Amanda's room. What makes her room interesting is that it is like many real teenagers' rooms. It is messy, piled high with clothes, books, and magazines.

Amanda's room is also where important events in the story take place. It is where we meet Amanda, her mom, Ellen, George, and Benji. Amanda and her classmates meet there each week to plan a science project, but they cannot decide on a project to do. When Amanda's mom brings snacks to the messy room for the kids to eat as they work, no one notices that Amanda's classmates are hiding parts of the snacks they don't like. But why? The reader wonders why Amanda still hasn't cleaned her room.

The setting is also the most important story element because the team members solve their problem in that room. A project is chosen and gets done there. This story just wouldn't be the same without this particular setting. I recommend this funny story so that readers can see how a messy room can change everything!

Reading as a Writer

What evidence did Amy add to support her argument? In your book review, what can you add to make the support for your argument stronger?

In my final book review, I added evidence to support my reasons. I made sure that I used coordinating conjunctions to form compound sentences.

Kensuke's Kingdom

Exploring Islands

✓ TARGET VOCABULARY

rudimentary

immaculately

defy

permeated

venture

poised

rigid

consequences

sparsely

array

Vocabulary Reader

Context Cards

 L.6.6 acquire and use general academic and domain-specific words and phrases/gather vocabulary knowledge for comprehension or expression

Vocabulary in Context

① rudimentary

This picture of a man on a beach gives a rudimentary, or simple, idea of a castaway on an island.

② immaculately

White sand on a tropical beach seems to sparkle immaculately, as if it were spotless.

③ defy

Only an emergency would force a resident of an island to defy, or challenge, a hurricane.

④ permeated

The sweet smells of tropical flowers have permeated, or spread through, many islands.

Go Digital

▶ Study each Context Card.

▶ Ask a question that uses one of the Vocabulary words.

5 venture

Few adult hermit crabs will venture, or dare to go, very far from the safety of their shells.

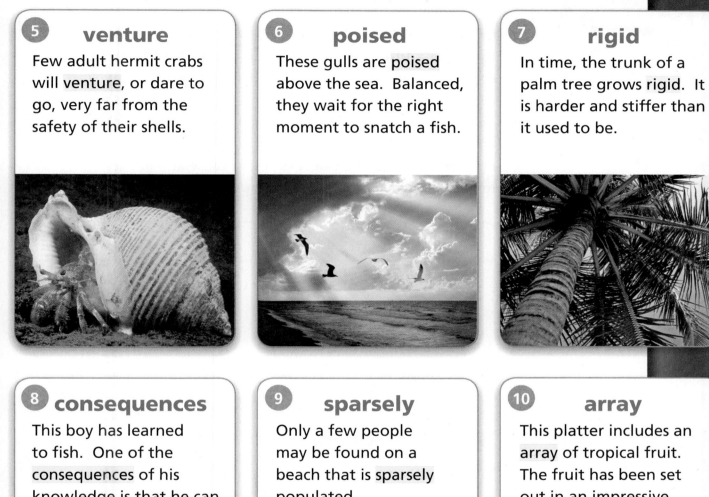

6 poised

These gulls are poised above the sea. Balanced, they wait for the right moment to snatch a fish.

7 rigid

In time, the trunk of a palm tree grows rigid. It is harder and stiffer than it used to be.

8 consequences

This boy has learned to fish. One of the consequences of his knowledge is that he can catch his own food.

9 sparsely

Only a few people may be found on a beach that is sparsely populated.

10 array

This platter includes an array of tropical fruit. The fruit has been set out in an impressive display.

Read and Comprehend

✓ TARGET SKILL

Cause and Effect When you read "Kensuke's Kingdom," look for **cause-and-effect relationships** as the plot unfolds and characters respond or change. To identify a **cause**, ask why an event happens; to identify an **effect**, ask what happens as a result. Remember that an effect can have more than one cause, and a cause can have more than one effect. Use a graphic organizer like the one below to record cause-and-effect relationships in "Kensuke's Kingdom."

Cause	Effect

✓ TARGET STRATEGY

Visualize Use text evidence to **visualize** the characters and events, forming pictures in your mind of the plot as it unfolds and moves toward a resolution.

Island Ecosystems

The living and nonliving things that interact with one another in an area make up an *ecosystem*. The living things include plants and animals. The nonliving things include air, water, and soil. An island is one example of an ecosystem.

Imagine that you are a castaway on an island. What would you need to survive? In "Kensuke's Kingdom," Michael is a castaway whose only company is a mysterious man who teaches him about the island's precious resources.

ANCHOR TEXT

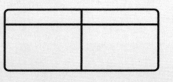

✓ TARGET SKILL

Cause and Effect Identify cause-and-effect relationships that lead to character changes and develop the plot.

✓ GENRE

Realistic fiction has characters and events that are like people and events in real life. As you read, look for:

▶ details that help the reader picture the setting
▶ a main character who overcomes a challenge

COMMON CORE
RL.6.3 describe how a story's or drama's plot unfolds and how characters respond or change; **RL.6.4** determine the meaning of words and phrases, including figurative and connotative meanings/analyze impact of word choice; **RL.6.6** explain how an author develops the point of view of the narrator or speaker; **RL.6.10** read and comprehend literature

Go Digital

MEET THE AUTHOR
Michael Morpurgo

British author Michael Morpurgo runs Farms for City Children, a program that allows children from British cities to spend time on his three farms. Many of his books center on an elderly man "giving back to nature more than he takes from it." An author of more than one hundred books, Morpurgo was Britain's Children's Laureate for 2003–2005.

MEET THE ILLUSTRATOR
William Low

Although he paints in a dark basement, William Low is known for his use of light. He once captured a sunset kayaking trip so accurately, viewers assumed he'd been there. Low's other books include *Old Penn Station* and *Chinatown*.

Kensuke's Kingdom

by Michael Morpurgo
selection illustrated by William Low

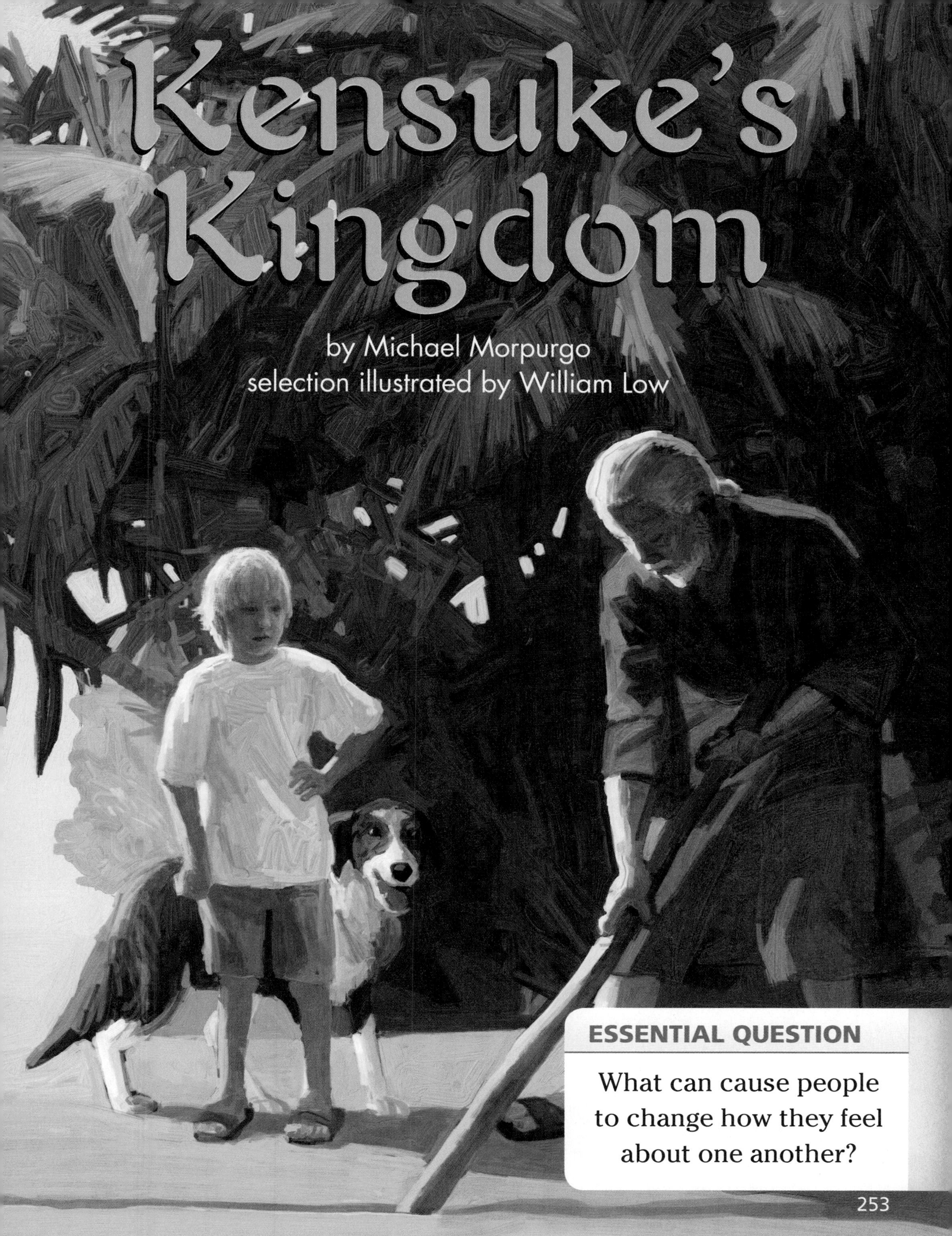

ESSENTIAL QUESTION

What can cause people to change how they feel about one another?

253

Sailing with his parents around the world, Michael and his dog, Stella, fall overboard during a wild storm. They are washed up on an island in the Pacific. A mysterious old man who has befriended the island's orangutans brings food and water to the boy and dog. But when Michael builds a signal fire to attract a passing ship, the man stomps it out. He draws a line in the sand beyond which Michael is not allowed to go and forbids him to swim in the ocean. Angry, the stranded boy waits for another chance to light a beacon.

With every day that passed, in spite of the fish and fruit and water he continued to bring me, I came to hate the old man more and more. Dejected and depressed I may have been, but I was angry, too, and gradually this anger fueled in me a new determination to escape, and this determination revived my spirits. Once again I went on my daily trek up Watch Hill. I began to collect a fresh cache of dry leaves and twigs from the forest edge and squirreled them away in a deep cleft in the rock so that I would always be sure they were dry when the time came. My beacon had dried out at last. I built it up, higher and higher. When I had done all I could I sat and waited for the time to come, as I knew it must. Day after day, week after week, I sat up on Watch Hill, my fireglass polished in my pocket, my beacon ready and waiting.

As it turned out, when the time did come, I wasn't up on Watch Hill at all. One morning, with sleep still in my head, I emerged from my cave, and there it was. A boat! A boat with strange red-brown sails—I supposed it to be some kind of Chinese junk—and not that far out to sea, either. Excitement got the better of me. I ran helter-skelter down the beach, shouting and screaming for all I was worth. But I could see at once that it was hopeless. The junk was not that far out to sea, but it was still too far for me to be either seen or heard. I tried to calm myself, tried to think . . . the fire! Light the fire!

I ran all the way up Watch Hill without once stopping, Stella hard on my heels and barking. All around me the forest was cackling and screeching and whooping in protest at this sudden disturbance. I readied my cache of dry leaves, took my fireglass, and crouched down beside the beacon to light my fire. But I was trembling so much with excitement and exhaustion by now that I could not hold my hand still enough. So I set up a frame of twigs and laid the glass over it, just as I had before. Then I sat over it, willing the leaves to smolder.

Every time I looked out to sea, the junk was still there, moving slowly away, but still there.

It seemed an age, but there was a wisp of smoke, and shortly afterward a glorious, wondrous glow of flame spreading along the edge of one leaf. I bent over it to blow it into life.

That was when I saw his feet. I looked up. The old man was standing over me, his eyes full of rage and hurt. He said not a word, but set about stamping out my embryo fire. He snatched up my fireglass and hurled it at the rock below, where it shattered to pieces. I could only look on and weep as he kicked away my precious pile of dry leaves, as he dismantled my beacon and hurled the sticks and branches one by one down the hill. As he did so the group of orangutans gathered to watch.

Soon nothing whatsoever now remained of my beacon. All about me the rock scree was littered with the scattered ruins of it. I expected him to screech at me, but he didn't. He spoke very quietly, very deliberately. "*Dameda* (dah meh dah)," he said.

"But why?" I cried. "I want to go home. There's a boat, can't you see? I just want to go home, that's all. Why won't you let me? Why?"

He stood and stared at me. For a moment I thought I detected just a flicker of understanding. Then he bowed very stiffly from the waist, and said, "*Gomenasai* (gah meh nah sy). *Gomenasai*. Sorry. Very sorry." And with that he left me there and went off back into the forest, followed by the orangutans.

I sat there watching the junk until it was nothing but a spot on the horizon, until I could not bear to watch anymore. By this time I had already decided how I could best defy him. I was so enraged that consequences didn't matter to me now. Not anymore. With Stella beside me, I headed along the beach, stopped at the boundary line in the sand, and then, very deliberately, I stepped over it. As I did so, I let him know precisely what I was doing.

"Are you watching, old man?" I shouted. "Look! I've crossed over. I've crossed over your silly line. And now I'm going to swim. I don't care what you say. I don't care if you don't feed me. You hear me, old man?" Then I turned and charged down the beach into the sea. I swam furiously, until I was completely exhausted and a long way from the shore. I trod water and thrashed the sea in my fury—making it boil and froth all around me. "It's my sea as much as yours," I cried. "And I'll swim in it when I like."

I saw him then. He appeared suddenly at the edge of the forest. He was shouting something at me, waving his stick. That was the moment I felt it, a searing, stinging pain in the back of my neck, then my back, and my arms, too. A large, translucent white jellyfish was floating right beside me, its tentacles groping at me. I tried to swim away, but it came after me, hunting me. I was stung again, in my foot this time. The agony was immediate and excruciating. It permeated my entire body like one continuous electric shock. I felt my muscles going rigid. I kicked for the shore, but I could not do it. My legs seemed paralyzed, my arms, too. I was sinking, and there was nothing I could do about it. I saw the jellyfish poised for the kill above me now. I screamed, and my mouth filled with water. I was choking. I was going to die, I was going to drown, but I did not care. I just wanted the pain to stop. Death I knew would stop it.

I smelled vinegar, and thought I was at home. My father always brought us back fish and chips for supper on Fridays and he loved to soak his in vinegar—the whole house would stink of it all evening. I opened my eyes. It was dark enough to be evening, but I was not at home. I was in a cave, but not my cave. I could smell smoke, too. I was lying on a sleeping mat covered in a sheet up to my chin. I tried to sit up to look around me, but I could not move. I tried to turn my neck. I couldn't. I could move nothing except my eyes. I could feel, though. My skin, my whole body, throbbed with searing pain, as if I had been scalded all over. I tried to call out, but could barely manage a whisper. Then I remembered the jellyfish. I remembered it all.

The old man was bending over me, his hand soothing on my forehead. "You better now," he said. "My name Kensuke. You better now." I wanted to ask after Stella. She answered for herself by sticking her cold nose into my ear.

I do not know for how many days I lay there, drifting in and out of sleep, only that whenever I woke, Kensuke was always there sitting beside me. He rarely spoke and I could not speak, but the silence between us said more than any words.

ANALYZE THE TEXT

Cause and Effect What does Michael do in the fourth paragraph on page 256 that might help explain why he is attacked by a jellyfish?

My erstwhile enemy, my captor, had become my savior. He would lift me to pour fruit juice or warm soup down my throat. He would sponge me down with cooling water, and when the pain was so bad that I cried out, he would hold me and sing me softly back to sleep. It was strange. When he sang to me it was like an echo from the past, of my father's voice, perhaps—I didn't know. Slowly the pain left me. Tenderly he nursed me back to life. The day my fingers first moved was the very first time I ever saw him smile.

When at last I was able to turn my neck I would watch him as he came and went, as he busied himself around the cave. Stella would often come and lie beside me, her eyes following him, too.

Every day now I was able to see more of where I was. In comparison with my cave down by the beach, this place was vast. Apart from the roof of vaulted rock above, you would scarcely have known it was a cave. There was nothing rudimentary about it at all. It looked more like an open-plan house than a cave—kitchen, sitting room, studio, bedroom, all in one space.

He cooked over a small fire that smoked continuously at the back of the cave, the smoke rising through a small cleft high in the rocks above—a possible reason, I thought, why there were no mosquitoes to bother me. There always seemed to be something hanging from a wooden tripod over the fire, either a blackened pot or what looked like and smelled like long strips of smoked fish.

I could see the dark gleam of metal pots and pans lined up on a nearby wooden shelf. There were other shelves, too, lined with tins and jars, dozens of them of all sizes and shapes, and hanging beneath them innumerable bunches of dried herbs and flowers. These he would often be mixing or pounding, but I wasn't sure what for. Sometimes he would bring them over to me so that I could smell them.

The cave house was sparsely furnished. To one side of the cave mouth stood a low wooden table, barely a foot off the ground. Here he kept his paintbrushes, always neatly laid out, and several more jars and bottles, and saucers, too.

Kensuke lived and worked almost entirely near the mouth of the cave house where there was daylight. At night he would roll out his sleeping mat across the cave from me, up against the far wall. I would wake in the early mornings sometimes and just watch him sleeping. He always lay on his back wrapped in his sheet and never moved a muscle.

Kensuke would spend many hours of every day kneeling at the table and painting. He painted on large shells but, much to my disappointment, he never showed me what he had done. Indeed, he rarely seemed pleased with his work, for just as soon as he had finished, he would usually wash off what he had done and start again.

On the far side of the cave mouth was a long workbench and, hanging up above it, an array of tools—saws, hammers, chisels, all sorts. And beyond the workbench were three large wooden chests in which he would frequently rummage around for a shell, perhaps, or a clean sheet. We had clean sheets every night.

Inside the cave he wore a wraparound bathrobe (a kimono, as I later knew it to be). He kept the cave house immaculately clean, sweeping it down once a day at least. There was a large bowl of water just inside the cave mouth. Every time he came in he would wash his feet and dry them before stepping inside.

The floor was entirely covered with mats made of woven rushes, like our sleeping mats. And everywhere, all around the cave, to head height and above, the walls were lined with bamboo. It was simple, but it was a home. There was no clutter. Everything had its place and its purpose.

As I got better, Kensuke would go off, and leave me on my own more and more but, thankfully, never for too long. He'd return later, very often singing, with fish, perhaps fruit, coconuts or herbs, which he'd bring over to show me proudly. The orangutans would sometimes come with him, but only as far as the cave mouth. They'd peer in at me, and at Stella, who always kept her distance from them. Only the young ones ever tried to venture in, and then Kensuke only had to clap at them and they'd soon go scooting off.

During those early days in the cave house I so much wished we could talk. There were a thousand mysteries, a thousand things I wanted to know. But it still hurt me to talk, and besides, I felt he was quite happy with our silence, that he preferred it somehow. He seemed a very private person, and content to be that way.

Then one day, after hours of kneeling hunched over one of his paintings, he came over and gave it to me. It was a picture of a tree, a tree in blossom. His smile said everything. "For you. Japan tree," he said. "I, Japanese person." After that, Kensuke showed me all the paintings he did, even the ones he later washed off. They were all in black-and-white wash, of orangutans, gibbons, butterflies, dolphins, and birds, and fruit. Only very occasionally did he keep one, storing it away carefully in one of his chests. He did keep several of the tree paintings, I noticed, always of a tree in blossom, a "Japan tree" as he called it, and I could see he took particular joy in showing me these. It was clear he was allowing me to share something very dear to him. I felt honored by that.

In the dying light of each day he would sit beside me and watch over me, the last of the evening sun on his face. I felt as if he were healing me with his eyes. At night, I thought often of my mother and my father. I so much wanted to see them again, to let them know I was still alive. But, strangely, I no longer missed them.

ANALYZE THE TEXT

Style and Tone How does the narrator's tone change as his opinion of Kensuke changes? What words does the author use to illustrate this?

In time I found my voice again. The paralysis gradually lost its grip on me, and my strength flowed back. Now I could go out with Kensuke, whenever he invited me, and he often did. To begin with, I would squat on the beach with Stella and watch him spearfishing in the shallows. So still he stood, and his strike was lightning fast. Then one day he made me my own spear. I was to fish with him. He taught me where the bigger fish were, where the octopuses hid under the rocks, how to stand still as a heron and wait, spear poised just above the water, my shadow falling behind me so that the fish were not frightened away. I tell you, spearing a fish for the first time was like scoring a winning goal for the Mudlarks back home—just about the best feeling in the world.

ANALYZE THE TEXT

Point of View From what point of view is this story told? How do you know? How does the author develop the narrator's point of view throughout the story?

Medusa Jellyfish: Look, but Don't Touch!

Michael learned the hard way that the stinging tentacles of a jellyfish can be excruciatingly painful; in fact, some jellyfish stings can be fatal. Jellyfish, which have inhabited the oceans for hundreds of millions of years, do not deliberately attack humans; swimmers are stung when they inadvertently make contact with one of these creatures as it is drifting along.

Though many species of jellyfish are quite toxic, some jellyfish can be exquisitely beautiful to behold, with their simple, translucent bodies in the radial shape of a bell, sometimes in luminescent hues of purple, pink, or blue. Jellyfish have long tentacles trailing from the rim of their bodies, and for this reason they are also called Medusa jellyfish, after a monster in Greek mythology who had venomous snakes for hair.

The tentacles of a jellyfish contain special stinging organelles called nematocysts. When a swimmer (or more typical prey, such as a small fish) brushes against a tentacle, the nematocysts spring out and pierce the victim's skin with tiny lances. This action paralyzes the prey and allows the jellyfish to pull the unfortunate fish into its mouth and digest it with special enzymes—no chewing necessary!

If you happen to visit a beach where jellyfish are present, take precautions, or avoid the water altogether, especially if the species concerned is among the more venomous ones. Refrain from touching a jellyfish that has washed up onto the shore; even dead jellyfish can sting! Jellyfish are best observed at a safe distance—or better yet, behind a thick sheet of glass, in an aquarium.

Dig Deeper

How to Analyze the Text

Use these pages to learn about Cause and Effect, Style and Tone, and Point of View. Then read "Kensuke's Kingdom" again to apply what you learned.

Cause and Effect

Being able to identify **causes and effects** can help you better understand a story's plot and its characters.

To identify a cause, ask yourself, "Why did this event happen?" To identify an effect, ask yourself, "What happened as a result of this cause?" Remember to look for multiple causes and multiple effects in a text.

What chain of events in the plot causes Michael and Kensuke to become closer? What other events are connected by cause-and-effect relationships?

Cause	Effect

COMMON CORE **RL.6.3** describe how a story's or drama's plot unfolds and how characters respond or change; **RL.6.4** determine the meaning of words and phrases, including figurative and connotative meanings/analyze impact of word choice; **RL.6.6** explain how an author develops the point of view of the narrator or speaker

Style and Tone

An author's word choice often helps to reveal the **tone** of a story. The story is told from Michael's perspective. Look back at the following text on page 256: "I trod water and thrashed the sea in my fury—making it boil and froth all around me." At this point in the story, Michael feels defiant—he does not want to obey Kensuke. The author's use of *thrashed, fury,* and *boil* helps to create Michael's tone of defiance.

Point of View

The term **point of view** gives us a way to identify a story's narrator, or speaker. In first-person point of view, the narrator is a story character who uses words like *I, me,* and *my* to describe his or her experiences. This point of view reveals only what the narrator is able to know, as well as the narrator's thoughts and feelings. As you reread "Kensuke's Kingdom," look for how the author uses the first-person point of view. For example, look for places where the author reveals Michael's thoughts and feelings.

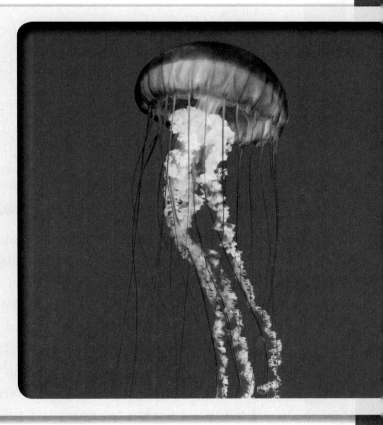

Your Turn

Turn and Talk Review the selection with a partner to prepare to discuss this question: *What can cause people to change how they feel about one another?* Ask and respond to questions that help you develop an answer based on the text.

Classroom Conversation

Continue your discussion of "Kensuke's Kingdom" by explaining your answers to these questions:

1 Why do you think Kensuke imposes such strict rules on Michael?

2 How does Kensuke teach Michael respect for the island and its resources?

3 How do you think Michael's feelings about being rescued may change from the beginning of the story to the ending?

INTERVIEW A CHARACTER

Role-Play Work with others to role-play Kensuke, Michael, and a Japanese-English translator. The students playing Kensuke and Michael should write a list of questions they would like to ask each other. The translator should read the questions in turn for Michael or Kensuke to answer. Students playing Kensuke and Michael should use story details and make inferences about the characters to answer the questions.

WRITE ABOUT READING

Response Do Michael's and Kensuke's attitudes toward each other begin to change at the ending of the story? Do they begin to trust each other more? Write one or two paragraphs to explain whether the characters share a mutual trust. Use stated details about how the characters respond to story events, along with inferences about what you have read in the story as text evidence to support your opinion.

Writing Tip

State your opinion at the beginning of your response. Use transition words and phrases to link the evidence for your opinion.

COMMON CORE **RL.6.1** cite textual evidence to support analysis of what the text says explicitly as well as inferences drawn; **RL.6.3** describe how a story's or drama's plot unfolds and how characters respond or change; **W.6.9a** apply grade 6 Reading standards to literature; **SL.6.1c** pose and respond to questions and make comments that contribute to the discussion

INFORMATIONAL TEXT

Exploring Islands

✓ GENRE

Informational text, such as this science magazine article, gives facts and examples about a topic.

✓ TEXT FOCUS

Diagrams Informational text may include a diagram, a drawing that explains how something works or how parts relate to each other.

COMMON CORE

RI.6.7 integrate information presented in different media or formats as well as in words; **RI.6.10** read and comprehend literary nonfiction

Exploring Islands

by Carole Gerber

Picture an island. What comes to mind? Maybe it's a sparsely inhabited Pacific island with immaculately white sand, where only a few seabirds venture. Maybe it's Greenland, the world's biggest island, at 822,000 square miles. It could be the island nation of Indonesia, home to 211 million people.

Islands come in all varieties. They defy one-size-fits-all descriptions—except for the rudimentary one that applies to all islands: a piece of land completely surrounded by water.

Ancient volcanoes formed the islands of Channel Islands National Park in California.

How Islands Form

There are two main types of island—oceanic and continental. Both types show the consequences of dramatic changes.

Oceanic islands, such as those found along the coast of Southern California, form from the peaks of undersea volcanoes. Some oceanic islands are created when coral reefs, made from rigid coral skeletons, build up around these volcanoes.

Continental islands form when the sea rises and surrounds a section of the mainland of a continent. One kind of continental island is the barrier island. This island forms from the action of water, wind, and tides that shape and move sand and sediment. Many barrier islands are found along the Atlantic coast of North America.

Barrier Island Zones

Barrier islands are always poised for change. A typical barrier island has five zones. Ocean waves bring sand to the beach. Wind forms the sand into dunes that are held in place by plants. Storms push water permeated with sediment over the dunes, forming a mud flat. Ocean tides make an area of salt marsh around the mud flats.

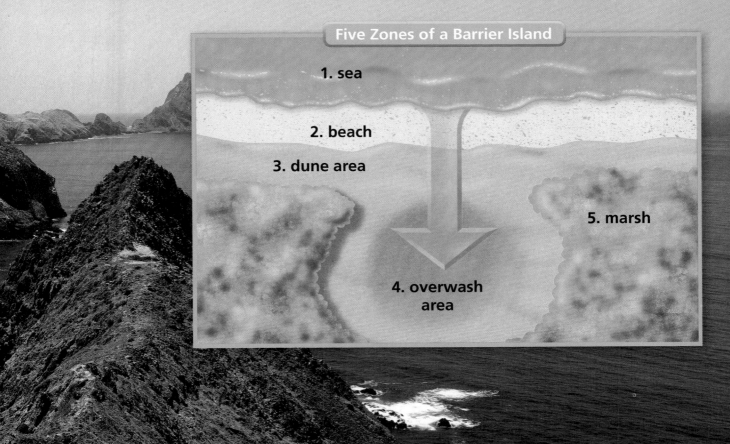

Five Zones of a Barrier Island

1. sea
2. beach
3. dune area
4. overwash area
5. marsh

The Island Ecosystem

The Outer Banks (left) are a chain of barrier islands along the North Carolina coast. This island ecosystem is the home of a rich array of plant and sea life.

Some animals live on the Outer Banks year-round, but others only visit. Often, the sky above the islands is filled with flocks of snow geese and other birds that arrive for the winter. Another visitor, the female loggerhead sea turtle, lives in the ocean but comes ashore in summer to dig a nest and lay her eggs.

To care for this ecosystem and protect its animals and plants, portions of the Outer Banks have been named federal wildlife refuges.

Female loggerhead sea turtles return to the Outer Banks every two to three years to nest.

Compare Texts

TEXT TO TEXT

Compare Island Texts "Kensuke's Kingdom" and "Exploring Islands" provide information about islands. Use the following questions to compare and contrast the texts: *Which text tells about barrier islands? How does each text tell about island ecosystems? How does each text describe the living things on the island?* Use evidence from the texts to support your answers.

TEXT TO SELF

Describe an Experience In "Kensuke's Kingdom," Kensuke's actions frustrate Michael. Write a paragraph about a time when someone's actions surprised, puzzled, or frustrated you. What did the experience teach you?

TEXT TO WORLD

Link Information Island ecosystems are found all over the world. "Exploring Islands" tells about barrier islands in North America. How does the text information and the diagram on page 269 give you a better understanding of the topic? Discuss why it is helpful to have information presented in more than one way.

COMMON CORE **RL.6.1** cite textual evidence to support analysis of what the text says explicitly as well as inferences drawn; **RI.6.1** cite textual evidence to support analysis of what the text says explicitly as well as inferences drawn; **RI.6.7** integrate information presented in different media or formats as well as in words; **W.6.10** write routinely over extended time frames and shorter time frames

Grammar

What Is a Subordinating Conjunction? Words such as *although, when, because, if,* and *since* are **subordinating conjunctions**. The part of a sentence that begins with a subordinating conjunction is the **dependent clause**. Dependent clauses are not complete sentences. A **complex sentence** consists of a dependent clause and an **independent clause**. An independent clause can stand alone as a sentence. It is the most important part of a complex sentence. Use a comma after a dependent clause that comes at the beginning of a sentence.

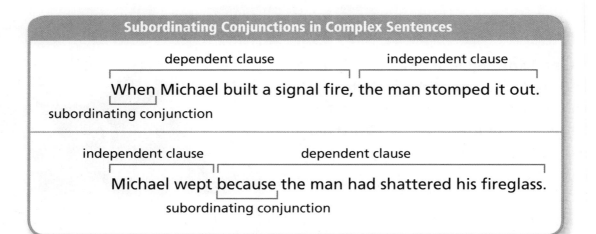

Subordinating Conjunctions in Complex Sentences

dependent clause   independent clause

When Michael built a signal fire, the man stomped it out.

subordinating conjunction

independent clause   dependent clause

Michael wept because the man had shattered his fireglass.

subordinating conjunction

Try This! Write the complex sentences below on a sheet of paper. Circle the subordinating conjunctions. Underline the independent clauses, and draw two lines under the dependent clauses.

1 Michael swam furiously until he was exhausted.

2 After the jellyfish stung him, Michael felt great pain.

3 Michael could not swim because his muscles had become rigid.

4 When Michael screamed, his mouth filled with water.

You can vary your sentence structure and make your writing smoother by using a subordinating conjunction to combine two related sentences into a complex sentence.

Separate Sentences

The boy lay motionless in bed.

His dog shoved her nose into his ear.

Complex Sentence

As the boy lay motionless in bed, his dog shoved her nose into his ear.

Connect Grammar to Writing

As you revise your argument next week, look for sentences that you can combine into a complex sentence by using a subordinating conjunction.

W.6.4 produce writing in which development, organization, and style are appropriate to task, purpose, and audience; **W.6.5** develop and strengthen writing by planning, revising, editing, rewriting, or trying a new approach

Argument Writing

Reading-Writing Workshop: Prewrite

✓ **Ideas**   In an **argumentative essay**, writers present a claim, or opinion, about a topic. The writers' purpose in an argument is to influence their audiences to do something or to think a certain way. Plan an argument by clearly stating an opinion. Then think of strong reasons that will support your claim. Support the reasons with evidence. Organize the reasons and evidence in a way that is logical and appropriate for your audience.

Maya explored the topic of island ecosystems and decided to write about protecting coral reefs. Once she stated her claim, she developed her argument by listing reasons and the evidence that supports the reasons. She deleted an idea to strengthen her writing. Later, she organized her ideas into an argument chart.

Writing Process Checklist

▶ **Prewrite**

- ✓ **Did I plan my argument with my audience in mind?**
- ✓ **Did I begin with a claim?**
- ✓ **Did I include strong reasons?**
- ✓ **Did I include enough evidence to support each reason?**
- ✓ **Did I organize my ideas in a clear way?**

Draft

Revise

Edit

Publish and Share

Exploring a Topic

Reefs are ecosystems that people depend on.

~~Reefs are found around the world.~~

Coral reefs should be protected.

Reefs can provide barriers around islands and coasts.

Reefs are almost impossible to replace when damaged.

274

Coral reefs are important to the environment. People should protect them.

Reason:
Reefs are ecosystems that people depend on.

Evidence:
Reef environments are home to many sea animals that are food sources for people.

Reason:
Reefs can provide barriers around islands and coasts.

Evidence:
Reefs protect beaches from the force of damaging waves.

Reason:
Reefs are almost impossible to replace when they are damaged.

Evidence:
Coral reefs grow at an extremely slow rate.

Reading as a Writer

How does Maya's evidence support her reasons? Where can you add evidence to support your own reasons in your argument?

When I developed ideas for my argument, I used strong reasons and evidence to support my claim.

Vocabulary in Context

☑ **TARGET VOCABULARY**

lore
abundance
altered
sophisticated
cultural
lush
teeming
retains
heritage
concept

Vocabulary Reader | Context Cards

L.6.6 acquire and use general academic and domain-specific words and phrases/gather vocabulary knowledge for comprehension or expression

276

---

1 lore

A tribe's lore, or collected knowledge, is passed on by adults who teach traditions to new generations.

2 abundance

These fishermen can feed many families with this abundance of salmon.

3 altered

Computers have changed Alaskan schools. They have altered how students learn.

4 sophisticated

This artwork is sophisticated. It shows many complex details.

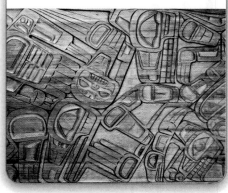

Go Digital

▶ Study each Context Card.

▶ Discuss one picture. Use a different Vocabulary word from the one on the card.

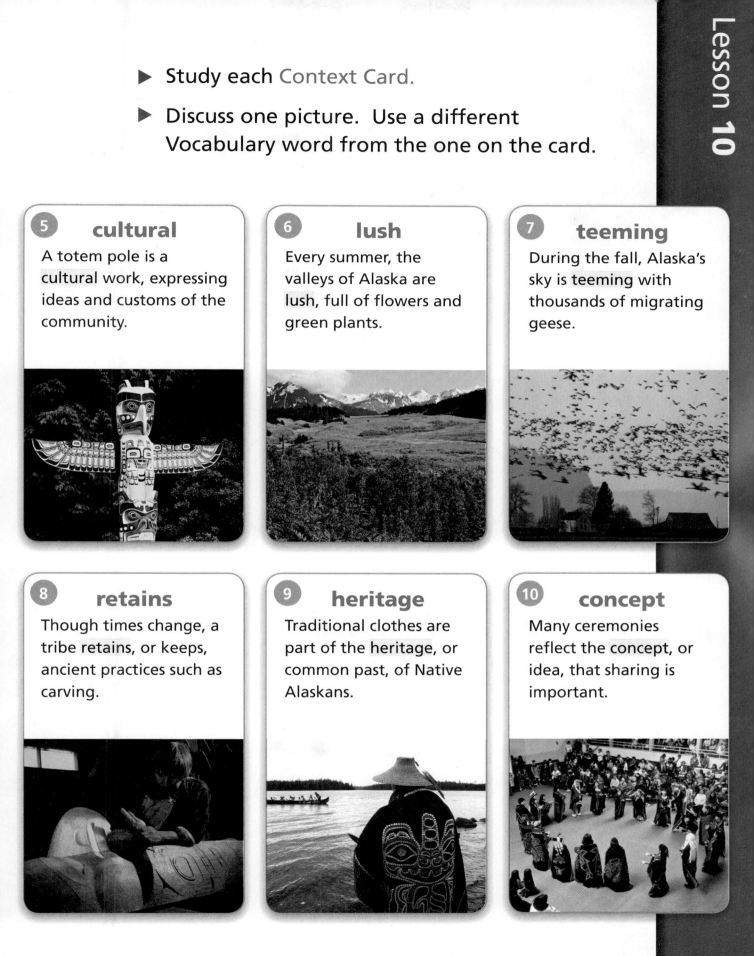

5 **cultural**

A totem pole is a cultural work, expressing ideas and customs of the community.

6 **lush**

Every summer, the valleys of Alaska are lush, full of flowers and green plants.

7 **teeming**

During the fall, Alaska's sky is teeming with thousands of migrating geese.

8 **retains**

Though times change, a tribe retains, or keeps, ancient practices such as carving.

9 **heritage**

Traditional clothes are part of the heritage, or common past, of Native Alaskans.

10 **concept**

Many ceremonies reflect the concept, or idea, that sharing is important.

Read and Comprehend

✓ TARGET SKILL

Compare and Contrast When you **compare**, you analyze how things are the same. When you **contrast**, you look for differences. As you read "Children of the Midnight Sun," notice how people, places, or historical periods are alike and different. Look for clue words such as *in common*, *similar*, and *all* to help you find likenesses. Look for clue words such as *but*, *each*, and *better* to help you find differences. Use a graphic organizer like this one to gather your ideas.

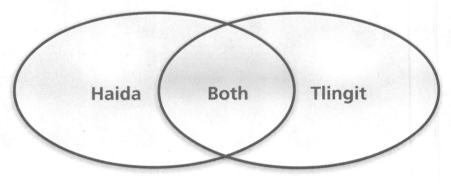

Haida | Both | Tlingit

✓ TARGET STRATEGY

Question Ask **questions** about a selection before you read, as you read, and after you read. Then look for text evidence to help you answer the questions.

COMMON CORE

RI.6.1 cite textual evidence to support analysis of what the text says explicitly as well as inferences drawn

PREVIEW THE TOPIC

Traditions

People of different cultures have their own traditions that are followed and honored over time. Traditions are often handed down from parents and grandparents to children. Some traditions come out of the history of a people and the places where they live. Other traditions develop as families come together to celebrate.

In "Children of the Midnight Sun," you'll learn about the culture and way of life of two native Alaskan children. You'll also learn about southeastern Alaska and its natural beauty and richness.

ANCHOR TEXT

Compare and Contrast
Examine how two or more things are alike and different.

Literary nonfiction tells about people, places, or things that are real. As you read, look for:

▶ factual information that tells a story
▶ text features such as photographs and captions
▶ events organized in time order

COMMON CORE **RI.6.6** determine the author's point of view or purpose and explain how it is conveyed; **RI.6.8** trace and evaluate the argument and specific claims in a text; **RI.6.10** read and comprehend literary nonfiction

MEET THE AUTHOR

Tricia Brown

Tricia Brown has lived and worked in Alaska since the 1970s. A writer and an editor, she has published books on a wide range of topics, including the Iditarod sled-dog race, quilt making, and the Alaska Highway. She has won numerous awards for her writing and continues to write for both adults and children.

MEET THE PHOTOGRAPHER

Roy Corral

Roy Corral has explored and photographed much of Alaska, including some of its most remote regions. At one point, he lived in a wilderness area above the Arctic Circle in a log home he built himself. His photographs have appeared in *National Geographic Magazine, Sports Illustrated for Kids,* and many children's books.

Children of the Midnight Sun:
Young Native Voices of Alaska

by Tricia Brown   photographs by Roy Corral

ESSENTIAL QUESTION

What kinds of things might two different cultures have in common?

These portraits of two Native American children growing up in Alaska reveal how they each celebrate their culture's ancient traditions in the context of modern life.

Selina Tolson Haida

Belly down on the Hydaburg dock, Selina Tolson, nine, and her cousin Jamie peer into the shadowy water beneath them. The girls identify seaweed, jellyfish, and salmon while they wait for Selina's teenage brother Charles to come with his skiff. Selina's family left earlier on the *Haida* (HY duh) *Girl*, her grandfather's fifty-six-foot commercial seiner, and the girls are anxious to join them at a picnic across the water.

"Look at those fish!" says Selina. "I wish I had my brother's rod." She loves to fish for salmon, although she admits that a brother helps reel them in. Selina has three brothers and two sisters, a cat named Fatso, a pen pal, a treehouse, and a *chanáa* (chah NAH), or grandfather, who tells her wonderful stories.

This late August day is sunny and dry, a rare occasion. Hydaburg, a village of about 400 Haida Indian people, lies in rain forest country on Prince of Wales Island in Southeast Alaska. Each year, the area normally gets about 150 inches of rain and a little snow.

Rows of totem poles stand next to Selina's school. Some are new poles; others are very old, collected from other places on the island.

Minutes pass slowly. The girls roll onto their backs to stare at the clouds. On Selina's wrist are two broad, engraved silver bracelets that tinkle whenever they touch. The Eagle clan symbol adorns one. Selina wears a silver ring too.

"My uncle gave me this ring," Selina says. "This bracelet was my dad's mother's, and when she died, he gave it to me. I don't take them off, ever."

Art and Culture

Artistically, the Haidas have much in common with their neighbors, the Tlingits (KLIHNG its) and Tsimshians (SIHM shee uhns). Their styles vary so slightly that only a clan member or a fellow artist might notice the differences. All three groups carve totem poles and follow similar customs in clan organization. But each group retains its own identity and tribal lore, and each is known for its artistic specialty. Historically, for the Haidas, it was dugout canoes, made from the biggest cedar trees in the region—found about forty miles south on Canada's Queen Charlotte Islands.

In Selina's village there is an abundance of artists. Rosa Alby makes beautiful button blankets. Her brother, Warren, carves Haida-style boats and totems. Viola Burgess teaches Haida art to the children. Selina's mom, Christine, is among those who teach Haida dance.

"Our dance costume is a special blanket with our clan on it," says Selina. "Jamie and I are Eagle. There's Eagle, Frog, Bullhead, and Beaver.

"We don't use the same dance steps for every song," she explains. "We practice what we're going to do. Our teachers teach us Haida words, like *kwáadaa* (KWAH dah). That means 'quarter,' and *dáalaa* (DAH lah) means 'money,' and *dúus* (doos) means 'cat.' *Háw'aa* (huh WAH) means 'thank you.'"

ANALYZE THE TEXT

Author's Purpose What do you think is the author's purpose for writing this selection? What text evidence supports your answer?

Selina loves to fish. Although she'd rather have a coho salmon on the end of her line, she'll settle for this rockfish. ▶

Next to Selina's school is a grassy lot lined with totem poles. Life in a rain forest means there are always plenty of large trees for carving. The frequent rain and constant dampness speed the natural decay of these valuable pieces of history and art. Some were moved from other places on Prince of Wales; others were carved here. Historically, the totems served as storytellers, memorials, or signs of clan ownership.

Finally, Selina spots Charles on the horizon and jumps to her feet. Within minutes, he motors in and helps his passengers aboard for a twenty-minute ride.

At the picnic, three generations of adults—Selina's aunts, uncles, grandparents, older cousins, and family friends—sit on driftwood logs, talking, laughing, and feeding a bonfire. Over the flames, they roast hot dogs and marshmallows. Tupperware containers of salads, smoked *chíin* (cheen), or salmon, and desserts are opened. A few grown-ups keep their eyes on the young ones romping in the chilly ocean. Selina can't be tempted to jump in, but wades instead, squealing when the cold water laps against her ankles.

Occasionally, a shivering child runs up to a parent for a rubdown with a towel. A few head into the woods to look for berries. Seated in nearby lawn chairs are Selina's grandparents, Sylvester and Frieda Peele, respected tribal elders who are passing on stories, language, and dance, teaching the Haida ways in daily life and in cultural heritage classes for children.

Selina poses with her mother, Christine, and grandparents Sylvester and Frieda Peele. Because clan membership is passed from mother to child, Frieda, Christine, and Selina are all Eagles.

Haida History

Sylvester was born in Hydaburg, but his parents were not. His mother came from British Columbia, and his father was from Kilnkwun, a village about ten or twelve miles away from Hydaburg. Kilnkwun and another village were abandoned in 1911 when the government forced the residents to move to Hydaburg.

"It was mostly for school purposes," Sylvester says gently. "But this was a better place to live, with a river and lots of salmon." At one time his ancestors all lived in Canada. Some tribal stories say that about 400 years ago there was a food shortage, and one group came north to Prince of Wales Island.

The Alaska Haidas settled in villages that had been abandoned by Tlingits. However, other storytellers say the new arrivals warred with the Tlingits, driving them to the northern part of the island. Today, an invisible boundary splits the island, with Tlingit country in the north and the Haidas in the south. But wars? None lately.

The third largest American island, Prince of Wales Island, lies just across the border from Canada.

The Haidas found plentiful food when they arrived: deer, berries, fish eggs, crab, salmon, halibut, and seaweed. And even though Hydaburg's children can walk to the little Do Drop grocery store for candy, pop, crackers, or other snacks, their families still mostly rely on the ocean to feed them.

"I like coho eggs and dog salmon eggs," says Selina. "We dry them and save them for the winter. I help pick the berries, and I help with drying seaweed, too.

"My brothers usually go out on the boat and get seaweed on the beach somewhere. At home, they grind it up in the grinder and lay it out on the roof of the house to dry. Then we seal it in plastic bags."

The picnic is wrapping up, and as mothers and aunties are replacing lids and gathering children, the men fold up chairs and carry supplies to the water's edge.

In the middle of the cove, the beautiful *Haida Girl* waits, anchored in the still, gray water. Charles shuttles the party from the beach to the seiner, a handful at a time. Voyaging home to Hydaburg, Selina turns her face toward the bow of the *Haida Girl*. Her long, black hair flutters in the wind like a flag.

A member of the Eagle Clan, Selina models her ceremonial regalia.

Josh Hotch  Tlingit

Josh Hotch doesn't know whom he'll marry when he grows up, but he knows she'll be a Raven, so his children will be Ravens. That's because Josh is a member of the other Tlingit clan—the Eagle clan—just like his mother.

"You are what your mother is," he explains. "An Eagle can't marry an Eagle, and a Raven can't marry a Raven." Marrying within your clan would be like marrying a member of your family.

At ten, Josh may not know the word *moiety* (MOY uh tee), but he understands the concept. Throughout Tlingit territory—nearly all of Alaska's Southeast Panhandle—the Natives historically were born into two moieties, or membership groups, called Eagle and Raven, and further divided into subclans with animal symbols such as Killer Whale, Wolf, or Frog.

The clan shared responsibilities. If one clan organized to build a house, the other clan finished the work. Then the first hosted a potlatch, a ceremonial feast that focused on gift-giving memorials, and displays of wealth. If a clan member died, the other clan prepared the dead for cremation or burial. Later, the deceased's clan would show their thanks by hosting a potlatch. And so it went, back and forth, sharing labor and gifts, with each clan helping and honoring the other.

Josh is robed in a Chilkat blanket, part of his dance regalia.

These customs are among the ancient Tlingit traditions woven into daily life in Klukwan, Josh's home village of 140 people in the northern part of the state's Panhandle. So, too, are practices such as smoking and drying fish, carving totem poles and masks, weaving Raven's Tail robes and Chilkat blankets, dancing and singing, storytelling, and celebrating in potlatches. Nothing is done for the sake of tourists—it's just everyday living. The residents also drive cars and own fax machines in a village that mixes past and present in a postcard setting.

Living with Nature

"Klukwan is a nice place," says Josh. "We have the biggest mountains in the U.S.A. We have evergreen and cottonwood trees and glaciers. Salmon, fish, and deer, too. In the spring, the hooligans are here—they're the teeny fish that you can't catch in salmon fishing nets. We make hooligan oil out of them. We dip dried fish or dried hooligan in it—it's a snack!"

Klukwan is indeed a beautiful, bountiful place to live. That's probably why Chilkat Tlingits have lived in this valley for thousands of years. They were sophisticated artisans who often traded with their Athabascan (ath uh BAS kuhn) neighbors. They also held the rights to the trails later used by the Gold Rush prospectors headed for the Klondike.

At the edge of Josh's backyard, beyond the swing set and the fringe of cottonwoods, beyond the smoke house and the skiff, the Chilkat River rolls by in a broad, braided pattern. In the distance, snow-capped mountains tower above a lush, green valley teeming with fish and wildlife.

The people of Klukwan depend on fish and game as their food staples, and drive twenty-one miles to Haines for any other groceries, to pick up mail, see a movie, or board the ferry on the Inside Passage. The villagers share this valley with the largest gathering of bald eagles in North America. Each October and November, up to 4,000 eagles congregate to glut themselves on late-run salmon in the Chilkat River. "Eagles fight with eagles for fish," Josh says.

Klukwan is so small that there are ten children in Josh's class of second- through fourth-graders.

Josh's village is long and narrow, laid out parallel to the river along one unpaved street with weathered cabins and newer frame homes sprinkled on each side. Near the middle is the community center, used for potlatches and other special events. Josh and his cousins like to explore, run, play hide-and-seek, and go bike riding around town. There's plenty of room and little traffic. And everybody knows everybody else.

Growing Up Tlingit

Even though Josh is still young, he has learned the rules of his society, not from books, but from the Ravens and Eagles around him. And if he'd been born a century ago, he would have practiced another Tlingit tradition, the "avunculate." At about age six, Tlingit boys used to go live with their mother's brother, who taught them as they grew to manhood. It was believed that fathers would be too easy on their sons, but that an uncle was the right combination of softness and strictness.

Josh's dad, Jones, is a tribal government leader who's teaching his son with assistance from a special uncle. Today, Tlingit children don't leave home for the avunculate, but uncles still help to instruct them, and not just the boys in the family. When Josh's mom, Lani, was growing up, she and her brothers learned from their mother's brother, Albert Paddy. And when Josh was born, Lani gave him Uncle Albert's Tlingit name: *Kaan-kai-da* (kahn KY dah).

"He still watches out for us now, even though we're grown," Lani says. "And he's been training Josh on the fishing boat on the river. He also had an important role in showing me how to make dried fish, along with my grandmother, my mom, and my dad."

ANALYZE THE TEXT

Arguments and Claims On page 288, the author makes the claim that Klukwan is "a beautiful, bountiful place." What evidence in the text supports this claim?

Josh uses a spotting scope to watch for eagles in trees along the river. ▶

Contact with non-Native settlers, gold miners, missionaries, and educators in the last two centuries has altered the ancient ways of the Tlingit people. Especially in the 1900s, the loss of traditional dancing, singing, and weaving was sorely felt.

"Josh's grandparents weren't taught to dance and sing," Lani says. "If they used their language, they were punished." And as old weavers died, few young people were trained to follow. Only in the last decade has Lani's generation learned the songs and dances of their ancestors by listening to old recordings and experimenting with movements. "We had a lot of encouragement from the elders," she says.

Josh and his uncle, Albert Paddy, leave the village for a fish site on the Chilkat River.

From the adults around him, Josh has learned the meaning of the symbols on totem poles and on his special dance clothing. He's learned how to bead, dance, sing, and prepare salmon for smoking.

"You cut off the head, tail, and fins," Josh says. "You use cottonwood to burn in the smokehouse. There's a screen so that no bugs can get in. It's just like how it sounds: dried fish would be dry; smoked fish would taste like smoke. What I like are herring eggs. They're crunchy. They're better than potato chips!"

On his way to becoming a man, Josh is surrounded by a village full of Eagles and Ravens who will make sure he knows who he is: *Kaan-kai-da*, a Tlingit, a son of Klukwan.

ANALYZE THE TEXT

Compare and Contrast How are the Haida and the Tlingit cultures alike and different? What details in the text support your answer?

Dig Deeper

How to Analyze the Text

Use these pages to learn about Compare and Contrast, Arguments and Claims, and Author's Purpose. Then read "Children of the Midnight Sun" again to apply what you learned.

Compare and Contrast

In "Children of the Midnight Sun," author Tricia Brown presents two portraits of Native American children in Alaska. Comparing and contrasting can help you understand the subjects and their unique cultures. To **compare,** identify similarities between details in the two portraits. To **contrast,** identify the differences between details.

Look back at the selection. One aspect of the portraits is the author's description of what the subjects like to do. The author includes details about activities that Selina and Josh enjoy. What do Selina and Josh like to do that is similar? What does each like to do that is different?

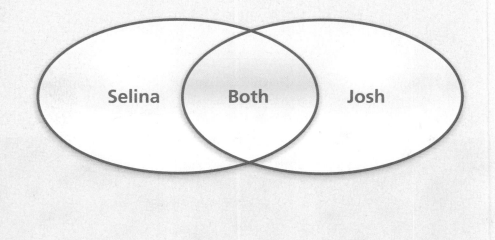

Selina   Both   Josh

RI.6.1 cite textual evidence to support analysis of what the text says explicitly as well as inferences drawn; **RI.6.6** determine the author's point of view or purpose and explain how it is conveyed; **RI.6.8** trace and evaluate the argument and specific claims in a text

COMMON CORE

Arguments and Claims

Authors of informational texts often state a **claim,** or an opinion. To convince readers to share the opinion, authors develop an **argument.** A strong argument contains reasons and evidence. As you read informational text, look for the author's claims and the evidence that supports them. Evaluate the strength of an argument by identifying the claims that are supported by evidence and those that are not.

Author's Purpose

Tricia Brown had a reason, or **purpose,** for writing about Native American children in Alaska. Although her reason for writing is not stated in the selection, readers can use text evidence such as details and descriptive words to figure out whether the author's purpose is to inform, persuade, or entertain readers. Look back at page 291. Tricia Brown includes Josh's opinion that herring eggs are "crunchy" and are "better than potato chips." Why does Brown include these details? How do these details help you figure out the author's purpose?

Your Turn

RETURN TO THE ESSENTIAL QUESTION

Turn and Talk
Review the selection with a partner to prepare to discuss this question: *What kinds of things might two different cultures have in common?* As you discuss, reflect on answers and ask questions of each other to clarify.

Classroom Conversation

Continue your discussion of "Children of the Midnight Sun" by explaining your answers to these questions:

1. How do the photographs and captions support the author's purpose for writing?

2. What do the words *honor* and *respect* mean to Selina and Josh?

3. In what ways would the selection be different if the author had chosen to write it as interviews with the two children?

LAND AND CULTURE

Write an Explanation Both Selina and Josh live in the Alaskan Pacific Northwest. How does this location shape the way of life for both the Haida people and the Tlingit people? Write an explanation of how the two groups are affected by the place where they live. Use text evidence in your explanation.

WRITE ABOUT READING

Response With a partner, choose who will write about the Haida and who will write about the Tlingit. Then write a summary of the culture you chose. Use information from the selection. When finished, trade summaries with your partner. Be sure to avoid personal opinions or judgments. Rely entirely on the information presented in the selection.

Writing Tip

As you write, make sure you use correct punctuation and capitalization. Ask yourself if each sentence makes sense.

COMMON CORE **RI.6.1** cite textual evidence to support analysis of what the text says explicitly as well as inferences drawn; **RI.6.2** determine a central idea of a text/provide a summary; **RI.6.7** integrate information presented in different media or formats as well as in words; **W.6.9b** apply grade 6 Reading standards to literary nonfiction; **SL.6.1a** come to discussions prepared/explicitly draw on preparation to probe and reflect on ideas under discussion; **SL.6.1d** review key ideas expressed and demonstrate understanding of multiple perspectives

POETRY

NATIVE AMERICAN POETRY

GENRE

Poetry uses the sound and rhythm of words to suggest images and express feelings in a variety of forms.

TEXT FOCUS

Imagery Poetry includes figurative language so readers can picture the images the poet wants to evoke.

The Native American poems in this selection connect to a rich cultural past. The Makah Nation of Washington State retains tribal dancing as an important part of its heritage. "Song" honors that tradition. "Twelfth Song of Thunder" celebrates the Navajo of the American Southwest and their connection to all living things above, on, and below the land. The Maidu of California's Sierra Nevada are represented in "Lesson in Fire," a poem teeming with dreamlike images that recalls the lore of making fire.

Song

Mine is a proud village, such as it is,
We are at our best when dancing.

Makah

COMMON CORE **RL.6.4** determine the meaning of words and phrases, including figurative and connotative meanings/analyze impact of word choice; **RL.6.10** read and comprehend literature

Twelfth Song of Thunder

Navajo Tradition

The voice that beautifies the land!
The voice above,
The voice of thunder
Within the dark cloud
Again and again it sounds,
The voice that beautifies the land.

The voice that beautifies the land!
The voice below,
The voice of the grasshopper
Among the plants
Again and again it sounds,
The voice that beautifies the land.

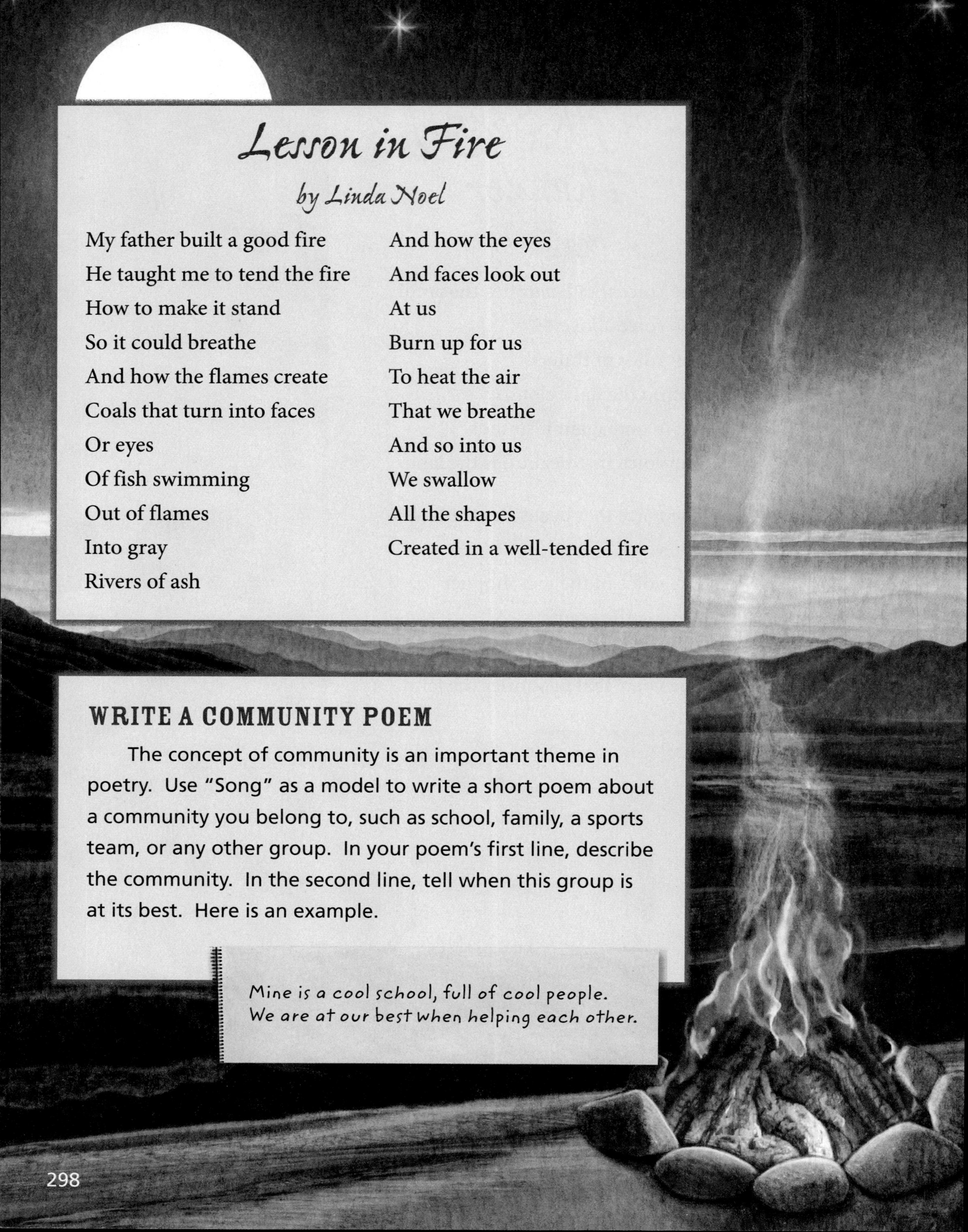

Lesson in Fire

by Linda Noel

My father built a good fire

He taught me to tend the fire

How to make it stand

So it could breathe

And how the flames create

Coals that turn into faces

Or eyes

Of fish swimming

Out of flames

Into gray

Rivers of ash

And how the eyes

And faces look out

At us

Burn up for us

To heat the air

That we breathe

And so into us

We swallow

All the shapes

Created in a well-tended fire

WRITE A COMMUNITY POEM

The concept of community is an important theme in poetry. Use "Song" as a model to write a short poem about a community you belong to, such as school, family, a sports team, or any other group. In your poem's first line, describe the community. In the second line, tell when this group is at its best. Here is an example.

Mine is a cool school, full of cool people.
We are at our best when helping each other.

Compare Texts

TEXT TO TEXT

Compare and Contrast Compare and contrast how "Children of the Midnight Sun" and "Native American Poetry" tell about Native American traditions and culture. In what ways do the forms of writing impact how the information is presented? Discuss with a partner.

TEXT TO SELF

Describe Favorite Activities Selina and Josh enjoy doing many activities with their families and people from their villages. What activities do you enjoy doing with your own family, friends, or neighbors? Write a paragraph describing those activities.

TEXT TO WORLD

Plan a Visit Imagine that your class can visit a Native American community anywhere in the United States. Choose a region to visit, and identify one or more native groups in the area. Create a map and an itinerary, or plan, for your trip. List highlights of what you might see and learn. Share this information with other members of a small group.

COMMON CORE **RL.6.1** cite textual evidence to support analysis of what the text says explicitly as well as inferences drawn; **RI.6.1** cite textual evidence to support analysis of what the text says explicitly as well as inferences drawn; **RI.6.7** integrate information presented in different media or formats as well as in words; **W.6.10** write routinely over extended time frames and shorter time frames

Grammar

What Is a Compound-Complex Sentence? You have learned that two simple sentences can be joined by a **coordinating conjunction** to form a **compound sentence.** You have also learned that two simple sentences can be joined by a **subordinating conjunction** to form a **complex sentence.** A **compound-complex sentence** is a long sentence created by joining a compound sentence and a related complex sentence.

Complex Sentence	Although no official dividing line is visible, the people live separately.
Compound Sentence	The Tlingits live on the northern part of the island, and the Haidas live on the southern part.
Compound-Complex Sentence	Although no official dividing line is visible, the Tlingits live on the northern part of the island, and the Haidas live on the southern part.

 **With a partner, read aloud each sentence below. Identify each sentence as compound, complex, or compound-complex. Then identify the coordinating and subordinating conjunctions.**

1. Prince of Wales Island is in Alaska, and the Queen Charlotte Islands are in Canada.

2. When the Haidas needed trees for dugout canoes, they traveled to the Queen Charlotte Islands.

3. Because the biggest cedar trees in the region grow on the Queen Charlotte Islands, the Haidas traveled there often, but it was a long journey.

4. The Haidas carve totem poles, but their specialty is dugout canoes.

You can avoid choppy writing and vary your sentence structure by using conjunctions to combine simple sentences into longer sentences. When you create a compound sentence, a complex sentence, or a compound-complex sentence, be sure that your new sentence is clearer than the short sentences you combined. Also, be sure to use commas correctly.

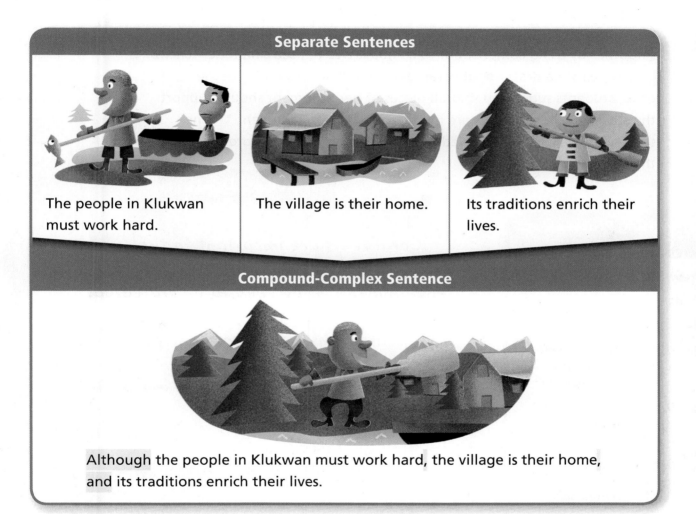

Separate Sentences

The people in Klukwan must work hard.

The village is their home.

Its traditions enrich their lives.

Compound-Complex Sentence

Although the people in Klukwan must work hard, the village is their home, and its traditions enrich their lives.

Connect Grammar to Writing

As you revise your argument, look for sentences that you can combine to form compound, complex, or compound-complex sentences. Check to see that each longer sentence you write is clear and properly punctuated.

W.6.1a introduce claim(s) and organize reasons and evidence clearly; **W.6.1b** support claim(s) with reasons and evidence, using credible sources and demonstrating understanding of the topic or text; **W.6.1c** use words, phrases, and clauses to clarify relationships; **W.6.1e** provide a concluding statement or section; **W.6.4** produce writing in which development, organization, and style are appropriate to task, purpose, and audience

Argument Writing

Reading-Writing Workshop: Revise

✓ **Sentence Fluency** To write a strong **argument,** begin by clearly stating a claim (an opinion or belief). Support that claim with reasons. Use facts, examples, and other details as evidence for each reason. When you revise, ask yourself: Are the development and organization appropriate for my task, purpose, and audience? Make your writing smoother by using conjunctions to combine two related simple sentences.

   May wrote a draft about coral reefs. Feedback from her teacher and other students suggested that all pieces of her argument should support the statement "Coral reefs are important to the environment." When she revised her draft, May tried a new approach to focus more on animals than on people.

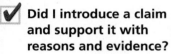

Writing Process Checklist

Prewrite

Draft

▶ **Revise**

✓ **Did I introduce a claim and support it with reasons and evidence?**

✓ **Did I organize my reasons and evidence clearly?**

✓ **Did I use words, phrases, and clauses to clarify relationships?**

✓ **Did I end with a conclusion?**

Edit

Publish and Share

Revised Draft

Coral reefs are important to the

environment. ~~They~~ , so t̂hey need to be protected.

One reason why is that so many ~~people~~ animals depend

on reefs for food and ~~making a living.~~ a place to live. The

protective reefs serve as safe nurseries for

fish and other marine animals that have their

young there.

Saving Coral Reefs

by May Owens

Coral reefs are important to the environment, so they need to be protected. One reason why is that so many animals depend on reefs for food and a place to live. The protective reefs also serve as safe nurseries for fish and other marine animals that have their young there.

Second, reefs can provide barriers around islands and coasts. The reefs protect the beaches and coasts from the waves' force during severe storms. As a result, the reefs save the habitats of beach and marine animals from being flooded, eroded, or destroyed.

A third reason why coral reefs need to be protected is that they are almost impossible to replace when they are damaged. Reefs grow at an extremely slow rate, and animals that rely on the reefs cannot "wait" until they grow back. Reef managers are currently working to rebuild reefs destroyed by warmer waters, higher sea levels, pollution, and intense storms. However, if sea life cannot be sustained, animals will likely die.

It is very important that fragile coral reefs are protected. Without them, animals of this ecosystem may not survive.

Reading as a Writer

Which changes did May make to her draft to try a new approach and strengthen her writing? What can you change to reflect feedback you get from others?

In my final paper, I tried a new approach based on the feedback I got. I also added words to connect my ideas. I made sure my argument had a claim supported by reasons and evidence.

Test POWER

Read the passage "Schooling on the American Frontier." As you read, stop and answer each question using text evidence.

Schooling on the American Frontier

On the American frontier, just one room was usually large enough to hold all the children in a district. One-room schoolhouses were common in rural areas from the early 1800s through the 1940s. Only one teacher taught all the children in grades one through eight. Because many families depended on farming, school schedules were structured around the growing season. School might be held for four or five months of the year when there was less work to do on the farms. For the rest of the year, children were needed at home. They worked right along with the adults in the fields and doing household chores.

The Schoolhouse

Each frontier community was responsible for creating its own schoolhouse. Sometimes log cabins or barns were used as school buildings. Often, local schools were built and maintained by the people who lived in the area. An entire one-room schoolhouse would in many cases have been no larger than a modern classroom. Usually, a wood or coal stove kept the room warm in winter. At the back of the room, there were pegs where students would hang their coats, and a shelf for the lunch buckets they brought from home. There was also a pail of fresh drinking water with children's cups nearby.

> **1** Why do you think the author chose the schoolhouse as the topic for the first section of this article?

In early days, the children sat on rows of benches facing the teacher's big desk in the front of the room. Later, students in most schools had wooden desks of their own. Near the teacher's desk in many schools you would find a "recitation bench." Groups of students sat there while the teacher listened to them recite their schoolwork. Other students were expected to work quietly at their desks until it was their turn. Usually, younger children sat near the front of the room and older children near the back. Boys and girls sat on separate sides of the room. At many frontier schoolhouses, boys and girls were separated at recess, too.

RI.6.1 cite textual evidence to support analysis of what the text says explicitly as well as inferences drawn; **RI.6.5** analyze how a sentence, paragraph, chapter, or section fits in the overall structure; **RI.6.6** determine the author's point of view or purpose and explain how it is conveyed; **RI.6.7** integrate information presented in different media or formats as well as in words; **RI.6.8** trace and evaluate the arguments and specific claims in a text

The schoolhouse often served a second function, too, as a community building. It was a meeting place where various social events were held. Debates, plays, and lectures might be offered there to the public.

The Teachers

It was not uncommon in the early 1800s for teachers to have very little education themselves. Their teaching lessons consisted of having the students memorize and recite facts. The only subjects taught in the frontier schools were reading, writing, and arithmetic.

Later in the century, would-be teachers attended a "normal school," an early type of teachers' college, after which they were given an exam by a local school board. They had to earn a passing score to be hired. Teaching methods and lessons still emphasized memorizing sets of facts.

In the early 1800s, most teachers were men. By the second half of the century, however, the need for teachers was growing very quickly. Many women moved to the western frontier regions to fill vacant teaching jobs, even though they received much lower pay than male teachers.

In general, most teachers were young. Families whose children attended school were expected to arrange for housing and food for the teacher. Sometimes teachers lived right there in the schoolhouses. Usually, though, they boarded with their students' families, spending a few months at a time with each one. Local school boards often had strict rules limiting how teachers could spend their free time.

Challenges of Teaching on the American Frontier

Frontier teachers were expected to arrive at school at 8 A.M. to hoist the flag and bring in drinking water and fuel for the stove. While school was in session, teachers had to keep order in a room full of restless children who preferred to be outdoors. Maintaining order in a classroom with students of varying ages was not always easy. Often, older children were expected to help the teacher keep control of the class.

> **2** What is the author's point of view in the preceding paragraph? Explain how the author conveys that point of view.

Another challenge that teachers on the frontier faced was the lack of supplies. Most schools on the frontier did not have what we now consider to be basic supplies, such as pencils, pens, and paper. Blackboards did not become common in frontier schoolhouses until the end of the 1800s.

SCHOOL SUPPLIES THEN AND NOW	
Frontier Schools	**Modern Schools**
few books	many books, periodicals, computers, and other electronic reading devices
wooden boards to write on	paper, notebooks, chalkboards to write on; also computers and tablets
pieces of charcoal to write with, pens made from goose quills	pencils, markers, pens, keyboards
ink made from bark or berries; point of pen had to be dipped in ink before writing	ballpoint pens or printers

3 How does the chart add to your understanding of this article?

The most popular textbooks of the time were the "readers" written by William H. McGuffey and the spelling book written by Noah Webster (who also wrote a famous dictionary). Webster's spelling book was nicknamed the "Blue-Backed Speller" for the color of its cover. It was first published in 1783, and it continued to be used in American schools for over 100 years.

Textbooks were expensive to purchase. As a result, in some frontier areas, students brought their own books from home. It was a challenge for teachers to teach students who had different books or, in some cases, no books at all.

4 What reasons or evidence does the author give to support the claim that frontier teachers faced challenges?

Even though there were many obstacles, communities with one-room schoolhouses worked hard to provide an education for their children. These children would go on to become the citizens who shaped American society as the United States grew and developed.

Unit 3

Vocabulary in Context

stifling
ambled
intense
smolder
ornately
proclaimed
hazards
unrelenting
flared
alleviate

Vocabulary Reader   Context Cards

COMMON CORE **L.6.6** acquire and use general academic and domain-specific words and phrases/gather vocabulary knowledge for comprehension or expression

---

1 stifling

Firefighters wear oxygen masks to breathe during the stifling conditions of a fire.

2 ambled

The couple talked about old times as they ambled slowly through the park.

3 intense

The wildfire was so intense that firefighters could only approach it from the air.

4 smolder

Everyone watched the volcano smolder and hoped that it would not erupt.

 Go Digital

▶ Study each Context Card.

▶ Use a dictionary to confirm the meanings of these words.

5 ornately

The ornately designed gardens, with their elaborate mazes, were breathtaking to see.

6 proclaimed

In a speech, the mayor proclaimed that a new fire station would be built to make neighborhoods safer.

7 hazards

These oil drums present many hazards, or dangers, to nearby neighborhoods.

8 unrelenting

The fire was unrelenting. It did not stop until it had burned up the entire forest.

9 flared

I roasted my marshmallow until it flared, and then I blew it out.

10 alleviate

Firefighters wear special suits and equipment to alleviate, or lessen, the danger.

Read and Comprehend

☑ TARGET SKILL

Sequence of Events Authors often introduce and elaborate events in **sequence**, or time order. Each event contributes to the text's overall structure, or organization. As you read "The Great Fire," pay attention to the sequence, or time order, of events before and during the fire. Days of the week, dates, and signal words such as *first*, *after*, *later*, and *at about this time* can help you understand the sequence of events. Use a graphic organizer like this one to help you.

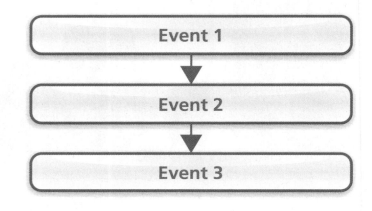

☑ TARGET STRATEGY

Summarize Briefly retell, or **summarize,** the most important parts of the text in your own words.

COMMON CORE **RI.6.3** analyze how a key individual, event, or idea is introduced, illustrated, and elaborated; **RI.6.5** analyze how a sentence paragraph, chapter, or section fits in the overall structure

Fire

Fires can be dangerous and fast-moving; therefore, knowing ways to prevent them is the best way to stay safe. When fires do occur, people must respond quickly. Television and radio broadcasts and text messages can quickly alert us if a fire occurs. Fire drills using planned escape routes help people practice how to reach safety. In the late 1800s, however, such precautions and alert systems did not exist.

In "The Great Fire," you will learn about events that led up to the historic 1871 Chicago fire. You'll also learn how people responded when they discovered the flames.

ANCHOR TEXT

MEET THE AUTHOR

Jim Murphy

Jim Murphy grew up in New Jersey as a curious boy with a wide range of interests and talents. His research and writing skills have resulted in more than thirty-five books for young readers, beginning with *Weird and Wacky Inventions* in 1978. He has twice won Newbery Honors (for *The Great Fire* and *An American Plague*) as well as numerous other writing awards.

✅ TARGET SKILL

Sequence of Events
Identify the time order in which events take place.

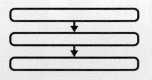

✅ GENRE

Literary nonfiction gives factual information by telling a true story. As you read, look for:

▶ elements of nonfiction and fiction

▶ information about a topic

▶ a story that involves real people or events

COMMON CORE **RI.6.3** analyze how a key individual, event, or idea is introduced, illustrated, and elaborated; **RI.6.4** determine the meaning of words and phrases, including figurative, connotative, and technical meanings; **RI.6.8** trace and evaluate the argument and specific claims in a text; **RI.6.10** read and comprehend literary nonfiction

THE GREAT FIRE

by Jim Murphy

ESSENTIAL QUESTION

What things can people do to help prevent fires?

It was Sunday and an unusually warm evening for October eighth, so Daniel "Peg Leg" Sullivan left his stifling little house in the West Side of Chicago and went to visit neighbors. One of his stops was at the shingled cottage of Patrick and Catherine O'Leary. The one-legged Sullivan remembered getting to the O'Learys' house at around eight o'clock, but left after only a few minutes because the O'Leary family was already in bed. Both Patrick and Catherine had to be up very early in the morning: he to set off for his job as a laborer; she to milk their five cows and then deliver the milk to neighbors.

Sullivan ambled down the stretch of land between the O'Learys' and their neighbor, crossed the street, and sat down on the wooden sidewalk in front of Thomas White's house. After adjusting his wooden leg to make himself comfortable, he leaned back against White's fence to enjoy the night.

The wind coming off the prairie had been strong all day, sometimes gusting wildly, and leaves scuttled along the street; the sound of laughter and fiddle music drifted through the night. A party was going on at the McLaughlins' to celebrate the arrival of a relative from Ireland. Another neighbor, Dennis Rogan, dropped by the O'Learys' at eight-thirty, but he, too, left when he learned the family was in bed.

Fifteen minutes later, Sullivan decided to go home. As the driver of a wagon, he would need every ounce of strength come morning. It was while pushing himself up that Sullivan first saw the fire—a single tongue of flame shooting out the side of the O'Learys' barn.

Sullivan didn't hesitate a second. "FIRE! FIRE! FIRE!" he shouted as loudly as he could. Running clumsily across the dirt street, Sullivan made his way directly to the barn. There was no time to stop for help. The building was already burning fiercely and he knew that in addition to five cows, the O'Learys had a calf and a horse in there.

The barn's loft held over three tons of timothy hay, delivered earlier that day. Flames from the burning hay pushed against the roof and beams, almost as if they were struggling to break free. A shower of burning embers greeted Sullivan as he entered the building.

> **ANALYZE THE TEXT**
>
> **Figurative Language** How does the author use figurative language on this page? What does it describe? Where else does the author use figurative language in this selection?

Sightseers visiting the O'Leary neighborhood

An overhead view of Chicago as it appeared before the Great Fire. Lake Michigan is in the foreground, and the Chicago River branches left and right. The South Side is on the left, while the North Side is to the right.

He untied the ropes of two cows, but the frightened animals did not move. On the other side of the barn, another cow and the horse were tied to the wall, straining to get loose. Sullivan took a step toward them, then realized that the fire had gotten around behind him and might cut off any chance of escape in a matter of seconds. The heat was fiercely intense and blinding, and in his rush to flee, Sullivan slipped on the uneven floorboards and fell with a thud.

He struggled to get up and, as he did, Sullivan discovered that his wooden leg had gotten stuck between two boards and come off. Instead of panicking, he began hopping toward where he thought the door was. Luck was with him. He had gone a few feet when the O'Learys' calf bumped into him, and Sullivan was able to throw his arms around its neck. Together, man and calf managed to find the door and safety, both frightened, both badly singed.

A shed attached to the barn was already engulfed by flames. It contained two tons of coal for the winter and a large supply of kindling wood. Fire ran along the dry grass and leaves, and took hold of a neighbor's fence. The heat from the burning barn, shed, and fence was so hot that the O'Learys' house, forty feet away, began to smolder. Neighbors rushed from their homes, many carrying buckets or pots of water. The sound of music and merrymaking stopped abruptly, replaced by the shout of "FIRE!" It would be a warning cry heard thousands of times during the next thirty-one hours.

Chicago in 1871 was a city ready to burn. The city boasted having 59,500 buildings, many of them—such as the Courthouse and the *Tribune* Building—large and ornately decorated. The trouble was that about two-thirds of all these structures were made entirely of wood. Many of the remaining buildings (even the ones proclaimed to be "fireproof") looked solid, but were actually jerry-built affairs; the stone or brick exteriors hid wooden frames and floors, all topped with highly flammable tar or shingle roofs. It was also a common practice to disguise wood as another kind of building material. The fancy exterior decorations on just about every building were carved from wood, then painted to look like stone or marble. Most churches had steeples that appeared to be solid from the street, but a closer inspection would reveal a wooden framework covered with cleverly painted copper or tin.

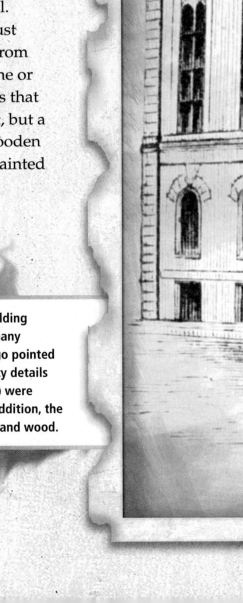

The Chamber of Commerce Building before the fire. It was one of many buildings the citizens of Chicago pointed to with pride. Many of the fancy details (such as those above the clock) were really carved out of wood. In addition, the mansard roof was made of tar and wood.

The situation was worst in the middle-class and poorer districts. Lot sizes were small, and owners usually filled them up with cottages, barns, sheds, and outhouses—all made of fast-burning wood, naturally. Because both Patrick and Catherine O'Leary worked, they were able to put a large addition on their cottage despite a lot size of just 25 by 100 feet. Interspersed in these residential areas were a variety of businesses—paint factories, lumberyards, distilleries, gasworks, mills, furniture manufacturers, warehouses, and coal distributors.

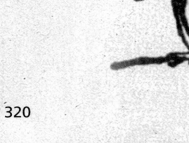

Wealthier districts were by no means free of fire hazards. Stately stone and brick homes had wood interiors, and stood side by side with smaller wood-frame houses. Wooden stables and other storage buildings were common, and trees lined the streets and filled the yards.

The links between richer and poorer sections went beyond the materials used for construction or the way buildings were crammed together. Chicago had been built largely on soggy marshland that flooded every time it rained. As the years passed and the town developed, a quick solution to the water and mud problem was needed. The answer was to make the roads and sidewalks out of wood and elevate them above the waterline, in some places by several feet. On the day the fire started, over 55 miles of pine-block streets and 600 miles of wooden sidewalks bound the 23,000 acres of the city in a highly combustible knot.

ANALYZE THE TEXT

Arguments and Claims The author makes the claim that "Chicago in 1871 was a city ready to burn." How does the author support this claim with text evidence?

A steam pumper and crew race to a fire.

Fires were common in cities back then, and Chicago was no exception. In 1863 there had been 186 reported fires in Chicago; the number had risen to 515 by 1868. Records for 1870 indicate that fire-fighting companies responded to nearly 600 alarms. The next year saw even more fires spring up, mainly because the summer had been unusually dry. Between July and October only a few scattered showers had taken place and these did not produce much water at all. Trees drooped in the unrelenting summer sun; grass and leaves dried out. By October, as many as six fires were breaking out every day. On Saturday the seventh, the night before the Great Fire, a blaze destroyed four blocks and took over sixteen hours to control. What made Sunday the eighth different and particularly dangerous was the steady wind blowing in from the southwest.

Chicago was built on marshland as this scene from 1833 makes clear. As the city grew in size, the roads, sidewalks, and buildings were gradually raised to alleviate the muddy conditions.

It was this gusting, swirling wind that drove the flames from the O'Learys' barn into neighboring yards. To the east, a fence and shed of James Dalton's went up in flames; to the west, a barn smoldered for a few minutes, then flared up into a thousand yellow-orange fingers. Dennis Rogan had heard Sullivan's initial shouts about a fire and returned. He forced open the door to the O'Learys' house and called for them to wake up.

Moments later, Patrick emerged from the cottage, still half asleep. "Kate!" he screamed the moment he saw what was happening. "The barn is afire!"

Their first action was to get their children out of the house and into the street safely away from the fire. The barn was already engulfed in flames, so Patrick and a group of neighbors began pouring water on the cottage. It would catch fire several times during the night, but the flames would be smothered before they could get out of control. Strangely enough, the cottage on the O'Leary property would survive with little damage.

At about this time William Lee, who lived down the block from the O'Learys', went into his seventeen-month-old son's room to see why the child was crying. After comforting his son, Lee went to fasten the window blind. Outside, he saw a crimson night sky lit up by flames and flying embers. Already some of those embers were landing in his yard and igniting the grass and leaves.

Lee hesitated a moment before shouting to his wife to take care of the baby and rushing out of the house. He ran the three blocks to Bruno Goll's drugstore, determined to do what no one else in the neighborhood had thought about doing: turn in a fire alarm. At this point, the fire was barely fifteen minutes old. What followed was a series of fatal errors that set the fire free and doomed the city to a fiery death.

• •

The Great Chicago Fire of 1871 burned for two days, finally dying out when rain began to fall on the morning of October 10, 1871. The fire claimed at least 300 lives, left 100,000 people homeless, and caused $200 million in property damage. The entire business district of the city was destroyed.

ANALYZE THE TEXT

Sequence of Events Where did the Chicago fire of 1871 start, and how did the fire get out of control?

Dig Deeper

How to Analyze the Text

Use these pages to learn about Sequence of Events, Arguments and Claims, and Figurative Language. Then read "The Great Fire" again to apply what you learned.

Sequence of Events

In "The Great Fire," author Jim Murphy includes dates, signal words, and references to time of day in hours and minutes to introduce and elaborate the **sequence,** or time order, of events. Paying attention to the sequence of events helps you understand where a paragraph fits in the overall structure of the text.

Look back at page 324. How does the paragraph in which William Lee dashes to Goll's drugstore fit in the overall structure of the selection? How does this text evidence add to the development of the selection's ideas?

COMMON CORE

RI.6.3 analyze how a key individual, event, or idea is introduced, illustrated, and elaborated; **RI.6.4** determine the meaning of words and phrases, including figurative, connotative, and technical meanings; **RI.6.5** analyze how a sentence, paragraph, chapter, or section fits in the overall structure; **RI.6.8** trace and evaluate the argument and specific claims in a text

Arguments and Claims

When authors want to influence an audience, they state a **claim.** A claim is a belief or an opinion an author has about a topic. To support a claim, authors develop an **argument.** They include reasons and text evidence to support their claim. The most convincing claims are supported by a great deal of evidence. Evidence consists of facts, examples, details, and other true information. As you read "The Great Fire" again, look for the author's claims and the text evidence used to support the author's argument.

Figurative Language

Authors often use **figurative language** to describe actions and objects. There are several kinds of figurative language, such as similes and metaphors. A writer describing a fire might say, "The wildfire approached the town like an advancing army." In this simile, a fire is compared to an army. Figurative language helps describe a scene by creating a vivid sensory image.

327

Your Turn

Turn and Talk Review the selection with a partner to prepare to discuss this question: *What things can people do to help prevent fires?* As you discuss, take turns posing questions, responding to them, and making comments. Support your ideas with text evidence.

Classroom Conversation

Continue your discussion of "The Great Fire" by explaining your answers to these questions using text evidence:

1. What did survivors likely learn from the fire as they faced rebuilding their city?

2. Why do you think people decorated buildings with wood painted to look like stone or marble?

3. Why do you think the author chose to write a story about real people instead of writing an informational report about the fire?

WHAT DOES IT MEAN?

Use Reference Sources Find these words in the selection: *fiercely, abruptly, boasted.* Then look up each word in a digital dictionary to clarify its precise meaning and pronunciation. Write a new sentence for each word that helps others know what the word means. Share your sentences with a partner.

Response Author Jim Murphy introduces Daniel Sullivan with an anecdote. An anecdote is a short account of some event. Write a paragraph to describe how the author introduces Sullivan. What do you learn about Sullivan from this anecdote? Include text evidence that supports your response.

Writing Tip

End your paragraph with a conclusion that follows logically from your response. Correct any vague pronouns in your writing.

RI.6.4 determine the meaning of words and phrases, including figurative, connotative, and technical meanings; **W.6.2f** provide a concluding statement or section; **W.6.9b** apply grade 6 Reading standards to literary nonfiction; **SL.6.1c** pose and respond to questions and make comments that contribute to the discussion; **L.6.1d** recognize and correct vague pronouns; **L.6.4c** consult reference materials, both print and digital, to find pronunciation and determine or clarify meaning or clarify part of speech

INFORMATIONAL TEXT

✓ GENRE

Informational text provides accurate information for readers. Informational text can take many forms, including essays, biographies, and historical accounts.

✓ TEXT FOCUS

An **argument** presents a claim and contains facts, details, and examples to support the claim.

COMMON CORE

RI.6.8 trace and evaluate the argument and specific claims in a text; **RI.6.10** read and comprehend literary nonfiction

FIRE
Friend or Enemy?
by Gerardo Benavides

A wildfire is a rapidly spreading fire that burns uncontrollably in the wilderness. In the past few years, many wildfires have burned in wild areas across the United States. Some are caused by lightning strikes, but most are caused by careless people.

Fire doctors using prescribed fires

For thousands of years, natural fires regularly burned huge areas of wild land. After a series of deadly fires in 1910, land managers would either prevent or quickly put out these fires. As a result, dry, dead plants piled up. During times of high fire risk, such as drought, wildfires could be started by something as simple as a spark from a piece of machinery. The dry, dead plants provided fuel for these fires, making the fire quickly burn out of control. Winds could hurl burning-hot embers miles away, igniting more fires.

Now scientists are helping land managers harness the power of fire. Just as medical doctors prescribe medicine, these "fire doctors" prescribe fire. They set prescribed fires to improve the health of wild lands.

In states that have had several wildfires, such as Florida and California, fire experts are working in national parks and other wild areas. They set fires to burn dry, dead plants on the forest floor.

Ashes from these fires add nutrients to the soil. As a result, trees become healthier and plants grow back stronger than before. For some plants, fire is necessary for survival.

When natural fires are stopped, forests become less diverse. In California, some pine and cypress trees cannot spread their seeds without fire. Their seed cones open only if they are heated.

The fire triangle shows the three ingredients of fire. Remove any of these ingredients, and a fire will die.

To promote different types of plant growth, fire experts burn away dead plants on the forest floor. The heated cones open up, allowing the seeds to drop onto bare soil where they can sprout.

Experts also use prescribed fires to help birds, animals, and other wildlife. In Florida, some species of birds, such as the Florida scrub jay, rely upon fire to maintain the conditions of their habitat. Prescribed fire helps the scrub jay and other species survive.

Herds of elk live in the Mendocino National Forest near Willows, California. Elk eat many different plants. A burn might be prescribed to encourage the growth of grasses, plants, and freshly-sprouted brush that elk like to eat. As a result, the elk find plenty to eat and their population grows.

Tule elk in Mendocino National Forest

Fires are always dangerous, even if they are set by experts to help the environment. A few prescribed fires have spread out of control, but thousands more have been safely contained. Wildfires are by far the most dangerous kind of fire. Many huge wildfires often burn across an entire state at the same time. Land managers can help prevent these dangerous wildfires by planning fires to burn dead plants.

Firefighters continue to bravely fight wildfires. Fire doctors continue to turn this wild enemy into a powerful friend.

Compare Texts

TEXT TO TEXT

Compare Fire Texts "The Great Fire" and "Fire: Friend or Enemy?" have the same subject: fire. Compare and contrast how the subject is treated in the literary nonfiction selection and the informational text. Explain how each author gives facts about fire within the form of each genre. Use text evidence from both selections in your explanation.

TEXT TO SELF

Put Safety First As you have grown older, you have practiced safety many times in many situations. These situations may have involved riding a bike, swimming, traveling, or walking to an unfamiliar location. Choose one situation, and write to reflect on what you did to practice safety for it.

TEXT TO WORLD

Clarify Points of View What is each author's viewpoint on the topic of fire? What are their attitudes about it? If the two authors met to discuss their points of view about famous fires in history, what might they say? What would each like the other to know? Share your thoughts with a partner.

COMMON CORE **RL.6.1** cite textual evidence to support analysis of what the text says explicitly as well as inferences drawn; **RI.6.6** determine the author's point of view or purpose and explain how it is conveyed; **RI.6.9** compare and contrast one author's presentation of events with that of another; **W.6.10** write routinely over extended time frames and shorter time frames

Grammar

Subject and Object Pronouns A **pronoun** is a word that can replace a noun; that noun is called the pronoun's **antecedent.** A **subject pronoun** replaces a noun as the subject of a sentence. An **object pronoun** replaces a noun following an action verb or a word such as *to, in, for, by,* or *at.* Use a subject pronoun when writing compound subjects. Use an object pronoun when writing compound objects. Avoid using **vague pronouns,** which have unclear antecedents.

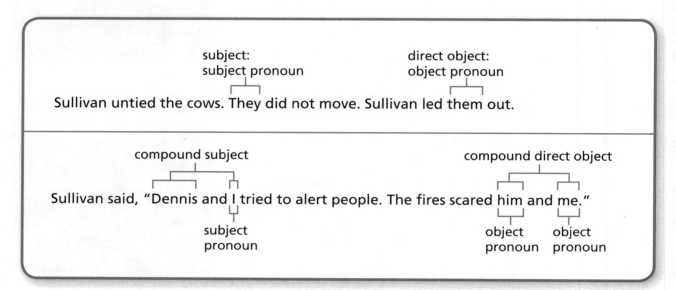

subject:
subject pronoun

direct object:
object pronoun

Sullivan untied the cows. They did not move. Sullivan led them out.

compound subject

compound direct object

Sullivan said, "Dennis and I tried to alert people. The fires scared him and me."

subject
pronoun

object
pronoun

object
pronoun

Try This! **Work with a partner. Read each sentence below. Tell which pronoun form is correct. Then tell why it is the correct form.**

1. Patricia and (she, her) went to bed early that night.

2. The campers shouted "Fire!" to the park ranger and (I, me).

3. Land managers value the "fire doctors" because of the information they provide to (they, them).

4. (They, Them) actually depend on fire to maintain the Florida habitat.

If you use the same subject too many times, you may bore your reader. When two sentences have the same subject, combine them into one, replacing the subject with a pronoun. Sometimes you can use a subordinating conjunction to form a complex sentence. Correct vague pronouns by clearly stating about whom or about what you are writing.

Vague Pronoun; Repeated Subject

Wildlife managers set fires. They help to save elk.
Wildlife managers burn grass. Wildlife managers want to save elk.

Combined Sentences with Subordinating Conjunctions and a Clear Pronoun

Wildlife managers set fires because the fires help to save elk.
Because wildlife managers want to save elk, they burn grass.

 Connect Grammar to Writing

As you revise your procedural essay, keep a list of subordinating conjunctions handy. Try to use a subject pronoun and a subordinating conjunction, such as *after*, *since*, or *because*, to combine sentences with the same subject. Avoid using vague pronouns.

Informative Writing

✔ **Word Choice** The purpose of a **procedural essay** is to help readers understand a process or procedure—that is, to tell them how to do something. The topic is usually developed with steps followed by details that support the steps. As you revise your essay, add transition words to clarify the order of steps to complete the task. Correct any variations from standard English. End with a strong concluding statement.

my **WriteSmart**

Go **Digital**

Ruby wrote a first draft of her procedural essay about making a 911 call. Then she revised her draft. She made sure she included transition words to show the sequence of steps. She corrected a sentence that did not use correct English.

Writing Traits Checklist

✔ **Ideas**
Did I clearly tell how to do something?

✔ **Organization**
Did I use time-order sequence?

✔ **Sentence Fluency**
Did I use transition words to clarify relationships?

✔ **Word Choice**
Did I use correct standard English?

✔ **Voice**
Did I show interest in my topic?

✔ **Conventions**
Did I use correct spelling, grammar, and punctuation?

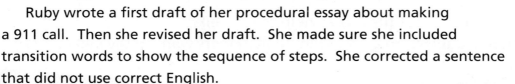

Revised Draft

First, make sure that you are safe yourself.

Next, take a deep breath. You need to be calm

in order to speak clearly and give accurate

information. ~~Thirdly;~~ _{Then,} dial 911. Report the

emergency to the dispatcher. Explain the

emergency and give your location and your

name. Also give your cell phone number on the

call so that the dispatcher has a record of ~~it~~ _{the number} in

case you get disconnected.

How to Report an Emergency

by Ruby Garland

You witness a fire at the side of the road as you're riding in the car with your dad. He asks you to call 911. Do you know what to do? If you have a cell phone, you can help by reporting the emergency quickly. A call to 911 from a cell phone is harder to track than a call from home, however, so you need to follow a specific process.

First, make sure that you are safe yourself. Next, take a deep breath. You need to be calm in order to speak clearly and give accurate information. Then, dial 911. Report the emergency to the dispatcher. Explain the emergency and give your location and your name. Also give your cell phone number on the call so that the dispatcher has a record of the number in case you get disconnected.

After the dispatcher knows who you are and where you are, wait for questions. Answer clearly and calmly. Let the dispatcher guide the conversation. If he or she gives instructions, follow them.

As the call finishes, do not hang up until the dispatcher says you can. By knowing how to make a 911 call from a cell phone, you will be able to alert emergency personnel to a problem.

Reading as a Writer

How did using correct standard English improve Ruby's paper? Which transition words did Ruby use to clarify the sequence? What words can you add to clarify the sequence in your procedural essay?

In my final paper, I used correct standard English. I organized the steps, added transitions to clarify relationships between ideas, and used correct pronouns. I provided a concluding statement.

KENNETH OPPEL
Author of the Internationally Best-Selling
SILVERWING TRILOGY

✓ TARGET VOCABULARY

engulf

supple

jostled

taut

careening

frail

undulating

falter

frayed

relishing

Vocabulary Reader

Context Cards

COMMON CORE **LA.6.6** acquire and use general academic and domain-specific words and phrases/gather vocabulary knowledge for comprehension or expression

Vocabulary in Context

1 engulf
Clouds will soon engulf, or swallow up, this blimp as it climbs higher into the sky.

2 supple
A hot air balloon is made of supple material that is flexible but strong.

3 jostled
As it flies, an ultralight aircraft may be jostled, or bumped, by the wind.

4 taut
Early gliders were covered with fabric stretched until it was taut, or tight, over a frame.

Go Digital

▶ Study each Context Card.

▶ Make up a new context sentence that uses two Vocabulary words.

5 careening

Caught in a gusty wind, a kite might go careening wildly from side to side.

6 frail

A monarch butterfly may look too frail to fly thousands of miles, but it is not as weak as one might think.

7 undulating

Undulating air currents, moving like a roller coaster, can cause clouds to form wavy patterns.

8 falter

A bird seems to falter, or hesitate, as it brakes with its wings when it comes in for a landing.

9 frayed

If the ropes holding down a hot air balloon became frayed, they could break, causing the balloon to escape.

10 relishing

Many people enjoy the hobby of skydiving, relishing the feeling of freedom it brings.

Read and Comprehend

☑ TARGET SKILL

Story Structure The elements of a story include **setting, characters,** and **plot.** The plot is made up of events or groups of events called **episodes.** In "Airborn," the characters and setting are introduced early on. As you read, look for text evidence that helps you identify the story elements and record them in a graphic organizer like this one. Remember what happens in the story so that you can record the episodes that make up the plot. Pay attention to how each episode fits into the overall development of the story.

Setting	Characters
Plot Episodes	

☑ TARGET STRATEGY

Infer/Predict You can use text evidence to figure out, or **infer,** what the author means. You can also use them to guess, or **predict,** what might happen in the future.

RL.6.1 analyze how a key individual, event, or idea is introduced, illustrated, and elaborated; **RL.6.3** describe how a story's or drama's plot unfolds and how characters respond or change; **RL.6.5** analyze how a sentence, chapter, scene or stanza fits in the overall structure

Air Travel

People travel by air in different ways. To get somewhere quickly, they may ride in jet planes and helicopters. For slower-paced flights and for enjoyment, they may ride in hot air balloons.

In "Airborn," you'll read a fantasy that features an airship and a hot air balloon. You'll learn how one young man works with both aircraft in an emergency.

Lesson 12

ANCHOR TEXT

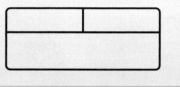

☑ TARGET SKILL

Story Structure Examine details about the setting, characters, and plot. Notice the episodes that make up the plot.

☑ GENRE

A **fantasy** is an imaginative story that may have unrealistic characters and events. As you read, look for:

▶ story events or settings that could not happen in real life
▶ characters who behave in an unrealistic way

COMMON CORE **RL.6.3** describe how a story's or drama's plot unfolds and how characters respond or change; **RL.6.4** determine the meaning of words and phrases, including figurative and connotative meanings/analyze impact of word choice; **RL.6.6** explain how an author develops the point of view of the narrator or speaker; **RL.6.10** read and comprehend literature; **L.6.5a** interpret figures of speech in context

Go Digital

MEET THE AUTHOR

Kenneth Oppel

At age fourteen, Kenneth Oppel, who was born in Port Alberni, Vancouver Island, British Columbia, but raised predominantly in Victoria, British Columbia, and Halifax, Nova Scotia, wrote a novel that a family friend showed to esteemed novelist, screenwriter, and poet Roald Dahl. As a result of Dahl's cogent recommendation to his own literary agent, *Colin's Fantastic Video Adventure* was reviewed, accepted, and successfully published a few years later in Great Britain, Canada, the United States, and France — an experience that Oppel has said paralyzed him with excitement. That exceptional experience encouraged Oppel to pursue a career in writing novels for an international audience as well as embellished his stature as a new author and gave him autonomy. Oppel's *Silverwing* trilogy, which was later written and published to great acclaim and has been one of the epitomes of his career so far, sold more than a million copies worldwide and was also awarded the Michael Printz Honor Book Award from the American Library Association as well as a Canadian Governor General's Award for Children's Literature. Oppel also published two sequels to *Airborn*, titled *Skybreaker* and *Starclimber*, as well as a screenplay version of *Airborn*. Oppel has lived in Newfoundland, Dublin, Ireland, and Toronto, Canada.

MEET THE ILLUSTRATOR

Greg Newbold

Greg Newbold says he "doesn't remember life without art" and that his supportive parents recognized and encouraged his creative persona and kept him well stocked with a raft of art supplies throughout his youth as he delved more and more deeply into art. Newbold earned a Bachelor of Fine Arts degree while working as a graphic illustrator in software technology. A fortuitous employment layoff did not make his art career go awry; rather with the blessing of his spouse he seized this new opportunity to plunge into a more directly artful lifestyle. His recognizable style and brand of art has been commissioned by many top corporations and international publishers, and Newbold has been honored with numerous art awards. His fine art has been exhibited in New York City, Los Angeles, Columbus, and around the Mountain west. As avocations, Newbold also enjoys vegetable gardening and participating actively in the outdoor life in Salt Lake City, Utah, and he was selected as a torchbearer for the 2002 Winter Olympics there.

AIRBORN

by Kenneth Oppel
selection illustrated by Greg Newbold

ESSENTIAL QUESTION

How do people react
to emergencies in
different ways?

Fourteen-year-old Matt Cruse is a cabin boy on the airship Aurora, *on which his father served as a crewman before dying in an accident. As the* Aurora *flies over a vast ocean, Matt, in the crow's nest, spots a hot air balloon drifting dangerously near. When the* Aurora *draws alongside, the crew can see the balloon's pilot lying on the floor of the gondola. The captain decides to attempt a rescue.*

Just then Captain Walken strode in. He was the kind of man everyone felt safer being around. If he'd been wearing a velvet robe and crown, he'd be the very image of a great king; if he were in a doctor's jacket, you'd trust your life to him; if he were in a carpenter's smock, you'd know he'd build you the finest house imaginable. But I preferred him in his blue captain's jacket with the four gold stripes on the sleeve and his cap encircled with thick gold cord. His beard and mustache were trim, and he had steady, kind eyes. He was approaching sixty, with a full head of gray curly hair, and wide in the shoulders. He wasn't a particularly big man or even tall, but when he walked into the room you could almost sense everyone exhaling in relief and thinking, There now, things will work out just fine.

The captain needed only to glance at the situation.

"Mr. Rideau, would you please return to the control car and assume my watch. I'll take over here, thank you."

"Yes, sir," said Mr. Rideau, but I could tell he didn't much like that.

"Ready the davit, please, gentlemen," Captain Walken said.

Centered before the bay doors was a davit, a small crane with an extendible arm that swung out and raised and lowered cargo when we were docked. The crew sprang to it at once, manning the lines and wheeling out the davit's arm to its full length.

"Let's see if she'll reach," the captain said. "Swing her out, please."

Breathless, I watched, wondering if it would be long enough. I knew what the captain had in mind.

I kept looking down at the man on the gondola floor. He was deathly white in the flare of the *Aurora*'s spotlight. But then I saw him stir slightly, a hand twitch.

The davit's arm slowly swung all the way out, as far as it would go.

It was still at least six feet shy of the gondola.

"Pity," said the captain calmly. "Bring her back in, please, gentlemen."

I looked down and saw the water close below us. The captain had vented a little hydrium to keep us level with the balloon, but now we had gone as low as we safely could. Any nearer was foolhardy, for you never knew when a sudden gust or rogue front might clutch the ship and thrust her down into the drink.

"Well, gentlemen, we've not much time," the captain said. "The situation is simple, and our course of action clear. Someone's going to need to hook himself to the end of the davit and swing across to the gondola. It's the only way to get her before she goes down."

He looked across at Mr. Kahlo and Mr. Chen, and the machinists and sailmakers, their faces gray in the starlight, none relishing the idea of careening out over the ocean.

I held my breath, hoping.

The captain stared straight at me and smiled.

"Mr. Cruse, I look at you, and of all the men, you're the one who shows not the slightest hint of fear. Am I right?"

"Yes, sir. I have no fear of heights."

"I know it, Mr. Cruse." And he did, for I'd served aboard his ship for more than two years, and he'd seen the ease with which I moved about the *Aurora*, inside and out.

"Sir," said Mr. Chen, "the lad shouldn't be the one. Let me go."

And all at once the other crewmen were vigorously offering themselves up for the job.

"Very good, gentlemen," said the captain, "but I think Mr. Cruse really is the best suited. If you're still willing, Mr. Cruse?"

"Yes, sir."

"We'll not tell your mother about this. Agreed?"

I smiled and gave a nod.

"Is your harness snug?"

"It is, sir." I was glowing with pride and hoped the others wouldn't see the flush of my cheeks. The captain came and checked my harness himself, his strong hands testing the straps and buckles.

"Be careful, lad," he told me quietly, then stepped back. "All right, Mr. Cruse. Hook yourself up to the davit, and we'll swing you over."

He said it as if he were proposing a stroll up to A-Deck to take in the view. He hadn't chosen me just because he thought I was least fearful. Any of the other crew would have done it. But I was light, too, the lightest here by sixty pounds. The captain was afraid the gondola might be too flimsy to carry her own weight once she was hooked and reeled in, and he didn't want anything heavy added to her. Above all, he needed someone light. But I was still honored he trusted me with the job.

The davit's cable ended with a deep hook, and onto this hook I shackled the ends of my two safety lines. They winched me up a little so it was like sitting on a swing. Up close, the davit's arm seemed a frail enough bit of metal to hang your life upon, but I knew she could carry fifty of me.

"I know you'll not falter," the captain told me. "Here. You'll need this to cut the balloon's flight lines." He passed me up his knife. I slid it through a buckle of my harness. "If you're ready, we'll send you over."

"Ready, sir."

With that the crew swung the davit's arm out. I saw the deck of the cargo bay give way to the ocean's silvered surface, dark and supple as a snake's skin, four hundred feet below. The arm swung to its farthest point and stopped. The gondola was still out of reach, its rim about six feet below me now. Inside, the man shifted again, and I thought he moaned, but that might have been the wind, or the creak of the cable unwinding, or maybe some whalesong out to sea.

"Lower me some, please!" I called over my shoulder.

Looking back at the ship did give me a moment's pause. It wasn't fear—more interest, really. Just the oddness of it. I'd never seen the *Aurora* from this angle, me dangling midair, the crewmen standing on the lip of the deck, staring down at me through the open cargo bay doors.

They paid out more cable until I was at the same level as the gondola, not six feet away.

I felt no fear. If someone had put an ear to my chest, he'd find it beating no faster than it had in the crow's nest. It was not bravery on my part, simply a fact of nature, for I was born in the air, and so it seemed the most natural place in the world to me. I was slim as a sapling and light on my feet. The crew all joked I had seagull bones, hollow in the center to allow for easy flight. To swing across this little gap, four hundred feet aloft, was no more to me than skipping a crack in the pavement. Because deep in my heart, I felt that if I were ever to fall, the air would support me, hold me aloft, just as surely as it did a bird with spread wings.

There was a bit of breeze building now, twirling me some at the end of the cable. I grabbed both my safety lines and started pumping my legs, a youngster on a playground swing. Back and forth, back and forth. At the forward end of my arc, when I looked down, I figured I was almost over the rim of the gondola. Just a little more. Back I went, legs folded tight.

Then: that moment when you're almost motionless, just hanging there for a split second before you start swinging forward again.

"Let run the line!" I shouted. I kicked forward, body flat, legs shooting out, and felt myself drop suddenly—and keep dropping. I sat up quickly as the cable paid out, and I was slanting down toward the gondola fast but—

Falling short.

I flung myself forward, stretching, and just hooked my forearms over the gondola's lip. My body slammed into the side, scratching my face against the wicker and knocking all my breath out. It took a moment to suck some air into me. My arms sang with pain. I heard the crew above in the *Aurora*, cheering me. I heaved myself up, scrabbling with my feet for purchase, and then crashed over into the gondola.

Beside the man.

But there was not time to tend to him. I stood, grabbed hold of the davit's hook, and unshackled my two safety lines. Then I cast about for somewhere secure to attach the hook—it had to be something strong, for it would be bearing the gondola's entire weight once I cut the balloon free. Above my head was a metal frame that supported the burners. The frame had four metal struts that were welded to the gondola's iron rim. It all seemed a little rickety, but it would have to be good enough; I saw nothing better. I curled the hook around the burner frame, as close to its center as I could manage.

"Reel her in!" I bellowed up at the *Aurora*. I saw the line quickly swing up and become taut. The hook grabbed. The gondola shuddered. A long, nasty squeal came from the burner frame. I didn't like the sound of that at all. I stared, breath stoppered in my throat, at those four bits of metal that tethered the burner frame to the gondola. They were never supposed to support the gondola's entire weight. That's what the balloon was meant to do.

But now the balloon was coming down, slowly collapsing toward the gondola—and the burner. The whole lot might go up in flames, with me and the pilot caught beneath.

ANALYZE THE TEXT

Personification In the third paragraph, the author uses personification when he writes that Matt's arms "sang with pain." What is the meaning of this phrase? Find a similar example of personification on page 355 and tell what it means.

ANALYZE THE TEXT

Point of View From whose point of view is the story told? How does the author develop the narrator's perspective on events throughout the story?

Flight lines. Flight lines.

I'd never sailed a balloon, and the rigging was unfamiliar to me.

There were eight lines holding the balloon to the gondola, two stretching up from each corner.

"Take care, Mr. Cruse!" I heard the captain shout down at me.

I glanced overhead. Despite being hooked to the davit, the gondola was dragging the great balloon ever closer to the *Aurora*'s hull and engines. In a few minutes, they'd collide. I had to be quicker.

The knife glinted in the starlight as I sawed away at the first flight line. It was thick braid, and my heart sank when I began, but the captain's sharp knife bit deep and kept going. Snap went that first line, and the gondola didn't even shift. I did the line opposite, not wanting the gondola to start hanging crooked.

The balloon was sagging now almost to the burner. I didn't have time to fuss about looking for the gas valve to shut it down, but I was sorely afraid of a fire.

The third and fourth lines went.

At my feet, the man moaned again and his arm twitched and knocked against my boot.

I slashed through the fifth line.

I looked up and saw the balloon slowly billowing down toward me, all but blotting out my view of the *Aurora*. It was awfully close to the engine cars and their propellers.

The sixth line went, and now there were but two lines tethering the balloon to the gondola, attached to opposite corners.

Suddenly the burner came on, triggered by its clockwork timer, and a geyser of blue-hot flame leaped up and scorched the fabric of the balloon. It caught immediately, spreading high. I checked the davit hook, for once I cut these last two lines, the only thing holding us would be that hook and the *Aurora*'s crane.

My wrist throbbed as I began slashing through the seventh line. With a mighty crack the frayed rope snapped high into the air, and the entire gondola slewed over. The unconscious pilot slid toward me and crumpled up against the low side.

Without the crane's cable holding us, we would have been tipped out into the sea. I hauled myself to the high side and the last light flight line. The smell of burning fabric was terrible now, though luckily the smoke and flames were mostly dancing up away from me. But the weight of the blazing balloon was oozing down over the frame now, starting to engulf the gondola.

Frantically I slashed at the last flight line. Something burning hit my shoulder and I struck it off, and then I saw with a panic that a bit of the wicker was alight. I'd deal with it later. That last flight line needed cutting.

Furiously, I attacked it with my knife, severed it, then grabbed hold of the gondola's side as it jerked violently down. The metal burner frame shrieked with stress as it took the full weight. Suspended only on the davit's hook, the gondola swung out from underneath the blazing balloon, and just in time. Aflame, it seeped quickly downward, cut lines trailing, undulating like a giant jellyfish intent on the ocean's bottom. I held my breath as it fell past the gondola.

Fire crackled in the wicker, and I grabbed a blanket from the floor and smothered the flames. There was a sharp tug from the cable, and we were being reeled in, rocking. I made sure the fire was out and then knelt down beside the man. I felt badly that he'd been jostled about so roughly.

Gently I turned him over onto his back and put a blanket beneath his head. He looked to be in his sixties. Through the whiskers, his face had a sharpened look to it, all cheekbones and nose. Lips scabbed over by wind and lack of water. A handsome gentleman. I didn't really know what else to do, so I just held his hand and said,

"There now, we're almost aboard, and Doc Halliday will take a look at you and get you all sorted out." For a moment it looked like his eyes might open, but then he just frowned and shook his head a little, and his lips parted and he mumbled silently for a bit.

Scattered on the floor were all manner of things. Empty water bottles and unopened cans of food. An astrolabe, dividers, a compass, and rolled up charts. From overhead came a terrible shriek, and I looked up to see one of the burner frame's metal struts rip loose from the gondola's rim. We were too heavy. I stared in horror, watching as the frame began twisting from the stress of her load.

"Hurry!" I bellowed up at the *Aurora*. We were getting reeled up fast, but not fast enough, for with a mighty jerk, a second strut ripped clean out. The entire gondola started to slowly keel over as the remaining struts weakened.

We were level with the cargo bay now but still needed to be swung inside, and the gondola was slewing over, about to dump us into the drink. The metal frame was groaning and shrieking. I grabbed hold of the gondola's side with one hand and the man's wrist with the other, knowing I had not the strength to hold us both in if the gondola tried to tip us out.

I looked up and saw the hook screeching along the burner frame, sparking, about to come off the ripped metal strut and we would surely fall—

A violent bump—

And we set down onto the deck of the cargo bay. Inside.

I heard the captain's voice. "Bay doors closed, please! Mr. Kahlo, call the bridge and tell them to take her back to seven hundred feet."

And then everyone was at the side, looking over into the gondola. Doc Halliday was climbing in beside me, and I stepped back to make room for him. A hand clapped me on the shoulder, and I turned to see Captain Walken smiling at me.

"Good work, Mr. Cruse. Very good work, indeed."

I felt terribly thirsty all of a sudden and tired all the way through my bones, and then remembered that I'd been on duty for more than sixteen hours, and normally would have been in my bunk asleep. Instead I'd been swinging across the sky. I started to climb out, but my knees went wobbly, and Captain Walken and Mr. Chen grabbed me under the arms and swung me to the deck.

"You're a brave man, Matt Cruse," Mr. Chen said.

"No, sir. Just light."

"Lighter than air, that's our Mr. Cruse," said one of the sailmakers. "Cloud hopping next, it'll be!"

Hands tousling my hair, clapping me on the back, voices saying, "Well done," and me trying not to smile but smiling and laughing anyway because it felt so good to know I'd brought the gondola in, saved the pilot, and impressed everyone. All these men who had known my father. They would have called him Mr. Cruse too.

Doc Halliday and another crewman were lifting the pilot out of the gondola to a waiting stretcher.

"Is he going to be all right?" I asked the doctor.

"I don't know yet," was all Doc Halliday answered, and his young face looked so grave I felt a queer squeeze in my stomach. The wicker gondola looked odd and out of place in our cargo bay.

"Get some sleep, Mr. Cruse," the captain said to me.

I nodded, but didn't want to go. I watched them take the pilot away on the stretcher. I wondered who he was. I wanted to go through the gondola and find out what had gone wrong.

"Sleep first, Mr. Cruse," said the captain. "Your father would have been very proud of you."

I blinked away the hot tingle behind my eyes. "Thank you, sir."

My legs wobbled as I left the cargo bay and trudged aft along the keel catwalk to the crew quarters. Lighter than air, but I felt heavy as lead. I opened the door to my cabin, caught a glimpse of the clock. Five thirty-nine. I shrugged off my shirt and trousers and climbed into my bunk. And, as so often happened when I slept aloft, I drifted free of my body and glided alongside the *Aurora*, and my father came and joined me, and we flew.

ANALYZE THE TEXT

Story Structure How does the narrator respond to the problem in the story? How does he change because of it?

Dig Deeper

How to Analyze the Text

Use these pages to learn about Story Structure, Personification, and Point of View. Then read "Airborn" again to apply what you learned.

Story Structure

Fictional stories like "Airborn" always include a beginning, a middle, and an ending. In the beginning, the author introduces the **setting** and the **characters**. The author also identifies the **problem** that needs to be solved. In the **episodes,** or events, in the middle of the story, the author shows how the characters try to solve the problem. By the end of the story, the problem usually gets solved.

Look back at page 347 in "Airborn." In this section of text, the story problem is identified. What is the problem? How can identifying the problem help you recognize the most important plot events as they unfold?

Characters	Setting
Plot Episodes	

COMMON CORE   **RL.6.3** describe how a story's or drama's plot unfolds and how characters respond or change; **RL.6.4** determine the meaning of words and phrases, including figurative and connotative meanings/analyze impact of word choice; **RL.6.5** analyze how a sentence, chapter, scene or stanza fits in the overall structure; **RL.6.6** explain how an author develops the point of view of the narrator or speaker; **L.6.5a** interpret figures of speech in context

Personification

Personification is a figure of speech in which something is talked about as if it has human qualities or characteristics. Authors use personification to create images in the readers' minds—for example, *The fire raced across the dry forest, stomping out any signs of life.* This use of personification shows readers that the fire was moving across the forest very quickly, leaving much destruction in its path. Analyzing this type of figurative language helps readers better imagine the action in the story.

Point of View

A narrator tells a story from a **point of view.** In first-person point of view, the speaker, or narrator, is a character within the story. The story "Science Friction," which you read earlier, is told in first-person point of view by the main character, Amanda. In first-person point of view, the narrator uses the pronoun *I.* Readers know only what the narrator thinks, feels, and experiences. Understanding point of view can help readers better understand what characters are thinking.

Your Turn

RETURN TO THE ESSENTIAL QUESTION

Turn and Talk Review the selection with a partner to prepare to discuss this question: *How do people react to emergencies in different ways?* As you discuss, take turns reviewing the key story events and sharing different perspectives.

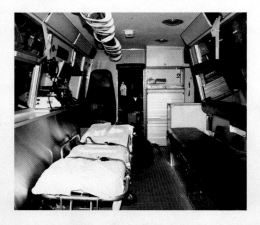

Classroom Conversation

Continue your discussion of "Airborn" by explaining your answers to these questions using text evidence:

1. Why doesn't the author tell the story from the captain's point of view?

2. What does the author do in telling the story that would make it a good live-action movie?

3. What might the hot air balloon pilot say if he were asked to tell what he remembers before the rescue?

RADIO BROADCAST

Be a Radio Announcer Work in small groups to write news stories that summarize the hot air balloon rescue in "Airborn." Then deliver the summaries during a mock radio show. Use background music and sound effects. After all groups have performed, discuss how reading "Airborn" is different from, and similar to, listening to broadcasts about it.

Response Matt Cruse starts his adventure as a "young lad" about to take on a risky rescue. As different events happen during the rescue, Matt responds to them. How is Matt changed by these events? Write a paragraph to describe how Matt changes from the beginning of the story to the end. Include text evidence to support your claim.

KENNETH OPPEL
Author of the Internationally Best-Selling
SILVERWING TRILOGY

Writing Tip

Introduce your paragraph by stating your claim. Use precise, vivid verbs to describe Matt's actions.

Go Digital

COMMON CORE **RL.6.2** determine a theme or central idea of a text/provide a summary; **RL.6.3** describe how a story's or drama's plot unfolds and how characters respond or change; **RL.6.7** compare and contrast the experience of reading to listening or viewing; **W.6.1a** introduce claim(s) and organize reasons and evidence clearly; **W.6.9a** apply grade 6 Reading standards to literature; **SL.6.1a** come to discussions prepared/explicitly draw on preparation to probe and reflect on ideas under discussion; **SL.6.5** include multimedia components and visual displays in presentations

INFORMATIONAL TEXT

✓ **GENRE**

Informational text, such as this magazine article, gives facts and examples about a topic.

✓ **TEXT FOCUS**

Headings help readers identify main ideas of text sections, such as chapters, paragraphs, or captions.

Riding on Air

Every year in early October, the sky above Albuquerque, New Mexico, fills with multicolored hot air balloons. The balloons rise by propane-heated air. They are guided—and sometimes jostled—by undulating wind currents. The International Balloon Fiesta is the largest gathering of hot air balloons in the world. In a way, it is also one of the world's biggest science experiments, demonstrating buoyancy, convection (moving heat), and wind power.

The annual Albuquerque International Balloon Fiesta began in 1972 with thirteen balloons launched from a shopping mall parking lot. Today thousands of visitors attend, relishing the sight of hundreds of balloons in the air.

RI.6.5 analyze how a sentence, paragraph, chapter, or section fits in the overall structure; **RI.6.10** read and comprehend literary nonfiction

The Rise of Ballooning

Ballooning began in France in 1783. The Montgolfier brothers, paper-makers, had noticed that paper bags rise when they are held over a fire. They experimented and that summer they launched a balloon made of linen and paper. It carried a rooster, a duck, and a sheep. Two months later, two human passengers went up in a Montgolfier balloon. If their nerves were frayed, who can blame them? Today we consider them ballooning pioneers.

Hot Air

How do hot air balloons go up? They rely on the same principle that the Montgolfiers used in 1783: convection, or heat in motion—in this case, hot air filling up a giant bag. Today the bag, or envelope, is made of supple nylon. Beneath it is a basket, the gondola, where the pilot and passengers ride. A frame on the gondola holds one or two burners, which heat liquid propane, turning it to gas. The gas ignites and the air heats up and rises, pulling the lines holding the balloon taut until it is ready to take off.

The Ups and Downs of Navigation

From a distance a hot air balloon might appear as frail as a toy. Clouds seem to engulf it as it climbs. What if the pilot should falter and send the balloon careening in the wrong direction? In fact, a balloon's pilot is controlling forces as much as being controlled by them. After going up, the pilot opens a valve at the top of the balloon, letting hot air escape, in order to go down. Meanwhile, wind currents are traveling crosswise in different directions at different altitudes. The pilot can go up or down to choose the right wind current and travel in the right direction.

To travel horizontally, the pilot of a hot air balloon uses the burner or valve to climb or drop to different altitudes. Air currents at those levels push the balloon in the desired direction.

Compare Texts

TEXT TO TEXT

Compare Aircraft Texts Talk with a partner about "Airborn" and "Riding on Air." Discuss these questions: *How does the author of "Airborn" use the topic of air travel in a fantasy? How is air travel treated in the informational text "Riding on Air"? In what way is the approach in both texts similar?* After you discuss your ideas, work together to write an answer to each question. Use text evidence to support your answers.

TEXT TO SELF

Write a Description In "Airborn," the *Aurora* flies over the ocean; in "Riding on Air," the balloons fly over land. Imagine you have the chance to ride in a hot air balloon. What scenery do you see below you? Write a paragraph describing what you might see from the basket of a hot air balloon.

TEXT TO WORLD

Do an Experiment Stretch a balloon over the top of an empty water bottle. Hold the bottle in a bowl of hot tap water. Draw a picture of what happens to the balloon. Write about how this relates to the way a hot air balloon works.

COMMON CORE **RL.6.1** cite textual evidence to support analysis of what the text says explicitly as well as inferences drawn; **RL.6.9** compare and contrast texts in different forms or genres on their approaches to themes and topics; **W.6.4** produce writing in which development, organization, and style are appropriate to task, purpose, and audience; **W.6.10** write routinely over extended time frames and shorter time frames; **SL.6.1c** pose and respond to questions and make comments that contribute to the discussion

Grammar

Using Pronouns Correctly A **pronoun** is a word that takes the place of a noun. **Personal pronouns** take the place of specific people or things. Personal pronouns have different forms for number and person. A **possessive pronoun** shows ownership. It is used to replace a possessive noun. Some possessive pronouns, such as *my, her,* and *our,* are always used with nouns. Others, such as *mine, hers,* and *ours,* stand alone. *His* and *its* can be used with nouns or can stand alone.

	Personal Pronouns		Possessive Pronouns	
	Singular	**Plural**	**Singular**	**Plural**
First person	I, me	we, us	my, mine	our, ours
Second person	you	you	your, yours	your, yours
Third person	he, him, she, her, it	they, them	his, her, hers, its	their, theirs

The **antecedent** of a pronoun is the noun or nouns to which the pronoun refers.

antecedent   pronoun   pronoun

Matt cut the line with his knife. Then he grabbed the gondola.

His and *he* refer to *Matt.*

Try This! **Write the sentences below on another sheet of paper. Underline each pronoun and circle its antecedent. Next to each sentence, write *possessive* or *personal* to identify the kind of pronoun.**

1 Because Captain Walken is a good leader, the crew respects him.

2 The men on the airship do their jobs well.

3 The notebook is Mr. Chen's, but Mr. Rideau is holding it.

4 Matt said, "The job of rescuing the man is mine."

A shift in pronoun number or person can confuse your readers. When you proofread your writing, be sure that your antecedents and pronouns match in number and person.

Shifts in Pronoun Number and Person

A person who flies in hot air balloons has fun because they get to fly to different places. Vera and I flew our balloon to an island. We flew over the ocean, and this always scares you a bit. We had to land on the beach. The beach was full of crabs. It didn't bother us.

Consistent Pronoun Number and Person

People who fly in hot air balloons have fun because they get to fly to different places.	Vera and I flew our balloon to an island. We flew over the ocean, and this always scares us a bit.	We had to land on the beach. The beach was full of crabs. They didn't bother us.

 Connect Grammar to Writing

As you edit your classification essay this week, look closely at each pronoun you use. Correct any errors you notice. Using pronouns correctly is an important part of good writing.

Informative Writing

☑ **Voice** In a **classification essay,** writers give information by organizing things into categories, or groups. Choose a topic that can be divided into categories. Then choose the categories. In the introduction, include a statement that reveals your interest in the topic. In the body, explain each category equally using facts, examples, definitions, and other informative details. End with a conclusion that summarizes the topic.

Eric wrote a first draft of his classification essay about balloon aircraft. Then he revised his draft. He deleted what he thought was not necessary. He added words appropriate to his topic and details that would make his essay more informative.

Writing Traits Checklist

☑ **Ideas**
Did I include a focus statement in my introduction?

☑ **Organization**
Did I explain each category equally?

☑ **Sentence Fluency**
Did I use transitions to clarify relationships?

☑ **Word Choice**
Did I use words about my topic?

☑ **Voice**
Did I reveal my interest in the topic?

☑ **Conventions**
Did I use correct spelling, grammar, and punctuation?

Revised Draft

A powered balloon is called an airship or blimp. It has ~~unique parts~~ an engine and propellers to power it.

It also has a rudder and instruments that allow a pilot to steer it. ~~Blimps are often flown over special events on the ground, sometimes to advertise something.~~ Several people can ride ~~in~~ in the enclosed gondola of a blimp because of its size.

Balloon Aircraft

by Eric Rodarte

There are many ways to ride in the sky, but one of the most exciting is by balloon. There are three types of balloon aircraft.

Captive Balloon

A captive balloon is a balloon that is anchored to the ground by a cable. A captive balloon is often used to give a few people the chance to be up in the air without flying to another location.

Free-Floating Balloon

A free-floating balloon goes wherever the wind blows it. The pilot can control the vertical movement of the balloon but can't steer it. Only a few people can fit in the gondola of a colorful, free-floating balloon.

Powered Balloon

A powered balloon is called an airship or blimp. It has an engine and propellers to power it. It also has a rudder and instruments that allow a pilot to steer it. Several people can ride in the enclosed gondola of a blimp because of its size.

As you see, there are many choices for balloon enthusiasts. Be it captive, free-floating, or powered, balloon aircraft offer you a unique flying experience and a great view of the sights below.

Reading as a Writer

How does Eric show his interest in the topic? What does he do to help his readers understand the topic? What can you do to show your interest in and knowledge of your topic?

When I planned my classification essay, I thought about how to show my interest in the topic. I also thought about what I wanted the reader to learn. I used specific vocabulary to develop my topic.

Vocabulary in Context

✓ **TARGET VOCABULARY**

expanse
sacrificed
durable
prime
frigid
participants
equivalent
deduced
affirmed
culmination

Vocabulary Reader

Context Cards

COMMON CORE

L.6.6 acquire and use general academic and domain-specific words and phrases/gather vocabulary knowledge for comprehension or expression

1 expanse

Explorer Matthew Henson sledged across a vast expanse of polar ice. It stretched for miles.

2 sacrificed

Polar explorers gave up many comforts for the sake of adventure. They sacrificed the pleasure of being in a warm home.

3 durable

An explorer's equipment needs to be durable. It has to last a long time and hold up under extreme conditions.

4 prime

Members of a mountain expedition might prime, or prepare, themselves by taking hikes in high elevations.

Go Digital

▶ Study each Context Card.

▶ Discuss one picture. Use a different Vocabulary word from the one on the card.

5 frigid

Mountain climbers wear layers of clothing to protect themselves from frigid, or extremely cold, weather.

6 participants

The participants in an expedition can be old or young and don't need to travel far from home.

7 equivalent

For European explorers, coming to America may have been the equivalent of visiting the moon—equally strange.

8 deduced

Henry Stanley deduced, or concluded, that he had found the long-missing British explorer, David Livingstone, in Africa.

9 affirmed

The presence of Native Americans affirmed, or proved, that Europeans were not the first people in the "New World."

10 culmination

Reaching the top of a mountain at last may be the culmination of a long, hard climb.

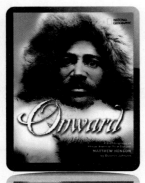

Read and Comprehend

✓ TARGET SKILL

Main Ideas and Details The biography "Onward" tells about Matthew Henson's expedition to the North Pole. As you read about each stage of the expedition, think about the most important point the author is trying to make about that stage. Use text evidence, or **details** in the text, to infer the central idea, or **main idea.** Use a graphic organizer like this one to help you record the main idea and its supporting details.

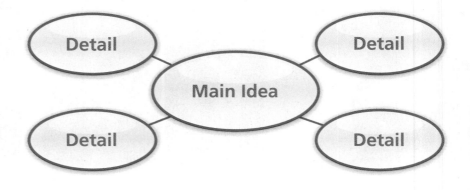

✓ TARGET STRATEGY

Monitor/Clarify As you read "Onward," **monitor,** or pay attention to, your understanding of the text. Find ways to **clarify,** or make clear, any parts that do not make sense.

RI.6.1 cite textual evidence to support analysis of what the text says explicitly as well as inferences drawn; **RI.6.2** determine a central idea of a text/provide a summary

374

Exploration

Exploration means "the act of traveling into an unfamiliar place for the purpose of discovery." For centuries, people have traveled the world to discover new lands, resources, and hidden treasures left behind by lost civilizations. Exploration has even reached beyond earth and into space.

Explorations can happen anywhere—in caves, in jungles, even in your own backyard. In "Onward," you will learn about Matthew Henson and Commander Robert Peary's mission to explore the North Pole.

ANCHOR TEXT

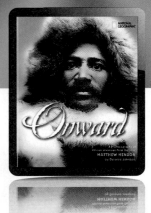

✓ TARGET SKILL

Main Ideas and Details
Identify the central ideas in the selection. Find the details that support those ideas.

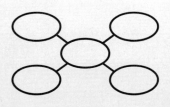

✓ GENRE

A **biography** is the story of a person's life written by another person. As you read, look for:

▶ information that tells why the person is important

▶ opinions and personal judgments based on facts

▶ time-ordered events

COMMON CORE **RI.6.2** determine a central idea of a text/provide a summary; **RI.6.4** determine the meaning of words and phrases, including figurative, connotative, and technical meanings; **L.6.5c** distinguish among connotations of words with similar denotations; **L.6.6** acquire and use general academic and domain-specific words and phrases/gather vocabulary knowledge for comprehension or expression

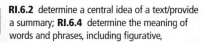

MEET THE AUTHOR

Dolores Johnson

Dolores Johnson has written several historical books about African Americans. *She Dared to Fly* tells the true story of Bessie Coleman, the first African American woman to become a licensed pilot. Johnson has also written and illustrated two books of fiction that bring the historical events of slavery vividly to life—*Now Let Me Fly: The Story of a Slave Family* and *Seminole Diary: Remembrances of a Slave.*

Onward

A Photobiography of African-American Polar Explorer Matthew Henson

by Dolores Johnson

I n July of 1908, Matthew Henson and Commander Robert F. Peary
set sail from New York City in a heavily fortified ship, the Roosevelt,
*bound for Ellesmere Island in far northern Canada. Over the past
sixteen years, Henson and Peary have made four attempts to cross the
Arctic ice and be the first to reach the North Pole. Henson has become good
friends with the native Inuit who live nearby, but the explorers have been
blocked by stretches of open water called leads, especially one called the
Big Lead. Now, with a crew of five—Ross Marvin, Robert Bartlett, and
newcomers George Borup, Dr. John Goodsell, and Donald MacMillan—the
expedition is bringing its sledges, or dogsleds, to the Arctic for another try.*

The newcomers seemed to view the coming adventure as a
sporting event. Henson, who by this time was 42 years old, thought
differently. He had devoted practically his whole adult life to the
mission. He had teetered close to death. He had lost, and nearly
lost, fellow crew members who had fallen into crevasses or the inky
black waters of an Arctic Ocean lead. And he had sacrificed a stable
family life so that he could be part of history. This was serious
business. Yet Henson's mood brightened by the time the ship
arrived at Etah, Greenland. He was to be reunited with his Inuit
friends once again.

*Much of the warm spirit and
decent character that endeared
him to many of the people he
encountered, such as the Inuit
and the people who became
his benefactors, is shown in
this candid photo of Matthew
Henson. It was shot on the deck
of the* Roosevelt.

The specially built ship, the Roosevelt, *contributed to the expedition's eventual success because it got the crew members closer to the North Pole than any previous ship. Here the ship is being unloaded of its cargo, after proceeding so far north it became trapped in the ice.*

After Henson and Peary persuaded Inuit families to join the expedition, they all sailed to Cape Sheridan in an ice-busting, gut-wrenching voyage that took two weeks. Then the men unloaded the ship and sledged the supplies to Cape Columbia, on Ellesmere, which was only 413 miles south of the Pole.

By February 1909, the entire expedition was prepared to begin the march to the Pole. The novices had practiced their sledging and hunting and had spent enough time outdoors to prime themselves for the frigid Arctic conditions.

Henson supervised the Inuit women in the preparation and sewing of the garments the crew would wear. Each man had a long red flannel shirt and soft bearskin trousers lined with flannel. The soft cloth absorbed sweat and kept the roughness of the fur away from the skin. The pants were wrapped with a band of bearskin that held the legs snugly. A deerskin coat with a hood covered the torso. Bearskin mittens and sealskin boots completed the wardrobe. The outfit was easily transformed into a fur-lined sleeping sack.

> ### ANALYZE THE TEXT
>
> **Connotation** The author describes the expedition as an "ice-busting, gut-wrenching voyage." Do those words have a positive or a negative connotation? How can you tell?

On past expeditions, Commander Peary had sent sledges forward to store provisions along the trail. But he realized how unreliable that technique could be if the supplies got buried in deep snow. On this expedition, Peary proposed that a pioneering team would break the trail up ahead. Then six relay teams would follow, each carrying enough food, tools, weapons, and clothes for the whole expedition for five days. The entire expedition would consume supplies from the equivalent of one of the sledges. When those provisions were gone, one team and the weakest dogs would be sent back to headquarters. Until the actual participants of the last relay team were sent back, no one but Commander Peary would know who was to accompany him to the Pole.

Bartlett and Borup were sent out to break the trail. Then Henson and his Inuit team were sent out. Marvin, Goodsell, MacMillan and their teams followed, with Peary trailing. The Commander stayed in touch with the units by leaving notes in igloos for retreating teams so that they could forward information to teams bringing up more supplies.

Men pause while driving a sledge pulled by teams of dogs harnessed in a fan formation.

The sledge teams had to confront pressure ridges and steep hummocks of ice, tremendous obstacles in their effort to reach the North Pole. Often they had to lift the sledges and dogs to go forward. Stormy weather, blinding snow, and wide expansive leads would often stop onward progress completely.

The assault began with difficulty. Between March 2nd and 3rd, the temperature fell so low that no one got much sleep. The men had to beat their arms and feet to keep the blood circulating. The next day, the only way the crews could advance was to use their pickaxes to carve through rough ice studded with pressure ridges and sharp hummocks, or projections of ice. Some sledges broke down, and the drivers often had to prod the dogs forward when they balked. Harsh winds stung their faces. Giant fissures in the ice threatened every step.

Henson's party followed Bartlett's tracks as far as the Big Lead. While camped beside the lead, the men woke to the thunderous crack of shifting ice grinding beneath them. At any moment, men, equipment, and dogs could be thrown into the flowing water that was passing below. The crews shifted their campsite.

> **ANALYZE THE TEXT**
>
> **Domain-Specific Vocabulary** The author uses technical terms such as *pressure ridges* and *sledges*. What are the meanings of these words? How can you find out?

The team waited six days for the icy path spreading across the lead to freeze solid. They then advanced four days' marches until they caught up with Bartlett, who was stopped again by another wide lead. They had to set up camp and wait.

On March 11, a passable lane across the lead finally formed. But steep, rocky ice ridges studded the trail, and their supply of fuel was dwindling. One by one, the supporting parties and their Inuit crews were sent back to base camp to conserve the remaining fuel and supplies.

First, Dr. Goodsell was sent back with his team, and then MacMillan. Borup was sent back on March 20. The remaining crew crossed plains of deep ice littered with pressure ridges and ice rubble. The temperature rose to 20 degrees below zero; that turned the ice hard and smooth. But the warmer temperature opened up more leads.

Robert Peary, an engineer, used his training to reconfigure the design of the Inuit sledge so that it could carry heavier loads and be more durable. Henson was instrumental in building the sledges that Peary designed, and repairing those that disintegrated in the below-zero temperatures.

Marvin finished five marches, and then Bartlett moved up again as the trail breaker. The temperature dropped. On March 26, a disappointed Marvin was ordered back to land. The expedition had gotten past Peary's record of farthest north. Then on March 30 Bartlett was told to retreat. Bartlett was so frustrated by not being picked to go all the way to the Pole that he walked 5 or 6 miles farther north to reach the 88th parallel, the record up until that date. It was only at Bartlett's departure that Henson knew he would accompany Peary to the North Pole.

The final assault team was made up of Henson, Peary, and the Inuit Ootah, Ooqueah, Egingwah, and Seegloo. Henson, Ootah, and Ooqueah were to break the trail over the last 133 miles. Peary, still crippled by the frostbite that had taken his toes 11 years earlier, took turns riding Egingwah's sledge and walking beside it. The conditions varied from stretches of smooth ice to steep ice ridges. Henson lengthened his marches to a back-breaking 18 to 20 hours a day. Peary caught up to Henson's team at day's end on April 1.

ANALYZE THE TEXT

Main Ideas and Details What is the main idea on pages 382–383? What details support this idea?

On April 5, Peary checked the position of the sun with his sextant. It told him that the Pole was only 35 miles away. The next morning, he alerted Henson to begin the march. Henson's progress was so successful that by the time he had covered 20 miles, he was an hour ahead of Peary. As Henson drove his team across thin ice bridging a lead, the ice suddenly cracked. Henson, along with his dogs and sledge, was plunged into the frigid water. Henson began floundering about, trying to grasp onto jutting ice to save himself. He swallowed frigid water, and his lungs felt like they would burst. Then he found himself being lifted out of the water. It was Ootah who saved him and his sledge and dogs. Ootah slipped off Henson's wet boots and warmed his feet in the Inuit way, against Ootah's bare stomach.

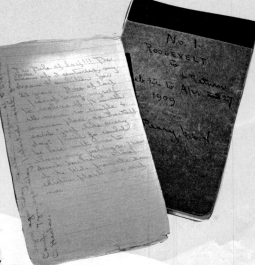

Peary's journals recording the day he and Henson and the four Inuit finally reached their goal. The entry at left says, "The Pole at last!!! The prize of three centuries. My dream and ambition for 20 years. Mine at last!"

They continued the march for four more hours until Henson deduced that they must have reached the North Pole. Henson, who had learned to steer a ship by the stars, had often played a game with Peary that he could estimate their position at the end of marches. "Knowing that we had kept on going in practically a straight line, [I] was sure that we had more than covered the necessary distance to insure our arrival at the top of the earth," wrote Henson later. He, Ooqueah, and Ootah built igloos.

Peary arrived forty-five minutes later. When the clouds parted in the sky, he was able to take a latitude sighting with his sextant that affirmed they were at 89°57'. (The North Pole is at 90°N.) They probably got as close to determining their position as their navigational gear allowed—within five miles of the North Pole. For all intents and purposes, the expedition had reached its goal. It was April 6, 1909. In a whisper, Peary announced his reading to Henson. Then the two explorers, weary with the culmination of so many years of effort, crawled into an igloo, lay down, and went to sleep.

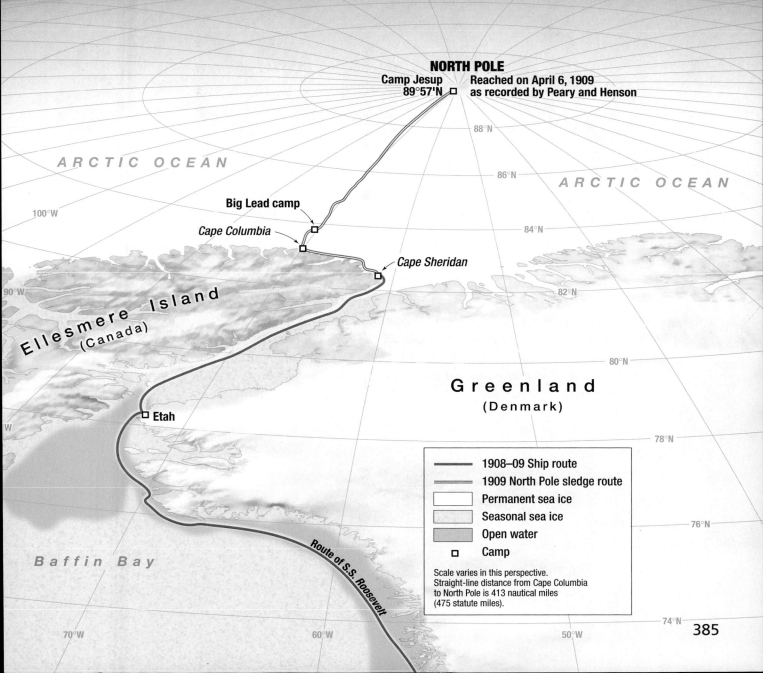

have attempted to travel in such weather. Our breath was frozen to our hoods of fur and our cheeks and noses frozen . . ." —Matthew Henson

NORTH POLE

Camp Jesup 89°57'N — Reached on April 6, 1909 as recorded by Peary and Henson

88°N

ARCTIC OCEAN

86°N

ARCTIC OCEAN

100°W

Big Lead camp

84°N

Cape Columbia

Cape Sheridan

82°N

90°W

Ellesmere Island
(Canada)

80°N

Greenland
(Denmark)

Etah

78°N

76°N

Baffin Bay

Route of S.S. Roosevelt

—— 1908–09 Ship route
═══ 1909 North Pole sledge route
☐ Permanent sea ice
☐ Seasonal sea ice
☐ Open water
☐ Camp

Scale varies in this perspective.
Straight-line distance from Cape Columbia
to North Pole is 413 nautical miles
(475 statute miles).

74°N

70°W   60°W   50°W   385

Peary had Matthew Henson and the four Inuit, Seegloo, Egingwah, Ooqueah, and Ootah, pose for photographs holding the four banners he carried to commemorate their reaching the North Pole. The Inuit were amazed that the culmination of so many years of effort was just another expanse of ice. "There is nothing here," Ootah said.

When Peary awoke, he wrote in his diary, "The Pole at last!!!" He unpacked a thin silk American flag he had been carrying with him all of his many years of exploration and planted it on top of his igloo.

Peary, Egingwah, and Seegloo then sledged several miles beyond the camp, covering a rectangular area, to ensure that an inaccurate reading would not spoil their achievement. Peary had Henson thrust an American flag into a large pressure ridge, and he took a photo of the five men holding flags that the Commander had carried with him for the occasion. Henson held an American flag that Josephine Peary had sewn by hand. Ooqueah held a flag of the Navy League. Ootah held a banner from Peary's college fraternity. Seegloo waved a flag of the Red Cross. And Egingwah held a Daughters of the American Revolution peace flag. They all joined in an exhilarated chorus of "Hip, hip, hooray." Then Peary said, "Let us go home, Matt."

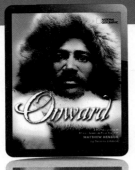

Dig Deeper

How to Analyze the Text

Use these pages to learn about Main Ideas and Details, Connotation, and Domain-Specific Vocabulary. Then read "Onward" again to apply what you learned.

Main Ideas and Details

The topic of "Onward" is Matthew Henson's role in the exploration of the North Pole. **Main ideas** are the central, or most important, points the author makes about the topic. **Details** are facts, examples, and other text evidence that support the main ideas.

Authors often do not state main ideas directly. Readers must use details in the text to figure them out. As you reread "Onward," use the details to figure out the main ideas.

Look back at the last paragraph on page 386. All the sentences are details that support an unstated main idea. What is the main idea of this paragraph?

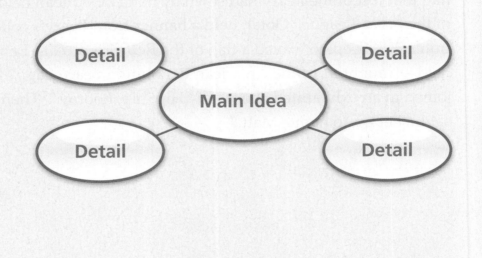

COMMON CORE

RI.6.1 cite textual evidence to support analysis of what the text says explicitly as well as inferences drawn; **RI.6.2** determine a central idea of a text/provide a summary; **RI.6.4** determine the meaning of words and phrases, including figurative, connotative, and technical meanings; **L.6.5c** distinguish among connotations of words with similar denotations; **L.6.6** acquire and use general academic and domain-specific words and phrases/gather vocabulary knowledge for comprehension or expression

Connotation

Have you ever read a word that made you think of something pleasant or maybe unpleasant? **Connotations** are the feelings and associations connected with words. For example, in its dictionary meaning, a *home* is just a place where a person lives. Over time, though, the word has gained the positive connotations of safety, love, comfort, and family. As you reread "Onward," think about the words the author uses to describe the expedition. Think about the dictionary meanings of the words and whether they have positive or negative connotations.

Domain-Specific Vocabulary

Authors of biographies and other informational texts often use **technical terms,** the vocabulary specific to a profession or area of knowledge. For example, an author writing about caves might use the technical term *spelunker* to refer to someone who explores caves. Readers can use context clues, photos and captions, a dictionary, or a glossary to determine the meanings of technical terms. As you reread "Onward," look for technical terms related to the topic. Look for clues in the text to determine the meaning of each term.

Your Turn

RETURN TO THE ESSENTIAL QUESTION

 Turn and Talk

Review the selection with a partner to prepare to discuss this question: *What drives people to explore remote places?* As you discuss, ask questions of each other and reflect on the ideas presented. Cite text evidence to support your ideas.

Classroom Conversation

Continue your discussion of "Onward" by using text evidence to explain your answers to these questions:

1. What contributions did Matthew Henson make that made him so valuable to Commander Peary?

2. Why do you think Commander Peary and his team were finally able to reach the North Pole on the fourth attempt?

3. In what ways did the Inuit contribute to the team's success in the Arctic?

EXPLORERS

Explore Motivation With a partner, discuss the details that show why the final push to reach the North Pole was so challenging. What do you think drove the explorers to give up the comforts of home and pursue this quest? Write a paragraph that explains your ideas. Provide text evidence about the expedition team, along with inferences about the explorers' motivations, to support your ideas.

Response Matthew Henson devoted much of his adult life to reaching the North Pole. What did he do to make his dream come true? Why do you think Henson decides to give up a comfortable life in order to pursue this goal? Write a paragraph to present and explain your claim. Use facts from the biography as evidence to support your ideas.

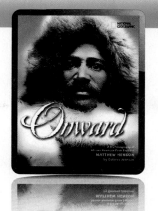

Writing Tip

State your claim at the beginning of your response. Provide clear reasons, supported by text evidence, to explain your opinion.

Go Digital

COMMON CORE **RI.6.1** cite textual evidence to support analysis of what the text says explicitly as well as inferences drawn; **W.6.1a** introduce claim(s) and organize reasons and evidence clearly; **W.6.9b** apply grade 6 Reading standards to literary nonfiction; **SL.6.1a** come to discussions prepared/explicitly draw on preparation to probe and reflect on ideas under discussion; **SL.6.1c** pose and respond to questions and make comments that contribute to the discussion

The Pole!

by Matthew Henson

In the spring of 1909, Commander Robert Peary's long-held dream was about to come true. The North Pole was only 130 frozen miles away. Captain Bartlett and his team had returned from breaking the trail and leaving supplies. As the captain headed south and home, Commander Peary, Matthew Henson, and four native Inuit would undertake the final assault on the North Pole. Three years after returning from the Arctic, Matthew Henson wrote a memoir about his adventures and described their fearful and exhilarating journey to the top of the world.

Commander Peary's team climbing an Arctic ice ridge

Go Digital

It was during the march of the 3rd of April that I endured an instant of hideous horror. We were crossing a land of moving ice. Commander Peary was in the lead setting the pace, and a half hour later the four Esquimos and myself followed in single file. They had all gone before, and I was standing and pushing at the upstanders of my sledge, when the block of ice I was using as a support slipped from underneath my feet. Before I knew it, the sledge was out of my grasp, and I was floundering in the water of the lead. I did the best I could. I tore my hood from off my head and struggled frantically. My hands were gloved and I could not take hold of the ice, but before I could give the "Grand Hailing Sign of Distress," * faithful old Ootah had grabbed me by the nape of the neck, the same as he would have grabbed a dog. With one hand he pulled me out of the water and with the other hurried the team across.

Matthew Alexander Henson

He had saved my life, but I did not tell him so, for such occurrences are taken as part of the day's work. The sledge he safeguarded was of much more importance, for it held, as part of its load, the Commander's sextant, the mercury, and the coils of piano-wire that were the essential portion of the scientific part of the expedition.

My *kamiks* (boots of sealskin) were stripped off, and the congealed water was beaten out of my bearskin trousers, and with a dry pair of kamiks, we hurried to overtake the column. When we caught up, we found the Esquimos gathered around the Commander, doing the best to relieve him of his discomfort, for he had fallen into the water also. While he was not complaining, I was sure that his bath had not been any more voluntary than mine had been.

---

* *Grand Hailing Sign of Distress:* a distress gesture made with both arms

When we halted on April 6, 1909, and started to build the igloos, the dogs and sledges having been secured, I noticed Commander Peary at work unloading his sledge and unpacking several bundles of equipment. He pulled out from his *kooletah* (thick, fur outer-garment) a small folded package and unfolded it. I recognized his old silk flag, and I realized that this was to be a camp of importance. Our different camps had been known as Camp Number One, Number Two, etc., but after the turning back of Captain Bartlett, the camps had been given names such as Camp Nansen, Camp Cagni. etc. I asked what the name of this camp was to be—"Camp Peary"? "This, Henson, is to be Camp Morris K. Jesup, * the last and most northerly camp on the earth." He fastened the flag to a staff and planted it firmly on top of his igloo.

---

*Camp Nansen, Camp Cagni, Camp Morris K. Jesup: Fridtjof Nansen, a Dane, and Umberto Cagni, an Italian, were renowned Arctic explorers. Morris K. Jesup financed Peary's expedition.

A lead is a stretch of open water in the ice.

For a few minutes it hung limp and lifeless in the dead calm of the haze. Then a slight breeze, increasing in strength, caused the folds to straighten out, and soon it was rippling out in sparkling color. The stars and stripes were "nailed to the Pole." A thrill of patriotism ran through me, and I raised my voice to cheer the starry emblem of my native land.

The Esquimos gathered around and, taking the time from Commander Peary, three hearty cheers rang out on the still, frosty air, our dumb dogs looking on in puzzled surprise. As prospects for getting a sight of the sun were not good, we turned in and slept, leaving the flag proudly floating above us.

Commander Robert Peary in 1909

Matthew Henson and four Inuit pose with flags at the North Pole. Color has been added to the original black-and-white photograph.

This was a thin silk flag that Commander Peary had carried on all of his Arctic journeys, and he had always flown it at his last camps. It was as glorious and as inspiring a banner as any battle-scarred, blood-stained standard of the world. This badge of honor and courage was also blood-stained and battle-scarred, for at several places there were blank squares marking the spots where pieces had been cut out at each of the "Farthests" of its brave bearer, and left with the records in the cairns,* as mute but eloquent witnesses of his achievements. At the North Pole, a diagonal strip running from the upper left to the lower right corner was cut, and this precious strip, together with a brief record, was placed in an empty tin, sealed up and buried in the ice, as a record for all time.

---

*cairns: mounds of stones built as landmarks or memorials

Matthew Henson in a photo taken shortly after the North Pole expedition

Compare Texts

Compare Events Author Dolores Johnson describes Matthew Henson's expedition to the North Pole in "Onward." Matthew Henson provides his own account in the memoir "The Pole!" Use these questions to compare and contrast the authors' presentations of the events: *In what way is Johnson's version of events the same as Henson's? In what way is it different?* Use text evidence to support your answers.

Make a Wish List Henson and Peary traveled to the North Pole. Where in the world would you like to travel? On a sheet of paper, list three places that you would visit if you could. For each destination, note what you would like to see or do there. Post your list in the classroom.

Research Travel Facts Choose one of the places you listed in "Make a Wish List" above. Use print and digital sources to research information about its landscape, climate, and other geographic features. Write a fact file about the location, and add an illustration.

COMMON CORE **RI.6.1** cite textual evidence to support analysis of what the text says explicitly as well as inferences drawn; **RI.6.9** compare and contrast one author's presentation of events with that of another; **W.6.7** conduct short research projects to answer a question, drawing on several sources and refocusing the inquiry when appropriate; **W.6.8** gather information from print and digital sources/asses credibility of sources/quote or paraphrase data and conclusions of others/provide bibliographic information

Grammar

 Go Digital

What Are Verb Tenses? The tense of a verb tells when an action or a state of being takes place. The **present tense,** the **past tense,** and the **future tense** are called the simple tenses. The **present perfect tense,** the **past perfect tense,** and the **future perfect tense** are called the perfect tenses. Each perfect-tense verb is made up of a form of the helping verb *have* and a simple past-tense verb.

Simple Tenses	Perfect Tenses
present tense Explorers seek new discoveries.	present perfect tense Polar explorers have made many discoveries.
past tense Peary and Henson sailed to Greenland.	past perfect tense They first had sailed to Greenland eighteen years before they began this expedition.
future tense Readers will learn about their trek.	future perfect tense Our class will have read two other books about explorers by the end of the year.

Try This! **Find the verb in each sentence. On another sheet of paper, write each verb and name its tense.**

1. Peary chose Henson for this expedition because of his skills and experience.

2. The temperature will drop far below zero.

3. Inuit women sew warm clothes for the explorers.

4. Matthew Henson had become a friend of the Inuit on earlier trips.

Different tenses of the same verb show when an action or a state of being occurs. As you write, your verb tenses tell readers when events take place. You may confuse readers if your verb tenses do not match other time clues in your writing.

Time Clues

Now they stand on the icy expanse.

All last week, they imagined this trek.

Tonight, they will dream about the snowy landscape.

Connect Grammar to Writing

As you edit your definition essay, examine the verbs. Make sure you used the proper tenses. To determine the correct tense, ask yourself when the action or state of being occurs. Be sure to use the proper verb form for each tense.

W.6.2a introduce a topic and organize ideas, concepts, and information/include formatting, graphics, and multimedia; **W.6.2b** develop the topic with facts, definitions, details, quotations, or other information and examples; **W.6.2d** use precise language and domain-specific vocabulary; **W.6.2e** establish and maintain a formal style; **W.6.2f** provide a concluding statement

Informative Writing

✔ Organization In a **definition essay,** writers explain a word, a term, or an idea by using one or more definitions, examples, facts, and other details. As you revise your essay, make sure that you have organized ideas in a logical way. Also check that you have ended your essay with a strong concluding statement.

Felice drafted a definition essay on an interesting place to explore. Later, she revised her essay to add details and precise terms that helped her extend the definition.

Writing Traits Checklist

✔ Ideas
Did I clearly explain a word, term, or concept?

✔ Organization
Did I define the term, extend the definition, and end with a concluding statement?

✔ Sentence Fluency
Did I use verb tenses correctly?

✔ Word Choice
Did I use precise words and terms?

✔ Voice
Did I write in a formal voice?

✔ Conventions
Did I use correct spelling, grammar, and punctuation?

Revised Draft

A cenote (suh-NOH-tee) is a deep hole in the ground that opens to water below. Some types of cenotes have an entrance into caverns that contain an underground river. People can explore the caverns and the underground river of these cenotes.

~~The hole~~ may be filled with water, or it may lead to underground pools of water and a maze of underwater ~~caves.~~ cave tunnels.

A cenote is formed when limestone rocks soften and collapse inward, forming a large sinkhole, or pit in the earth. The sinkhole

400

Discovering Cenotes

by Felice Cruz

A cenote (suh-NOH-tee) is a deep hole in the ground that opens to water below. Some types of cenotes have an entrance into caverns that contain an underground river. People can explore the caverns and the underground river of these cenotes.

A cenote is formed when limestone rocks soften and collapse inward, forming a large sinkhole, or pit in the earth. The sinkhole may be filled with water, or it may lead to underground pools of water and a maze of underwater cave tunnels.

A cenote is home to rock formations called stalagmites and stalactites. Stalagmites jut upward from the floor of a cave. Stalactites hang downward from the ceiling of the cave. People travel into cenotes to investigate these rock formations. The more adventurous explorers dive the deep water that fills the cave tunnels.

A cenote can contain miles and miles of river and caves. For those who want to learn about the mysteries of the underground world, cenotes are waiting to be explored.

Reading as a Writer

How does Felice develop her topic? How can her strategy help you organize the information in your definition essay?

In my final paper, I began with a definition and used other definitions to help me extend it. I also used precise words and terms to explain my topic.

✓ TARGET VOCABULARY

emulate
motive
anonymous
bland
skeptical
veered
reception
aim
understatement
fanatic

Vocabulary
Reader

Context
Cards

402

Vocabulary in Context

1 emulate

A good person can serve as a role model whom others want to emulate. They want to be like that person.

2 motive

The motive of volunteers is not to make money. The reason for their actions is to help those in need.

3 anonymous

When a donation is from someone who wants to remain anonymous, no one knows who gives it.

4 bland

A day without a visit from a friend can be as bland as pasta without sauce.

Go Digital

▶ Study each Context Card.

▶ Ask a question that uses one of the Vocabulary words.

5 skeptical

People who are skeptical about learning a skill may need a friend to help them overcome their doubts.

6 veered

Many people have veered from their normal routine, changing their path to help someone in need.

7 reception

Those who attend a reception, a welcoming gathering, get a chance to meet others whom they admire.

8 aim

The aim, or purpose, of many fundraisers is to raise money to help people in need.

9 understatement

Saying "I helped" after saving someone's life is an understatement. It describes a big event in a few plain words.

10 fanatic

A sports fanatic may act too wild for some in a crowd, but the home team often appreciates the enthusiasm.

Read and Comprehend

Go Digital

☑ TARGET SKILL

Theme You have learned that the **theme** of a fiction story is the central idea or message that the author wants readers to understand and remember. The theme is most often a message about life or human nature. Readers usually must infer, or figure out, the theme from details such as plot episodes, dialogue, character changes, and characters' thoughts and feelings. As you read "Any Small Goodness," look for text evidence that helps you infer the theme. Use a graphic organizer like the one below to record the details and the theme.

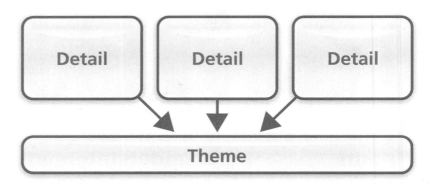

☑ TARGET STRATEGY

Visualize Use text evidence and your own senses to **visualize,** or form a mental picture of what is happening in the story.

COMMON CORE

RL.6.1 cite textual evidence to support analysis of what the text says explicitly as well as inferences drawn; **RL.6.2** determine a theme or central idea of a text/provide a summary

Community Helpers

Everyone in a community has a part to play in making it a better place to live. From doctors to coaches in the neighborhood soccer league, people make the difference.

Have you ever thought about how to make your community a better place to live? Something as small as picking up trash helps. In "Any Small Goodness," Arturo meets a community helper who makes an unexpected contribution to Arturo's basketball team.

ANCHOR TEXT

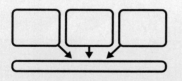

TONY JOHNSTON
Any Small
Goodness
a novel of the barrio

✓ TARGET SKILL

Theme Infer the theme from plot episodes, dialogue, character changes, characters' thoughts and feelings, and other story details.

✓ GENRE

Realistic fiction has characters and events that are like people and events in real life. As you read, look for:

▶ a setting that is a real place
▶ characters who have feelings that real people do

RL.6.2 determine a theme or central idea of a text/provide a summary; **RL.6.4** determine the meaning of words and phrases, including figurative and connotative meanings/analyze impact of word choice; **RL.6.5** analyze how a sentence, chapter, scene or stanza fits in the overall structure; **L.6.5a** interpret figures of speech in context

MEET THE AUTHOR
Tony Johnston

Born in California, Tony Johnston spent fifteen years in Mexico. As she traveled, she collected handmade Indian belts. Her notes and stories about the belts became a collection of poems called *My Mexico*. Johnston usually works on several ideas at once and has published more than seventy-five books, including *The Harmonica* and *Uncle Rain Cloud*.

MEET THE ILLUSTRATOR
David Diaz

David Diaz developed his bold art style while making sketches on a trip down the Amazon River. His first illustrated children's book was Gary Soto's *Neighborhood Odes*. Diaz's illustrations for *Smoky Night*, by Eve Bunting, won the 1995 Caldecott Medal.

Any Small Goodness

by Tony Johnston

selection illustrated
by David Diaz

ESSENTIAL QUESTION

What can people do to
help their communities?

Arturo is a basketball fanatic, just like the rest of his family and everyone else in the barrio, his Spanish-speaking neighborhood in Los Angeles. He gets up at the crack of dawn nearly every morning to attend practice at his school. This day will be a little different.

Ours is a barrio of basketball maniacs. Our fans don't wear cheese hunks on their heads like some of those *idiotas* (ee DYOH tahs) on TV. But they get pretty into the game. When the season approaches, like now, too-worn shoes stop and start, with no squeak. Too-soft balls loft through the air. The whole neighborhood starts dribbling and jumping around. Like a great big popcorn machine. Guess that's another reason I signed up. Like the ad says, "I love this game!"

Now we're in the gym, waiting for Coach. He comes late a lot because he owns a watch as primitive as a sundial and a car that's easily Jurassic.

"I count on every one of you players," Coach pounds into us again and again. "I can't count on my watch; I can't count on my car; I've *got* to count on something."

Everyone's about as zoned-out as me. So there's a spurt of talk now and then, but mostly pretty senseless mumblings. Some kids stretch out on the bleachers for extra z's.

Our school colors are orange and green. Our mascot's the tiger. What *menso*-heads thought these things up? Tigers don't exist in that color combination. Tigers don't exist in L.A.

ANYWAY, dressed like peas and carrots, our basketball class's waiting for Coach, *again*.

Unbelievable! Coach strolls into the gym—in a suit! With a tie! (Off to one side, like a skinny, wind-flopped flag.) He usually wears grey oversized sweats that make him look like a melting elephant. Today he's dressed sharp.

The reason's standing beside him. Seven-foot plus, with the build of a post, and bald as a light bulb. An NBA basketball player once so famous he made Santa Claus seem like a total unknown. He's been out of the game a while, but any true fan knows him. *¡Ay!* The day's shaping up!

What I notice most about this guy is his eyes. Like owls'. It seems there are deep things in them. Deep and mysterious.

What's he doing lost among the Tigers? He must have really veered off the road from Beverly Hills!

"Listen up, everybody," Coach says. As if he needs to grab our attention. We're all gaping like apes.

"You all know who this is, right?" His face looks completely satisfied. Like a cat who's swallowed an entire turkey. Man, do we know this guy.

He's here, says Coach, to hang out with us. Watch our moves. Instruct us. To be our *assistant coach*. Wow! At this news, it's amazing all the Tigers don't swoon to the floor. But we don't. We're too stupefied.

"One thing," Coach adds, "nobody breathes his name, understood? Our new assistant wants to remain anonymous—to keep cameras from snooping around."

Right now nobody can breathe anything. But somehow guys pipe up with "*Yo juro,*" (yoh HOO roh) "Scout's honor"—even though there are no scouts here—and "I swear on the grave of my hamster."

Then Coach Tree (my name for the wandering all-star) steps forward and says, "*Buenos días.*" (BWAY nohs DEE ahs) That snaps the spell. The Tigers can no longer control themselves. They totally swarm the guy. He hugs everyone and they hug him. And he laughs and laughs.

At home we're discussing this coach thing over supper. *Chiles rellenos* (CHEE lehs reh YEH nohs), which Mami and Abuelita prepared together. For this dish you need *poblano* (poh BLAH noh) chilies, the black-green glossy kind. Abuelita says you count the veins to pick the hottest ones. Some people prefer bland, but we want those strong enough to blow your head off. Once the skins are roasted and steamed off, you stuff the rest with meat or cheese and dunk them in flour. Then, with stiff coats of egg whites, they fry in oil, floating like hot islands. Last touch, a drizzle of tomato sauce.

To help out, I usually chop the onions, wearing ski goggles that Abuelita and I got at a yard sale. So my tears don't dilute the sauce. One thing I know, if on my own, *por lo menos* (pohr loh MEH nohs), I could always fix *chiles rellenos*.

Our whole family loves basketball. Even Abuelita. Probably even our cat, who sits in Abue's skimpy lap to watch all games. Especially we love the Lakers. We know the names of all the players, their numbers, their stats. We are wild for their announcers, Chick and Stu, and given the chance, we would vote Chick in for president.

My brother's both excited and skeptical about Coach Tree, the barrio interloper. Luis is three years older than me. Maybe that's why he's untrusting.

"His motive must be money," Luis says, studying his mangled fork, a garbage-disposal victim. But his eyes say no way can that be. The school district's wish list has a focus on *books*, not on NBA coaches.

"Yeah," I say, "like we've got a gushing oil well at school to turn into dollars at will."

Luis burns me a look, so I say, "So cut my heart out and fry it for dinner."

Everyone, including him, laughs at this Aztec humor.

Papi finishes his stuffed chili pepper. "*Ay, qué delicia.*" (KEH deh LEE syah) He almost sings about how delicious it is. Instead, he exclaims, "You are such a good cook, *mi vida* (mee VEE *th*ah)! It's that *mole* (MOH leh) runs in your veins."

All happy, Mami laughs and goes a little red. Then she grows serious and says, "I believe this basketball man has all he will ever need. I believe he is doing this coaching for love only."

That sends Luis' eyes spinning in his skull. I can nearly hear his brain grinding: *Love! Man, don't you know? The world goes on* verde (VEHR deh)—*the green of dollars.* But he says nothing disrespectful. Neither do I. I plan to just dribble my brains loose while this guy's here. To gain every possible tip. Maybe, with buckets of sweat, I'll become *excelente* (ehk seh LEHN teh) at this game.

ANALYZE THE TEXT

Hyperbole In paragraph four, Papi praises Mami's cooking by saying that she has *mole* in her veins. What is the meaning of this phrase? Find another example of hyperbole on this page and explain what it means.

Coach Tree arrives every morning just about before anyone. He slips into the parking lot in some anonymous car and slowly unfolds himself out. Like a giant and rusted pocketknife. I say he's there *before* most everyone. Actually, at first just about the whole school's waiting for a glimpse of him.

He takes that easily. Just strides along, talking to crowding kids and smiling. Like he's found himself a good home. From a distance, where I'm watching, this reception looks like a tall, calm ship riding a choppy sea.

The new basketball program affects everyone. Not just the big kids. From kinder on up, anyone can play. (Our school is so old, kinder to eighth, all grades are there.)

And they do play—if the ball doesn't bog them down. And even if it does. They just keep trying and trying. That's Coach Tree's real aim.

Though everyone gets a shot at basketball, against other schools it's the older kids who suit up. I'm not world-class, but somehow I make the team. For Coach Tree, the Tigers work like crazy. We don't have much height. But speed, we've got *muchísimo* (moo CHEE sih moh). And we're okay shooters, too.

To say Coach Tree helps us a lot is the understatement of the millennium. No whistles. No yells. No heaving of chairs. From steady practice and from his calm voice, the fundamentals sink in.

Once, between classes, he stops me in the hall. My nerves get tangled as a fistful of paper clips.

"You're working hard, Arturo," he says, quiet as ever. "Doing good."

¡Ay! Like a warm look from a girl (rare for me), I can live on these words forever.

Before long we're actually winning some games. That's partly due to one guy. José. A natural, you could say. He can steam past all defenders. Fake one way, stutter-step, elevate, shoot, and *swish*! All day, all night, if he has to. Like breathing. José, he can flat *play*.

José's a smooth player, but a real troublemaker. His family's a mess, so he bears a chip on his shoulder the size of a sequoia stump. He's been kicked out of school more times than there are numbers. He'd as soon spit on you as talk. Has *pleitos* (PLAY tohs), fights, for fun. José's a strong reason why we win. Still, for survival, after practice, wherever he is, our team pretty much vacates the area.

There's a sign on my door: NO SE ACEPTAN CHISMES (noh seh ah SEP tahn CHEES mehs). But, actually, in my room I allow carloads of gossip. *Chismes* bloom at school, too. Soon everyone knows that Coach Tree's losing things. A pen. A handkerchief. A key chain. Once even a tennis shoe! Next thing I hear, the culprit's José. Word is, he's vending Coach Tree-abilia to guys. Wow! Stealing from Coach Tree's like stealing from God. My opinion? José's the undisputed king of the *menso*-heads.

If it's true, we all expect that this is the last of him. He ought to depart the team fast. But, after all, it must be a story invented for excitement, because José keeps playing. Weird thing, though. *Mucho muy* (MOO choh MWEE) strange. Sometimes he asks to shoot hoops with us. Sometimes he says hello.

One night Alicia comes over. To do homework. And snack on Mexican cooking. Crunchy *chicharrón* (chee cha ROHN), with lime juice squeezed on. We gouge it into guacamole, while we're sort of studying.

ANALYZE THE TEXT

Author's Word Choice Why do you think the author includes Spanish words? How do they impact the meaning of the story?

"Sort of" because immediately concentration slips away. The air feels crackly as the pork rinds. Like Alicia's got something to say.

I mark my book with a tomato, the only thing around.

From nowhere she plunges in. "Coach Tree caught José stealing his stuff."

"Yeah?" I say, low-key, to see where this's going.

"Yeah. And he's letting it slide."

"¡*Mentirosa!*" (mehn tee ROH sah) She's gotta be lying. Amazement must fill my face like the look of a stuffed deer.

"Well, not exactly letting it slide," she says. "Coach Tree sees promise in José. He's spending free time with him. Making him practice ball. Making him study. Coach Tree says he won't *let* him toss his life into the Dumpster."

So Coach Tree works with José, one-on-one. I let that sink in. "Think it'll work?" I ask.

"Yeah, I do."

"Why?"

"Because for the first time in forever, José trusts someone."

After Alicia goes, I'm in my room thinking. About Coach Tree and José. Coach doesn't have to do this. He's lost by choice in our nothing barrio, helping a kid with not many chances.

Even though he's a hardcase, I have hope if Alicia does. And she ought to know. José's her brother.

My grandmother takes a decision. "I prepare *chiles rellenos* for this Coach man."

That said, there's no stopping her. I'm ordered to tell him (*tell* the ex-NBA champ!) that the peppers will arrive today after school—along with my whole family. And they do. In a see-through tub. (Not my family, the chilies.)

ANALYZE THE TEXT

Theme Coach Tree coaches José even though he knows José stole from him. What does this event say about the theme of this story?

Coach Tree's waiting in the lunch court with a mob of curious kids when Abuelita gets there. Like a little broom, she sweeps right up and says, "I am happy to meet. You play basket real good. *Chiles muy excelentes.* Eat."

"Yes, ma'am."

He samples a *chile relleno* with Abuelita cheerfully breathing down his neck and prodding, "¿*Excelente?* ¿*Excelente?*"

Suddenly, Coach Tree's like some cartoon character, steam puffing from his ears, strangling out words in speech balloons: "Agh! Agh!" I say, "Agh!" too, casting an arrowy stare at Abuelita. She's brought the hottest chilies in the universe! Man. My basketball days are over. Probably my life's over.

"CPR!" some kid shouts. What a *menso*-head! There's no CPR for peppers.

Abuelita turns away, totally mortified. I take that back. She's giggling.

We all hold our breath. Then—"*Graa-ci-us, Sonora. Ex-ell-en-tees,*" Coach Tree gasps.

Everyone loses it, *muriendo de la risa* (moo RYEN doh deh lah REE sah). Then Coach Tree wipes tears from his face and bows and shakes Abuelita's hand. He shakes hands with everybody in my family. He laughs and laughs. And over the haze of the hot blacktop, carrying the leftover chili peppers, he walks to his car. Slowly, a tall ship of (smoking) calm.

Luis's right. I find out from Alicia, Coach Tree *is* coaching for money. His relative's a teacher here, so he said he'd help out our school—for the salary-shattering price of one dollar.

I know my limits. In pickup games I hold my own, but I'm not NBA-bound. Still, maybe I could do something like Coach Tree. Something for love. Something that's mine. Though right now, I've got zero idea what. To use one of Papi's favorite words, Coach Tree's a person to emulate.

Dig Deeper

How to Analyze the Text

Use these pages to learn about Theme, Hyperbole, and Author's Word Choice. Then read "Any Small Goodness" again to apply what you learned.

Theme

Tony Johnston, the author of "Any Small Goodness," shares an important message about life through her writing. This message is called the **theme,** or **central idea.**

The author of a fiction story usually does not state the theme directly. Readers must connect story details, or text evidence, to infer a central idea about life or about human nature.

Look back at page 412. In the last section of text, Arturo tells the ways that Coach Tree helps Arturo's basketball team. What do these details say about Coach Tree? Does he set a good example for the team to follow? How does this scene contribute to the development of the theme?

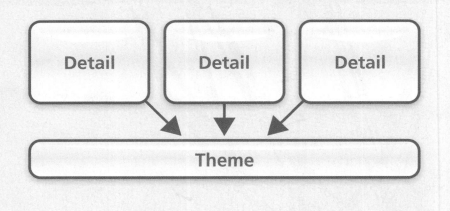

COMMON CORE   **RL.6.2** determine a theme or central idea of a text/provide a summary; **RL.6.4** determine the meaning of words and phrases, including figurative and connotative meanings/analyze impact of word choice; **RL.6.5** analyze how a sentence, chapter, scene or stanza fits in the overall structure; **L.6.5a** interpret figures of speech in context

Hyperbole

Hyperbole is a figure of speech that uses extreme exaggeration. An example of hyperbole is an expression such as "I'm so tired I could sleep for a year." This figure of speech expresses how very tired a person is. Authors use hyperbole to add humor or to make a strong impression on readers. As you read, look for examples of hyperbole. What text clues help you understand its meaning?

Author's Word Choice

In a fiction story, the narrator's tone can reveal his or her attitude toward what is happening in the story. "Any Small Goodness" is about the ways that Coach Tree changes Arturo's neighborhood school. The **author's word choice** includes words and phrases that tell how the characters are feeling and help readers get to know them. As you read the story, think about how the author's word choice helps reveal things about each character.

Your Turn

RETURN TO THE ESSENTIAL QUESTION

 Turn and Talk Review the selection with a partner to prepare to discuss this question: *What can people do to help their communities?* As you review the selection's key ideas, take turns asking and answering questions about the text. Use text evidence to support your ideas.

Classroom Conversation

Continue your discussion of "Any Small Goodness" by using text evidence to explain your answers to these questions:

1. In what ways does Coach Tree make the community better?

2. Why do you think Coach Tree wants to remain anonymous?

3. How does the new basketball program affect the school?

WHAT DOES IT MEAN?

Determine Figurative Meanings Think about the effects that figurative language can have on a story. Look back at the simile "like a giant and rusted pocketknife" on page 412 and the metaphor "a tall ship of (smoking) calm" on page 416. Then write a sentence explaining the meaning of each figure of speech as it relates to the text. Then make up two similes or metaphors and write the literal meaning next to each one.

WRITE ABOUT READING

Response Do you agree or disagree with Coach Tree's decision to continue coaching José after he is caught stealing? What evidence from the text influences the way you think about this event? Write a paragraph to explain why you agree or disagree with Coach Tree. Use evidence from the text to support your claim.

Writing Tip

State your claim in the first sentence of your paragraph. Check for the proper use of subject, object, and possessive pronouns in your sentences.

COMMON CORE **RL.6.1** cite textual evidence to support analysis of what the text says explicitly as well as inferences drawn; **RL.6.4** determine the meaning of words and phrases, including figurative and connotative meanings/analyze impact of word choice; **W.6.1a** introduce claim(s) and organize reasons and evidence clearly; **W.6.9a** apply grade 6 Reading standards to literature; **SL.6.1c** pose and respond to questions and make comments that contribute to the discussion; **L.6.1a** ensure that pronouns are in the proper case; **L.6.5a** interpret figures of speech in context

LITERARY NONFICTION

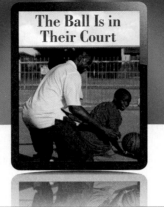

The Ball Is in Their Court

☑ GENRE

Literary nonfiction, such as this newspaper article, gives factual information by telling a true story.

☑ TEXT FOCUS

Primary Sources Nonfiction may include a primary source, an original document such as a quote or photo, to give more information about the topic.

RI.6.10 read and comprehend literary nonfiction

TODAY'S

MONDAY, SEPTEMBER 16

The Ball Is in Their Court

by Jeff Morse

What would you do if you became rich and famous? Would you choose to keep your wealth to yourself, or would you use your resources to help others?

Many players from the National Basketball Association (NBA) have chosen the second path. They give time and money to community outreach programs like Es Tu Cancha (It's Your Court) that help young people. A skeptical observer might wonder if athletes just want to polish their image. In fact, most have found that doing good means feeling good. Their motive is to give back to the communities they play for.

A young athlete almost veers around the Lakers' Andrew Bynum.

The Lakers hold court at the Nueva Maravilla Housing Development.

The NBA founded *Es Tu Cancha* (It's Your Court) in 2004. The program's aim is to build or renovate basketball courts in Latino communities across the country.

How do basketball courts help kids? If you're a young hoops fanatic, it helps to have a place to emulate your favorite stars. But playing sports is also a great way for kids to get in shape. Los Angeles Lakers' player Andrew Bynum says that *Es Tu Cancha* is "an initiative we hope will encourage kids to get up and get moving in a local environment that is both safe and fun."

So far, *Es Tu Cancha* has opened more than a dozen courts in cities across the nation. On September 26, 2006, the Lakers helped open a new court in the Nueva Maravilla Housing Development in Los Angeles.

Perhaps the best part of the event was when Bynum and coach Craig Hodges hosted a passing and shooting clinic for local kids.

COMMUNITY

To say that the kids are excited at these court-opening ceremonies is an understatement. But athletes also say that being part of Es Tu Cancha helps to keep their lives from becoming bland. Rather than be anonymous donors, many stars are proud to show up at the neighborhood courts.

"It is an honor for us to contribute to such a great cause," says former Women's NBA (WNBA) player Sheila Lambert.

Former New York Knicks' guard John Starks agrees. "It's a great feeling to be a part of something that's so positive," he says.

A ribbon-cutting ceremony at the opening reception for a new basketball court in Mexico

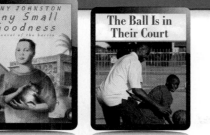

Compare Texts

TEXT TO TEXT

Compare Basketball Texts Talk with a partner about "Any Small Goodness" and "The Ball Is in Their Court." Then use these questions to compare and contrast the texts: *How does Coach Tree give back to the community? How do the professional NBA players give back to their communities?* Use text evidence to support your answers.

TEXT TO SELF

Make an Activity List Coach Tree in "Any Small Goodness" and the NBA players in "The Ball Is in Their Court" give back to their communities. How can you give back to your community? Make a list of volunteer activities you already do or would like to do. Choose one and tell why the activity is a good match for your talents or strengths.

TEXT TO WORLD

Write About Culture and Community Use text evidence to write a short summary of what you have learned about Arturo's family life, neighborhood, and culture. Include a list of Spanish words and phrases and give their definitions.

¡Es tu cancha!

COMMON CORE **RL.6.1** cite textual evidence to support analysis of what the text says explicitly as well as inferences drawn; **RL.6.2** determine a theme or central idea of a text/provide a summary; **RL.6.9** compare and contrast texts in different forms or genres on their approaches to themes and topics; **RI.6.1** cite textual evidence to support analysis of what the text says explicitly as well as inferences drawn; **W.6.10** write routinely over extended time frames and shorter time frames

Grammar

What Is the Active Voice? What Is the Passive Voice? A verb in the **active voice** puts the focus on the subject, the doer of the action. A verb in the **passive voice** tells what was done to, or what happened to, the subject. The doer of the action becomes not as important as the receiver of the action. Passive voice combines a form of the verb *be* and a simple past-tense verb.

Verbs in the Active and Passive Voice	
active-voice verb The players notice a tall visitor. doers of the action	passive-voice verb A tall visitor is noticed by the players. receiver of the action

A passive-voice verb, like an active-voice verb, must agree with the subject. If the subject is a personal pronoun, a special verb form may be required.

plural   plural form of
subject   helping verb
Decisions are made by the coach.

singular subject: helping verb: special
personal pronoun   form used with *you*
You were elected captain by your teammates.

Try This! **With a partner, read aloud each sentence below. Identify each verb, and say whether it is in the active or passive voice. Then explain how the subject and verb agree.**

1 You are applauded by the fans often.

2 Spectators appreciate your skill and hustle.

3 I am feared by our opponents.

4 They are intimidated by my strength.

The use of an incorrect verb form can confuse your readers. When a personal pronoun is the subject of a sentence, be sure to use the correct verb form with it.

Correct Subject-Verb Agreement with Personal Pronouns

Active-Voice Verbs

A local sportswriter mentions you in this week's sports section. She praises you for your footwork.

Passive-Voice Verbs

I am included in the article, too. We are called a "dynamic duo."

Connect Grammar to Writing

As you revise your informational essay next week, remember to use the correct verb form when the subject of a sentence is a personal pronoun.

W.6.4 produce writing in which development, organization, and style are appropriate to task, purpose, and audience; **W.6.5** develop and strengthen writing by planning, revising, editing, rewriting, or trying a new approach

COMMON CORE

Informative Writing

Reading-Writing Workshop: Prewrite

my **WriteSmart**

Go Digital

✓ **Ideas**   The purpose of an **informational essay** is to inform readers about a topic. An informational essay includes an introduction, body, and conclusion. The introduction contains a focus statement that gives the main idea for the essay. Each paragraph in the body should support this main idea. Use transition words to connect ideas. Be sure to use precise, or specific, words and phrases throughout your writing.

Corey wanted to tell his audience, his classmates, how to get involved in community-service projects. After he chose his topic, he used an idea-support map to organize his ideas into paragraphs.

Writing Process Checklist

▶ **Prewrite**

✓ **Did I include a focus statement, or main idea?**

✓ **Did I include facts, examples, and other informative details to support the main idea?**

✓ **Did I organize ideas in a logical way?**

Draft

Revise

Edit

Publish and Share

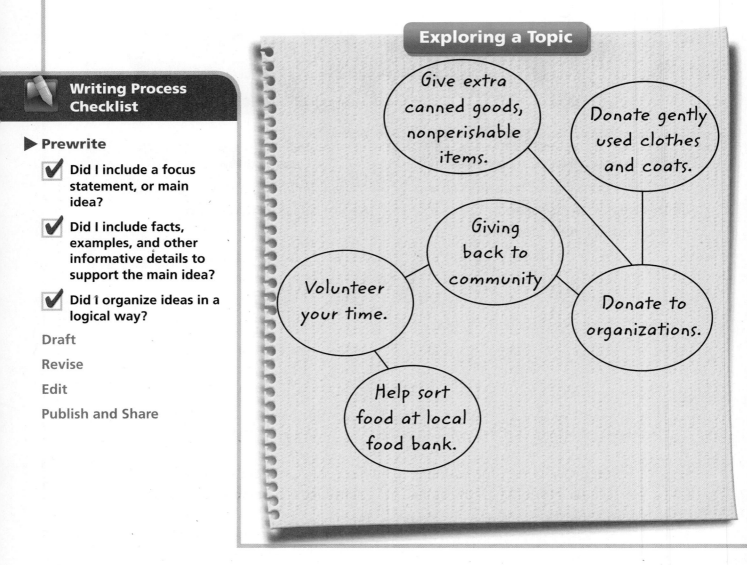

Exploring a Topic

Give extra canned goods, nonperishable items.

Donate gently used clothes and coats.

Giving back to community

Volunteer your time.

Donate to organizations.

Help sort food at local food bank.

Topic: Giving back to your community is important, and it feels good. You can give back to your community in different ways.

> Volunteer your time to help others.

↓

> Help sort and organize food at your local food bank.

↓

> Care for the plants in a nearby community vegetable garden.

↓

> Volunteer to be a tutor at your school or an elementary school.

> Donate to organizations.

↓

> Buy and give extra canned goods and other nonperishable items to your local food bank.

↓

> Donate gently used clothes and winter coats to charity organizations.

Reading as a Writer

How does Corey's idea-support map help him develop his paragraphs? What can you do to organize your ideas into paragraphs?

When I planned my informational essay, I thought about what I wanted the reader to learn. I chose details that would develop my main idea.

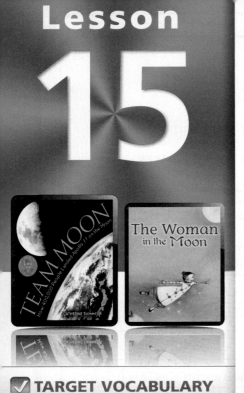

Vocabulary in Context

Vocabulary Reader

Context Cards

430

1 ascent

A rocket's ascent stage, or climb into space, begins with a powerful, fiery liftoff.

2 perilous

Movies and comic books often portray outer space as perilous, or full of danger.

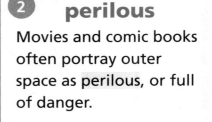

3 unpredictability

Even though astronauts are well prepared, there is always unpredictability about a mission. No one knows what will happen.

4 lunar

Astronauts have brought back moon rocks that they gathered from the lunar surface.

▶ Study each Context Card.

▶ Tell a story about two or more pictures, using Vocabulary words of your choice.

5 likelihood

After animals successfully traveled in space, there was a strong likelihood, or probability, that people would be next.

6 hovering

This lunar module seems to be hovering over the surface of the moon. It looks as though it is hanging in space.

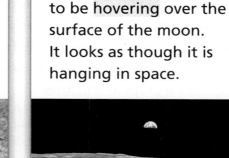

7 impending

Impending bad weather may threaten to delay the launch of a space shuttle flight.

8 presumably

Presumably, people knew the moon was not made of green cheese before *Apollo 11* landed there. That is a safe guess.

9 option

In the future, space travelers may have the option of a window or an aisle seat. Which would you choose?

10 random

Because of dust in the atmosphere, stars twinkle in a random order, not following a pattern.

Read and Comprehend

Go Digital

☑ TARGET SKILL

Text and Graphic Features When authors use **text features** and **graphic features,** they give readers added information about a topic. As you read "Team Moon," look for text features such as headings, captions, and special type. Also notice graphic features such as photographs. Note how the text and graphic features work together to help you learn more about the moon landing. Use a graphic organizer like this one to help you.

Text	Text Feature or Graphic Feature	How They Work Together

☑ TARGET STRATEGY

Analyze/Evaluate As you read "Team Moon," **analyze** and **evaluate** text evidence and graphic features in the selection to decide how well each fills its role. Analyzing and evaluating give you a critic's-eye view of what you are reading.

COMMON CORE

RI.6.1 cite textual evidence to support analysis of what the text says explicitly as well as inferences drawn; **RI.6.7** integrate information presented in different media or formats as well as in words

Moon Exploration

People have always been fascinated by the moon. Seeing the moon in the night sky, they have long wondered what it would be like to go there. They have asked many questions about that mysterious place, but they have received very few answers.

Finally, in 1969, American astronauts set out to be the first people to walk on the moon. In "Team Moon," you'll learn about the risks those astronauts faced in order to accomplish this dangerous and historic mission.

Lesson 15

ANCHOR TEXT

✓ TARGET SKILL

Text and Graphic Features
Examine how the arrangement of text and visuals makes ideas clearer.

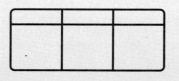

✓ GENRE

Literary nonfiction gives information by telling a true story. As you read, look for:

▶ factual information
▶ a story that involves real people or events
▶ events in time order

 RI.6.4 determine the meaning of words and phrases, including figurative, connotative, and technical meanings; **RI.6.7** integrate information presented in different media or formats as well as in words; **RI.6.10** read and comprehend literary nonfiction; **L.6.3b** maintain consistency in style and tone; **L.6.6** acquire and use general academic and domain-specific words and phrases/gather vocabulary knowledge for comprehension or expression

MEET THE AUTHOR

CATHERINE THIMMESH

Catherine Thimmesh, who lives in Minneapolis, Minnesota, is categorically a big fan of space exploration and its related technological accoutrements but, more importantly, she is interested in the thousands of contributors behind the scenes who make such daunting and mesmerizing feats possible—everyone from the hundreds of seamstresses to the thousands of lunar module engineers. While researching the Sibert Medal-winning *Team Moon*, Thimmesh regretted having been born too late to witness the dramatic Apollo missions in person as well as the space boon and euphoria for space exploration that followed immediately afterward. However, Thimmesh is dedicated to saving enough money herself to travel up into the firmament as a space tourist, which is estimated to cost $98,000 or more. Thimmesh's other books include *Madam President: The Extraordinary, True (and Evolving) Story of Women in Politics* and *Girls Think of Everything: Stories of Ingenious Inventions by Women*. Some of the many other accolades and awards Thimmesh has accrued include the IRA Children's Book Award, the Children's Book of the Month Club Best Nonfiction Book Award, Outstanding Science Trade Book for Children, and a Smithsonian Notable Book Award. It will be interesting in the future to witness the results of Thimmesh's own astral explorations and how her observations affect her writing for young adults.

TEAM MOON

How 400,000 People Landed *Apollo 11* on the Moon

BY CATHERINE THIMMESH

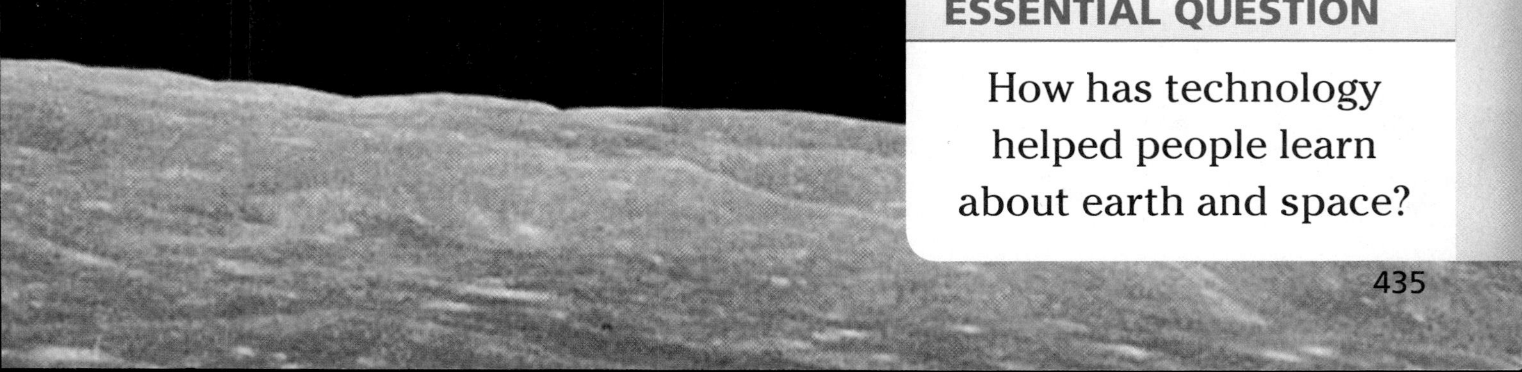

ESSENTIAL QUESTION

How has technology helped people learn about earth and space?

The year is 1969. After years of preparation, **Apollo 11** *is minutes away from being the first space expedition to land a man on the moon. With only 3,000 feet to go, a software alarm from* **Eagle** *, the* lunar *module* **(LM), puts astronauts Neil Armstrong and Buzz Aldrin and Mission Control on high alert.**

Their voices were rapid-fire. Crisp. Assured. There was no hesitation. But you could practically hear the adrenaline rushing in their vocal tones, practically hear the thumping of their hearts as the alarms continued to pop up.

Then the *Eagle* was down to 2,000 feet. Another alarm! 1202. Mission Control snapped, "Roger, no sweat." And again, a 1202! Then the *Eagle* was down to 700 feet, then 500. Now, they were hovering— helicopter-like—presumably scouting a landing spot.

In hundreds of practice simulations, they would have landed by now. But Mission Control couldn't see the perilous crater and boulder field confronting Neil and Buzz. Those things, coupled with the distraction of the alarms, had slowed them down.

More than eleven minutes had passed since they started down to the moon. There was only twelve minutes' worth of fuel in the descent stage.

Telescopic views showing the area of the *Apollo 11* landing site: *Tranquility Base*

ANALYZE THE TEXT

Text and Graphic Features How does the close-up photo of the moon on this page contribute to your understanding of the moon expedition?

An interior view of the LM cockpit, showing the 16 mm film camera out Buzz's window

Almost Empty

"Sixty seconds!"

Not sixty-one. No wiggle room. No "just a couple more seconds—we're almost there." And no second chances. They had just sixty seconds to land on the moon.

Absolutely no one expected it to happen. They painstakingly planned so it absolutely wouldn't-couldn't happen. But here they were, less than 500 feet from the moon, and just about plumb out of fuel.

Robert Carlton, the CONTROL position in Mission Control, who was in charge of monitoring fuel consumption among other things, had just sent the shocking sixty-second notice through the voice chain up to the astronauts. Both Neil and Buzz knew when they heard the words "sixty seconds," that was how much time remained until they *had* to abort. Until they *had* to push the button, fling themselves away from the moon, never to land. Or else, they could possibly die.

"We wanted to give him [Neil] every chance to land," explained Robert Carlton. "So we wanted it [the LM] to be as near empty as it could possibly get, but on the other hand, we didn't want him to run out of gas ten feet from the surface. That would have been a bad thing to do, you know. So you had to hit both. You wanted to make the mission, but you didn't want to jeopardize your crew, and you wanted to play it just as tight as you could safely."

The heavier the spacecraft, the harder it is to launch. And fuel is heavy. So it was critical to pinpoint the fuel needed, add a cushion, then take no more than necessary. But now, because the landing was taking far longer than planned, the fuel was almost gone. Mission Control wanted Neil to take as much time as he needed and fly the LM as near empty as possible *only* because they wanted him to make the landing. But if he ran out of fuel above the surface, in all likelihood, the LM would crash onto the moon. So they were trying to time it to the last possible second before calling an abort—calling off the landing.

If they aborted, if they flung themselves away from the moon (never to land), they would be slung into lunar orbit, where they would meet up with Mike Collins in the command module and head home to Earth. If they landed, though, leaving the moon wouldn't be a problem because there was a full tank of fuel in the ascent stage for liftoff (an abort also used the ascent stage). But the ascent and descent stages were completely separate. When the supply for the descent stage was empty, that was it. Sharing fuel was not an option.

In every simulation, the LM had been landed well before the low-level sensor was tripped, indicating 120 seconds of fuel left. Bob Nance, backroom support for CONTROL, was calculating the seconds of fuel remaining on his paper strip chart. (Flight Director Gene Kranz would write in his memoir, "I never dreamed we would still be flying this close to empty and depending on Nance's eyeballs.") Bob Carlton backed up the backup with a stopwatch.

Thirty seconds!

Now would not be the time for the two Bobs to miscalculate, miscount, or lose their superhuman powers of concentration. They could not afford to be wrong.

"When we tripped low level, things really got quiet in that control center," recalled Bob Carlton. "We were nervous, sweating. Came to sixty seconds, came to thirty seconds, and my eyes were just glued on the stopwatch. I didn't see [the control center as a whole]. The system could have [fallen] apart at that instant, and I wouldn't have [known] it. I was just watching the stopwatch."

Eighteen seconds!

Click.

ANALYZE THE TEXT

Domain-Specific Vocabulary The author uses several technical words. Why do you think she has chosen to do that? How can you determine their meanings?

"People [were] concerned about the amount of fuel you had left, the master alarms. . . . I don't believe anybody in the room breathed for the last five minutes. We were just hanging on every word. And trying to force the vehicle down by sheer willpower. Get down! Get down! *Neil, get down. Turn off that engine.*"

— *Charlie Mars, chief lunar module project engineer; listening in on a headset in one of the backrooms at the Mission Control complex*

"*Forty feet, down two and a half, picking up some dust...*"
— *Apollo 11 astronaut Buzz Aldrin, from the LM*

You know it's real when you walk in [to the Mission Contr. of building]. Then you sit down and start doing what you've done a hundred times and it becomes surreal—you don't know or care if it's real, you're just doing your thing. And then all of a sudden it doesn't go quite the same. Somebody calls out something that brings you . . . wakes you up—and says . . . 'It is real!' And that was what happened when he said 'We've got some dust.' We'd never heard that before."

— AGC Jack Garman, in Mission Control

"Houston, Tranquility Base here. The Eagle has landed."
—Apollo 11 *commander Neil Armstrong, from the LM*

"Roger, Tranquility. We copy you on the ground. You got a bunch of guys about to turn blue. We're breathing again. Thanks a lot." ("I was so excited," Duke later said. "I couldn't get out Tranquility Base. It came out sort of like Twangquility.")
—CapCom (and astronaut) Charlie Duke, in Mission Control

Frozen Slug

After eight challenging years and countless hours, man was finally on the moon. Flight Director Gene Kranz would soon "go around the horn" for the very first Stay/No Stay decision.

"You know, they landed, and everybody's cheering and everything and then all of a sudden somebody notices that something's gone wrong. Temperature's building up. Uh-oh! It shouldn't be like that," explained Grumman engineering manager John Coursen.

Up, up, up went the temperature in a fuel line on the descent engine. Up, up, up went the pressure. Rocket science rule number one? Do *not* allow the fuel to become unstable. Instability equals unpredictability—and unpredictability is just another word for random explosions and all sorts of unwanted chaos.

Engineers John Coursen, Manning Dandridge, and a whole lot of others sprang into action. Back at the Grumman plant in Bethpage, New York (where Coursen was stationed), there was a frenetic burst of engineering pandemonium:

from table to table, rushing;

blueprints and schematics, unfurling;

telephones, dialing;

telephones, ringing . . .

Do you remember that one test? What about when such and such happened? Remember when so-and-so talked about . . . Any ideas? . . .

At 300 degrees, the fuel was quickly approaching its 400-degree instability rating. Engineers at Grumman, and their counterparts at NASA in Houston (like Grumman manager Tom Kelly), simultaneously deduced the likely culprit: a slug. A solid slug of frozen fuel had trapped a small amount of the descent fuel in the line. This caused the temperature and pressure in the line to rise rapidly—and dangerously.

"First thing we did was get the drawings out so you could see," recalled John Coursen. "All kinds of functional diagrams, say of the heat exchanger; the line that runs from there to the valve of the tank. . . . You want to get all of the data before you that you can; and that's the purpose for having a good call room back at the plant—because there's more data there that the people didn't take with them [to Houston]."

Up went the pressure; the temperature—now 350 degrees. Terrified of an impending explosion (even a small blast could damage vital engines or components), Coursen and the Grumman engineers argued their options. They could (1) abort now and leave the problem on the moon. (The slug was isolated in the descent stage—and liftoff relied on the separate ascent stage. The descent stage—no longer necessary—would be left behind.) Or they could (2) try to "burp" the engine—give the valve a quick open-close to release the built-up pressure.

The trouble with option 2 was that venting might push the fuel to an unstable condition. Or, another possible outcome of the "burping": what if the landing gear hadn't deployed correctly? Could any movement, or any resulting burst—no matter how small—tip the LM over? Many a voice in the debate thought the safest option was to abort—now! But that opinion was quickly overruled by the Grumman and NASA leadership (who were confident of the landing gear), and the consensus of the leaders was that it would be safe to gently, *gently* burp the engine.

ANALYZE THE TEXT

Style and Tone How does the author's word choice maintain a consistent tone of suspense on pages 442–443?

"I'm going to step off the LM now."
—Neil Armstrong, from the moon

"That's one small step for man,
one giant leap for mankind."
—Neil Armstrong, first man on
the moon

444

Suddenly, though, just as the procedure was about to be relayed to the astronauts, the pressure . . . the temperature . . . dropped! And . . . stayed down. The frozen slug, apparently, had melted! (Probably due to the extreme heat in the fuel line.) Problem solved. And only now—a solid, panic-stricken, gut-wrenching, heart-palpitating ten minutes by clock but feeling like an eternity later—did it sink in for John Coursen, Tom Kelly, and a lot of the other Grumman folks who had poured years of their lives into building the lunar module: Their baby was on the moon. Let the cheering begin!

Dig Deeper

How to Analyze the Text

Use these pages to learn about Text and Graphic Features, Domain-Specific Vocabulary, and Style and Tone. Then read "Team Moon" again to apply what you learned.

Text and Graphic Features

Nonfiction selections like "Team Moon" often contain both **text features** and **graphic features.** Authors use text features such as headings to organize information, captions to provide explanations, and boldfaced, capitalized, or italicized type to highlight important vocabulary or ideas. Authors use graphic features such as photographs, charts, graphs, diagrams, and maps to add to or explain what is in the text.

Look back at page 437 in "Team Moon." On this page, a heading identifies the problem to be explained in the text. The caption and photograph give details about the LM cockpit. What purpose does the use of italics serve in the fourth paragraph?

Text	Text Feature or Graphic Feature	How They Work Together

RI.6.4 determine the meaning of words and phrases, including figurative, connotative, and technical meanings; **RI.6.6** determine the author's point of view or purpose and explain how it is conveyed; **RI.6.7** integrate information presented in different media or formats as well as in words; **L.6.3b** maintain consistency in style and tone; **L.6.6** acquire and use general academic and domain-specific words and phrases/gather vocabulary knowledge for comprehension or expression

Domain-Specific Vocabulary

Authors of nonfiction text often use **domain-specific words.** These are words that relate to the selection's own field, or domain, of knowledge. Domain-specific words often come from science or social studies. Look back at page 443. The science vocabulary is specific to parts of the lunar module and how those parts should work. What clues does the author provide to help readers understand the meaning of these words?

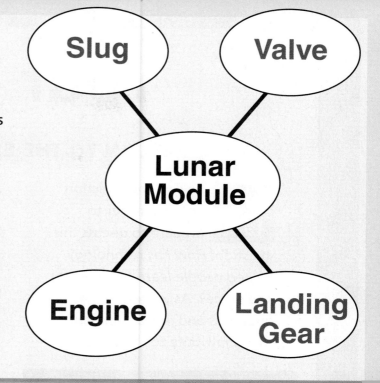

Style and Tone

When authors write about true events, they reveal their **point of view** by choosing words and phrases carefully. Their word choices along with writing **style** show the feelings they have toward their subjects. An author who wants to maintain a consistent **tone** of respect for a soldier might use words such as *brave, fearless, courageous, daring*, and *heroic* throughout a text. What other words can you think of that would maintain a tone of respect? Would you expect the author's style to be formal or informal?

Your Turn

 **my WriteSmart**

RETURN TO THE ESSENTIAL QUESTION

Turn and Talk Review the selection with a partner to prepare to discuss this question: *How has technology helped people learn about earth and space?* As you discuss, ask questions and make comments that contribute to the topic.

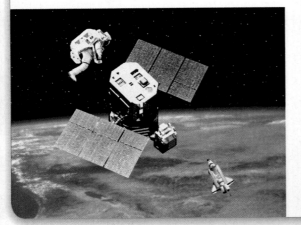

Classroom Conversation

Continue your discussion of "Team Moon" by explaining your answers to these questions using text evidence:

1. Since the author tells a true story, how did she likely get the information she needed to write about the event?

2. How do sixty seconds play an important role in this story?

3. What message does Catherine Thimmesh send through her choice of title and subtitle?

MEASURING UP

By the Numbers "Team Moon" includes several words that refer to units for measuring time, temperature, or distance. With a partner, scan the selection to find four "measurement" words. Create a word search, using each word twice. Then trade with another pair of students and complete their word search. After finishing, identify what each unit measures.

WRITE ABOUT READING

Response Do you think that the crew of *Apollo 11* should have accepted the risks of the lunar mission? Write a paragraph that gives your opinion. State your claim and make an argument to convince others. Include text evidence to support your reasons. End with a concluding statement.

Writing Tip

State your claim in the topic sentence of your paragraph. End with a concluding sentence that summarizes your argument. Then evaluate whether you have made a good argument.

COMMON CORE **RI.6.1** cite textual evidence to support analysis of what the text says explicitly as well as inferences drawn; **RI.6.4** determine the meaning of words and phrases, including figurative, connotative, and technical meanings; **W.6.1b** support claim(s) with reasons and evidence; **W.6.9b** apply grade 6 Reading standards to literary nonfiction; **SL.6.1a** come to discussions prepared/explicitly draw on preparation to probe and reflect on ideas under discussion; **SL.6.1c** pose and respond to questions and comments that contribute to the discussion

PLAY

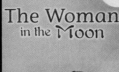

The Woman in the Moon

✓ **GENRE**

A **folktale** is a story that the people of a country tell to explain or to entertain. The story may be told in a dramatic, or **play,** form.

✓ **TEXT FOCUS**

Scenes Most plays are divided into scenes, separate episodes that reflect changes in the setting, characters, or plot.

COMMON CORE **RL.6.5** analyze how a sentence, chapter, scene or stanza fits in the overall structure; **RL.6.10** read and comprehend literature

The Woman in the Moon

retold by Cynthia Benjamin

Cast of Characters
Narrator
Chang E
Hou Yi
Emperor
Hare

SCENE 1

Narrator: The moon is a popular subject in folktales. In China, the tale of Chang E is a central part of the Moon Festival, or Mid-Autumn Festival, which takes place on the fifteenth day of the eighth lunar month. Here is one version of the tale.

According to legend, long ago ten suns circled Earth, threatening to destroy all living things with their perilous heat. A frightened emperor called Hou Yi to the palace.

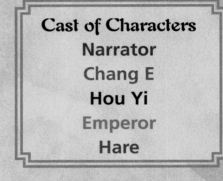

  Go Digital

Emperor: (*fanning himself*) Ooh, it is hot! These ten suns are hovering in the sky, cooking us alive. Hou Yi, you are a famous archer. Help us!

Hou Yi: I could try to shoot the suns down, Emperor.

Emperor: (*clapping his hands together*) Then do it and save us from impending doom!

Hou Yi: (*pointing to one of the suns*) May I leave one sun so we can still see what we're doing?

Emperor: Yes, good point.

(*Hou Yi points his bow and arrow to the sky and shoots down all but one of the suns. The Emperor smiles and hands Hou Yi a bottle.*)

Emperor: This potion will grant eternal life, but be careful. This bottle contains enough for two. Do not drink more than half.

SCENE 2

Narrator: Hou Yi rushed home and began to tell his wife, Chang E, about their good fortune. But before he could finish explaining, Chang E grabbed the bottle and drank it all.

Chang E: (*alarmed*) What's happening? Hou Yi, help me!

Hou Yi: You weren't supposed to drink the entire bottle!

Narrator: Chang E flew out the door and began an ascent to the heavens, never to return. Her journey took her to the moon, where her only companion was a hare.

Hare: I wasn't expecting company.

Chang E: I wasn't expecting to end up on the moon.

Hare: (*laughing softly*) Ah, the unpredictability of life!

Narrator: Back on Earth, Hou Yi gazed up at the full moon.

Hou Yi: What are those shadowy shapes on the lunar surface? One of them looks like Chang E, and the other looks a lot like a hare!

Narrator: For generations, the tale of Chang E has explained why there is only one sun and why people see shapes on the lunar surface.

Emperor: Presumably, they are not just random patterns.

Narrator: Meanwhile, it is said that once a year, on the fifteenth day of the eighth lunar month, Hou Yi is able to fly to the moon and visit his wife.

Hou Yi: I'm coming, Chang E!

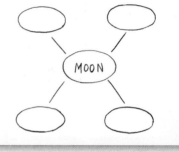

Compare Texts

Compare Presentations Write *moon* at the center of a word web. Complete the web with a partner by brainstorming a list of books, movies, stories, articles, myths, computer and video games, songs, and other works you know that focus on the moon. Compare and contrast how they present the moon in different ways.

MOON

Write Interview Questions Make a list of interview questions for someone who would remember watching or reading about the moon landing in 1969. Make sure your questions ask about the details of the moon landing. Share your interview questions with the class.

Discuss Space Travel Imagine that in the future, it becomes common for ordinary people to travel to the moon. Think of the positive and negative effects this travel might have on both our planet and the moon. Share your thoughts with a small group.

 Go Digital

COMMON CORE **RI.6.9** compare and contrast texts in different forms or genres on their approaches to themes and topic; **W.6.10** write routinely over extended time frames and shorter time frames

Grammar

What Are Regular and Irregular Verbs? A **regular verb** adds *-ed* to its present form to show action that happened in the past. A regular verb also adds *-ed* when it is used with the helping verb *has, have,* or *had.* An **irregular verb** does not add *-ed* in these situations. It changes in other ways. You must memorize the spellings of irregular verbs.

Regular and Irregular Verbs Showing Past Action	
regular verbs	The lunar module *approached* the moon. A difficult situation *had developed*. The astronauts *had* not *identified* a landing site.
irregular verbs	The lunar module *had* little fuel in its tank. An engineer *had sent* the "sixty seconds" message. The astronauts still *had* not *found* a suitable landing spot.

Try This! With a partner, read aloud each sentence below. Find the verb or main verb in each sentence. Say whether it is regular or irregular.

1. The astronauts chose a landing site just in time.

2. Soon they had become the first humans on the moon!

3. A few minutes later, another problem arose.

4. The temperature in a fuel line increased steadily.

When you write, use vivid verbs and consistent tenses to communicate action precisely. Vivid verbs help make your writing more lively, and consistent tenses eliminate confusion for your audience.

Vague Verbs, Confusing Tenses	Vivid Verbs, Consistent Tenses

The lunar module is over the surface of the moon. While the fuel level was falling, Neil and Buzz will make a difficult landing.

The lunar module hovered over the surface of the moon. While the fuel level plunged, Neil and Buzz tackled a difficult landing.

Connect Grammar to Writing

As you revise your informational essay, look for vague verbs that you can replace with vivid verbs. Use these verbs, in the correct tense, to create clear and lively pictures in your writing.

Informative Writing

Reading-Writing Workshop: Revise

✔ **Voice** In an **informational essay,** writers help readers better understand a topic. They develop a main idea with facts, examples, and other informative details. When you draft your essay, organize the information in paragraphs, and use transition words to link them. End with a concluding paragraph. To give your essay a voice, show your personal interest in the topic, but maintain a formal writing style. As you revise, check your use of precise language and domain-specific vocabulary.

Corey wrote a first draft of an informational essay about giving back to the community. Then he revised his draft. He added details to make the essay more informative.

Writing Process Checklist

Prewrite

Draft

▶ **Revise**

✔ **Did I state my main idea clearly?**

✔ **Did I develop my topic with facts, examples, and other informative details?**

✔ **Did I use precise language and link paragraphs with transitions?**

✔ **Did I show my personal interest?**

✔ **Did I maintain a formal writing style?**

Edit

Publish and Share

Revised Draft

Another way to give back is to ~~You could~~ donate to organizations. If you can, buy extra canned goods and other non-perishable items to donate to your local food bank. Look through your closet for gently used clothes, shoes, and winter coats that don't fit. You may have some ~~other things~~ games and books you could donate, too.

Giving Back to the Community

by Corey Barnes

Giving back to the community is important. Many people need help. There are many different ways to benefit your community. One way to give back is to volunteer your time. Find out whether your local food bank needs help. You could easily help sort and organize food so that it could be distributed. Many cities have community gardens, and they depend on volunteers to plant and care for the gardens. Ask about volunteer programs at your school, such as tutoring or cleaning up around the school. Volunteer to clean up a local park.

Another way to give back is to donate to organizations. If you can, buy extra canned goods and other nonperishable items to donate to your local food bank. Look through your closet for gently used clothes, shoes, and winter coats that don't fit. You may have some games and books you could donate, too.

In conclusion, volunteering your time and donating items are excellent ways to give back to your community. You'll make it a better place, and you'll help others in need.

Reading as a Writer

Which words did Corey add to make his writing clearer? How can you make your essay more informative?

In my final paper, I replaced vague words with specific ones and added examples. I also added transition words to link the paragraphs.

Test POWER

Read the passage "The Record-Setting Popcorn String." As you read, stop and answer each question using text evidence.

The Record-Setting Popcorn String

The whole idea began with a book that Chima had received for her birthday, *Guinness World Records*. Chima became absorbed in the facts and records involving nature, the universe, sports, and many other topics. She learned fascinating facts about the fastest roller coaster, the tallest horse, the deepest valley, the smallest bee, and the largest flea.

Chima also discovered there were hundreds of unusual records set by people, such as the most cartwheels in one minute or the most kites flown at the same time. Chima could hardly believe that someone had actually run a mile in just over seven minutes while balancing a baseball bat on one finger! She thought *Guinness World Records* was the most fascinating book she had seen in a long time. She was eager to share it with her two best friends, Mei-Mei and Max.

> **1** What is the narrator's point of view about Chima's book? Explain how this point of view is expressed in the passage.

At first, Mei-Mei and Max didn't think a bunch of world records would be very interesting, but Chima found something to appeal to each of them. She pointed Mei-Mei to the section about nature and animals. Max, who loved sports, was amazed to read that the fastest recorded baseball pitch was clocked at 100.9 miles per hour. "You're right, Chima, these world records really are fascinating," Max admitted.

The three friends became especially interested in the records set by friends working together, like the group that made the longest chain of pipe cleaners. "Wouldn't it be fun to try to set our own Guinness record?" Chima suggested. She challenged her friends to help her. Mei-Mei was enthusiastic and agreed at once. Max was hesitant, saying he thought setting a new world record would probably be too difficult and time-consuming.

RL.6.1 cite textual evidence to support analysis of what the text says explicitly as well as inferences drawn; **RL.6.2** determine a theme or central idea of a text/provide a summary; **RL.6.3** describe how a story's or drama's plot unfolds and how characters respond and change; **RL.6.6** explain how an author develops the point of view of the narrator or speaker

Chima and Mei-Mei began to consider records they might attempt to break. Chima suggested they could set a record for hopping the longest distance. Mei-Mei checked to see if there was a record for the tallest sand castle, thinking that perhaps they could build an even-taller one. Then Chima came up with the perfect idea. She had often made strings of popcorn to hang from trees to feed the birds. Why not try to make the world's longest string of popcorn? Even Max agreed that this was something they might be able to accomplish and that it would be fun, too.

For the remainder of the day, the friends mapped out a plan and bought the supplies they needed for their challenge. They finally parted, looking forward to setting a new world record and eventually seeing their names in the book.

Over the next month, the three friends spent weekend mornings popping popcorn and long afternoons in Chima's garage stringing the popped kernels. The project was proving more challenging than they had anticipated. Mei-Mei complained that the stringing was boring. Max said he had come to detest the smell of popcorn and planned never to eat it again. Chima had to admit that she agreed with both of them.

---

2 How has Chima's attitude changed since the beginning of the passage?

Finally, one Saturday afternoon, the friends realized they had finished stringing 5,280 feet of popcorn. Their popcorn string was a mile long! They had tracked the length of the string by recording how many spools of thread they used. They called their families to come and admire the impressive string of popcorn and to share in the proud moment. Everyone agreed that the world record was sure to be theirs.

The next morning, Chima was awakened by strange noises coming from the garage. As she hurried to discover the source of the noise, she realized it sounded like birds squawking. With a sinking feeling, Chima remembered how she had gotten the idea for the popcorn string in the first place. She tried to recall whether she had shut the garage door the night before, but she couldn't remember.

---

3 What inference can you make about what may have happened? Identify information in the passage that you used to draw the inference.

A flock of birds scattered when Chima walked through the open door of the garage. She gasped when she saw what the birds had done. All that remained of the fabulous record-setting popcorn string were long half-empty threads and kernels of popcorn strewn on the garage floor. Chima knew that she was the one who was responsible because she had forgotten to close the garage door. She wished with all her heart that she could somehow undo her mistake. She dreaded having to call Max and Mei-Mei and tell them the bad news.

When Max and Mei-Mei arrived and saw the bits of popcorn and lengths of exposed string, they knew the possibility of setting a world record had ended. Chima apologized tearfully.

"It was just an accident, Chima," said Mei-Mei, trying to comfort her. "We forgive you, don't we, Max?"

Max said yes, of course he forgave Chima. He reminded them about the time he had forgotten to latch the gate at Mei-Mei's house. The three of them had had to search all over the neighborhood before finding Mei-Mei's puppy, Peanut. "Losing Peanut would have been much worse than losing our popcorn string," Max pointed out.

After a while, the friends began talking about the experience of trying to set a world record. Although they were disappointed, they felt good that they had set a goal and had worked hard to achieve it. In their own minds, they knew they really had set a world record, even if their feat would never make it into the book. "I'm sure nobody else ever created a string of popcorn a whole mile long," Mei-Mei said.

The friends even talked about other records they could try to set. "But let's agree on one thing right now," said Chima. "Any record-setting challenges in the future will not involve popcorn!"

---

4 What did the characters in this passage learn from their experience? Support your response with details from the text.

unit 4

Vocabulary in Context

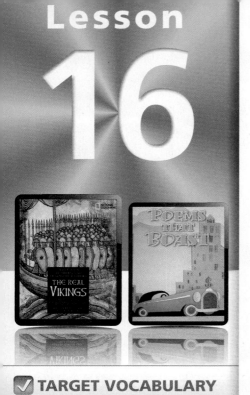

☑ **TARGET VOCABULARY**

ruthless
unearthed
ancestral
forge
embodied
artistry
recreational
saga
majestic
destiny

1 ruthless
During raids, Vikings sometimes acted in a ruthless fashion. At other times, they were peaceful.

2 unearthed
Remains of Viking settlements have been unearthed, or dug up, in Greenland.

3 ancestral
The descendants of this lord lived on ancestral land that he had owned many generations ago.

4 forge
Viking friends worked to forge, or build, a strong bond by helping each other through hard times.

Vocabulary Reader

Context Cards

LA.6.6 acquire and use general academic and domain-specific words and phrases/gather vocabulary knowledge for comprehension or expression

Go Digital

► Study each Context Card.

► Make up a new context sentence that uses two Vocabulary words.

5 embodied

Viking ships had snake heads carved into their prows. These embodied, or gave form to, the Vikings' warrior spirit.

6 artistry

Early books had decorated pages that showed the artistry of the illustrator who created them.

7 recreational

This early chess piece shows that games were one type of recreational activity that Vikings found relaxing.

8 saga

The poem *Beowulf* tells the saga of a hero. It is a tale of his great deeds.

9 majestic

The mountains and inlets of former Viking lands are still a majestic, or impressive, sight.

10 destiny

This stone shows Vikings in Valhalla, a paradise they saw as their destiny, where they would go if they died in battle.

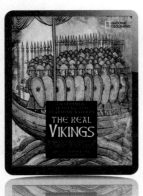

Read and Comprehend

✓ TARGET SKILL

Compare and Contrast Some informational texts **compare** and **contrast** two or more things. As you read "The Real Vikings," notice how the author has organized information to show how categories of people, settings, and objects are alike and different. Look for clue words and other text evidence that signal comparisons, such as *both* and *most*. Also look for words that signal contrasts, such as *instead* and *although*. Use a graphic organizer like the one below to help you compare and contrast people, settings, and other details in the selection.

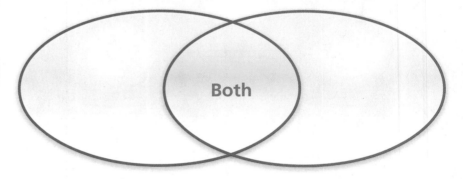

✓ TARGET STRATEGY

Summarize As you read "The Real Vikings," **summarize** the text, or briefly retell it in your own words.

COMMON CORE **RI.6.1** cite textual evidence to support analysis of what the text says explicitly as well as inferences drawn; **RI.6.2** determine a central idea of a text/provide a summary; **RI.6.5** analyze how a sentence, paragraph, chapter, or section fits in the overall structure

Fact and Legend

Long ago, people did not write about important events or about heroic actions. Instead, people memorized stories and repeated them orally. As these stories were passed down from generation to generation, each storyteller told a different version. Some of the facts and other details changed. Over time, some of the oral stories grew to become legends.

When you read a legend, it is important to consider what is true in it and what is fiction. In "The Real Vikings," you'll learn about a legendary people—the Vikings from Scandinavia—and about their true culture.

THE REAL VIKINGS

✓ TARGET SKILL

Compare and Contrast
Examine how two or more things are alike and different.

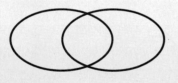

✓ GENRE

Informational text gives facts and information about a topic. As you read, look for:

▸ headings that begin sections of related information

▸ photographs and captions

▸ the way in which ideas are organized

COMMON CORE **RI.6.2** determine a central idea of a text/ provide a summary; **RI.6.5** analyze how a sentence, paragraph, chapter, or section fits in the overall structure; **RI.6.6** determine the author's point of view or purpose and explain how it is conveyed; **RI.6.10** read and comprehend literary nonfiction

MEET THE AUTHORS
Melvin Berger and Gilda Berger

As a husband-and-wife author team, Melvin Berger and Gilda Berger have written more than sixty books, including another title about early history: *Mummies of the Pharaohs: Exploring the Valley of the Kings.* They began collaborating fifty years ago, but their careers have included teaching special education (Gilda) and playing viola for the New Orleans Philharmonic (Melvin). The Bergers live and write near the ocean in East Hampton, Long Island.

THE REAL VIKINGS

Craftsmen, Traders, and Fearsome Raiders

by Melvin Berger and
Gilda Berger

ESSENTIAL QUESTION

How can learning
about history help
people today?

The Vikings often sailed their majestic longships from Scandinavia and swarmed ashore to rob their neighbors—including the monks of Lindisfarne, England, in 793 C.E. Raiding, however, does not tell the whole story of the Vikings.

Who Were the Vikings?

From the Lindisfarne attack and the many other attacks that followed arose the popular—though now disputed—belief that all Vikings were cruel, ruthless pirates and murderers.

Archaeologists have recently uncovered many remains from the Viking Age, the period from around 800 to 1100, that give a more balanced view of Viking life than previously held. As experts dig in the places where Vikings lived, they are finding many everyday objects preserved in the soil. These include coins and silver jewelry, carved animal bones, furniture, clothing, boots, and weapons. Archaeologists are also uncovering the foundations of buildings and the remains of large ships.

From studies of these finds, scholars have learned that the majority of Viking Age Scandinavians did not go out raiding. Instead, most of them stayed home, where they farmed, raised cattle, and hunted and fished. Some built ships. Viking craftsmen produced a variety of goods in their workshops. Viking merchants traveled widely, trading these goods for materials from other lands.

Egil (AY gihl) Skallagrimsson, the hero of Egil's Saga, *embodied both sides of the Viking character. According to the saga, he was tough and cruel, but at the same time he won fame as a merchant, farmer, and great poet.*

A dig in what is now Dublin, Ireland, revealed the wooden planks of a Viking road and the remains of houses and shops.

Evidence from Viking graves tells us about everyday life. Some men and women were buried with their most valuable possessions and occasionally with their horses and dogs. Some people were buried in fine wooden ships or within enclosures of stones arranged in boat shapes. The ship settings suggest that the Vikings thought that death was followed by a voyage to the next world.

Clues to Viking life and beliefs also come from their ancestral histories and heroic legends, which families once passed on by word of mouth. On long, dark, cold winter evenings in Viking lands, family elders repeated these stories, sometimes known as sagas, again and again. Later, long after the end of the Viking Age, scribes wrote down the sagas. Among the most famous tales are *Egil's Saga, Erik the Red's Saga,* and *The Greenlanders' Saga,* all of which people still enjoy reading.

The few written records left by the Vikings consist of inscriptions on gravestones, road markers, weapons, and jewelry. The Vikings wrote in letters called runes, which also served as magic symbols. The 16 letters of the runic alphabet were angular in shape, which made them easy to carve into hard surfaces, such as stone or metal. Although many runic stones were memorials to dead relatives, other inscriptions marked property boundaries, noted important events, or offered thanks to a god.

From archaeological excavations, sagas, runes, and the writings of their enemies and victims, we've learned much about the Vikings, a people who triumphed over the cold and isolation of their homelands to forge a distinctive culture and destiny.

At Home in Scandinavia

Hedeby, a large, important town in Viking times, is the most thoroughly explored of all Viking sites. From remains that archaeologists have uncovered there, we have a fairly good idea of what a Viking town looked like and of how ordinary people lived there.

Both a fort and a trading center, Hedeby is located at the southeast corner of Denmark, facing the Baltic Sea. In Viking times, a high wall of earth surrounded the town. In some places the wall was 40 feet tall—the height of a four-story building. People had to walk through tunnels in the wall to get in or out of Hedeby. A small brook ran through the center of the town, providing the residents with water for drinking and washing.

Hedeby had at least two main streets, both paved with planks of wood. Most houses were built of wattle and daub—flexible willow branches threaded in and out of posts and covered with mud and cow dung. Wealthy people lived in wooden houses built from tree trunks, which were split lengthwise and placed upright in the ground to form a continuous wall. Other houses were made with wooden planks placed horizontally. Covering the houses were roofs of reed thatching or sod—thick, matted grass growing in a thin layer of earth. Behind each house was an outhouse, a well, a cesspool, and a pit for garbage.

Reconstructions of ninth-century buildings, these houses are found in Hedeby, Denmark, once the largest Viking town. A busy trading center, Hedeby had a population of about 1,000 to 1,500 people in Viking times. A bird's-eye view of Hedeby shows the many houses crowded together, the farms on the outskirts of town, and the sea.

Perched amid metalworking tools, a delicate animal ornament reflects the artistry of a Viking jeweler. Viking craftsmen used molds, such as the dragon's head mold at left, to produce a variety of metal objects.

Rich merchants and craftsmen in Hedeby lived in large wooden houses that measured about 16 by 40 feet. The living room had a central fireplace with a cooking pot hanging over the hearth. The fireplace provided both heat and light. A small hole in the roof let the smoke out. Low earth platforms, built up on both sides of the fireplace, served as benches for sitting and sleeping.

The houses had no windows. Light came from the fireplace or from lamps, which were small iron or soapstone bowls holding wicks, probably made of plant fibers, for burning oil. Still, it must have been dark indoors—as well as smelly and smoky—so many tasks were probably done outside.

The wattle-and-daub huts of the poorer people of Hedeby were about 9 by 12 feet. They had a fireplace in one corner and earthen benches along the walls.

From objects found at Hedeby, it appears that many of the townspeople worked as merchants and craftsmen. Some of the craftsmen made jewelry. Others were expert glassblowers, who produced everything from glass beads for necklaces to drinking cups. Some craftsmen carved objects of horn or bone. Still others made their living weaving and sewing cloth.

Archaeologists have found two important tools that Viking craftsmen used to make marvelous objects from metal: the crucible and the mold. The crucible, a pot of hard-fired clay, allowed workers to melt metal at very high temperatures before shaping it. Molds, also made of clay, made it possible to easily produce a great many objects, from pots to rings to battle-axes to statues.

> **ANALYZE THE TEXT**
>
> **Compare and Contrast** Use information on these pages to compare and contrast the houses of the poorer and the wealthier people in Hedeby.

Viking merchants brought fine goods from Germany, France, England, Constantinople, and Persia to trade in Hedeby. Indeed, people from all over Scandinavia visited the town's bustling market to buy jewelry, silk, lace, and other luxuries. Slaves captured on raids were also traded at Hedeby.

While some Vikings lived in towns such as Hedeby, most people were farmers in the countryside. A typical farm contained the family house, stables and barns for the farm animals, a workshop to make metal tools, and small huts for slaves. Farms on the coast usually had a shed to hold the farmer's boat during the winter months.

Farmers raised mainly corn, peas, cabbage, barley, and oats. They kept cattle both for meat and for milk. The farmers' wives churned the milk into butter or made cheese, which they kept in cold storerooms, using the winter snow as a kind of deep freeze. They also pickled and smoked meat and stored dried peas and beans. Without these preserved foods, the people would have had nothing to eat during the winter.

Every member of a farm family shared in the work. Men worked in the fields, hunted and fished, and looked after the livestock. Women preserved and cooked the food, cared for the children and the sick, spun and wove wool, and sewed, embroidered, and washed clothes. They ran the farm while their husbands and sons were away fishing or on trading or raiding voyages—sometimes for months or years at a time. Children helped their parents around the house and farm. Even the youngest ones contributed by feeding the animals or gathering firewood.

Viking family groups were large. A man and his wife, their children—including older sons with their wives and children—and the grandparents all lived together on the family farm. When a daughter married, she usually left home to join her husband's family.

Vikings ate two main meals a day. The women served the first meal at about eight or nine o'clock in the morning, which was after the farmers had already worked in the fields for about two hours. The other meal, which they ate at about seven or eight o'clock in the evening, marked the end of the day's work.

At dinner, members of the family sat around the table, sometimes on the same benches they slept on at night. They ate off rectangular

In this scene of a Viking home, a woman stirs a cooking pot over a hearth. The fire provides both heat and light. The hole in the roof allows smoke to escape and serves as another source of light for the windowless house.

wooden platters or from soapstone bowls, using only spoons and knives, which they carried in their belts. Forks were a later invention.

In good times, Viking families supped on soups and stews of beef or mutton or on fish from the sea. Women roasted meat on huge spits over the hearth and cooked vegetables in big iron cauldrons. They baked bread in stone ovens or on long-handled flat metal griddles placed on the ashes of the fire.

When not working, Vikings played games such as chess and went swimming and skiing. A board game called *merils*, which is similar to checkers, has been found in Viking graves. Other recreational activities included fencing, running, and wrestling, as well as training falcons to hunt wild birds and animals.

Winter sports included racing on snowshoes and ice-skating. Skates were made of sharpened animal bones attached to shoes with leather straps. Skaters used long, sharpened poles to push themselves on the ice. In warmer weather, ball games were popular.

ANALYZE THE TEXT

Main Ideas and Details What is the main idea of this selection? What details do the authors give to convey the main idea?

The Vikings were fond of music. They celebrated victories and festivals in song, which might be accompanied by harps or lyres. From findings at various archaeological sites, we know that the Vikings also had simple wind instruments. Pipes unearthed in Sweden were made of hollowed-out animal bones, with holes drilled along the length to produce the different tones.

Carved from walrus tusks, these ivory chess pieces date back to 12th-century Norway.

If a girl wanted to marry into a good family, she had to be able to sing and play an instrument. Boys also had to be musical, but they needed to master other skills as well, especially the use of weapons. One young Viking man boasted:

> "There are nine skills known to me—
> At the chessboard I am skillful,
> Runic writing I know well,
> Books I like; with tools am handy,
> Good with snowshoes,
> Rowing, and shooting,
> And expert with harp and verse."

Life was hard in Viking times—but there was obviously still time to relax and have fun.

ANALYZE THE TEXT

Author's Purpose What is the authors' perspective on the Vikings? How do the authors communicate this in the text?

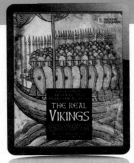

Dig Deeper

How to Analyze the Text

Use these pages to learn about Comparing and Contrasting, Author's Purpose, and Main Ideas and Details. Then read "The Real Vikings" again to apply what you learned.

Compare and Contrast

Authors of informational texts organize their writing in different ways. One way of organizing information is to provide details that tell how things are alike and different.

When you **compare,** you determine the ways in which two or more things are alike. When you **contrast,** you determine how two or more things are different. Look for clue words in the text that may signal comparisons and contrasts.

Look back at pages 471–473 of "The Real Vikings," where the authors describe how Viking townspeople and Viking farmers lived. Use the text evidence on these pages to compare and contrast how townspeople and farmers spent their time.

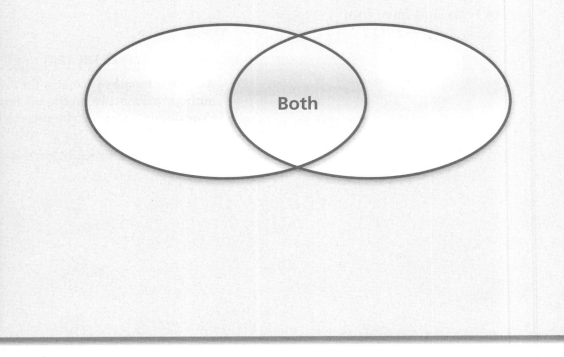

Both

COMMON CORE **RI.6.1** cite textual evidence to support analysis of what the text says explicitly as well as inferences drawn; **RI.6.2** determine a central idea of a text/provide a summary; **RI.6.5** analyze how a sentence, paragraph, chapter, or section fits in the overall structure; **RI.6.6** determine the author's point of view or purpose and explain how it is conveyed

476

Author's Purpose

Every author has a reason, or **purpose,** for writing. The author may want to entertain, to provide information, or to persuade the reader to believe something. Authors' opinions and beliefs about a subject are expressed through their **point of view.** Authors may use words and phrases that express their point of view about a topic without stating it directly.

Main Ideas and Details

The **main idea** of a nonfiction text is the central idea the author is trying to convey about the topic or subject. The main idea of a text is always supported by **details.** Authors may state main ideas directly, but many times readers must use text evidence and make inferences to determine the main idea.

Your Turn

Turn and Talk Review the selection with a partner to prepare to discuss this question: *How can learning about history help people today?* Develop your answer by asking questions and responding to your partner's questions using text evidence.

Classroom Conversation

Continue your discussion of "The Real Vikings" by explaining your answers to these questions:

1. How have archaeologists provided us with a more balanced view of the Vikings of Scandinavia?

2. How do the facts provided by the authors affect your own beliefs about Vikings?

3. Viking families were large. What were some advantages of having a large family? What might have been some disadvantages?

WHAT'S THE CLAIM?

Analyze the Argument At the beginning of "The Real Vikings," the authors claim that the common belief that "all Vikings were cruel, ruthless pirates and murderers" is not true. Work with others to analyze the authors' claim. Discuss whether you agree or disagree with it. Support your opinion about the Vikings with evidence from the text.

WRITE ABOUT READING

Response In their daily lives, Vikings were sailors, storytellers, craftsmen, and farmers. Choose one aspect from the Vikings' daily lives that is the same in the lives of people today. Then choose an aspect of their daily lives that is different in people's lives today. Write one paragraph to explain the similarities and another paragraph to explain the differences. Use facts and other details from the selection as text evidence to support your comparisons.

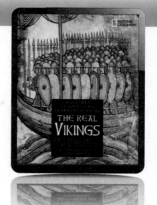

Writing Tip

Use concrete, specific, real-world details to support your ideas. Use words that signal comparisons and contrasts.

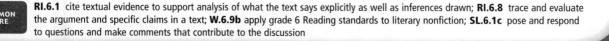

COMMON CORE

RI.6.1 cite textual evidence to support analysis of what the text says explicitly as well as inferences drawn; **RI.6.8** trace and evaluate the argument and specific claims in a text; **W.6.9b** apply grade 6 Reading standards to literary nonfiction; **SL.6.1c** pose and respond to questions and make comments that contribute to the discussion

☑ GENRE

Poetry uses the sound and rhythm of words to show images and express feelings in a variety of forms.

☑ TEXT FOCUS

Imagery Poetry often creates a vivid description by using exact words that appeal to the senses.

COMMON CORE **RL.6.4** determine the meaning of words and phrases, including figurative and connotative meanings/analyze impact of word choice; **RL.6.10** read and comprehend literature

 Go Digital

POEMS THAT BOAST

The poet at the end of "The Real Vikings" doesn't brag that he is a ruthless raider. Instead, he boasts about his artistry with words and how well he plays chess. These poems also boast. "A Mighty Fine Fella" and "Super Samson Simpson" embody the idea of bigness in their majestic images. In "A Song of Greatness," the narrator honors the sagas of her ancestral heritage. She is confident about her destiny.

A MIGHTY FINE FELLA

by Eloise Greenfield

I don't want to be
Mr. Big
with a hundred different suits
counting my money in public
and showing off
in my new sports car
I'm a mighty fine fella
And I don't need things
to prove it

Super Samson Simpson

by Jack Prelutsky

I am Super Samson Simpson,
I'm superlatively strong,
I like to carry elephants,
I do it all day long,
I pick up half a dozen
and hoist them in the air,
it's really somewhat simple,
for I have strength to spare.

My muscles are enormous,
they bulge from top to toe,
and when I carry elephants,
they ripple to and fro,
but I am not the strongest
in the Simpson family,
for when I carry elephants,
my grandma carries me.

A SONG OF GREATNESS
CHIPPEWA TRADITIONAL

by Mary Austin

When I hear the old men
Telling of heroes,
Telling of great deeds
Of ancient days,
When I hear that telling
Then I think within me
I too am one of these.

When I hear the people
Praising great ones,
Then I know that I too
Shall be esteemed,
I too when my time comes
Shall do mightily.

POEM OF CELEBRATION

Use a poem in this selection as a model to help you write a poem. Think about your talents. Once you have brainstormed your special skills, write about them in a poem that celebrates you! Include imagery in your poem.

Compare Texts

TEXT TO TEXT

Compare Topics With a partner, talk about "The Real Vikings" and "Poems That Boast." Discuss how the informational text "The Real Vikings" and the poetry in "Poems That Boast" present the idea of greatness, and what the texts have to say about pride and accomplishments. Use evidence from the texts to support your ideas.

TEXT TO SELF

Write a Description Archaeologists use objects as clues to the Vikings' daily life. Imagine that two of *your* possessions are dug up a thousand years from now. Write a description an archaeologist might write for each object, explaining its use.

TEXT TO WORLD

Discuss Viking Culture Most young people in the Viking culture lived on farms. Think about how a typical young person would spend his or her day. What might young people in modern times enjoy most about the Viking way of life? What might they find to be most difficult? Use text evidence to support your ideas. Share your thoughts with a partner.

COMMON CORE **RL.6.1** cite textual evidence to support analysis of what the text says explicitly as well as inferences drawn; **RL.6.9** compare and contrast texts in different forms or genres on their approaches to themes and topics; **RI.6.1** cite textual evidence to support analysis of what the text says explicitly as well as inferences drawn

Grammar

What Are the Four Principal Parts of Verbs? Every verb has four basic forms called **principal parts.** You use the principal parts to form all verb tenses. You use some of these principal parts in other ways, too. For example, you can use the **present participle** and **past participle** forms of verbs as describing words. The chart below shows the four principal parts of some regular and some irregular verbs.

Principal Parts of Regular Verbs			
Present	**Present Participle**	**Past**	**Past Participle**
learn	(is) learning	learned	(has) learned
stay	(is) staying	stayed	(has) stayed
raise	(is) raising	raised	(has) raised
Principal Parts of Irregular Verbs			
Present	**Present Participle**	**Past**	**Past Participle**
dig	(is) digging	dug	(has) dug
come	(is) coming	came	(has) come
know	(is) knowing	knew	(has) known

Try This! Copy the chart below onto another sheet of paper. Fill in the missing principal parts.

	Present	**Present Participle**	**Past**	**Past Participle**
1	uncover	(is) _____	uncovered	(has) _____
2	run	(is) _running_	_____	(has) _____
3	build	(is) _____	_____	(has) _built_
4	carve	(is) _carving_	_____	(has) _____

Present participles and past participles can be used to describe nouns. To vary your sentence patterns, you can sometimes combine two sentences into one by using a participle to describe a noun.

Two Sentences

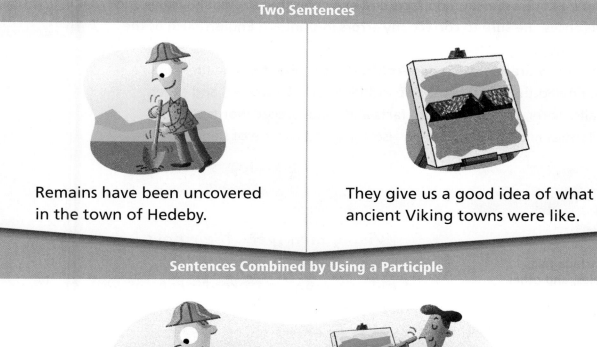

Remains have been uncovered in the town of Hedeby.

They give us a good idea of what ancient Viking towns were like.

Sentences Combined by Using a Participle

Uncovered remains in the town of Hedeby give us a good idea of what ancient Viking towns were like.

Connect Grammar to Writing

As you revise your compare-contrast essay, look for ways to add a variety of sentence patterns. Try to combine some sentences by using participles to modify nouns.

W.6.2a introduce a topic and organize ideas, concepts, and information/include formatting, graphics, and multimedia; **W.6.2b** develop the topic with facts, definitions, details, quotations, or other information and examples; **W.6.2c** use transitions to clarify relationships; **W.6.2d** use precise language and domain-specific vocabulary; **L.6.1e** recognize variations from standard English and identify/use strategies to improve expression

COMMON CORE

Informative Writing

☑ **Word Choice** In a **compare-contrast essay,** writers explain how two or more things are alike and how they are different. As you revise your compare-contrast essay, add facts and examples that show similarities and differences. Be sure to correct any errors in standard English, such as the use of slang.

Whitney drafted a compare-contrast essay about Viking men and women and their farm jobs. She included facts, examples, and other details. Later, she added more facts and some precise words to show similarities and differences. She also corrected her use of slang.

Writing Traits Checklist

☑ **Ideas**
Did I include facts, examples, and other details that show similarities and differences?

☑ **Organization**
Does my organization follow the structure of a compare-contrast essay?

☑ **Sentence Fluency**
Did I use words to signal similarities and differences?

☑ **Word Choice**
Did I use correct standard English?

☑ **Voice**
Is my writing clear and informative?

☑ **Conventions**
Did I use correct spelling, grammar, and punctuation?

Revised Draft

Viking men spent their days harvesting

fields of many different crops as well as ~~doing~~
          hunting and
~~cool stuff like~~ fishing. They also tended to the

livestock, which included cattle. They raised
                              ¶On the other hand,
the cattle for meat and for milk. Viking women

spent their days storing dried peas and beans,
                    churning
preserving meats, ~~making~~ butter, and making
          In addition to these chores,
cheese. women cooked two meals a day. They
          and made clothes for the family.
also took care of the children

486

Men's Work, Women's Work

by Whitney Viers

Most Vikings lived on farms, and men and women alike worked to provide food and clothing for their families. Their jobs were similar in that both men and women performed chores that required physical strength and endurance. Both men and women were busy from dawn until dusk. However, the particular jobs that men and women did were very different.

Viking men spent their days harvesting fields of many different crops as well as hunting and fishing. They also tended to the livestock, which included cattle. They raised the cattle for meat and for milk.

On the other hand, Viking women spent their days storing dried peas and beans, preserving meats, churning butter, and making cheese. In addition to these chores, women cooked two meals a day. They also took care of the children and made clothes for the family.

Both Viking men and women were able to support their families by doing different jobs. Together they kept their families fed and clothed, especially during the harsh winter months.

Reading as a Writer

What facts did Whitney add to show the differences between men's work and women's work? What did she do to correct her English? What strategies can you use to find and correct errors in standard English?

In my final paper, I added facts and examples to make the similarities and differences clearer. I also made sure I replaced any slang with correct English words.

17

TARGET VOCABULARY

archaeologists
replicas
lustrous
elaborate
excavate
distinct
dignified
mythical
temperaments
precede

Vocabulary
Reader

Context
Cards

COMMON CORE **L.6.6** acquire and use general academic and domain-specific words and phrases/gather vocabulary knowledge for comprehension or expression

Vocabulary in Context

1 archaeologists

Archaeologists are scientists who study items left behind by cultures from the past.

2 replicas

Replicas, or copies, have been made of ancient Chinese pottery and statues.

3 lustrous

Chinese royalty wore lustrous silk robes. The material seemed to shine or gleam.

4 elaborate

The Great Wall of China was an elaborate building project. It involved a great deal of careful detail.

Go Digital

▶ Study each Context Card.

▶ Use a dictionary to confirm the meanings of these words.

5 excavate

To learn about ancient China, men and women excavate artifacts that have been buried for centuries.

6 distinct

The Chinese writing system has hundreds of distinct, or different, characters.

7 dignified

Members of the emperor's court acted in a manner that was dignified, or worthy of honor.

8 mythical

The Chinese dragon is a mythical creature, one that exists only in the imagination.

9 temperaments

According to Chinese astrology, people born in certain years have similar temperaments, or personalities.

10 precede

A horseman might precede, or go ahead of, the emperor during his travels.

489

Read and Comprehend

✓ TARGET SKILL

Fact and Opinion Authors of informational texts often make **claims** that are **opinions**—personal beliefs and feelings. Words and phrases such as *may*, *probably*, and *is considered* often signal opinions. As you read "The Emperor's Silent Army," look for claims the author makes. Notice whether the author supports the claims with facts and other text evidence. Use a graphic organizer like this one to help you.

Fact	Opinion

✓ TARGET STRATEGY

Question Ask **questions** about a selection before you read, as you read, and after you read. Look for text evidence to help you find answers.

COMMON CORE **RI.6.1** cite textual evidence to support analysis of what the text says explicitly as well as inferences drawn; **RI.6.8** trace and evaluate the argument and specific claims in a text

Ancient China

China is one of the oldest civilizations in the world. As a result, modern China has a rich cultural heritage. Artifacts, along with artwork, music, stories, and architecture of long ago, can tell us much about ancient China.

In the past, emperors were China's leaders. They ruled over millions of people, defining the country and its people. In "The Emperor's Silent Army," you will learn what the first emperor of ancient China left behind that provides clues to the nation's history.

Lesson 17

ANCHOR TEXT

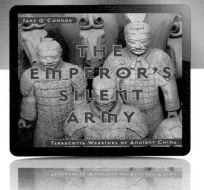

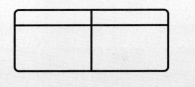

MEET THE AUTHOR
Jane O'Connor

Jane O'Connor is the author of more than thirty books for all age groups. Writing runs in O'Connor's family. Her younger son, Tim, is an author; she has collaborated with her husband, Jim (*The Magic Top Mystery*, *Slime Time*); and when her older son, Robert, was in sixth grade, the two of them wrote the book *Super Cluck*, about a chicken from outer space. O'Connor's nonfiction includes books on art, movie special effects, and the White House.

THE EMPEROR'S SILENT ARMY

Terracotta Warriors of Ancient China

by Jane O'Connor

ESSENTIAL QUESTION

How can people use clues to learn about ancient cultures?

A STRANGE DISCOVERY

LINTONG COUNTY, PEOPLE'S REPUBLIC OF CHINA, MARCH 1974

It's just an ordinary day in early spring, or so three farmers think as they trudge across a field in northern China. They are looking for a good place to dig a well. There has been a drought, and they must find water or risk losing their crops later in the year.

The farmers choose a spot near a grove of persimmon trees. Down they dig, five feet, ten feet. Still no water. They decide to keep on digging a little deeper. All of a sudden, one of the farmers feels his shovel strike against something hard. Is it a rock? It's difficult to see at the bottom of a dark hole, so the farmer kneels down for a closer look. No, it isn't a rock. It seems to be clay, and not raw clay but clay that has been baked and made into something. But what?

Now, more carefully, the men dig around the something. Perhaps it is a pot or a vase. However, what slowly reveals itself is the pottery head of a man who stares back at them, open-eyed and amazingly real looking. The farmers have never seen anything like it before. But they do remember stories that some of the old people in their village have told, stories of a "pottery man" found many years ago not far from where they are now. The villagers had been scared that the pottery man would bring bad luck so they broke it to bits, which were then reburied and forgotten.

The terracotta figures were discovered in the countryside of northern China.

ANALYZE THE TEXT

Figurative Language Find an example of hyperbole on page 495. Why would the author use this type of figurative language here? What does it mean?

The terracotta army was discovered when well-diggers found the head of a "pottery man" like this one. No photographs were taken that day.

The three well-diggers are not so superstitious. They report their discovery to a local official. Soon a group of archaeologists arrives to search the area more closely. Maybe they will find pieces of a clay body to go with the clay head.

In fact, they find much more.

During the weeks and months that follow, the archaeologists dig out more pottery men, which now are called by a more dignified term—terracotta figurines. The figurines are soldiers. That much is clear. But they come from a time long ago, when Chinese warriors wore knee-length robes, armor made from small iron "fish scales," and elaborate topknot hairdos. All of the soldiers are life-size or a little bigger and weigh as much as four hundred pounds. They stand at attention as if waiting for the command to charge into battle. The only thing missing is their weapons. And those are found too— hundreds of real bronze swords, daggers, and battle-axes as well as thousands of scattered arrowheads—all so perfectly made that, after cleaning, their ancient tips are still sharp enough to split a hair!

Today, after nearly thirty years of work, terracotta soldiers are still being uncovered and restored. What the well-diggers stumbled upon, purely by accident, has turned out to be among the largest and most incredible archaeological discoveries of modern times. Along with the Great Pyramids in Egypt, the buried army is now considered one of the true wonders of the ancient world. Spread out over several acres near the city of Xian (shee ahn), the soldiers number not in the tens or hundreds but in the thousands! Probably 7,500, total. Until 1974, nobody knew that right below the people of northern China an enormous underground army had been standing guard, silently and watchfully, for more than 2,200 years. Who put them there?

One man.

Known as the fierce tiger of Qin (chin), the divine Son of Heaven, he was the first emperor of China.

Although more than seven thousand strong, the terracotta army is small compared to the emperor's real army.

THE QUEST FOR IMMORTALITY

Before the time of Qin Shihuang (chin shir hwong), who lived from 259 to 210 B.C.E., there was no China. Instead there were seven separate kingdoms, each with its own language, currency, and ruler. For hundreds of years they had been fighting one another. The kingdom of Qin was the fiercest; soldiers received their pay only after they had presented their generals with the cut-off heads of enemy warriors. By 221 B.C.E. the ruler of the Qin kingdom had "eaten up his neighbors like a silkworm devouring a leaf," according to an ancient historian. The name China comes from Qin.

The king of Qin now ruled over an immense empire—around one million square miles that stretched north and west to the Gobi (GOH bee) desert, south to present-day Vietnam, and east to the Yellow Sea. To the people of the time, this was the entire civilized world. Not for another hundred years would the Chinese know that empires existed beyond their boundaries. To the ruler of Qin, being called king was no longer grand enough. He wanted a title that no one else had ever had before. What he chose was Qin Shihuang. This means "first emperor, God in Heaven, and Almighty of the Universe" all rolled into one.

No paintings exist of the emperor done in his lifetime, so there is no way to know how faithful this portrait is.

But no title, however superhuman it sounded, could protect him from what he feared most—dying. More than anything, the emperor wanted to live forever. According to legend, a magic elixir had granted eternal life to the people of the mythical Eastern Islands. Over the years, the emperor sent expeditions out to sea in search of the islands and the magic potion. But each time they came back empty-handed.

If he couldn't live forever, then Qin Shihuang was determined to live as long as possible. He ate powdered jade and drank mercury in the belief that they would prolong his life. In fact, these "medicines" were poison and may have caused the emperor to fall sick and die while on a tour of the easternmost outposts of his empire. He was forty-nine years old.

If word of Qin Shihuang's death got out while he was away from the capital, there might be a revolt. So his ministers kept the news a secret. With the emperor's body inside his chariot, the entire party traveled back to the capital city. Meals were brought into the emperor's chariot; daily reports on affairs were delivered as usual— all to keep up the appearance that the emperor was alive and well. However, it was summer, and a terrible smell began to come from the chariot. But the clever ministers found a way to account for the stench. A cart was loaded with smelly salted fish and made to precede the chariot, overpowering and masking any foul odors coming from the dead emperor. And so Qin Shihuang returned to the capital for burial.

The tomb of Qin Shihuang had been under construction for more than thirty years. It was begun when he was a young boy of thirteen and was still not finished when he died. Even incomplete, the emperor's tomb was enormous, larger than his largest palace. According to legend, it had a domed ceiling inlaid with clusters of pearls to represent the sun, moon, and stars. Below was a gigantic relief map of the world, made from bronze. Bronze hills and mountains rose up from the floor, with rivers of mercury flowing into a mercury sea. Along the banks of the rivers were models of the emperor's palaces and cities, all exact replicas of the real ones.

This detail of a silk robe shows an embroidered dragon, the symbol of Chinese emperors.

In ancient times, the Chinese believed that life after death was not so very different from life on earth. The soul of a dead person could continue to enjoy all the pleasures of everyday life. So people who were rich enough constructed elaborate underground tombs filled with silk robes, jewelry with precious stones, furniture, games, boats, chariots—everything the dead person could possibly need or want.

Qin Shihuang knew that grave robbers would try their best to loot the treasures in the tomb. So he had machines put inside the tomb that produced the rumble of thunder to scare off intruders, and mechanical crossbows at the entrance were set to fire arrows automatically should anyone dare trespass. The emperor also made certain that the workers who carried his coffin to its final resting place never revealed its exact whereabouts. As the men worked their way back through the tunnels to the tomb's entrance, a stone door came crashing down, and they were left to die, sealed inside the tomb along with the body of the emperor.

Even all these measures, however, were not enough to satisfy the emperor. And so, less than a mile from the tomb, in underground trenches, the terracotta warriors were stationed. Just as flesh-and-blood troops had protected him during his lifetime, the terracotta troops were there to protect their ruler against any enemy for all eternity.

THE FACES OF ANCIENT CHINA

About two thousand soldiers have been unearthed, yet, amazingly, so far no two are the same. The army includes men of all different ages, from different parts of China, with different temperaments. A young soldier looks both excited and nervous; an older officer, perhaps a veteran of many wars, appears tired, resigned. Some soldiers seem lost in thought, possibly dreaming of their return home; others look proud and confident. Although from a distance the figures appear almost identical, like giant-size toy soldiers, each is a distinct work of art.

Did real-life models pose for the figures? Probably not. But hundreds of craftsmen from all over the empire spent more than ten years in workshops set up near the pits creating the warriors. It is likely that they made the faces of the soldiers look like the faces of people that they knew from home.

The uniforms of the terracotta figures are exact copies in clay of what real soldiers of the day wore. The soldier's uniform tells his rank in the army. The lowest-ranking soldiers are bareheaded and wear heavy knee-length tunics but no armor. Often their legs are wrapped in cloth shin guards for protection.

ANALYZE THE TEXT

Text Structure How does the author organize the information on this page? How does this section of text fit in the overall text structure?

The generals' uniforms are the most elegant. Their caps sometimes sport a pheasant feather; their fancy shoes curl up at the toes; and their fine armor is made from small iron fish scales. Tassels on their armor are also a mark of their high rank.

The terracotta soldiers are now the ghostly grayish color of baked clay, clay that came from nearby Mount Li. Originally the soldiers were all brightly colored. Tiny bits of paint can still be seen on many of the figures and are proof that uniforms came in a blaze of colors—purple, blue, green, yellow, red, and orange. The colors of each soldier's uniform indicated not only which part of the army he belonged to—cavalry or infantry, for example—but also what his particular rank was. The terracotta horses were fully painted, too, in brown with pink ears, nostrils, and mouths. Unfortunately, when figures are dug out of the ground, most of the paint on them peels off and sticks to the surrounding earth. Also, when exposed to air, the paint tends to crumble into dust.

The colored computer image shows how the general would have looked originally.

Today groups of artisans in workshops near the three pits make replicas of the soldiers, following the techniques used 2,200 years ago. Their work helps archaeologists learn more about how the original figures were created. Even though the workers today have the advantages of modern kilns that register temperatures exactly, no copies have ever come out as hard or as lustrous as the ancient originals. (The workers of today are also not under the same kind of pressure as the emperor's potters—if they made a mistake, they were killed!)

Who were the potters who made the original soldiers? For the most part, they have remained anonymous. In ancient times, being a craftsman was considered lowly work. However, some soldiers are signed, probably by the master potter in charge of a workshop. The signature is like a stamp of approval, a sign of quality control.

Of course, the creators of the terracotta warriors never intended their work to be seen by anyone other than the emperor. That is a strange notion for twenty-first-century minds to accept. Artists today want their work to be seen, enjoyed, admired. But as soon as the emperor's army was completed, it was buried. Pits were dug twenty feet deep. Green-tiled floors were laid down. Dirt walls were constructed, creating tunnels in which the soldiers and horses and chariots were placed. A wooden roof was built overhead, and then ten feet of dirt was shoveled on top of the army. It was supposed to remain undisturbed for all eternity, but it did not turn out that way. How surprised the Qin sculptors would be by the crowds of people from all over the world who come to see their creations!

This cross-section drawing shows how soldiers in Pit 1 were placed in underground tunnels, which were separated by earthen walls and covered by a wooden roof.

ANALYZE THE TEXT

Fact and Opinion What claims does the author make on pages 502-503? Which claims are supported by facts and evidence? Which claims are not supported by evidence?

INSIDE THE EMPEROR'S TOMB

What exactly is the terracotta army guarding so steadfastly? What, besides the body of the dead emperor, is inside the tomb? The answer is that nobody knows. And the government of China has no plans to excavate and find out.

In ancient China it was the custom to build a natural-looking hill on top of a person's tomb. The more important a person was, the bigger the hill. Thousands of years of harsh weather have worn down the emperor's mound; originally it was four hundred feet high, almost as high as the biggest of the three Great Pyramids in Egypt.

Like the ancient Egyptians, the ancient Chinese believed that the body of a dead person should be preserved as a "home" for the soul. However, the Chinese did not make a person's body into a mummy. They believed that jade had magic powers, among them the ability to keep a dead body from decaying.

In Chinese tombs from the first century B.C.E., bodies of noblemen and princesses have been found wearing entire suits of jade. It is believed that Qin Shihuang is buried in just such a suit, the thousands of small tiles all beautifully carved and sewn together with gold thread. And over this jade burial outfit, his body is supposedly covered in a blanket of pearls.

As for all the things placed with the emperor, certainly they must be grand beyond imagining—silk robes embroidered with dragons, gem-encrusted crowns and jewelry, musical instruments, hand-carved furniture, lamps, beautiful dishes, cooking pots, and golden utensils. Like the pharaohs of ancient Egypt, the first emperor would have made certain that he had everything he might possibly want in the afterlife. But unless his tomb is excavated, what these treasures look like will remain a mystery.

The body of the emperor, which has never been recovered, may wear a jade funeral suit like this one found in the tomb of a Chinese princess from the late second century.

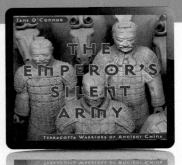

Dig Deeper

How to Analyze the Text

Use these pages to learn about Fact and Opinion, Figurative Language, and Text Structure. Then read "The Emperor's Silent Army" again to apply what you learned.

Fact and Opinion

Informational texts such as "The Emperor's Silent Army" often contain **claims** that may be **opinions**. Opinions express beliefs and feelings and cannot be proved true. **Facts,** on the other hand, can be proved true. They are a kind of **text evidence.** Knowing the difference between a fact and an opinion is important. Readers must evaluate the claims in a text to determine if they are supported with facts and other text evidence.

Look back at page 496 in "The Emperor's Silent Army." In the first paragraph, the phrase *is now considered* signals an opinion. What facts, if any, does the author include as evidence to support this claim?

Fact	Opinion

COMMON CORE **RI.6.4** determine the meaning of words and phrases, including figurative, connotative, and technical meanings; **RI.6.5** analyze how a sentence, paragraph, chapter, or section fits in the overall structure; **RI.6.8** trace and evaluate the argument and specific claims in a text; **L.6.5a** interpret figures of speech in context

Figurative Language

In **figurative language,** words have meanings beyond their dictionary definitions. In one kind of figurative language called **hyperbole,** people use extreme exaggeration, as in "It was a million degrees outside today!" In **personification,** human emotions, qualities, or characteristics are given to a thing or an idea. For example, in "The wind tugged at my coat and whispered in my ear," the wind is given two human abilities. Readers must use clues in the text to determine the meanings of figurative language.

Text Structure

Knowing how a piece of informational text is organized helps you understand it. **Text structure** is the way authors organize ideas. They may **compare** and **contrast** ideas. They may **sequence** ideas in time order. They may also explain what something is like through **description.** An informational text may have one overall text structure or several different text structures. Look for clues and other text evidence to detemine how a text is organized.

Your Turn

RETURN TO THE ESSENTIAL QUESTION

 Turn and Talk Review the selection with a partner to prepare to discuss this question: *How can people use clues to learn about ancient cultures?* As you review the text evidence in the selection, take turns posing questions and responding.

Classroom Conversation

Continue your discussion of "The Emperor's Silent Army" by using text evidence to explain your answers to these questions:

1. What does the author do to pull in readers at the beginning and end of the selection?

2. In what ways has the discovery of the silent army impacted the modern Chinese people?

3. Author Jane O'Connor calls the terracotta army "silent." How do the soldiers "speak" without talking?

WHAT WAS HE LIKE?

Emperor Qin Shihuang The emperor made many plans during his life to prepare for his death. With a small group, discuss what the emperor's plans for his death tell about him as a living person. What was he like? Use text evidence to support the conclusions you draw about Qin Shihuang.

WRITE ABOUT READING

Response Think about Qin Shihuang and life in ancient China. Would Qin Shihuang make a good leader today? Write a paragraph to express your argument. Introduce the paragraph with your claim, and then support the claim with facts and other evidence from the selection. End with a concluding statement.

Writing Tip

State your claim at the beginning of the paragraph. Make sure you use correct subject-verb agreement in each sentence of your paragraph.

COMMON CORE **RI.6.1** cite textual evidence to support analysis of what the text says explicitly as well as inferences drawn; **RI.6.3** analyze how a key individual, event, or idea is introduced, illustrated, and elaborated; **W.6.1e** provide a concluding statement or section; **W.6.9b** apply grade 6 Reading standards to literary nonfiction; **SL.6.1a** come to discussions prepared/explicitly draw on preparation to probe and reflect on ideas under discussion; **SL.6.1c** pose and respond to questions and make comments that contribute to the discussion

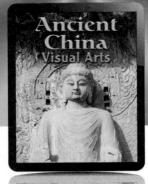

Ancient China Visual Arts

✓ GENRE

Informational text, such as this encyclopedia article, gives facts about a topic and is usually organized around main ideas and supporting details.

✓ TEXT FOCUS

Headings identify the main ideas of sections of a text, such as chapters, paragraphs, and captions.

RI.6.5 analyze how a sentence, paragraph, chapter, or section fits in the overall structure; **RI.6.10** read and comprehend literary nonfiction

Chinese civilization began about seven thousand years ago near a river, the Huang He. Over time, ruling families known as dynasties came to power. People skilled in calligraphy, pottery, carving, and metalworking created works of art. Archaeologists today continue to excavate burial sites and buildings. They are finding treasures that give us many details about ancient Chinese culture.

This 56-foot-tall statue of Buddha in northern China seems both powerful and dignified.

Shang Dynasty: 1650–1050 B.C.E.

Calligraphy, or the art of writing, developed during China's first recorded dynasty, the Shang. Chinese pictographs were engraved into bones or written on bamboo. Other artists from this time formed glazed pottery and bronze figures.

Shang leaders read cracks in oracle bones as answers to important questions. Spoken answers would precede the written ones. Then calligraphers would engrave the answers on the bones.

Han Dynasty: 202 B.C.E.–220 C.E.

Artists of the Han Dynasty created elaborate items from bronze and jade. Chinese crafts and silk fabrics traveled west on the trade route known as the Silk Road. Western ideas began to enter Chinese thought and art at this time.

The artist who created this bronze figure may have been inspired by mythical flying horses.

Tang Dynasty: 618–906 C.E.

During the Tang dynasty, the art of making porcelain was perfected. A white clay called kaolin was baked at high temperatures, creating a lustrous material like glass.

Buddhism became China's official religion at this time. Artwork reflected Buddhist ideas, and artists painted the life of the Buddha in colorful natural settings.

This glazed porcelain Tang vase comes from Henan province.

Song Dynasty: 960–1279 C.E.

The Song Dynasty emphasized the ideas of the philosopher Confucius. He taught that there should be harmony between individuals and society. Artists painted everyday pictures that showed people's temperaments. Landscape paintings reflected the ideas of Daoism, a religion that stressed balance between humans and nature.

(background) More than just replicas of nature, *shanshui* (mountain-water) landscapes show nature's distinct beauty.

The Qingming scroll is ten inches high and almost six yards long. Details in the scroll show parts of city life during the Song Dynasty.

Compare Texts

Compare Art and Information Talk with a partner about "The Emperor's Silent Army" and "Ancient China: Visual Arts." Discuss these questions: *What text structures are used in the selections? What points does each selection make about creative arts in ancient China? What kinds of information in the selections are similar?* After discussing your ideas, work together to write a paragraph that tells how the text and the photos and captions give you a better understanding of ancient China. Use text evidence in your paragraph.

Share Your Views Would you want to trade places with Qin Shihuang or another emperor? Why or why not? If you did trade places, how would you use your powers? Write your thoughts and then discuss them with a partner.

Locate Dig Sites Archaeological digs are taking place all over the world. Choose a country or continent. Use the Internet to find the location of any digs there. Find out what scientists have discovered. Share your findings with the class.

COMMON CORE **RI.6.1** cite textual evidence to support analysis of what the text says explicitly as well as inferences drawn; **RI.6.5** analyze how a sentence, paragraph, chapter, or section fits in the overall structure; **RI.6.7** integrate information presented in different media or formats as well as in words; **W.6.7** conduct short research projects to answer a question, drawing on several sources and refocusing the inquiry when appropriate

Grammar

More Kinds of Pronouns Words such as *someone* and *something* are **indefinite pronouns.** They refer to unidentified persons or things. *This, that, these,* and *those* are **demonstrative pronouns** when used as a subject or object in a sentence. When words such as *who, what,* and *which* begin questions, they are **interrogative pronouns.** Words such as *myself, himself, ourselves,* and *themselves* are **reflexive pronouns** when they refer back to the subject of a sentence. These same pronouns are **intensive pronouns** when they emphasize a noun or another pronoun in the sentence.

Kinds of Pronouns
indefinite pronoun The farmer's shovel strikes something.
demonstrative pronoun This could be an important discovery.
reflexive pronoun He asks himself what the object might be.
intensive pronoun I myself thought our teacher was right.
interrogative pronoun What will he and the other farmers find?

 **With a partner, read aloud each sentence. Identify each pronoun as reflexive or intensive.**

1 We found **ourselves** touring a pottery exhibit.

2 I **myself** do not care for pottery.

3 You **yourself** might really enjoy it.

4 The students arranged **themselves** into groups.

5 The pottery **itself** cannot tell the whole story.

514

The use of an incorrect pronoun can confuse your readers. When you proofread your writing, be sure to use the correct type of pronoun that refers to the antecedent.

Incorrect Pronouns

Emperor Qin Shihuang had a strong desire to become immortal. He wanted to find a potion that gave people eternal life. He couldn't do these hisself, so he sent explorers in search of the potion. The explorers found theirself with nothing to show for their efforts.

Correct Pronouns

Emperor Qin Shihuang had a strong desire to become immortal. He wanted to find a potion that gave people eternal life. He couldn't do this himself, so he sent explorers in search of the potion. The explorers found themselves with nothing to show for their efforts.

 **Connect Grammar to Writing**

As you revise your problem-solution essay, look for pronouns that may be incorrect. Correct any errors you notice. Using the correct forms of pronouns is an important part of good writing.

COMMON CORE **W.6.2a** introduce a topic and organize ideas, concepts, and information/include formatting, graphics, and multimedia; **W.6.2b** develop the topic with facts, definitions, details, quotations, or other information and examples; **W.6.2c** use transitions to clarify relationships; **W.6.2e** establish and maintain a formal style

Informative Writing

✓ **Organization** To write a powerful **problem-solution essay**, present a problem and one or more solutions in clearly organized paragraphs. Develop your ideas with facts, examples, and other informative details. In revising, be sure that transition words and phrases clarify the relationships between ideas and evidence.

my **WriteSmart**

Go **Digital**

Warren drafted a problem-solution essay about bike safety in Maplewood. He established and maintained a formal writing style and ended with a concluding section that summed up his ideas. When he revised his draft, he added another solution to make his essay stronger. He also made sure transition words and phrases connected his ideas.

Writing Traits Checklist

✓ **Ideas**
Did I include facts, examples, and details?

✓ **Organization**
Did I explain the problem first and then the solutions?

✓ **Sentence Fluency**
Did I use transition words and phrases to clarify relationships?

✓ **Word Choice**
Did I use pronouns correctly?

✓ **Voice**
Did I establish and maintain a formal style?

✓ **Conventions**
Did I use correct spelling, grammar, and punctuation?

Revised Draft

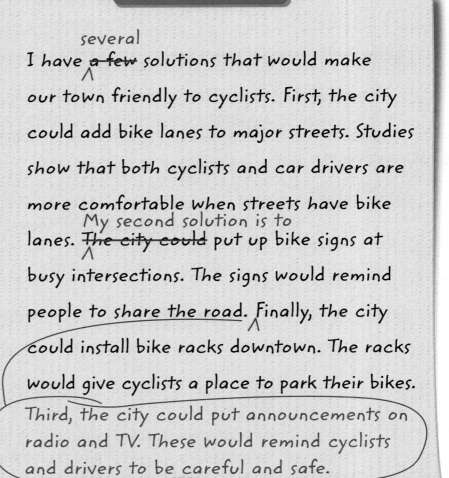

I have a few *several* solutions that would make our town friendly to cyclists. First, the city could add bike lanes to major streets. Studies show that both cyclists and car drivers are more comfortable when streets have bike lanes. ~~The city could~~ *My second solution is to* put up bike signs at busy intersections. The signs would remind people to share the road. Finally, the city could install bike racks downtown. The racks would give cyclists a place to park their bikes. Third, the city could put announcements on radio and TV. These would remind cyclists and drivers to be careful and safe.

Making Maplewood Bicycle-Friendly

by Warren Brown

Maplewood is a great community to live in, but it has a problem: it's not bicycle-friendly. Bicycling is dangerous here! When my friends and I ride our bikes to school, we have to travel on busy streets with no bike lanes. To get downtown, we have to cross three major intersections. Once we get there, we have nowhere to leave our bikes.

I have several solutions that would make our town friendly to cyclists. First, the city could add bike lanes to major streets. Studies show that both cyclists and car drivers are more comfortable when streets have bike lanes. My second solution is to put up bike signs at busy intersections. The signs would remind people to share the road. Third, the city could put announcements on radio and TV. These would remind cyclists and drivers to be careful and safe. Finally, the city could install bike racks downtown. The racks would give cyclists a place to park their bikes.

Maplewood is a great town that I love living in. With a few improvements, it could become a great town for bicycling, too!

Reading as a Writer

Which sentences did Warren add? What transition word did he add? How can you add sentences to improve the organization of your essay?

In my final paper, I explained the problem first; I followed it with my solutions. I also added a transition word to clarify my ideas. I ended my essay with a concluding section.

Vocabulary Reader

Context Cards

COMMON CORE **L.6.6** acquire and use general academic and domain-specific words and phrases/gather vocabulary knowledge for comprehension or expression

Vocabulary in Context

1 steadfast

The Greek hero Odysseus is steadfast. He stays true to his goal of returning home.

2 rash

Icarus acts in a rash, or foolish, manner when he chooses to fly close to the sun. The heat melts his wings, and he falls.

3 bitterly

The hero Heracles fights bitterly, in anger, with a fierce wild boar before he defeats it.

4 unravels

Each day, Penelope weaves a cloth while waiting for Odysseus to return. Each night, she unravels it again.

Go Digital

▶ Study each Context Card.

▶ Tell a story about two or more pictures, using Vocabulary words of your choice.

5 labyrinth

King Minos of Crete has a twisting labyrinth built. The maze is home for the Minotaur, a monster.

6 fury

The warrior Achilles fights bravely during the fury, or violence, of the Trojan War.

7 embrace

When Odysseus finally returns home, he hugs his wife, greeting her with a warm embrace.

8 abandon

A god in a myth might help a person in need, or might abandon that person to fate.

9 massive

During the Trojan War, Greek soldiers slip into Troy by hiding in a massive wooden horse.

10 somber

In a Greek myth, the somber, or gloomy, boatman, Charon, takes Psyche to the underworld.

Read and Comprehend

✓ TARGET SKILL

Story Structure "The Hero and the Minotaur, " like most stories, contains one or more characters and settings, along with a plot that unfolds across a series of episodes. As you read, look for text evidence that shows how the characters respond and change as the plot unfolds. Use a graphic organizer like the one below to help you keep track of the story's overall **structure**.

Characters	Settings
Plot	

✓ TARGET STRATEGY

Infer/Predict Use what you already know, along with text evidence, to help you **infer,** or figure out, what the author means or to **predict** what might happen in the story.

RL.6.1 cite textual evidence to support analysis of what the text says explicitly as well as inferences drawn; **RL.6.3** describe how a story's or drama's plot unfolds and how characters respond and change; **RL.6.5** analyze how a sentence, chapter, scene or stanza fits in the overall structure

Myths

In ancient times, myths were created to explain the world and human experience. These made-up stories include humans, gods and goddesses, and other creatures with special powers.

The ancient Greeks created a collection of myths. Many of the characters in these stories face difficult challenges. In "The Hero and the Minotaur," you will learn about a character named Theseus who sets out on a journey to face a deadly creature called the Minotaur.

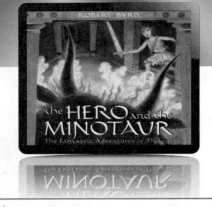

the HERO and the MINOTAUR
The Fantastic Adventures of Theseus

✓ TARGET SKILL

Story Structure Examine details about the story's plot and settings, as well as the characters and their responses.

✓ GENRE

A **myth** is a made-up story that tells what a group of people believed about the world. As you read, look for:

▶ characters with superhuman strength

▶ monster-like creatures

▶ unrealistic events

MEET THE AUTHOR AND ILLUSTRATOR

Robert Byrd

Robert Byrd's work combines simple storytelling with highly detailed illustrations. In this story he uses pen-and-ink and watercolor to bring ancient Crete to life. He says, "The most important thing is to have the small world I create in a picture perfectly match the words of the story, so that even if it is a make-believe world in the eyes and minds of the readers, everything you see is real." Byrd studies objects from the settings of his books, whether Crete or Leonardo da Vinci's Italy (*Leonardo: Beautiful Dreamer*), to make his illustrations as accurate as possible.

The HERO and the MINOTAUR

written and illustrated by
Robert Byrd

ESSENTIAL QUESTION

What is special about
characters in myths?

A Greek youth, Theseus, lifts a huge boulder, revealing a golden sword and sandals that were left for him by his father, King Aegeus. It is a sign that he is ready to join the king in Athens. On his journey, Theseus gains fame by killing three terrible giants who have been preying on travelers.

Word of Theseus' adventures soon reached Athens. As Theseus approached the city, crowds came out to greet him.

"Who performs these daring deeds?" Aegeus asked. "Let me meet the valiant champion." Aegeus decided to honor the stranger's bravery with a magnificent banquet in the Temple of Dolphins. When the prince stepped forward to present himself, the old king recognized the sandals and the golden sword, and he knew the youth before him was his son. He welcomed Theseus with a cry of wonder and a loving embrace. The sight of their happy reunion filled everyone with joy, and the people feasted, danced, and lit altars in every temple in Athens.

One morning shortly after the festivities ended, Theseus sensed a terrible sadness throughout the city. He also saw that his father's brow was creased with sorrow.

"Across the sea, a powerful king named Minos rules the island of Crete," Aegeus explained. "He keeps a beast called the Minotaur, a monster that is half-man, half-bull and feeds on human flesh. Many years ago, Minos' son visited our city and was killed here by a bull. In his rage, Minos made war on us and threatened to destroy Athens unless we sent him a tribute of seven young men and seven young women every year to sacrifice to the Minotaur. The time has come again to pay the tribute," he finished bitterly, "and though I am their king, I can do nothing to protect the fourteen who will draw unlucky lots and be sent to Crete, never to return."

Theseus, angered by King Minos' cruelty, replied, "Let me go with those to be sacrificed. I will slay the Minotaur and end the curse that hangs over our city." Aegeus pleaded with him to stay in Athens, but Theseus remained steadfast and prepared for the voyage to Crete.

The next morning, the old king was forced to bid his son farewell.

ANALYZE THE TEXT

Story Structure What problem do the people of Athens face? How does Theseus respond to this problem?

"In mourning for those to be sacrificed," said Aegeus, "your ship has a black sail. If the gods grant you the power to kill the Minotaur, hoist this white sail on your return. I will see it far out on the horizon and rejoice that you are safe." Theseus promised his father he would remember, then eagerly boarded the vessel. Many around him wept at the sad departure, but Theseus could think only of the thrilling adventure before him.

The ship sailed south and soon approached the shores of Crete. A towering figure ran back and forth across the harbor entrance.

"What is this marvel?" cried Theseus in wonder.

"That is Talus," replied the captain. "A senseless giant made of bronze. It moves as though it were alive and guards the harbor against King Minos' enemies. He would smash us to bits if it were not for our black sail, which even he can recognize." The mechanical man allowed the Athenians to pass him as they approached the king's immense palace, where Minos and the Minotaur were waiting for them.

Not only Talus watched the ship arrive. From a bluff, Ariadne, the daughter of King Minos, stood with her friend Icarus and gazed down at the somber ship. Icarus was the son of Daedalus, a famous inventor. Long ago at the king's command, it was Daedalus who built a labyrinth beneath the palace as a cage to hold the Minotaur.

ANALYZE THE TEXT

Analyze Setting How does the last sentence of paragraph 4 help you "see" the setting where this myth takes place? What other sentences describe the different settings in the myth?

"Who is that who stands so tall and unafraid on the Athenian ship?" Ariadne asked. She was impressed by the stranger's confidence.

"That must be Theseus, son of Aegeus," Icarus replied. He was pleased to be able to show off his knowledge to the beautiful princess, but he wondered at her admiration of Theseus. "I have heard he freely chose to come here and face the Minotaur."

Ariadne knew very well that no one had ever escaped the circling passages and corridors of her father's enormous stone maze. Gazing at the prince, she made up her mind to save him from the king's rash cruelty. "We must go to your father and ask for his advice," she said to Icarus. "If anyone knows the secrets of the maze and can help us rescue Theseus, it is Daedalus." The bold princess was right, for the brilliant inventor revealed to her a clever plan.

That night, while the others slept, Ariadne secretly entered the king's chamber, gathered up the palace keys and Theseus' sword, and crept down to the prisoner's cell. "Theseus," she whispered to him, "I am Ariadne. I have heard tales of your many good deeds. I can show you how to escape the labyrinth, but in return I ask that you help me to escape this island and my father, King Minos, who has grown wicked and pitiless."

Theseus agreed to help her, and so Ariadne explained Daedalus' secret. "You must secure one end of this ball of thread to the entrance of the labyrinth," she said, "and keep hold of the rest of the ball as the string unravels behind you. If you defeat the Minotaur, the thread's path will lead you back out of the labyrinth." Praying that the gods would help him, she led Theseus to the maze and watched as he descended the heavy stone steps. Then she returned to the prison hold to free the other captives.

In the corridors of the labyrinth, the odor was foul, the light dim. Theseus gripped his father's sword in one hand, and in the other he held the unraveling thread. The passages twisted and turned, leading him first one way and then another, winding around and around. Down, down he went, searching for the beast hidden deep in the black abyss. Finally he came to an open space where the Minotaur lay sleeping on the rough stone floor. Its hot breath shook the cavern walls. The creature had the chest and arms of a powerful man, but the rest of its body had the shape of a bull, and two great horns grew out of its head.

Then the Minotaur opened one glowing red eye and fixed it on Theseus. Its snore died away, and the chamber grew deathly still.

ANALYZE THE TEXT

Author's Word Choice How does the author's choice of words create a dark mood in this scene? What words create this mood?

With a thunderous bellow, the Minotaur rose to its feet and charged. Theseus leapt aside, but the deadly horns grazed his tunic. The Minotaur spun around, furious, and charged again. As the beast descended upon him, Theseus steadied himself, raised his golden sword, and with a great heave drove the blade through the Minotaur's heart. The monster dropped to the cold stone floor, silenced forever.

Shaken by the fury of the struggle, Theseus had dropped the ball of thread. Anxious to escape the gloomy maze, he picked it up again and followed the thread out of the labyrinth and into the cool night air.

Ariadne and Icarus were waiting for him. The princess cried out with delight to see Theseus unharmed.

"Let us waste no time in leaving. The king is sure to come after us," urged Ariadne. Theseus and the freed Athenians boarded the ship, but Icarus stepped back.

"Minos will blame Daedalus for your escape. I cannot abandon my father to the king's wrath," he explained, though it pained Icarus to see Theseus leave with Ariadne. "Daedalus and I will flee Minos together," he vowed. "Then we will join you in Athens."

Icarus watched from the bluffs as the ship set a course for Athens, but he was not the only one who followed the black sail in the breaking dawn. At the harbor entrance Talus spied the ship and raised his heavy club high to strike the boat. Theseus stepped forward with his sword, prepared to fight. But Poseidon, ever watchful, sent a massive wave smashing into the bronze giant. The Athenians watched in awe as the shining colossus, crushed into a heap of broken metal, sank to the bottom of the sea.

On his voyage to Athens, Theseus forgets to change the sails of his ship from black to white. Believing that his son is dead, King Aegeus throws himself into the sea. Theseus becomes the next king of Athens and names the surrounding waters the Aegean Sea, in honor of his father.

Dig Deeper

How to Analyze the Text

Use these pages to learn about Story Structure, Analyzing Setting, and Author's Word Choice. Then read "The Hero and the Minotaur" again to apply what you learned.

Story Structure

The myth "The Hero and the Minotaur" contains characters, settings, and plot, all of which work together to make up the **story structure.** The plot includes **episodes,** or scenes, that happen in a certain order. To understand a story's overall structure, use text evidence to trace how the characters respond to challenges as the plot unfolds. They must also identify the problem the main character faces and its solution.

Look back at page 531. What challenge or problem does Theseus face? How does he respond to this challenge?

Characters	Settings
Plot	

COMMON CORE

RL.6.1 cite textual evidence to support analysis of what the text says explicitly as well as inferences drawn; **RL.6.3** describe how a story's or drama's plot unfolds and how characters respond and change; **RL.6.4** determine the meaning of words and phrases, including figurative and connotative meanings/analyze impact of word choice; **RL.6.5** analyze how a sentence, chapter, scene, or stanza fits in the overall structure

Analyze Setting

Setting is often important to the plot of a story. The **setting** is where and when the episodes of a story take place. The setting can change in a story, so readers must look for sentences that describe each setting, or use evidence in the story to figure it out. As you reread "The Hero and the Minotaur," look for sentences that describe or give clues to each setting. Think about the way in which the setting is described and how the description helps you picture the story events that take place.

Author's Word Choice

Authors use particular words to develop **mood.** Mood is the atmosphere, or feeling, that a writer creates in readers. Each scene in a story can create a mood. Robert Byrd, the author of "The Hero and the Minotaur," creates mood through the words he chooses. As you read a particular scene in the myth, ask yourself: How does this part of the story make me feel? What words make me feel this way?

Your Turn

RETURN TO THE ESSENTIAL QUESTION

Turn and Talk Review the selection with a partner to prepare to discuss this question: *What is special about characters in myths?* Think about the characters in "The Hero and the Minotaur." Develop an answer by asking relevant questions and responding to your partner's questions.

Continue your discussion of "The Hero and the Minotaur" by using text evidence to explain your answers to these questions:

1. Why do you think the myth includes the tragic event that occurs at the end of the story?

2. Whom else might you consider to be a hero in this myth? Why?

3. What do you think motivates Theseus to slay the Minotaur?

WHAT'S THE MESSAGE?

Determine Theme Work in small groups to summarize "The Hero and the Minotaur." Then determine the theme of the story, the message the author wants readers to understand and remember. Discuss the following: *Theseus decides to face the Minotaur. How does this event contribute to the theme? What other story events reveal the theme?* Use story details as text evidence to support your answers.

WRITE ABOUT READING

Response Myths often reveal the values of the people who created them. Based on what you read in "The Hero and the Minotaur," what values do you think were important to the ancient Greeks? Do you think those values are important to people today? Write a paragraph to explain your argument. Use story details from the myth, along with inferences about the characters or events, as evidence to support your ideas.

Writing Tip

Begin your response by clearly stating a claim. Then give reasons supported by evidence to develop your argument.

COMMON CORE **RL.6.1** cite textual evidence to support analysis of what the text says explicitly as well as inferences drawn; **RL.6.2** determine a theme or central idea of a text/provide a summary; **W.6.1a** introduce claim(s) and organize reasons and evidence clearly; **W.6.9a** apply grade 6 Reading standards to literature; **SL.6.1a** come to discussions prepared/explicitly draw on preparation to probe and reflect on ideas under discussion; **SL.6.1c** pose and respond to questions and make comments that contribute to the discussion

NEWSPAPER ARTICLE

THE ANCIENT NEWS
Illustrated by Marilee Hayer

A **newspaper article** provides information about a current event. It usually answers the questions *Who? What? When? Where? Why?*

✓ **TEXT FOCUS**

Facts and details about a specific event are provided in newspaper articles. Facts can be proved true. Details support the facts in the article.

COMMON CORE

RL.6.10 read and comprehend literature

THE ANCIENT NEWS

illustrated by Marilee Heyer

Go Digital

The Cretan News

Minotaur Slain

The Minotaur is dead. According to reports, the fearsome half-man, half-bull was surprised in its sleep yesterday by Theseus, son of King Aegeus. After a brief struggle, Theseus was able to use a golden sword to end the Minotaur's life. This action will likely end the tradition of sending Athenian youth into the beast's lair. Cretans will recall that a son of King Minos was killed by an Athenian bull. This prompted the king's rage and his demand for revenge on Athens.

After the slaying, Theseus and the young men and women in his company escaped from the king's labyrinth. How they did this remains unclear as the maze was thought to be inescapable. The group set sail back to Athens along with a Cretan accomplice. Witnesses say this accomplice was Ariadne, a daughter of King Minos.

Theseus was able to use a golden sword...

In a related incident, Talus, the bronze guardian of the harbor entrance, was struck and destroyed by a massive wave. Talus was in the act of trying to stop the Athenian craft when the wave struck. The black-sailed craft, with all aboard, was able to navigate around Talus and complete its escape.

THE ATHENIAN NEWS

King Aegeus Drowns

King Aegeus, the long-reigning ruler of Athens, is dead. The king is reported to have plunged into the sea in despair at the sight of a black-sailed craft entering Athens's harbor today. Sources close to the king say Aegeus believed that his beloved son Theseus had been killed while on a quest to destroy the Minotaur of Crete. A distraught Prince Theseus, the heir to the Athenian throne, could not be reached for comment.

Compare Texts

Compare Text Forms "The Hero and the Minotaur" and "The Ancient News" present the same events. Use the following questions to compare and contrast the texts: *What approach do the newspaper articles use to tell the story of Theseus and the Minotaur? How is this different from the author's approach in "The Hero and the Minotaur"?* Write your answers. Use evidence from the texts to support your ideas.

Write to Reflect Theseus could not have escaped the labyrinth without the help of Ariadne and Icarus. Think of a time when friends helped you face a challenge or when you helped someone else do so. Write a paragraph describing the experience.

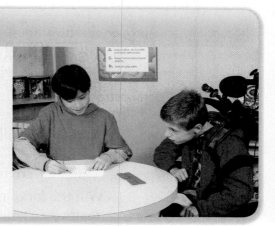

Use Patterns in Nature The labyrinth in "The Hero and the Minotaur" can be seen as a pattern, a form of visual math. Use patterns in nature, such as those in shells or leaves, to design a maze. Have a partner find the route out of your maze.

COMMON CORE **RL.6.1** cite textual evidence to support analysis of what the text says explicitly as well as inferences drawn; **RL.6.9** compare and contrast texts in different forms or genres on their approaches to themes and topics; **W.6.10** write routinely over extended time frames and shorter time frames

Grammar

 Go Digital

What Are Adjectives and Adverbs? An **adjective** gives information about a noun. Some adjectives are **descriptive adjectives** that tell *what kind*. One type of descriptive adjective, a **proper adjective,** is formed from a proper noun and is capitalized. Adjectives such as *this, that, these,* and *those* tell *which one* and are called **demonstrative adjectives.** An **adverb** is a word that modifies a verb, an adjective, or another adverb.

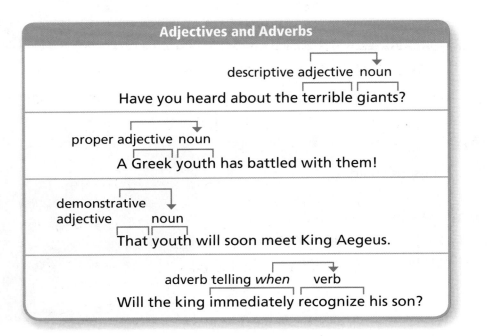

Adjectives and Adverbs

descriptive adjective noun
Have you heard about the terrible giants?

proper adjective noun
A Greek youth has battled with them!

demonstrative adjective noun
That youth will soon meet King Aegeus.

adverb telling *when* verb
Will the king immediately recognize his son?

Adverbs that modify verbs answer these questions: *How? Where? When?*

Try This! **Read the sentences below. List the adjectives and adverbs on another sheet of paper. Label each adjective as descriptive, proper, or demonstrative, and write the noun it modifies. Then write the verb each adverb modifies.**

1. Theseus freely chose a difficult task.

2. He stood on the deck of the Athenian ship.

3. A fearsome beast lived in a maze on Crete.

4. This beast leapt savagely at Theseus.

When you write, use precise adjectives and adverbs to create clear and vivid pictures for your readers. Also, be careful not to use the same adjectives or adverbs over and over.

Less Precise Adjective and Adverb

Greek myths tell good stories about characters who behave badly.

More Precise Adjective and Adverb

Greek myths tell cautionary stories about characters who behave foolishly.

✎ Connect Grammar to Writing

As you revise your cause-effect essay, look for opportunities to use precise adjectives and adverbs. Use those words to create clear pictures for your readers.

W.6.2a introduce a topic and organize ideas, concepts, and information/include formatting, graphics, and multimedia; **W.6.2b** develop the topic with facts, definitions, details, quotations, or other information and examples; **W.6.2c** use transitions to clarify relationships; **W.6.4** produce writing in which development, organization, and style are appropriate to task, purpose, and audience

COMMON CORE

Informative Writing

✔ **Sentence Fluency** In a **cause-effect essay,** writers use cause-and-effect relationships to explain a sequence of events. A cause can have more than one effect, and an effect can be the cause of another effect. As you revise your cause-effect essay, be sure you have used details from the text to develop the topic. Check that transition words and phrases such as *because*, *as a result*, *since*, and *so* clearly link ideas.

Michael explained the chain of events that led to Theseus' journey to Crete. Then he added transition words and phrases to make the relationship between the causes and effects clear.

Writing Traits Checklist

✔ **Ideas**
Did I develop the topic with details from the text?

✔ **Organization**
Are the events in a logical order?

✔ **Sentence Fluency**
Did I use transitions to link ideas?

✔ **Word Choice**
Did I use vivid adjectives and adverbs?

✔ **Voice**
Did I use my own voice?

✔ **Conventions**
Did I use correct spelling, grammar, and punctuation?

Revised Draft

The death of King Minos' son caused a ^tragic chain of events. A bull in Athens had killed Minos' son, ^so Minos declared war on Athens. His rage caused him to demand a terrible price: a yearly human sacrifice to the ^beastly Minotaur. ^As a result, seven Seven young men and seven young women traveled from Athens to Crete every year to die.

546

One Bad Thing Leads to Another

by Michael Wu

"The Hero and the Minotaur" tells of a young Greek hero named Theseus. The story begins as King Aegeus tells his son Theseus about King Minos, the death of King Minos' son, and the punishment that Minos inflicted on Athens.

The death of King Minos' son caused a tragic chain of events. A bull in Athens had killed Minos' son, so Minos declared war on Athens. His rage caused him to demand a terrible price: a yearly human sacrifice to the beastly Minotaur. As a result, seven young men and seven young women traveled from Athens to Crete every year to die.

When Theseus learned of the cruel practice, he was horrified and angry. Therefore, he vowed to his father, King Aegeus, that he would slay the Minotaur. Aegeus did not want him to go. Even though Aegeus begged him to stay, Theseus remained determined to end the senseless killings.

The next day, Theseus said goodbye to his father. Then he set out to kill the Minotaur so that he could end the curse forever.

Reading as a Writer

What transition words and phrases did Michael add to make the cause-and-effect relationships clearer? What transition words and phrases can you add to strengthen your essay?

In my final paper, I added transition words and phrases to connect ideas and sentences. I also added vivid adjectives to describe characters and events.

✓ **TARGET VOCABULARY**

divine
ceremonial
fragments
pondered
supportive
erected
mission
prosperity
emerge
depicted

Vocabulary
Reader

Context
Cards

COMMON CORE **L.6.6** acquire and use general academic and domain-specific words and phrases/gather vocabulary knowledge for comprehension or expression

Vocabulary in Context

1 divine
Pharaohs ruled Egypt by divine right. They claimed their power came from the gods.

2 ceremonial
Pharaohs wore special ceremonial robes when attending important events in their temples and palaces.

3 fragments
Digging in ancient ruins, archaeologists have found fragments of broken pottery and other objects.

4 pondered
For centuries people have pondered, or thought deeply about, the mystery of the Egyptian pyramids.

 Go Digital

▶ Study each Context Card.

▶ Use a dictionary to confirm the meanings of these words.

5 supportive

Hatshepsut was supportive of her husband, Thutmose II, and helped him rule Egypt wisely.

6 erected

Several impressive stone monuments were erected, or built, when Hatshepsut ruled Egypt.

7 mission

Hatshepsut sent traders on a mission. She asked them to bring goods back from the land of Punt.

8 prosperity

Crops flourished in the rich soil around the Nile River, making ancient Egypt a land of prosperity.

9 emerge

When historians learned to read ancient Egyptian hieroglyphics, new information about Egypt began to emerge.

10 depicted

In Egyptian art, the god Thoth is often depicted with the head of a bird—the ibis.

Read and Comprehend

☑ TARGET SKILL

Cause and Effect Authors of informational text often organize ideas by causes and effects to show relationships between events. As you read "The Princess Who Became a King," look for text evidence that shows the **causes**, or reasons why things happen, and their **effects**, or results. Look for clue words such as *because* and *when* to identify causes and effects. Remember that one cause can have several effects. Noting causes and effects in a section of text can help you better understand the ideas in a text. Use a graphic organizer like this one to keep track of the cause-and-effect relationships.

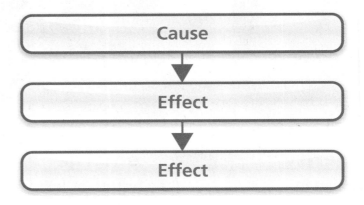

☑ TARGET STRATEGY

Monitor/Clarify As you read, **monitor,** or check, your understanding of the text. Look for text evidence to **clarify,** or make clear, any ideas that do not make sense.

RI.6.1 cite textual evidence to support analysis of what the text says explicitly as well as inferences drawn; **RI.6.5** analyze how a sentence, paragraph, chapter, or section fits in the overall structure

Ancient Egypt

Ancient Egyptians lived about 5,000 years ago. In ancient Egyptian culture, kings called *pharaohs* ruled the people and commanded armies. Egyptians believed a pharaoh's ruling power came from their gods.

Archaeologists have made many discoveries about ancient Egypt. In "The Princess Who Became a King," you'll learn about one surprising Egyptian pharaoh.

ANCHOR TEXT

✓ TARGET SKILL

Cause and Effect Explain how events are related and how one event causes another.

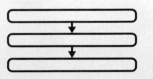

✓ GENRE

Informational text gives facts and other information about a topic. As you read, look for:

▶ details about a topic or subject

▶ photographs and captions

▶ the way in which ideas and information are organized

COMMON CORE **RI.6.1** cite textual evidence to support analysis of what the text says explicitly as well as inferences drawn; **RI.6.3** analyze how a key individual, event, or idea is introduced, illustrated, and elaborated; **RI.6.5** analyze how a sentence, paragraph, chapter, or section fits in the overall structure; **RI.6.10** read and comprehend literary nonfiction

MEET THE AUTHOR

Joyce Hansen

Joyce Hansen's career as an author spans three decades. As her many titles show, she is equally at home writing realistic fiction *(The Gift-Giver)*, historical fiction *(I Thought My Soul Would Rise and Fly)*, and nonfiction *(Women of Hope)*. A former teacher, Hansen is currently at work on a five-book series about a family of African Americans living in pre-Civil War New York City. Hansen has said, "Real success for me is when young people tell me that they were encouraged and helped by something I've written."

MEET THE ILLUSTRATOR

Laurie McGaw

A portrait painter and illustrator, Laurie McGaw lives and works in Ontario, Canada. She has illustrated many books for young people, including *To Be a Princess: The Fascinating Lives of Real Princesses* and *The Secrets of Vesuvius: Exploring the Mysteries of an Ancient Buried City.*

The Princess Who Became a King

from *African Princess: The Amazing Lives of Africa's Royal Women*

by Joyce Hansen   illustrated by Laurie McGaw

This limestone bust of Hatshepsut (hat SHEHP soot) wearing a pharaoh's beard was once part of an eighteen-foot statue that stood in the temple at Deir el-Bahri (dair ehl BAH ree), where her tomb was housed.

On a hot day in 1922, there was great excitement at a dig site in what had once been the Egyptian city of Thebes (theebz). The archaeologists had stumbled upon a pit containing hundreds of pieces of ancient granite statues. Some of the pieces were as small as fine gravel; others were so huge that a crane was needed to lift them. (The head archaeologist, Herbert E. Winlock, said later that putting the fragments together was like working on one hundred jigsaw puzzles, each one with pieces missing.) The statues were of a pharaoh wearing the traditional kilt and crown—as well as the beard—of an Egyptian ruler. But the pharaoh's face was that of a woman!

On some of the broken columns, the dig team found the name *Hatshepsut* written in hieroglyphs. Was this the same Hatshepsut who had reigned over Egypt around 1479–1457 B.C.E.? Herbert Winlock knew that her empty burial tomb had been found a few years earlier at Deir el-Bahri but that her mummy had yet to be discovered. If this was the same Hatshepsut, he wondered, why had so many statues of her been destroyed? As the archaeologists studied and pondered, the story of an extraordinary woman began to emerge after thousands of years of silence.

This set of Egyptian hieroglyphs represents the pharaoh Hatshepsut. The symbols are enclosed in an oval, called a cartouche (kahr TOOSH).

Statues of Hatshepsut stand at her Mortuary Temple in Deir el-Bahri. It was traditional to show a deceased pharaoh holding a shepherd's crook and flail (a rod with three strands of beads attached). These objects were symbols of a pharaoh's power and responsibilities.

The crowds on the banks of the river cheered wildly as the gilded royal barge came into view. Standing next to the pharaoh was a lovely young girl in white linen robes—his eldest daughter, the Royal Princess Hatshepsut. For Pharaoh Thutmose (thoot MOH suh) I, these trips along the Nile from Thebes to Memphis gave him an opportunity to inspect his kingdom and see his people. We can imagine him pointing out to his daughter the great monuments and temples, teaching her about the world they lived in. With Hatshepsut's mother, the Royal Wife Ahmose (AH mohs), and other members of the royal family, they would stay in temporary palaces called the "Mooring Places of Pharaoh."

The Nile River and its fertile valley (background) helped develop farming in Egypt. Along the Nile grew the royal cities of Memphis in the north of Egypt and Thebes in the south.

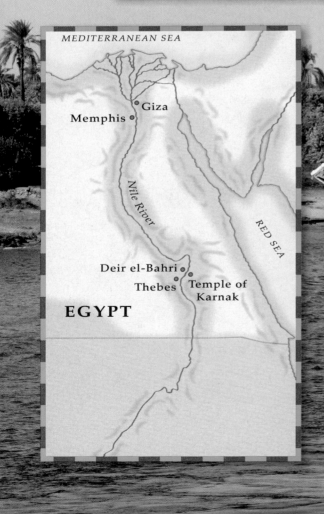

Throughout her childhood, Hatshepsut had a very close relationship with her father. She was the only surviving child of Ahmose. Sadly, with the exception of Hatshepsut's half brother, Thutmose II, all of the pharaoh's other children had died. Hatshepsut and Thutmose II, who would someday marry and rule Egypt together, must have been a great comfort to the pharaoh. Egyptian royalty married close family members in order to keep the royal blood "pure" and to keep wealth and power within the ruling family.

Hatshepsut's carefree days and nights spent in the palace at Thebes ended when she became a teenager. Her beloved father died, and her life changed completely. Historians are not certain whether Hatshepsut was older or younger than Thutmose II, but either way she could not become the new pharaoh because she was a woman. Pharaohs were not only supreme rulers; they were also divine. Their right to rule came directly from the gods. The pharaoh was the head of all the priests (a very powerful group of men) and was the only person who was allowed to communicate directly with the gods. Next in line to be the new pharaoh was Hatshepsut's half brother, Thutmose II. Princess Hatshepsut became his Royal Wife.

The goddess Mut (moot), shown here, was known as Mother of the Gods. Mut's crown often depicted a vulture, which was revered as a fierce protector of its young.

Ancient Egyptians worshiped the god Amun (AH moon) as the king of all gods.

Hatshepsut probably accepted her marriage to Thutmose II as her duty. If she refused to marry him, the Theban royal family would be weakened, and other people would try to claim the throne. She was only fourteen or fifteen years old when she married, but like her father, Hatshepsut had a deep sense of responsibility. Childhood things were put aside, and she gracefully stepped into her role as the "King's Great Wife," although she preferred the title "God's Wife of Amun." The title of God's Wife of Amun was politically important, as it gave Hatshepsut influence over the powerful priests and allowed the royal family to control the vast wealth and property of the Amun temples.

In the years that followed her marriage, the young queen had a daughter, Neferure (neh feh ROO ray), whom she loved very much. As well as being a mother, Hatshepsut seems to have been a supportive queen and wife. She might even have shared power with her husband.

This statue depicts Hatshepsut's daughter, Neferure, carried by her tutor, Senenmut (SEHN ehn moot). Senenmut served as a trusted adviser during Hatshepsut's reign.

ANALYZE THE TEXT

Conclusions and Generalizations
What inferences can you make to determine why Hatshepsut crowned herself as pharaoh? What text evidence supports your conclusions?

Almost every pharaoh from the 16th century B.C.E. to 30 B.C.E. added buildings, walls, or monuments to the Karnak temple complex, a religious site at Thebes.

Unfortunately, after a short reign of three years, Thutmose II died, and his son by a lesser wife, Thutmose III, became the new pharaoh. There was one serious problem—he was a small child. Hatshepsut was appointed Queen Regent. This was not an unusual situation. In the past, Egyptian queens had acted as regents, governing for their young sons or other male relatives.

But Hatshepsut was different. She had learned how to rule from her father and had taken on some of her husband's royal duties. For her, it must have seemed as though the gods had intervened in her life. She was finally going to be given a chance to rule on her own, at least until the young pharaoh was old enough to govern.

Although she was only seventeen or eighteen years old when her husband died, Hatshepsut was a successful ruler. She knew from her years at court how to deal with the important priests and nobles who helped run the country. Maybe it was a sign of things to come, but she had two obelisks built while she was Queen Regent. When these massive columns were completed seven years later, she did something that had never been done before. Hatshepsut had herself crowned as pharaoh!

Hatshepsut's Obelisks

Towering almost a hundred feet into the sky, one of two massive granite obelisks (AH buh lihsks) that Hatshepsut **erected** at the temple of Amun in Karnak still stands (at right, in photo) beside one built by her father. They were carved without any iron tools, and no one knows for certain how the Egyptians managed to raise them. Egyptian obelisks have been the model for many other structures, including the Washington Monument, which is almost six times taller than Hatshepsut's obelisk.

Hatshepsut became one of only a few female pharaohs to rule Egypt in three thousand years of history. She must have been confident, smart, and fearless to take such a bold step. She also must have had supporters among the powerful nobles and priests at court. Hatshepsut had obviously earned their respect and confidence. This would not have been an easy thing to do. She would have had to convince them that a female pharaoh would not anger the gods and bring terrible hardship to the Egyptian people.

Hatshepsut's reign did not bring down the fury of the gods. Historians believe she ruled for fifteen years, bringing peace and prosperity to her people. As a pharaoh, she is best known for her monuments at Karnak and Deir el-Bahri.

Hatshepsut was a builder. From the time she sat at her father's side gazing at the pyramids of Giza or visiting the temple complex at Karnak, she understood the importance of building monuments and temples to the gods. For the ancient Egyptians, life was a preparation for death, leading to eternal life in heaven. However, the Egyptians did not want to be forgotten on earth. They left grand monuments behind so that they would be remembered forever.

The three Pyramids of Giza are located near the modern capital of Cairo (KY roh). They were built, seven to ten centuries before Hatshepsut's reign, to house the mummies of Egyptian rulers.

Hatshepsut understood the importance of building strong trade relationships with other countries. She sent a mission to the fabled land of Punt, thought to be located in present-day Ethiopia or Somalia. The expedition returned from Punt with valuable goods such as gold, ebony, ivory, and myrrh (mur) trees (used for making incense). Hatshepsut was so proud of the successful mission that she had the entire story of the voyage carved on the walls of her mortuary temple.

This carving from Hatshepsut's temple shows the voyage to Punt. The land of Punt may have been located in one of several places on the Red Sea or on the Arabian Sea south of the Horn of Africa.

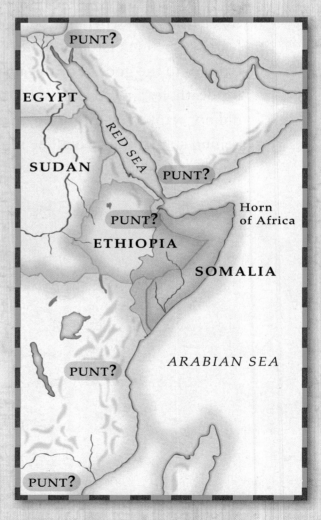

Hatshepsut's splendid mortuary temple at Deir el-Bahri

Hatshepsut asked her loyal and trusted adviser, Senenmut, to plan and build her mortuary temple at Deir el-Bahri. She named it Djeser-Djeseru (JEH sur jeh SEH roo), meaning "Holy of Holies." Nestled near her father's burial tomb, it was an elegant building. It was also very different from other styles of architecture at that time, just as Hatshepsut was so different from other women.

Fifteen years into her reign, Hatshepsut again broke with tradition. She celebrated her jubilee. Normally, a jubilee was held thirty years into a successful reign. After the celebration Hatshepsut followed in her father's footsteps and had two more obelisks built and placed in front of the temple at Karnak. One still stands there today.

ANALYZE THE TEXT

Analyze Historical Characters What examples and anecdotes does the author give to introduce and describe Hatshepsut on pages 561-563?

Hatshepsut may have been in her forties when she died—an old woman in those days. For years, scholars believed that Thutmose III was so angry at his aunt for crowning herself pharaoh that he knocked down her statues. But the time Hatshepsut spent training her nephew to become a successful ruler suggests that she was a loving woman, not a power-hungry one. And Hatshepsut's monuments were destroyed twenty years after her death. If Thutmose III had been angry with Hatshepsut, why did he wait so long to erase her memory? And why didn't he destroy the images and statues that showed her as a princess and a queen?

Perhaps Thutmose III was having political problems and his throne was threatened. Maybe he destroyed anything that depicted Hatshepsut as pharaoh in order to show that there was a direct line of kings from Thutmose I and II to himself, with no Hatshepsut in between.

We will probably never know who destroyed her statues or why. What we do know is that Pharaoh Hatshepsut can now take her place among the great kings and builders of Egypt.

The mortuary at Deir el-Bahri honors both Hatshepsut and the goddess Hathor, shown here. Ceremonial occasions celebrated Hathor as a joyful, loving protector of women.

ANALYZE THE TEXT

Cause and Effect What effects did Hatshepsut's reign have on Egypt's history? How do these effects help you better understand Hatshepsut's importance in history?

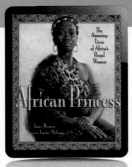

Dig Deeper

How to Analyze the Text

Use these pages to learn about Cause and Effect, Analyzing Historical Characters, and Conclusions and Generalizations. Then read "The Princess Who Became a King" again to apply what you learned.

Cause and Effect

In "The Princess Who Became a King," author Joyce Hansen uses **cause-and-effect relationships** to organize the key events in Hatshepsut's life. To understand the ideas in the text, look for sentences and sections of text that present **causes** and **effects.**

Look back at page 559 in "The Princess Who Became a King." The first paragraph in this section states that Pharaoh Thutmose II died after a short reign. What were the multiple effects that occurred as a result of his death? How does this section of text fit into the overall structure of "The Princess Who Became a King"?

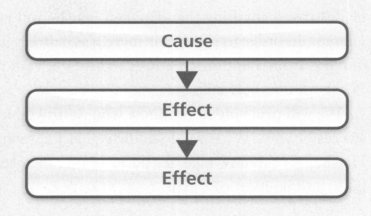

Cause

↓

Effect

↓

Effect

Analyze Historical Characters

Authors introduce and describe **historical characters** in a variety of ways. They may use descriptive language to illustrate, or reveal, a person's physical appearance or personality traits. They may also use examples and anecdotes, which are short stories about events in a person's life. As you reread "The Princess Who Became a King," pay attention to the ways that the historical characters are introduced and described.

Conclusions and Generalizations

When readers **draw conclusions** and **make generalizations,** they use their own experiences as well as text evidence to infer ideas that aren't stated or are generally true. For example, the author points out that Thutmose III did not destroy the images and statues of Hatshepsut as a princess and a queen, and that he waited twenty years to destroy her images as a pharaoh. One conclusion that can be drawn from this evidence is that Thutmose III was not angry with Hatshepsut.

Your Turn

RETURN TO THE ESSENTIAL QUESTION

Turn and Talk Review the selection with a partner to prepare to discuss this question: *What was life like in ancient Egypt?* As you review the text together, use text evidence to ask and respond to questions that help you develop your ideas.

Classroom Conversation

Continue your discussion of "The Princess Who Became a King" by explaining your answers to these questions:

1. Why do you think Hatshepsut built two obelisks when she was still Queen Regent?

2. What might have been Hatshepsut's reasons for celebrating her jubilee fifteen years into her reign?

3. What might have happened to Hatshepsut's legacy if she had not built her monuments and statues?

VIEWPOINT

Author's Perspective With a partner, determine the author's perspective, or **point of view,** on Hatshepsut. Discuss the following: *What information does Joyce Hansen share about Hatshepsut as a princess, as a queen, and as a pharaoh? Does she have a positive or negative view of Hatshepsut?* Use text evidence to support your ideas.

WRITE ABOUT READING

Response Queen Regent Hatshepsut had herself crowned as pharaoh. Do you agree or disagree that she should have declared herself ruler of Egypt? Write a paragraph to explain your claim. Use text evidence to support your argument.

Writing Tip

State your claim at the beginning of your response. Use transition words and phrases to link the evidence supporting your argument.

COMMON CORE **RI.6.1** cite textual evidence to support analysis of what the text says explicitly as well as inferences drawn; **RI.6.6** determine the author's point of view or purpose and explain how it is conveyed; **W.6.1b** support claim(s) with reasons and evidence, using credible sources and demonstrating understanding of the topic or text; **W.9.9b** apply grade 6 Reading standards to literary nonfiction; **SL.6.1c** pose and respond to questions and make comments that contribute to the discussion

☑ GENRE

Informational text, such as the article on these Web pages, gives facts and examples about a topic.

☑ TEXT FOCUS

Informational text may include a **map,** a detailed drawing that shows a place and its surroundings.

COMMON CORE

RI.6.7 integrate information presented in different media or formats as well as in words; **RI.6.10** read and comprehend literary nonfiction

---

File   Edit   View   Favorites

ANCIENT KINGDOMS ▶ KUSH   **GEOGRAPHY**

KUSH
LAND AND CLIMATE

Seven thousand years ago, a great society arose along the middle of the Nile River: the kingdom of Kush, also known as Nubia. Kush's civilization was as advanced as that of its neighbor, Egypt.

Hills separated Kush from Egypt and the Red Sea. To the south were the tropical forests of central Africa, but much of Kush had a desert climate. However, the yearly flooding of the Nile River provided fertile soil for animals and crops. In ancient times, Kush was actually wetter than Egypt is today. Huge herds of cattle grazed along the river.

Kush and the lands around it are in northeastern Africa. (See also page 571.)

AFRICA

QUEENS AND PHARAOHS

Kush began as a farming community, but over time, it gained in prosperity. The queens of Kush would emerge as powerful and supportive rulers. They shared the throne, and with the kings, they pondered problems facing the kingdom. A queen was known as a *kandake* (kahn DAH kee), or "strong woman."

The armies of Egypt wanted the gold and copper found in Kush. They conquered the kingdom during the reign of Thutmose (thoot MOH suh) I, around 1500 B.C.E. Then, after hundreds of years, Egypt's power began to decline. During the 700s B.C.E., the Kushite king Piankhi (PYAHNG kee) conquered Egypt. He began a line of Kushite pharaohs who used many Egyptian ceremonial rituals. Later, forced out of Egypt by the Assyrians, the Kushite kings erected a capital farther south, in Meroë (MEHR oh ee).

The Kingdom of Kush

Mediterranean Sea

ASSYRIA

EGYPT

0   250   500 Miles
0   250   500 Kilometers

ASIA

Key

Kush civilization
1000 B.C.E.–150 C.E.

⊙ Capital

Nile River

Kush

Red Sea

Kerma
First capital,
founded
c. 3000 B.C.E

Napata
Second capital,
700s B.C.E

Meroë
Third capital,
founded
c. 590 B.C.E

AFRICA

TRADE AND CULTURE

The kingdom of Kush carried on a busy trade in gold, ebony, and ivory. Traders on a mission to Egypt could exchange fabric, jewelry, and metal objects for Egyptian goods, such as glass. Kushites also melted down fragments of iron ore to make tools and weapons. Kush's achievements in art, technology, and trade helped it stay in power for nearly a thousand years.

Kushites borrowed many customs from Egypt. They accepted Egyptian ideas of divine figures, worshiping the god Amun. They also adapted what they took to create their own culture. At first, the people of Kush carved Egyptian hieroglyphics into the stone of their buildings. By the Meroitic period, they had begun to change the hieroglyphs to create different symbols and a cursive script that depicted their language. This script reduced the large number of Egyptian symbols to twenty-three signs—an alphabet.

Meroitic cursive script

Compare Texts

TEXT TO TEXT

Compare Informational Texts With a partner, compare and contrast how the authors of "The Princess Who Became a King" and "Kush" present the topic of life in ancient Egypt. How are the kingdoms of Kush and Egypt described? What can you learn from each text that you can't learn from the other? Work together to discuss and write your answers. Use evidence from the text to support your ideas.

TEXT TO SELF

Describe a Decision Hatshepsut made many important decisions while she ruled Egypt. Think of a time when it was your responsibility to be in charge. Describe a decision that you made and what resulted from that decision.

TEXT TO WORLD

Map Past onto Present With a partner, look at a map of present-day Africa. Identify the countries that now lie along the Nile River, including those in the region once known as Kush.

COMMON CORE **RI.6.1** cite textual evidence to support analysis of what the text says explicitly as well as inferences drawn; **RI.6.7** integrate information presented in different media or formats as well as in words; **RI.6.9** compare and contrast one author's presentation of events with that of another; **W.6.7** conduct short research projects to answer a question, drawing on several sources and refocusing the inquiry when appropriate

Grammar

What Are Nonrestrictive Elements? What Are Parenthetical Elements? In a sentence, a **nonrestrictive element** is a phrase or clause that gives nonessential information. If the phrase or clause is removed, the basic meaning of the sentence does not change. A nonrestrictive element is set off by commas. A **parenthetical element** is an expression that explains a word or phrase in the sentence. Parentheses or dashes are used to set off a parenthetical element.

Punctuating Nonrestrictive and Parenthetical Elements

nonrestrictive element

Ancient Egyptians built monuments, such as obelisks, and temples.

parenthetical element

Hatshepsut built massive obelisks (almost 100 feet tall) at Karnak.

parenthetical element with dash

Temple entrances were marked by obelisks—tall, four-sided monuments.

 **Copy each sentence. Use commas, parentheses, or dashes to punctuate the information in bold type.**

1. The statues **many of which were broken** lay in a pit.

2. The statues were of a pharaoh **a king of Egypt.**

3. The pharaoh wore a beard **which was a symbol of power** and a crown.

4. Hatshepsut **a female pharaoh** had the statues of herself built.

When you write, look for ways to vary your sentences to make them more interesting. Determine where you can add phrases or clauses to include or clarify information. Use commas, parentheses, and dashes correctly to punctuate nonrestrictive and parenthetical expressions.

Separate Sentences

Hatshepsut's temple, which was built to celebrate her reign, is grand.

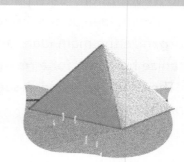

It is in the Valley of the Kings (the same place as her father's tomb).

Combined Sentence

Her burial tomb—a splendid temple dedicated to the gods— still stands today.

Connect Grammar to Writing

As you revise your research report next week, be sure you vary your sentences. Also be sure to fully explain or clarify information. Place commas, parentheses, and dashes correctly to help your readers understand the information in your report.

W.6.4 produce writing in which development, organization, and style are appropriate to task, purpose, and audience; **W.6.5** develop and strengthen writing by planning, revising, editing, rewriting, or trying a new approach

Informative Writing

Reading-Writing Workshop: Prewrite

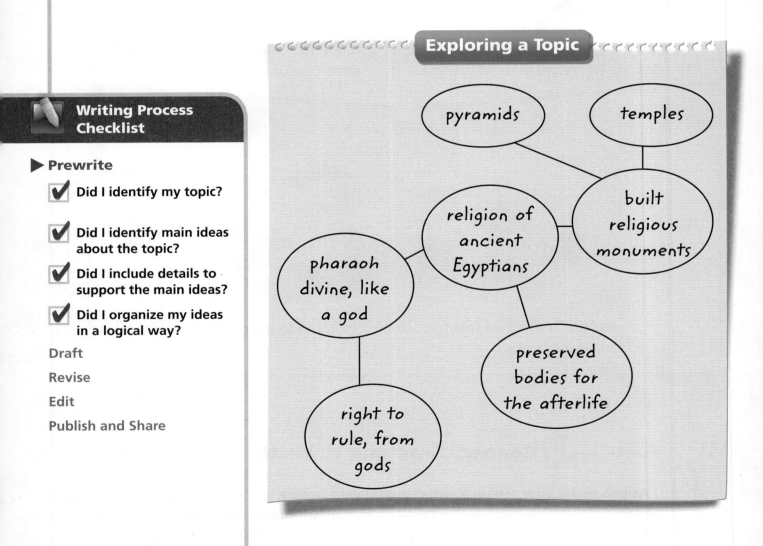

✓ Organization When you write a **research report,** you write to inform readers about a topic. A research report includes an introduction, a body, and a conclusion. Each paragraph in the body of a research report should give a main idea about the topic. Using a graphic organizer can help you organize the main ideas and details that you want to include.

To organize her ideas for a research report, McKenna first clustered her facts. Then she used an idea-support map to identify the main ideas and supporting details.

Writing Process Checklist

▶ **Prewrite**

✓ Did I identify my topic?

✓ Did I identify main ideas about the topic?

✓ Did I include details to support the main ideas?

✓ Did I organize my ideas in a logical way?

Draft

Revise

Edit

Publish and Share

Exploring a Topic

pyramids

temples

religion of ancient Egyptians

built religious monuments

pharaoh divine, like a god

preserved bodies for the afterlife

right to rule, from gods

The Egyptians believed that the pharaoh was not only a ruler but also a divine being, like a god.

The pharaoh's right to rule came from the gods.

The pharaoh communicated with the gods directly.

The pharaoh was the leader of all the priests.

The Egyptians built monuments and temples to the gods.

Hatshepsut had two obelisks built at the temple of Amun at Karnak.

Many pharaohs built pyramids and tombs so that their bodies could be placed there when they died.

Reading as a Writer

How can McKenna's idea-support map help her develop paragraphs? How might you use an idea-support map for your own research report?

To organize my research report, I began by clustering. This helped me identify the main ideas and supporting details for my idea-support map.

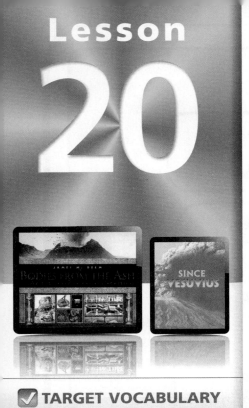

☑ TARGET VOCABULARY

unaffected
dormant
subjected
salvage
outlying
opulent
tremors
imprints
luxurious
meager

Vocabulary Reader | Context Cards

A City Buried in Time

COMMON CORE **L.6.6** acquire and use general academic and domain-specific words and phrases/gather vocabulary knowledge for comprehension or expression

Vocabulary in Context

① unaffected
Many of Rome's ancient buildings have changed little over the years. They seem to be unaffected by time.

② dormant
After centuries of being dormant, or inactive, the volcano Mt. Vesuvius awoke with a bang.

③ subjected
The city of Pompeii was subjected to, or made to experience, severe damage from the volcano.

④ salvage
Archaeologists have worked to salvage, or save, relics such as this head from a Roman statue.

 Go Digital

▶ Study each Context Card.

▶ Discuss one picture. Use a different Vocabulary word from the one on the card.

5 outlying

Outside Rome's city gates were roads that carried people to outlying areas, away from the city center.

6 opulent

Some bathhouses in ancient Rome were opulent, or richly decorated.

7 tremors

Tremors from earthquakes have damaged important buildings in Rome, such as the Colosseum.

8 imprints

Imprints, or impressions of items people used during the Roman Empire, have been found in England.

9 luxurious

Hadrian's Villa near Rome was luxurious, with expensive, comfortable furnishings and decorations.

10 meager

These bronze coins had a low value. A Roman citizen could buy only a meager amount of goods with them.

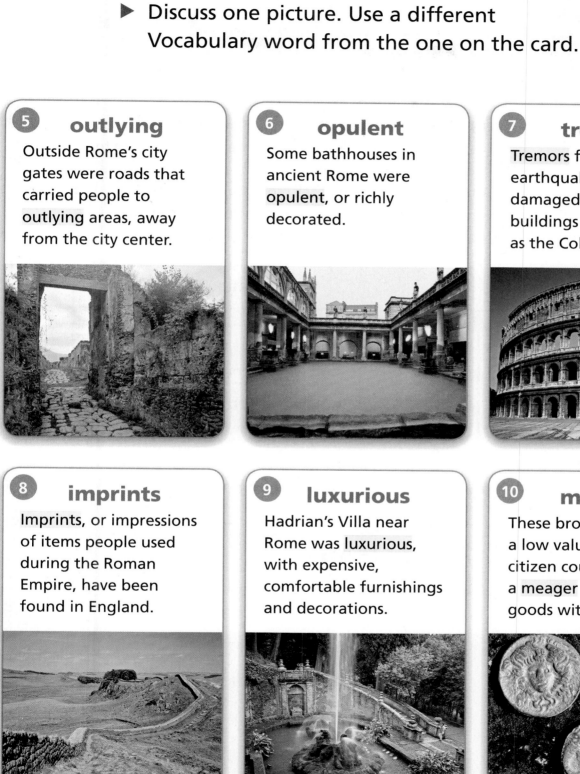

Read and Comprehend

Main Ideas and Details As you read "Bodies from the Ash," look for the **main idea,** or the central idea, about the topic. Note the **supporting details**, which are facts, examples, and other text evidence that tell more about the main idea. Use a graphic organizer like this one to help you record main ideas and supporting details.

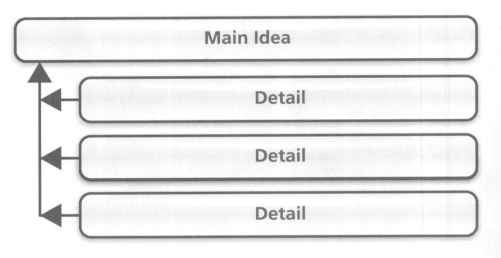

Main Idea

Detail

Detail

Detail

☑ **TARGET STRATEGY**

Visualize Use text details to help you **visualize,** or form pictures in your mind of, what you are reading.

COMMON CORE

RI.6.1 cite textual evidence to support analysis of what the text says explicitly as well as inferences drawn; **RI.6.2** determine a central idea of a text/provide a summary

580

Volcanoes

A volcano is a landform that opens to a pool of molten rock deep below the earth's surface. When pressure builds up, the molten rock rises toward the earth's crust. Gases, dust, rocks, ash, and steam or lava travel up through the opening. Then they spill over or explode into the air.

In "Bodies from the Ash," you'll learn about the eruption of a volcano in ancient Pompeii, near Rome, Italy. You'll also learn what people have found out about Pompeii through excavation and study.

Lesson 20

ANCHOR TEXT

✓ TARGET SKILL

Main Ideas and Details
Identify a text's central idea and supporting details.

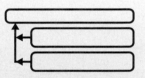

✓ GENRE

Informational text gives facts and other information about a topic. As you read, look for:

▶ headings that begin sections of related information

▶ photographs, illustrations, and captions

▶ text structure—the way ideas are organized

COMMON CORE

RI.6.2 determine a central idea of a text/provide a summary; **RI.6.3** analyze how a key individual, event, or idea is introduced, illustrated, and elaborated; **RI.6.10** read and comprehend literary nonfiction; **L.6.3b** maintain consistency in style and tone

MEET THE AUTHOR

James M. Deem

James M. Deem's writing career began in the fifth grade, when he and a group of friends found some strange tracks in the snow. He began a story called "The Strange Tracks Mystery," which stopped after the first page. However, it led to future books about such subjects as buried treasure, American presidents, and the Vikings. Like *Bodies from the Ash*, Deem's books *Bodies from the Bog* and *How to Make a Mummy Talk* explore the secrets that history has to tell us.

Bodies from the Ash
LIFE AND DEATH IN ANCIENT POMPEII

BY JAMES M. DEEM

ESSENTIAL QUESTION

What do we know today about volcanoes that people in ancient times did not?

August 24 and 25, 79 c.e.

On August 24, the last Tuesday that they would live in their town, the people of ancient Pompeii awoke to a typical hot summer's morning. Four days earlier, a series of small tremors had begun to shake the area, but people were not very concerned. The region had been subjected to so many earthquakes over the years that residents had grown accustomed to them.

What they didn't know is that the region's frequent earthquakes had been caused by nearby Mount Vesuvius. Roman writers had commented on the mountain's strange appearance; one had compared it to Mount Etna, an active volcano in Sicily. A writer named Strabo even concluded that Vesuvius had once "held craters of fire." But because Mount Vesuvius had been dormant, or sleeping, for more than eight hundred years, no one realized that it still had deadly power. What's more, no one understood that the region's frequent earthquakes were actually signs that Vesuvius was building up pressure and getting ready to erupt.

That morning, Vesuvius provided a clearer warning that an eruption was beginning. Between nine and ten o'clock, the volcano shot a small explosion of tiny ash particles into the air. To the residents of Pompeii, ten miles southeast of the volcano, this may have felt like a minor earthquake, but to the people living in the immediate vicinity of Vesuvius, it was terrifying. The ash streamed up and fell like fine mist on the eastern slope of Vesuvius. A woman named Rectina who lived at the foot of the volcano was so alarmed that she quickly sent a letter with a servant to Elder Pliny, the commander of the Roman naval fleet stationed some eighteen miles away, urging him to rescue her.

People in Pompeii might have noticed the small cloud that morning and may have felt tremors, but they continued with their daily activities until early that afternoon. At one o'clock, eighty-one loaves of bread were baking in the ovens of the Modestus bakery, and vendors were selling fruit and other products in the macellum, or marketplace. The priests in the Temple of Isis were preparing to eat an afternoon meal of eggs and fish. It was then that Vesuvius finally awoke with a massive explosion.

This cloud blasted from Vesuvius during its last eruption in 1944, but the cloud from the 79 c.e. eruption was much larger. Since 79 c.e., Vesuvius erupted thirty times before becoming dormant again.

An enormous pine-tree-shaped cloud of ash, pumice, and larger rock fragments blasted into the air. Within a half-hour, the cloud had risen over ten miles high, and winds had blown it toward the southeast—in the direction of Pompeii. The cloud blocked the sun and turned the sky over Pompeii to night. Then it began to release a deluge of ash, lightweight white pumice stones, and some larger, heavier volcanic rocks on Pompeii. At the same time, earth tremors continued to shake the town.

At first, most people would have taken shelter in their homes or other buildings. But as the volcanic fallout began to accumulate at the rate of five or six inches per hour and the pumice grew to an inch in size, many decided to escape. Protecting themselves as best as they could from the falling stones, they headed down the narrow city streets, stepping on the accumulated fallout, toward one of the city gates. Some people used pillows and blankets tied to their heads; others shielded themselves with pans or even baskets. After reaching the gates, many took the coast road; others tried to escape by sea. But the buoyant pumice floated in the water, filling the harbor and making a seagoing escape more difficult. During this time, some were killed on their way out of the city, hit by larger rocks falling from the eruption cloud.

585

(left) As the fallout continued, Pompeians made their way to one of the eight city gates, hoping to escape the deadly rain of Vesuvius. (right) Most Pompeii streets were narrow and paved with stones. They quickly filled with pumice and ash as the eruption progressed.

By five-thirty that afternoon, two feet of ash and stones had accumulated in the streets, on roofs, and in open areas such as the courtyards of houses and gardens. In fact, so much pumice had built up on roofs that some buildings began to collapse, especially when the loose pumice was shaken by strong earth tremors. Many Pompeians were crushed in their houses when the roofs caved in on them.

As the evening progressed, the raining pumice turned from white to gray and grew bigger, some pieces almost three inches in size. By midnight, first-story doors and windows were completely blocked by fallout. Anyone who had delayed escape would have had to use a second-floor window to reach the street and then walk atop five feet or more of collected stones and ash. Fires were burning on the slopes of Vesuvius. Lightning filled the sky around it, and the eruption cloud had risen almost twenty miles high. But no one in Pompeii would have been able to see this.

ANALYZE THE TEXT

Style and Tone How does the author maintain a consistently formal style when describing the events of the eruption on pages 585–587? How is a formal style of writing different from a casual, conversational style?

At about one o'clock on the morning of August 25, twelve hours after the first major explosion, the eruption shifted to its second—and deadlier—phase. Vesuvius was losing strength and its eruption cloud was beginning to weaken. As the cloud collapsed completely over the next seven hours, it would fall in six separate stages, each one producing a *pyroclastic surge and flow*. With each partial collapse, a surge of superhot gas and ash blew down the slopes of Vesuvius at speeds between 60 and 180 miles per hour and at temperatures ranging between 350 and 650 degrees Fahrenheit, each surge larger than the last, each one spreading farther. The surge cloud destroyed everything in its path, leaving behind a layer of ash. This was quickly followed by a very rapid pyroclastic flow of volcanic debris that covered the area like a hot avalanche. The flow itself was not lava (that is, a melted rock that would have moved slowly and burned everything it touched); rather, it was a mixture of rock fragments and gas that rolled over the ground at temperatures up to 400 degrees Fahrenheit. This combination of surge and flow is sometimes referred to as *nuée ardente,* or glowing cloud; it is the most deadly type of volcanic activity because of its high temperature and speed.

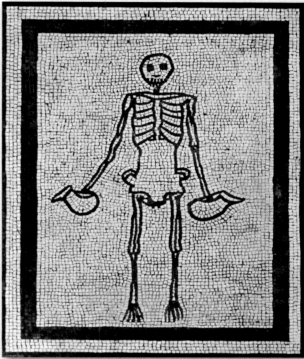

Skeleton images were frequently found in floor mosaics, wall paintings, and even on drinking cups in Pompeii. Such designs served as a reminder that life was short.

The first and second surges in the early morning hours did not reach as far as Pompeii, but they did destroy other towns closer to Vesuvius. At about six-thirty, a third surge ended at the northern edge of Pompeii, destroying some of the walls surrounding the city and suffocating anyone who had taken shelter in any of the outlying buildings.

This calix, a silver two-handled cup, was recovered by archaeologists from the ruins of Pompeii.

By morning, nine feet of pumice and other volcanic debris had accumulated, but the estimated two thousand people in and around Pompeii who had survived the night might have thought that they still had an opportunity to escape. By then, the rain of pumice had lessened so noticeably that many residents took to the streets, which were still darkened by the volcanic cloud, trying to get out of town. Many were carrying lanterns to help them see in the darkness.

But they were cut down around seven-thirty, when a fourth surge engulfed the city and the area beyond it, immediately killing everyone still alive, whether they were inside or out. Some fifteen minutes later, a fifth surge exploded through. Both of these surges deposited a layer of hot ash and a larger amount of pyroclastic flow.

Finally, at about eight o'clock that morning, a final surge—the largest and most violent—shook the area as the remainder of the volcanic cloud collapsed, crushing the top stories of buildings. Bricks, tiles, stones, and other debris were blown through the town. The last surge deposited two more feet of ash and debris on top of the town. But by then there was no one left alive to notice what had happened.

When the eruption ended, Pompeii was covered with more than twelve feet of volcanic debris. Only the very tops of a few ruined buildings were visible; most of the higher stories had been blown down during the pyroclastic surges.

In the days that followed, residents who returned hoping to find their city would have been lost in an unfamiliar landscape. Valleys were filled in; new hills had grown; and the course of the nearby river Sarno had changed. Even Vesuvius had a new look. The volcano's conelike top had collapsed, leaving a gaping crater.

And everywhere they would have looked, the landscape was blanketed by a ghostly covering of ash.

ANALYZE THE TEXT

Analyze Events How is the eruption of Vesuvius introduced in the text? Give examples of how the author elaborates on these events through page 588.

Rediscovering Pompeii

No one knows what happened to the residents of Pompeii who managed to escape, since no written record from any survivor of the town has ever been found. Some people may have left the area; others may have relocated to nearby towns unaffected by the tragedy. Some researchers believe that a few people returned and tunneled into the ruins, trying to salvage what they could, since tunnels have been found during excavations within the ruins. But no one tried to rebuild the city.

By the fourth century C.E., some 220 years after Vesuvius erupted, Pompeii's name no longer appeared on maps. Instead, the area was called Civitas. The volcanic ash that buried the town became fertile soil, and farmers planted olive trees and grapevines there. Sometimes they would come across bricks and other building materials that poked out of the ground. On rare occasions, a farmer might even find a statue hidden in the undergrowth. In 1594 an attempt to build an underground canal brought workers tantalizingly close to the ancient city. They found pieces of marble, parts of painted walls, and statues. But no one realized that the discoveries might lead to the site of the long-buried town.

In 1865 the artist Edouard Sain painted an imaginary version of the excavations at Pompeii. In reality, slaves and convicts were often used to excavate the ruins during the early years that it was explored.

This model depicts the theater in Herculaneum before early excavators looking for treasure plundered it.

Pompeii and its secrets remained hidden for centuries. It was only after the town of Herculaneum, which was also buried by Vesuvius in 79 C.E., was discovered that excavators began digging for Pompeii. In 1709, a group of well diggers came across some beautiful marble. Since the prince in charge of the region was building a new villa nearby, he was told of the discovery. No one knew that the marble was part of a theater or that it was situated in the ancient town of Herculaneum. Instead, the prince ordered an excavation, hoping to find even more marble for his house. Seven years later, when the prince's opulent villa was completed, he ordered workers to stop digging. During that time, they had stripped the theater of its statues and marble façade, without even knowing what they had found.

In 1738, after the Bourbon king Charles III took control of the region, he was eager to find more buried treasures from the same site, so he hired a Spanish military engineer named Alcubierre (al koo BYEH reh). In short order, Alcubierre widened the entrance to the site, quickly discovering that the treasure was part of a theater. He also found an inscription that finally identified the location as Herculaneum. But in his haste to please Charles, Alcubierre essentially turned the site into a tunnel-filled coal mine. Soon, workers were hauling beautiful statues and other treasures out of the tunnels and sending them to the palace of Charles III.

After fourteen years, workers began to find fewer objects, but Alcubierre was not about to give up. Instead, he planned to try another site: the underground canal that had been attempted in the late 1500s. He hoped that it might lead to the ruins of Pompeii—and further favor from Charles III.

On March 30, 1748, a small crew of twenty-four men, twelve of them convicts, began work. Digging was easier at the canal site, but it was filled with areas of firedamp—that is, toxic gasses trapped in the layers being excavated. Every time a pocket of firedamp was exposed, the diggers would have to run away to escape breathing the poisonous gas, and their work could be interrupted for many days.

Twenty days later, the workers discovered something unexpected: the skeleton of a man who had died during the eruption. The excavation report for that day read only: "Found a skeleton and 18 coins." Although this was the first recorded sign of the human tragedy at Pompeii, Alcubierre was more interested in the coins than the man. A few days later, another entry read: "Nothing was found, and only ruined structures were uncovered." Eventually, he became so disappointed with the meager discoveries that he returned to the excavations at Herculaneum, leaving only a small crew to work at the canal site. No more than fifty men—some of them Algerian and Tunisian slaves, chained together in pairs—seemed to have been used at any time, even after the site was finally identified as Pompeii in 1763.

But Pompeii was about to get much more attention. In 1771 excavators made a dramatic find: a large, luxurious house, now called the Villa of Diomedes (dy uh MEE deez), complete with two skeletons near the garden. These skeletons were of much greater interest, thanks to the riches found with them. Next to one man, who held a key and wore a gold ring, was a hoard of coins wrapped in a cloth: ten gold, eighty-eight silver, and nine bronze. This turned out to be one of the largest collections of money found at Pompeii and certainly a dazzling find in 1771.

The next year, as excavations of the house continued, workers discovered twenty more skeletons (eighteen adults and two children) piled together in a nearby underground room. The volcanic debris that had oozed into the room during the pyroclastic flows had hardened around the bodies and created imprints of the people, their clothing, and even their hair. Excavators studied the impressions and concluded that they had found a family and its servants. The woman of the house wore beautifully woven clothing and was adorned with a great deal of jewelry (multiple necklaces, armbands, bracelets, and rings).

This early photo shows the Villa of Diomedes after it was excavated.

She carried a young boy in her arms. A young girl wearing golden jewelry accompanied her; as the fourth surge hit, she had covered her face with her clothing, gasping for breath.

The rest of the victims were dressed quite differently. Most wore canvas or cloth socks that were more like leggings; many had no shoes. The excavators concluded that they were slaves or servants. They also came to believe that the two skeletons found the previous year were the male head of the family, who carried the family's most valuable possessions, and another slave.

Word of this discovery and others traveled around the world. Pompeii and its Villa of Diomedes became part of the grand tour for wealthy American and English travelers. As a result, many tourists flocked to the ruins, not only to watch the excavators, but also to see the skeletons. They would wander through the ruins to encounter tableaux; that is, little scenes arranged by excavators that featured skeletons and objects found at the site. Two victims that fascinated early visitors to the site, according to the writer Jennifer Wallace, were found in the Gladiator's Barracks in 1766. These two men, either prisoners or gladiators, were said to have still been in shackles and chained to the wall when they died in the eruption. Excavators placed their skulls on shelves for all visitors to see.

Unfortunately, some tourists stole bones from the skeletons and other artifacts as souvenirs, since the large site was poorly guarded. It is not surprising, therefore, that of all the coins and jewelry found at the Villa of Diomedes, only two items have been preserved to this day: a necklace and a gemstone. The rest have disappeared without a trace.

ANALYZE THE TEXT

Main Ideas and Details What is the central idea of pages 589–593? What details does the author provide to support this idea?

Dig Deeper

How to Analyze the Text

Use these pages to learn about Main Ideas and Details, Style and Tone, and how to Analyze Events. Then read "Bodies from the Ash" again to apply what you learned.

Main Ideas and Details

Informational texts such as "Bodies from the Ash" contain a **main idea** and **supporting details.** Main ideas are the central ideas of a text. To explain the topic, authors use supporting facts and other details that develop the main ideas.

Some informational texts have one central idea. Others have more than one. Notice that "Bodies from the Ash" contains two sections of very different kinds of information. What is the main idea of the first section? What details does the author give to support it?

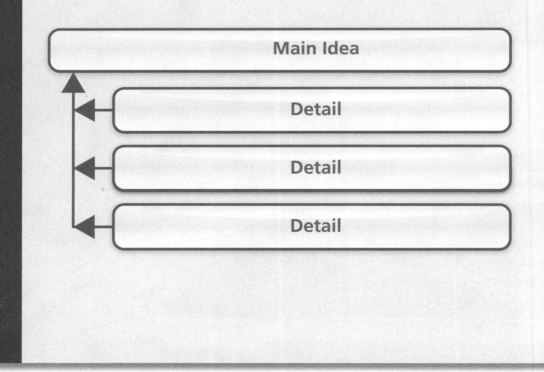

Main Idea

Detail

Detail

Detail

 RI.6.2 determine a central idea of a text/provide a summary; **RI.6.3** analyze how a key individual, event, or idea is introduced, illustrated, and elaborated; **L.6.3b** maintain consistency in style and tone

Style and Tone

In writing, an author's **tone** is the author's attitude, or feeling, toward his or her subject. When authors use a serious tone, they often use a formal writing **style**. They are polite, and they avoid humor. They use third-person point of view, not first, so you won't find authors using *I* in a formal style. Their vocabulary is varied and precise, and they avoid slang words and contractions. Authors keep the tone and style consistent in their writing.

Analyze Events

When authors write about **historical events**, they begin by introducing the events. They then elaborate by providing additional facts and other details. Authors may introduce and elaborate on events in a variety of ways. They may give background information, describe people and places, and give examples. They may tell what eyewitnesses said and make guesses about what people thought and did. Analyzing how events in "Bodies from the Ash" are introduced and elaborated helps you better understand what really happened.

Your Turn

RETURN TO THE ESSENTIAL QUESTION

Turn and Talk Review the selection with a partner to prepare to discuss this question: *What do we know today about volcanoes that people in ancient times did not?* As you discuss, reflect on your partner's responses.

Classroom Conversation

Continue your discussion of "Bodies from the Ash" by explaining your answers to these questions:

1. What did the author likely have to do to prepare to write this selection?

2. James M. Deem subtitled his work *Life and Death in Ancient Pompeii*. What did you learn about life in Pompeii?

3. What text evidence explains how unprepared the people of Pompeii were when Vesuvius erupted?

WHAT DOES IT MEAN?

Use Reference Sources Choose three of these words from the selection: *erupt, particles, pumice, fallout, surge*. Find each word in the selection. Then look up the pronunciation and meaning of each word in a digital dictionary. Write a new sentence for each word. Share your sentences with a partner.

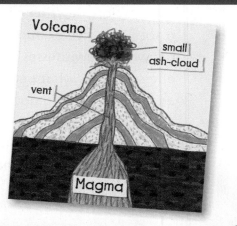

Volcano
small ash-cloud
vent
Magma

WRITE ABOUT READING

Response Some historic changes occur slowly over time, and others occur suddenly. Would we know as much about everyday life in Pompeii if Vesuvius had not erupted? Write an argument paragraph to express your ideas. Begin the paragraph by stating your claim, and use evidence from the selection to support it. End with a concluding sentence.

Writing Tip

State your claim at the beginning of your response. Use adjectives and adverbs correctly as you present and support your claim.

W.6.1a introduce claim(s) and organize reasons and evidence clearly; **W.6.9b** apply grade 6 Reading standards to literary nonfiction; **SL.6.1c** pose and respond to questions and make comments that contribute to the discussion; **L.6.4c** consult reference materials, both print and digital, to find pronunciation and determine or clarify meaning or part of speech; **L.6.6** acquire and use general academic and domain-specific words and phrases/gather vocabulary knowledge for comprehension or expression

INFORMATIONAL TEXT

SINCE VESUVIUS

☑ GENRE

Informational text, such as this science article, gives facts and examples about a topic.

☑ TEXT FOCUS

Informational text may include a **diagram**, a drawing that explains how something works or how parts relate to each other.

SINCE VESUVIUS

Since the middle of March of 1980, Mount St. Helens in southern Washington State had been producing steam explosions and tremors. Scientists feared that an eruption was coming—and soon.

On May 18, Mount St. Helens did erupt. The volcano spewed ash and pumice over a 22,000-square-mile area. People who lived nearby had already moved to outlying areas. They were not able to salvage their homes, but most escaped with their lives.

The citizens of ancient Pompeii were not as lucky. Vesuvius's ashes buried both luxurious homes and meager dwellings. We have learned from their experience. Scientists today closely study active volcanoes to learn more about why and when they erupt.

Mount St. Helens: May 18, 1980

COMMON CORE **RI.6.7** integrate information presented in different media or formats as well as in words; **RI.6.10** read and comprehend literary nonfiction

OUR FLUID EARTH

Today we know what the Pompeiians didn't: that Earth's interior is always in motion. The theory of plate tectonics tells us that Earth's outermost layer, or *crust*, is made of huge slabs of rock called *plates*. These plates fit together like puzzle pieces. They are thousands of miles across and about fifty miles thick. They float on a bed of molten rock, or *magma*. Magma is part of Earth's *mantle*, the layer that surrounds its core.

The plates don't fit together exactly. They push against each other and slip past each other. This movement can create volcanoes.

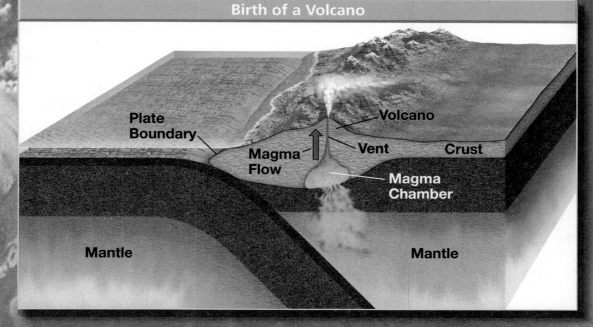

Birth of a Volcano

Plate Boundary

Magma Flow

Volcano

Vent

Crust

Magma Chamber

Mantle

Mantle

When two plates crash into each other, a chain reaction may begin that melts rock in the mantle. The liquid magma can rise through a surface opening called a *vent*. Lava, rocks, and ash build up around the vent, and a new volcano is born.

VOLCANO SPOTTING

No part of Earth is unaffected by plate movement. However, volcanoes usually leave their imprints at or near the edges of tectonic plates. These areas are subjected to more volcanic activity and earthquakes than other areas are. The edges of the plates surrounding the Pacific Ocean are especially active. Scientists call this area the "Ring of Fire."

LESSONS LEARNED

Scientists can now recognize some volcano warning signs, such as groups of small earthquakes. Lassen Peak, a volcano in northern California, erupted in 1915, a year after steam blasted through the ground near its summit.

We will probably never be able to predict the exact time of a volcanic eruption. Volcanoes can remain dormant for hundreds of years. Lassen Peak was quiet for 27,000 years before erupting! Still, because we know some of the warning signs, we are much safer than the people who lived in Pompeii's opulent villas.

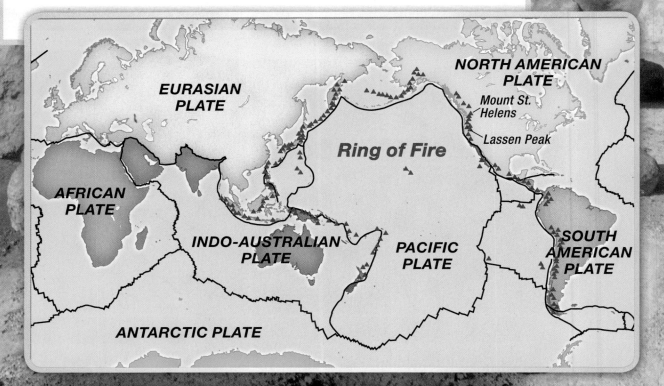

One of the active volcanoes (red triangles) in the Ring of Fire is Lassen Peak. Lassen's boiling mud pots show its volcanic activity.

Compare Texts

Compare Volcano Texts Talk with a partner about "Bodies from the Ash" and "Since Vesuvius." Discuss these questions: *How do both selections tell about the events during volcanic eruptions? How are the selections different from each other?* After discussing your ideas, work together to write a paragraph that compares and contrasts how the two authors treat volcanic eruptions in their texts. Use evidence from the texts in your paragraph.

TEXT TO SELF

Be Prepared What types of natural disasters happen in the state or region in which you live? With a partner, discuss what you have done or could do to prepare for a disaster. Then write a list of instructions to follow in an emergency.

TEXT TO WORLD

Discuss Technology Think about advances in technology since the time of ancient Pompeii. What are some ways that technology keeps people safe during natural disasters today? Research the topic, and share your thoughts with a small group.

COMMON CORE **RI.6.1** cite textual evidence to support analysis of what the text says explicitly as well as inferences drawn; **RI.6.9** compare and contrast one author's presentation of events with that of another

Grammar

Prepositions and Prepositional Phrases A **preposition** is a word that shows a relationship between a noun or pronoun (the **object of the preposition**) and another word. A **prepositional phrase** includes the preposition, the object of the preposition, and the modifiers of the object. An **adjective phrase** is a prepositional phrase that modifies a noun or pronoun. An **adverb phrase** is a prepositional phrase that modifies a verb, adjective, or adverb.

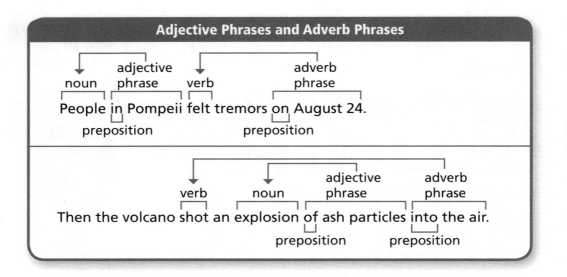

Adjective Phrases and Adverb Phrases

noun | adjective phrase | verb | adverb phrase
People in Pompeii felt tremors on August 24.
preposition — preposition

verb | noun | adjective phrase | adverb phrase
Then the volcano shot an explosion of ash particles into the air.
preposition — preposition

Try This! With a partner, read aloud each sentence below. Tell whether each prepositional phrase in bold type is an adjective phrase or an adverb phrase. Then identify the noun or verb it modifies.

1. **Throughout the morning,** most people ignored the warnings from the volcano.

2. **At one o'clock,** bakers were baking loaves **of bread.**

3. Suddenly the volcano erupted **with a massive explosion.**

4. A thick cloud **of ash and rock** rose **from Vesuvius.**

When you write, you can use prepositional phrases as modifiers to give details to your readers. Use adjective phrases to tell *what kind* or *which one* about nouns. Use adverb phrases to tell *how*, *where*, or *when* about verbs.

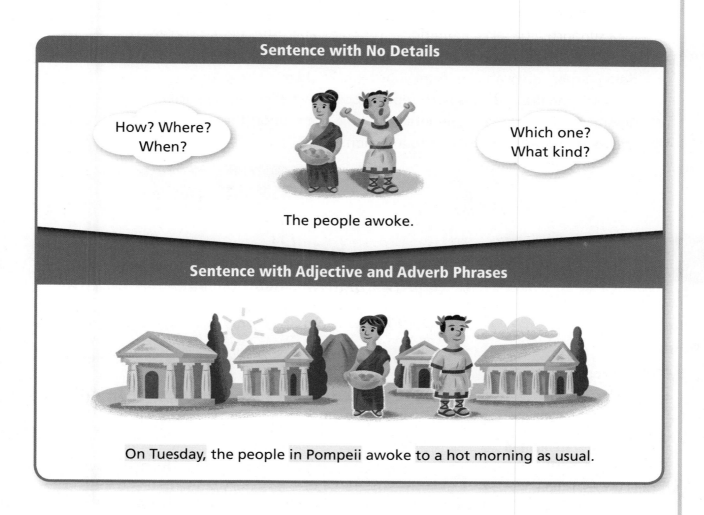

Sentence with No Details

How? Where? When?

Which one? What kind?

The people awoke.

Sentence with Adjective and Adverb Phrases

On Tuesday, the people in Pompeii awoke to a hot morning as usual.

Connect Grammar to Writing

As you revise your research report, look for sentences that can be improved by adding adjective phrases to describe nouns or by adding adverb phrases to describe verbs. Make sure the meaning is clear in your new sentences.

W.6.2a introduce a topic and organize ideas, concepts, and information/include formatting, graphics, and multimedia; **W.6.2b** develop the topic with facts, definitions, details, quotations, or other information and examples; **W.6.2c** use transitions to clarify relationships; **W.6.2d** use precise language and domain-specific vocabulary; **W.6.2e** establish and maintain a formal style; **W.6.2f** provide a concluding statement or section

COMMON CORE

Informative Writing

Reading-Writing Workshop: Revise

my WriteSmart

Go Digital

✓ **Ideas** In a **research report**, good writers identify the topic with a title, and they use headings to organize the information. When you write your research report, make sure each body section has a main idea supported by facts, definitions, examples, and other details you've gathered. End each section with a concluding statement. Be sure to use domain-specific vocabulary from your topic's field of knowledge.

McKenna drafted a research report about the beliefs of the ancient Egyptians. Then she deleted details that did not support the topic and added a concluding statement to a section.

Writing Process Checklist

Prewrite

Draft

▶ **Revise**

✓ Did I introduce the topic clearly?

✓ Did I include a main idea, details, and concluding statement in all body sections?

✓ Did I use transition words to clarify relationships?

✓ Did I maintain a formal style and objective tone?

✓ Did I use domain-specific vocabulary?

Edit

Publish and Share

Revised Draft

The Pharaoh Ruled

The ancient Egyptians believed that the pharaoh was not only a ruler but also a divine being, like a god. ~~The ancient Greeks also believed in gods and goddesses.~~ In addition, they thought the pharaoh was given the right to rule by the gods. Only the pharaoh was allowed to communicate directly with the gods. He was also the leader of all the priests in Egypt. ~~The most famous of all the pharaohs is King Tutankhamen.~~ The royal pharaoh led the Egyptians in their religion and governed how they lived their lives.

604

Religious Beliefs of the Ancient Egyptians

by McKenna Mare

Archaeologists sift through ruins like detectives looking for clues. As archaeologists piece together bits of broken pottery or parts of statues, they also piece together facts. They have pieced together many fascinating facts about Egyptian religious beliefs. The ancient Egyptians believed in gods and the afterlife, and their beliefs shaped the way they lived.

The Pharaoh Ruled

The ancient Egyptians believed that the pharaoh was not only a ruler but also a divine being, like a god. In addition, they thought the pharaoh was given the right to rule by the gods. Only the pharaoh was allowed to communicate directly with the gods. He was also the leader of all the priests in Egypt. The royal pharaoh led the Egyptians in their religion and governed how they lived their lives.

Reading as a Writer

Which sentences did McKenna delete from her draft? Does your research report include any details that do not support your topic?

In my final report, I deleted details that do not support the topic. I also made sure that each section in the body ends with a concluding statement.

Test POWER

Read the passage "The Legend of the Rice" and the poem "The Song of Rice." Stop and answer each question using text evidence.

The Legend of the Rice

Ajay Dutt sat at the kitchen table trying to concentrate on his math homework, but the pot of basmati rice simmering on the stove was making it difficult. The delicious fragrance was distracting him and making him hungry. Tonight Ajay's mother was cooking vegetable biryani for dinner. She often repeated the saying, "Grains of rice should be like two brothers, close but not stuck together." His mother had moved to Washington from India before she had married his father. Ajay always enjoyed hearing the wise old sayings and eating the foods of his mother's native land.

1 What is the meaning of the saying about grains of rice?

Now his mother cut potatoes, carrots, green beans, and cauliflower into small thin pieces for frying. She put oil into a pan and added mustard seeds, chili, cinnamon, and other seasonings. More mouth-watering smells filled the room as she asked, "Ajay, have I ever told you the Indian legend of the rice?"

Ajay gladly set aside his homework and prepared to listen to another of his mother's fascinating tales.

His mother continued to prepare the meal as she began retelling the ancient legend. "Long, long ago, when the Earth was still young, life was better in every way. Women and men and children were stronger and more beautiful. Trees were taller and greener, and the fruit they bore was sweet beyond belief. Even the rice was larger. In fact, it was so large that all a person needed for an entire meal was one single grain of rice."

Ajay thought about how odd it would be to eat just one grain of rice for a meal. He tried to imagine a single grain of rice large enough to fill up his whole plate. He wondered how long it would take to cook a grain of rice that size, but he didn't want to interrupt the story to ask his mother's opinion.

RL.6.1 cite textual evidence to support analysis of what the text says explicitly as well as inferences drawn; **RL.6.3** describe how a story's or drama's plot unfolds and how characters respond and change; **RL.6.4** determine the meaning of words or phrases, including figurative and connotative meanings/analyze impact of word choice; **RL.6.5** analyze how a sentence, chapter, scene, or stanza fits in the overall structure; **RL.6.9** compare and contrast texts in different forms or genres on their approaches to themes and topics

Mrs. Dutt put some of her homemade yogurt in a blender and flipped the switch. After that, she heated the yogurt in a pan and added the fried vegetables. "In those days, the people did not even have to gather the rice," she continued. "When it was ripe, it simply fell from the stalks and rolled directly into the village storehouses."

Ajay got up to set the table while his mother added the cooked rice to the vegetables and continued telling the story.

"One year there was so much rice growing in the fields that a widow said to her daughter, 'Our storehouse is too small to hold all that rice. We must build a larger one.' They demolished the old storehouse and started to build a new one, but the rice began rolling into the village before the new storehouse was ready. The widow became angry and struck one of the grains of rice, which you remember were much larger than grains of rice today. 'Couldn't you have waited a few more days? We are not ready for you yet!' the widow shouted angrily at the rice."

Ajay's mother put the biryani into an attractive ceramic dish and garnished it with dried fruits and green coriander leaves. She carried it to the table, called to Ajay's dad that dinner was ready, and the family sat down to dinner. As he took the first bite of the delicious food, Ajay asked, "What happened after that?" He was eager to hear the outcome.

"That large grain of rice broke into a thousand pieces," his mother answered. "The rice announced, 'From now on, we will wait until you decide you're ready to come and get us.' And from that day forth," Ajay's mom concluded, "rice has been a small grain, and people must toil to harvest it."

---

2 Describe how episodes from two different plots in two different settings are woven together in the passage.

"That is an excellent legend," Ajay said, "but I wish that widow hadn't been so bad-tempered. I would like to see how you would cook one of those giant grains of rice!"

The Song of Rice

Each one of us alone is tiny, insignificant,

But together with our sisters, brothers,

and cousins, we are powerful.

We are a magnificent multitude.

We are known by many names

In many languages and places.

We appear in many forms

And many guises.

We are in Italy's risotto with broth and cheese;

In Greece and Turkey's dolma, wrapped in grape leaves;

In India's biryani with spices and mustard seeds.

We are in Spain's paella with saffron, peppers, and peas.

We are in Japan's sushi, wrapped snugly in seaweed.

3 How does the third stanza develop the theme of the poem?

We are puffed and crisped into cereals,

Dried and ground into flour,

Used to make puddings and candy,

Our straw for paper, hats, and mats!

Each one of us alone is tiny, insignificant,

But together with our sisters, brothers,

And cousins, we are powerful.

We are a magnificent multitude.

4 How are the topics and themes of the passage and the poem similar to each other? How are they different?

unit 5

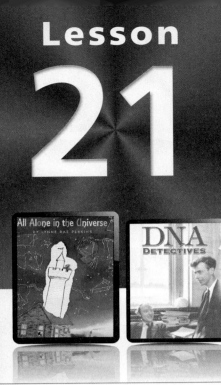

Vocabulary in Context

1 jeopardy

If two friends can't talk about problems, their friendship may be in jeopardy. It may be in danger of ending.

2 stable

In a stable relationship, family members stick together through good times and bad.

3 blurted

A friend who has blurted a remark, saying it without thinking, may regret it afterwards.

4 eventually

On a relay race team, the last runner has to wait but eventually receives the baton from a teammate.

► Study each Context Card.

► Use two Vocabulary words to tell about an experience you had.

5 scrounged

When friends drop in unexpectedly, someone might serve a meal scrounged together from leftovers.

6 spiteful

Spiteful words are spoken or written for the purpose of hurting or angering someone.

7 comprehension

In a classroom, a teacher might feel relieved when a smile of comprehension shows that a pupil understands.

8 abrupt

A bus driver who has to come to an abrupt, or sudden, stop might call out a warning to the passengers.

9 exhilaration

A volunteer might feel a lift of exhilaration, or joy, after finishing a job that others appreciate.

10 oracle

You wouldn't need the Greek oracle at Delphi to predict that being kind and attentive will keep a friendship going.

611

Read and Comprehend

☑ TARGET SKILL

Compare and Contrast As you read "All Alone in the Universe," think about how the characters in the story are alike and different. Note what the characters say and do as well as their feelings and reactions toward each other as the plot moves along. Use text evidence about the characters, along with inferences about what you have read in the story, to help you **compare** and **contrast.** Use a graphic organizer like the one below to help you compare and contrast story characters.

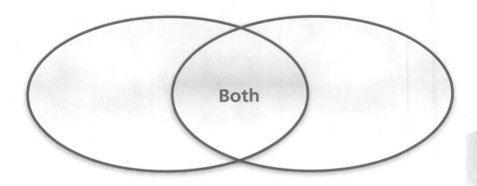

Both

☑ TARGET STRATEGY

Infer/Predict Combine what you already know with text evidence to help you **infer,** or figure out, what the author means and to **predict,** or guess, what might happen in the future.

 RL.6.1 cite textual evidence to support analysis of what the text says explicitly as well as inferences drawn; **RL.6.3** describe how a story's or drama's plot unfolds and how characters respond or change

Working Together

Think about a shared goal you may have had with a friend, a classmate, or a family member. To achieve the goal, you both had to collaborate, or work together, to accomplish what you set out to do.

Friendship is much like a shared goal. Friends work together to maintain trust and communication. In "All Alone in the Universe," you'll learn about two best friends who experience a change in their close friendship.

Lesson 21

ANCHOR TEXT

All Alone in the Universe
BY LYNNE RAE PERKINS

✅ TARGET SKILL

Compare and Contrast
Use stated details and make inferences to compare and contrast story characters.

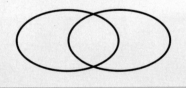

✅ GENRE

Realistic fiction has characters and events that are like people and events in real life. As you read, look for:

▶ settings like those in real life
▶ characters who have feelings that real people have
▶ real-life challenges and problems

COMMON CORE **RL.6.1** cite textual evidence to support analysis of what the text says explicitly as well as inferences drawn; **RL.6.3** describe how a story's or drama's plot unfolds and how characters respond or change; **RL.6.6** explain how an author develops the point of view of the narrator or speaker; **RL.6.10** read and comprehend literature

 Go Digital

MEET THE AUTHOR
Lynne Rae Perkins

Lynne Rae Perkins spent her youth in Cheswick, Pennsylvania, a town on the Allegheny River—in her words, "a paradise of uninterrupted backyards with unlimited playmates." Although she considers her hometown idyllic, Perkins vividly recalls the more anxiety-ridden aspects of adolescence and recaptures those moments, counterbalanced with moments of peaceful reflection, in her novels for young adults. Perkins's hometown of Cheswick forms the setting of both this selection and its companion novel *Criss Cross*, for which Perkins won the 2006 Newbery Medal. Both *Criss Cross* and *All Alone in the Universe* use poetic devices, drawings, and experimental writing techniques to develop realistic narratives about friendship, identity, transformation, adolescence, and coming of age. Says Perkins, who writes and illustrates picture books as well as writing novels for older readers, "I think making books is a way of having conversations with people."

MEET THE ILLUSTRATOR
Margaret Lee

Margaret Lee lives and works in Toronto, Canada. To create an illustration, she often photographs a subject and then manipulates the photograph to create a new image, using computer and collage techniques. Lee has also worked in animation and created title sequences for movies.

All Alone in the Universe

by Lynne Rae Perkins   selection illustrated by Margaret Lee

ESSENTIAL QUESTION

How does a new friendship affect an old one?

Debbie and her best friend, Maureen Berck, have grown up together in the same small town, and it seems as if they will be inseparable forever. One summer, though, Maureen's new relationship with classmate Glenna Flaiber puts their friendship in jeopardy. The day after Debbie returns from a family vacation, the three girls go to a carnival.

Three is a lousy number in a lot of ways. One of those ways is that carnivals always have rides with seats that hold two people, so one person has to act as if she doesn't mind waiting by the fence or riding in a seat by herself or with some other leftover. This is why the Three Musketeers became friends with D'Artagnan. Not because of carnivals but because the number three is not a happy number. I know that in geometry the triangle is supposed to be an extremely stable shape, as in the pyramids, but in real life triangles are almost never equilateral. There are always two corners that are closer together, while the third is off a little ways by itself.

I was off a little ways eating some french fries from a paper boat, watching Glenna and Maureen ride the Calypso, when the idea first came to me that Maureen actually liked Glenna. Glenna was shouting over the noise and music of the ride. Whatever she shouted, it made Maureen laugh, and Glenna was laughing, too. They were spinning around together and laughing, their hands up in the air, slammed together by centrifugal force against the painted metal shell of their twirling car. I was in some other not-laughing universe, leaning on a fence that was standing perfectly still. The ride ended, and they tumbled and spun, still laughing, out of the car and through the gate. It seemed as if they might tumble right past me then, and I blurted out, "Anyone want a french fry?"

Maureen spun my way and said, "Oh, yum!"

Glenna said, "No, thanks, I don't like greasy food."

This was wise, because I was planning to put a curse on her french fry that would make her throw up on the next ride.

"Oh, well." I shrugged. "More for us."

Then I said, "I love greasy food."

"Especially when it's salty," added Maureen.

We gobbled up the french fries, and now it was Maureen and I who were together while Glenna remained on her greaseless, unsalted planet.

"Let's go on the Zipper," I said to Maureen.

"Okay," she said.

So we did, and then we all played a game of tossing quarters onto plates balanced on bottle tops. I won a lime green cross-eyed bunny, which I gave to Maureen. I said, "Here, I want you to have this because you mean so much to me. And because I don't want to carry it around."

She grinned and said, "Oh, wow. Thanks a lot."

She glanced down at the bunny as she took it, then held it up to Glenna and said, "Does this remind you of anything?" Glenna crossed her eyes, they both laughed, and that was one for Glenna. Then it was her turn to ride with Maureen, and that was two. Glenna and I weren't taking any turns together, but no one mentioned that.

Maureen was too busy having a great time to notice. Glenna was having a great time, too. I wasn't exactly having a great time. I felt off-balance, as if someone kept borrowing my right foot for a few minutes. As if someone were moving into my house while I still lived there.

The three of us wobbled around the dinky midway like a triangle trying to walk. I could see the grass already turning yellow under the parked trailers and their thick, tangled piles of extension cords. I could feel some odd new feelings—uneasy, spiteful, shapeless ones—creeping in.

I hate this stupid carnival, I thought, sitting on a bench across from the Ferris wheel as the other two points of the triangle rose up into the blue sky.

When we had spent all the money Mrs. Berck was willing to throw down the drain, we walked back to the car, where she was waiting, reading a book. It made sense geographically for me to be dropped off first. I got out and watched the car pull away. It was no different from a million times before. Through the rear window, beyond the collapsed tissue box and the green bunny, I saw Maureen's and Glenna's heads turn toward each other, and I felt myself falling away behind. But what could I do? I lived here; it was where I had to get out.

I walked over to rinse my feet off under the spigot. I didn't know how to wash away a crumminess that seemed to be swimming around in my heart. The garage door opened, and my dad pushed the lawn mower out from inside. He put a pretend surprised look on his face.

"Why, hello there, long-lost daughter," he said. "How's every little thing?"

"Okay," I said. I mustered up a smile from somewhere, mostly from his words and the sound of his voice. His words and his voice and my scrounged-up smile pushed the crummy feeling a little way off to the side, and I thought, Probably it was all in my mind.

618

It's because I was on vacation, I thought. I'm back now.
Don't be a dope, I thought. Maureen is your best friend.

But something was happening; something I couldn't see was shifting. When Maureen and I were together without Glenna, everything seemed fine. Almost. We had fun. We still laughed a lot. But before, when we laughed, we were just laughing. We couldn't help it; it just happened. Laughing and other kinds of thoughts or feelings traveled between us like breathing. Now I found myself holding on to good moments as if I could save them up and prove something to somebody.

It was getting hard even to *be* with Maureen without Glenna because Glenna was there so much. When I called Maureen on the phone, Glenna had already called. Or Maureen wasn't at home because she was sleeping over at Glenna's. Or I could hear Glenna's dippy voice in the background. Maureen always invited me to come along. And I would go, even though being together with Maureen *and* Glenna was not that much fun.

I couldn't figure out how Glenna managed to make so many plans so far ahead all the time.

On summer mornings, when you first wake up, you hear the birds chirping, and a shady green light filters through the leaves, and a coolness in the air means it still feels good to have at least a sheet pulled up over your shoulders. Maybe there is the faint whining and clanking of a garbage truck on a nearby street. For a minute or two you don't even think of any personal facts, like what your name is, or what town you live in, or what kind of life you might be having. Then you hear your mother outside talking to a neighbor or banging around in the kitchen, or you roll over and see your sister, still asleep in the other bed. You know who you are now, and your mind eventually gets around to what you might be doing that day. Which is when your heart feels light or sinks a little bit, depending.

ANALYZE THE TEXT

Point of View How does the author develop Debbie's point of view of Glenna? What clues tell you how Debbie feels about her?

From the backseat of the Flaibers' car, Glenna asked her mother what day they would be leaving for their vacation. My ears pricked up. An unexpected ray of hope lit up little dioramas in my head: happy pictures of a week (or two?) without Glenna. A scrap of song from a passing radio furled through the open window.

Finally, I thought. Finally.

Trying to keep my face calm, I waited for Mrs. Flaiber's answer.

"Saturday," she said. "But early. So probably Maureen should stay over Friday night."

What for? I thought giddily. So she can wave good-bye?

"That way she'll be sure to get up in time," Mrs. Flaiber went on. She threw a quick grin over her shoulder at Maureen. Maureen and Glenna grinned at each other. "We'll just roll you out of bed and into the car, Maureen!" said Mrs. Flaiber in a jolly way.

A tide of comprehension rushed in all around me, separating my little island from the shore where the three of them stood, getting into the car to drive away.

"Where are you going?" I couldn't help asking.

Apparently they could still hear my voice, although it sounded far away, even to me. At least Mrs. Flaiber could.

ANALYZE THE TEXT

Characters' Motivations What does Debbie say and do when she finds out Maureen will be going on vacation with Glenna's family?

"Borth Lake!" she answered. "We have a camp up there! We decided to let Glenna take along a friend this year! We'll be sitting on each other's laps, but we figure, the more the merrier!"

I don't know what else she said, but all the sentences had exclamation points at the end. The water rose over my island and lapped around my ankles. I pressed my fingers into my knees, then lifted them and watched the yellow-white spots disappear. Maureen's knees were right next to mine. There was her hand on the car seat, with the fingernails bitten down below the nubs, as familiar to me as my own. I looked out the window at whatever was passing by. I felt mean and small, like something wadded up. Weightless, like something that doesn't even matter.

Mrs. Flaiber's voice chorbled merrily away, cramming the air with colorful pictures of capsizing rowboats and dinners of fish fried with their heads still on and the eyeballs looking right at you. I could hear Glenna telling Maureen that Borth Lake was the seventh largest man-made lake in the state.

"Really?" I heard myself say. "That is so interesting."

Suddenly it seemed to me that if I didn't get out of the car, I might completely disappear, and I said, "Mrs. Flaiber, can you let me off here?"

All three heads turned my way, and the abrupt quiet told me that I had probably interrupted someone.

"I just remembered," I said. "There's something I have to do. For my mom. I have to pick something up for her."

"Where do you need to go?" she asked. "We can take you there and wait while you run inside."

"No, no—that's okay," I said. "Actually I feel like walking."

"Are you sure?" she said, pulling adroitly over to the curb.

"Yep," I said. "Thanks. See you guys later. Have fun on your vacation."

Then, looking right into Maureen's eyes, I said, "Call me when you get back."

I tried to keep my voice steady, but my eyes were shooting out messages and questions and SOSs. I saw them reach her eyes and spark there in a flash of surprise. She turned to Mrs. Flaiber and Glenna and said, "I'm going to get out here, too."

She was out of the car and closing the door before Glenna could follow. She leaned her head inside to say good-bye. Glenna and her mother wore the startled expression of fish twitching in the bottom of a rowboat or fried on plates. Mrs. Flaiber turned forward, and the car moved slowly back into traffic, crunching pebbles and grit musically beneath its tires.

I was surprised, too. A rush of exhilaration went through me. Maybe Maureen just hadn't seen what was happening, what Glenna was doing. Maybe I just needed to tell her. She dropped her beat-up tennis shoes onto the sidewalk and slid her toes inside.

"Are you mad?" she asked.

I just needed to explain it to her. Make her see. That was all. "Not mad," I said. Then I said it, what was in my heart:

"I just miss when we were friends."

I waited for her to get it.

622

"We're still friends," she said, standing on one foot to pull the back of her shoe up over her heel. She looked at me as if I had said something really humorous. "You goof," she said. "Hey, let's go down by the river."

She started off across the spongy, shimmering parking lot of the Seldem Plaza, leading the way through the canyons of wavy heat made by the parked cars. I followed her, like maybe I had my whole life. But wanting only to keep on doing that.

"You know what I mean," I said. A few shades less certain, though, that she would. "I miss the way we used to be friends. Before Glenna."

It crossed my mind that to anyone who happened to see us there, we would look the same as we always had. Debbie and Maureen. There they are. "Frick and Frack," my dad said. We would look the same. Did that mean something?

"You should give Glenna a chance," said Maureen. "She tries to be nice to you."

We moved through a short tent of shade next to the supermarket and then the scrubby weeds that are the native flora of Seldem, the kind that can grow up through concrete as long as it's not the middle part that cars drive over all the time. The kinds of scratchy weeds that grow about ten inches high, then branch out and blossom forth in stiff, itchy exploded seedpods.

"Glenna doesn't want to be my friend," I said. "Glenna wants to be *your* friend. Glenna would be happy if I disappeared from the face of the earth in a puff of smoke."

We looked at each other. We both knew it was sort of true, and we smiled a little bit the way you can smile at something that is true when it is said out loud for the first time. It was a relief, in a way, to know that Maureen saw that part of it.

For the moment that seemed enough. Going further seemed dangerous, like stepping off a cliff. Because I could also tell that Maureen wasn't going to be deciding right then and there to dump Glenna. She didn't see why she should.

I realize now that Maureen saw something in Glenna that I could not see. (I leave it to her biographers, or maybe to microbiologists, to discover what that is.) Not that I was trying too hard.

Anyhow, it felt safer then to leave that topic behind and take this bit of time with Maureen any way I could get it. To add it to the little pile of proofs that I hoped would add up to some charm that could eventually ward off Glenna.

So we squeezed between the dusty bushes to get to the riverbank, where we sank our feet into the silty mud, and sat on the low, bouncing branch of a big old tree that leaned out over the water. We crossed our legs like yogis and tried to balance there with our eyes closed. The shallow part of the river flowed along steadily, but in no hurry, about a foot below our branch, greenish brown, the color of a dollar bill. We opened our eyes and dangled our feet, making whirls and eddies form around them, talking about whatever, one thing or another. The sun must have been moving along up above the trees because the patches of sunlight shifted bit by bit over the moving surface of the water, lighting up patches of our shoulders and legs and the tops of our heads. In a way it was the best afternoon of the summer. But it was also like a prediction from the oracle at Delphi; it could mean practically anything.

ANALYZE THE TEXT

Compare and Contrast What details in the story show how Debbie and Maureen are alike and different?

Award-Winning Literature for Independent Reading

If you enjoyed this excerpt from Lynne Rae Perkins's *All Alone in the Universe*, you might want to read the rest of the novel—and perhaps also seek out other novels by the same author. Reading additional works by the authors you encounter in this anthology is one way to find literature you might appreciate outside of school. One other way to find worthwhile literary and informational texts for independent reading purposes is to seek out award-winning pieces in your local library.

The following awards have earned the respect of reading teachers and librarians around the country for successfully identifying and honoring young people's reading material that is of exceptional quality and likely to be loved by many:

* The **Newbery Medal** is named for John Newbery, an eighteenth-century bookseller, but there is nothing antiquated or outdated about this honor. Only one title per year is graced with this prestigious award, considered by many librarians and other experts to be the premier award in young people's literature.

* Several books annually are designated as **American Library Association (ALA) Notable Children's Books,** which ALA defines as worthy of note or notice, important, distinguished, or outstanding. ALA Notable Books are conveniently divided into three categories: for younger children, for children in a middle age group, and for older children. ALA Notable Books include informational texts as well as fiction, although fiction usually dominates each annual list.

* The American Library Association also administers the **Coretta Scott King Book Awards,** named to commemorate the life and works of Dr. Martin Luther King, Jr., and to honor his widow, Mrs. Coretta Scott King, and the work she has continued to do in the name of peace and brotherhood. The Coretta Scott King Book Awards honor African American authors and illustrators for outstanding educational and inspirational contributions to the field of young people's literature.

* Each year, the staff of *School Library Journal* (SLJ), a periodical intended for school librarians and media specialists, reviews thousands of books for children and teens and lists those they find most deserving of young readers' attention. The **SLJ Best Books** include dozens of realistic fiction novels, works of fantasy and science fiction, and informational texts on subjects likely to interest many young people.

Of course, the fact that a book has been given an award does not mean that a potential reader will find that book interesting or appropriate. You will still need to investigate for yourself, finding the book in your library or sample pages and reviews online and gauging whether the subject matter and reading level seem right for you. If your school has a librarian or media specialist, he or she can also help steer you toward promising titles. Good luck, and may you open many doors onto the world of great literature and inspiring informational text—for it's a fascinating, enlightening, and often entertaining world to explore!

Dig Deeper

How to Analyze the Text

Use these pages to learn about Comparing and Contrasting, Character Motivations, and Point of View. Then read "All Alone in the Universe" again to apply what you learned.

Compare and Contrast

Authors of realistic fiction like "All Alone in the Universe" write stories about challenges and problems that can occur in real life. The characters in these stories are realistic—their thoughts, feelings, and actions are much like those of people in real life.

As you read "All Alone in the Universe," think about what the characters say and do. Use text evidence and make inferences about the characters to **compare** and **contrast** them.

Look back at pages 616–619. Look for details that help you understand Debbie and Glenna. How are Debbie and Glenna alike and different?

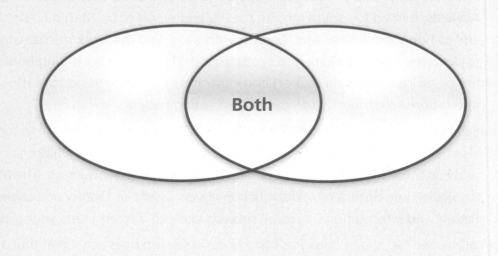

Both

COMMON CORE

RL.6.1 cite textual evidence to support analysis of what the text says explicitly as well as inferences drawn; **RL.6.3** describe how a story's or drama's plot unfolds and how characters respond or change; **RL.6.6** explain how an author develops the point of view of the narrator or speaker

Characters' Motivations

When you read realistic fiction, it is important to understand a **character's motivation,** or what the character wants and why the character wants it. Look back at page 617. Debbie feels jealous of Glenna and Maureen's new friendship, so she gives Maureen the carnival prize in order to reach out to her. Debbie is also trying to make the point that she, not Glenna, is Maureen's best friend. In rereading "All Alone in the Universe," analyze each character's motivations as the plot unfolds and the characters respond and change.

Point of View

In "All Alone in the Universe," the narrator is a story character, Debbie. This means that the story is told in first-person **point of view**. In first-person point of view, the narrator is a character who shares his or her thoughts and feelings with readers. As you reread the selection, think about how the author develops Debbie's point of view. For example, look for similes and metaphors in the text that help you understand Debbie's feelings. Also look for places where Debbie's outward reactions and behavior do not reflect what she is feeling inside.

Your Turn

my **WriteSmart**

RETURN TO THE ESSENTIAL QUESTION

Turn and Talk

Review the selection with a partner to prepare to discuss this question: *How does a new friendship affect an old one?* Ask clarifying questions as needed to help you understand your partner's answer. Use text evidence to defend your own answer.

Classroom Conversation

Continue your discussion of "All Alone in the Universe" by explaining your answers to these questions:

1. What do you think the author of "All Alone in the Universe" wants readers to understand about friendship?

2. What do Glenna's actions reveal about her true feelings toward Debbie?

3. Do you think Debbie will befriend Glenna in order to stay close to Maureen? Give text evidence to support your answer.

DESCRIPTIVE LANGUAGE

Infer a Character's Feelings The author of "All Alone in the Universe" allows readers to infer Debbie's feelings through the use of descriptive language, including similes and metaphors, instead of simply telling readers how she feels. Write a paragraph in which you evaluate how effective this method is in helping you understand the main character's feelings. Use text evidence and inferences you have made to support your evaluation.

WRITE ABOUT READING

Response Debbie and Maureen's close friendship changes when Maureen and Glenna start up a new friendship. Do you think Maureen continues to be a good friend to Debbie even though she becomes friends with Glenna? Write a paragraph to explain your opinion. Provide evidence stated in the text about how the characters respond to story events, along with your inferences about the characters, to explain your opinion.

All Alone in the Universe
BY LYNNE RAE PERKINS

Writing Tip

State your opinion at the beginning of your response. Support your opinion with clear reasons and relevant evidence from the text.

Go Digital

COMMON CORE **RL.6.1** cite textual evidence to support analysis of what the text says explicitly as well as inferences drawn; **RL.6.2** determine a theme or central idea of a text/provide a summary; **RL.6.3** describe how a story's or drama's plot unfolds and how characters respond or change; **W.6.9a** apply grade 6 Reading standards to literature; **SL.6.1a** come to discussions prepared/explicitly draw on preparation to probe and reflect on ideas under discussion; **SL.6.1c** pose and respond to questions and make comments that contribute to the discussion

LITERARY NONFICTION

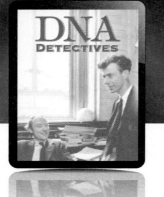

☑ **GENRE**

Literary nonfiction, such as this magazine article, gives factual information by telling a true story.

☑ **TEXT FOCUS**

Photos and Captions
Nonfiction articles often contain photos to illustrate the text and captions to tell more about what is in the photos.

DNA DETECTIVES

BY DOLORES HURLEY

In the 1950s, a race was taking place in England. Two teams of scientists, including one researcher who worked alone, were on their way to making one of the most important discoveries of the century: the structure of the DNA molecule. DNA carries the chemical code that determines the characteristics of all living things.

At Cambridge University, James Watson, an American, and Francis Crick, an Englishman, were friends and partners. Watson and Crick knew what DNA was, but they didn't know how its parts were connected. They built models of the molecule, using materials scrounged around their lab, but they couldn't make all the pieces fit.

Francis Crick

THE TWISTED LADDER

Meanwhile, at King's College in London, Rosalind Franklin was using x-rays to try to photograph a DNA molecule. Unlike Watson and Crick, Franklin did not have a friendly, stable relationship with her colleague, Maurice Wilkins. Wilkins had an abrupt manner and often treated Franklin like an assistant.

Despite the tension, Franklin continued to work. It took one hundred tries, but eventually, in 1952, she was able to create a clear photograph of DNA. Without her knowledge, however, Wilkins showed the photo to Watson. Some believe that Wilkins did this to be spiteful because of his dislike for Franklin.

Franklin's photo showed a blurry "X." It was a moment of exhilaration for Watson. "The instant I saw the picture my mouth fell open," he said. The photo led Watson and Crick to a new comprehension. It helped them build a twisting, ladder-shaped model of the DNA molecule. On February 28, 1953, Crick walked into a Cambridge restaurant and blurted that he and Watson "had found the secret of life."

James Watson

Rosalind Franklin's famous x-ray, "Photograph 51," of a DNA molecule

THE MISSING NOBELIST

In 1962 a Nobel Prize in Medicine was awarded to James Watson, Francis Crick, and Maurice Wilkins for their work on DNA. Sadly, the woman whose photo was important to their success was not awarded the prize. Rosalind Franklin had died of cancer in 1958, and the Nobel Prize is given only to living recipients. Some people think that Franklin's work with x-rays put her health in jeopardy. Crick has said that, had she been alive, Franklin should have received the prize because "she did the key experimental work."

Rosalind Franklin

WHAT IS DNA?

DNA is like an instruction book for creating living things. DNA molecules contain four chemicals that attach to each other across the twisted-ladder shape known as a double helix. The pairs of chemicals are the "steps" on the "ladder," and the chemicals can pair up in different patterns. Each pattern is a kind of oracle, predicting what many of the features of a plant or animal will be.

The double helix structure of a DNA molecule

2

Compare Texts

TEXT TO TEXT

Draw Parallels "DNA Detectives" explains that "DNA is like an instruction book for creating living things." Think about how "All Alone in the Universe" might be an instruction book for friendships. Do you believe that a friendship can be considered a living thing? Are there similarities between the two? Explain your opinion to a partner. Use details and inferences drawn from both selections as evidence to support your ideas.

TEXT TO SELF

Write a Letter Maureen seems not to notice that she is ignoring Debbie. Think of or imagine a time when you ignored someone, even if by accident. Write a letter to this person, explaining the situation from your viewpoint. Be sure to keep in mind your audience and your purpose for writing.

TEXT TO WORLD

Research Cells DNA supplies the code for plant cells as well as animal cells. Research and draw a plant cell, including the nucleus and chloroplasts. Show how the cell is involved in the process of photosynthesis. Share your project with a small group.

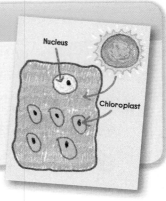

Nucleus

Chloroplast

COMMON CORE **RL.6.1** cite textual evidence to support analysis of what the text says explicitly as well as inferences drawn; **RI.6.1** cite textual evidence to support analysis of what the text says explicitly as well as inferences drawn; **W.6.4** produce writing in which development, organization, and style are appropriate to task, purpose, and audience; **W.6.7** conduct short research projects to answer a question, drawing on several sources and refocusing the inquiry when appropriate

Grammar

What Are Progressive Forms of Verbs? Verb phrases such as *is running* and *has been sleeping* tell about action that is continuing, or *in progress*. These verb phrases are called **progressive forms.** Each of the six verb tenses has a progressive form.

Present Progressive	I am talking with my friend about summer vacation.
Past Progressive	I was talking with her about it yesterday.
Future Progressive	I will be talking with her again later today.
Present Perfect Progressive	I have been talking with her for two hours.
Past Perfect Progressive	I had been talking with her only a few minutes when we had to leave.
Future Perfect Progressive	I will have been talking with her for three weeks by the time vacation starts.

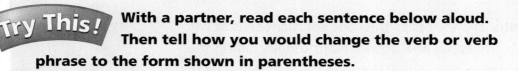 **With a partner, read each sentence below aloud. Then tell how you would change the verb or verb phrase to the form shown in parentheses.**

1 My friend and I walked to school. (past progressive)

2 I had told her about a cute dog on this street. (past perfect progressive)

3 She has taken photos of dogs. (present perfect progressive)

4 We will look at the photos together. (future progressive)

Using verb tenses and forms correctly will help you communicate clearly in your writing. If you are writing about events that are occurring at the same time or that are ongoing, use the same tense. Change from one tense to another only if events happen at different points in time.

Inconsistent Tenses	**Consistent Tenses**
My friends and I have wanted to go to the carnival for ages. We had waited for this day for weeks! After much discussion, we are agreeing on which rides we will try.	My friends and I have wanted to go to the carnival for ages. We have waited for this day for weeks! After much discussion, we have agreed on which rides we will try.

Connect Grammar to Writing

As you edit your opinion essay, look for verbs whose tenses should be changed to make your meaning clear.

COMMON CORE

Argument Writing

✔ **Voice** In an **opinion essay,** writers voice their feelings about a topic. As you write your opinion essay, state your opinion, or claim, at the beginning. Show a clear understanding of the topic by providing relevant reasons as well as evidence that supports the reasons. Connect with readers by using reasons they will be familiar with. Use transition words and phrases to clarify the relationships between your ideas.

Oliver drafted an opinion essay on why people should have close friends. Later, he added evidence to support his claim.

Writing Traits Checklist

✔ **Ideas**
Did I support my claim with reasons and evidence?

✔ **Organization**
Did I organize my reasons and evidence?

✔ **Sentence Fluency**
Did I use a variety of sentence structures?

✔ **Word Choice**
Did I use transition words to link reasons and evidence?

✔ **Voice**
Did I connect with my readers?

✔ **Conventions**
Did I use correct spelling, grammar, and punctuation?

Revised Draft

reason for
Another ~~great thing about~~ having close

friends is that they can cheer you up. They

try to do this whenever you are down. ~~My~~

e
friends know just the kinds of jokes that

would
make me laugh.

For example, when I got a disappointing grade on my math test last week, my

Nothing Beats Having Close Friends

by Oliver Drummond

Having close friends is one of the best things in life. In fact, everyone should have a couple of close friends. They make life better when it's good, and better when it's not so good.

One reason to have close friends is that you always have someone to do things with. For instance, I like to make up songs. My friends and I often write songs together. One of us thinks of a line of lyrics or the start of a tune. Someone else jumps in. Before long, we've written a great song!

Another reason for having close friends is that they can cheer you up. They try to do this whenever you are down. For example, when I got a disappointing grade on my math test last week, my friends knew just the kinds of jokes that would make me laugh.

Life is better with close friends. They help us enjoy life sometimes and help us get through it at others. The next time your friends do something nice for you, smile and say, "Nothing beats having close friends."

Reading as a Writer

How did Oliver connect with his readers? What can you do to connect with readers in your opinion essay?

In my final paper, I used words that my readers would know. I also used transition words and phrases to connect my reasons and evidence.

Vocabulary in Context

elusive

frustration

instinct

conditions

barren

harsh

decrepit

arose

vertical

lurched

Vocabulary Reader   Context Cards

COMMON CORE **L.6.6** acquire and use general academic and domain-specific words and phrases/gather vocabulary knowledge for comprehension or expression

1 elusive

The "aha!" moment that leads to an invention may be elusive. It may not be easy to achieve.

2 frustration

Inventors may feel frustration, or angry impatience, at their slow pace of progress.

3 instinct

Thomas Edison and other inventors relied on instinct, a natural sense of what to do, to solve problems.

4 conditions

At Kitty Hawk the Wright brothers found the ideal conditions of wind and landscape to test their airplane.

Go Digital

▶ Study each Context Card.

▶ Use a dictionary to confirm the meanings of these words.

5 barren

This jet-powered car achieved a speed of 763 miles per hour on an empty, barren desert in Nevada.

6 harsh

Firefighters' equipment was invented to protect them from the harsh, brutal heat of a blaze.

7 decrepit

After a car becomes old and decrepit, its owner might replace it with a newer, stronger model.

8 arose

When a storm suddenly arose, Benjamin Franklin flew a kite and proved that lightning is a form of electricity.

9 vertical

Communications devices, such as cell phones, require tall vertical towers to pick up signals in the air.

10 lurched

The cars of this early locomotive have lurched forward with a sudden burst of steam power.

Read and Comprehend

Go Digital

☑ TARGET SKILL

Conclusions and Generalizations As you read "First to Fly," use text evidence as well as your own experience to draw a **conclusion,** a judgment based on details. Use details to make a **generalization,** which is a broad statement about a range of facts that is true most of the time, but not always. A graphic organizer like this one can help you.

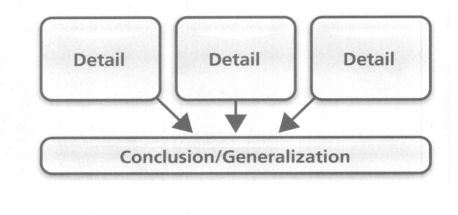

☑ TARGET STRATEGY

Monitor/Clarify As you read, **monitor** your understading of the text. Use text evidence to **clarify,** or figure out, the parts that are confusing.

RI.6.1 cite textual evidence to support analysis of what the text says explicitly as well as inferences drawn

Flight

People have long wanted to fly like birds. In the early days of aviation, many attempts were made to conquer the air. Gliders and hot air balloons were early inventions that inspired others to build flying machines. Today, helicopters, jet airplanes, and other aircraft carrying passengers and cargo fill the sky. Flight has become a common experience.

In "First to Fly," you'll learn about the Wright brothers and their challenges as they tried to create the first piloted, engine-driven aircraft.

ANCHOR TEXT

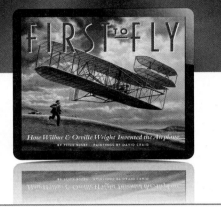

✓ TARGET SKILL

Conclusions and Generalizations Use details in the text to figure out ideas that aren't stated or are generally true.

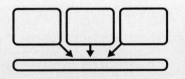

✓ GENRE

Literary nonfiction gives factual information by telling a true story. As you read, look for:

▶ elements of nonfiction and fiction

▶ information about a topic

▶ a story that involves real people or events

RI.6.1 cite textual evidence to support analysis of what the text says explicitly as well as inferences drawn; **RI.6.4** determine the meaning of words and phrases, including figurative, connotative, and technical meanings; **RI.6.5** analyze how a sentence, paragraph, chapter, or section fits in the overall structure; **L.6.5a** interpret figures of speech in context

MEET THE AUTHOR
Peter Busby

A former teacher, Peter Busby struck gold with his first children's book when *First to Fly* received the James Madison Book Award for excellence in explaining United States history. Busby, from Vancouver, British Columbia, and artist David Craig received the honor while standing beneath the 1903 Wright *Flyer*, which is displayed in the Smithsonian National Air and Space Museum.

MEET THE ILLUSTRATOR
David Craig

David Craig grew up in Ottawa, Ontario, the capital of Canada. A keen student of Canadian and United States history, he has designed coins for the Canadian Mint and has illustrated books about the Alamo, World War II, the Battle of Gettysburg, and the 1906 San Francisco earthquake.

FIRST TO FLY
How Wilbur & Orville Wright Invented the Airplane

by Peter Busby • paintings by David Craig

It's the spring of 1900, and brothers Wilbur and Orville Wright have traded bicycle making for the elusive dream of building a piloted aircraft. They're setting up camp to test their latest glider at Kitty Hawk, on a barren, windswept island in North Carolina.

It was far from perfect, but the brothers would learn to love it. There were two lifesaving stations, a weather bureau, a post office, and about twenty little houses among the sand dunes—but not much else. Wilbur's trip to Kitty Hawk, with the glider packed in a crate, was an incredible journey, by train, ferry, then fishing boat. The last part of Wilbur's trip, in a decrepit, flat-bottomed fishing schooner, was a nightmare. It started off calm enough, but when they reached the open sea, a storm arose. The cabin was so filthy that Wilbur spent the whole night on deck. Soaked to the skin, shivering cold, and ravenously hungry, with nothing to eat but a jar of jam, Wilbur wondered if he'd ever set foot on land again. Finally they docked at Kitty Hawk just before dawn. His hosts—the local postmaster Bill Tate and his wife—greeted him with a splendid breakfast of ham and eggs.

Orville arrived two weeks later, bringing supplies of tea and coffee, and they pitched their tent on the sand dunes, close to where they would fly the glider. Their mechanic, Charles Taylor, was left in charge of the bicycle shop back home.

"We certainly can't complain of the place," Orville wrote to his sister, Katharine. "We came down here for wind and sand, and we have got them." Some nights, when the wind came in from the Atlantic, they would have to jump out of their cots and hold the tent to keep it from blowing away, with sand stinging their hands and faces.

Wilbur and Orville pitched a tent on the dunes.

Wilbur and Orville carry the 1900 glider back to camp.

The brothers started off cautiously, flying the glider as a kite. They simply held it up off the sand and let the wind take it, then they played out ropes attached to the struts (the parts between the wings). They pulled on other ropes that moved the wing-warping (side to side movement) and elevator (upward and downward movement) controls, practicing keeping the craft level and bringing it safely down to land, learning the skills of a pilot from the ground.

Each flight brought the moment closer when Wilbur would take his life in his hands and pilot the glider himself.

One day in early October, he was ready. He positioned himself in the cockpit of the glider with his hands on the elevator controls and his feet against the wing-warping controls. Orville grasped one wing tip, and Bill Tate the other, and the two hoisted Wilbur and the glider into the air. Wilbur heard a dry crack as the twenty-five-mile (40 km) per hour wind filled the fabric of the wings, and then he felt a sudden weightlessness. Orville and Bill played out the ropes, letting Wilbur soar higher and higher.

The next few seconds passed in a blur. He'd thought there would be all the time in the world to plan his moves, to look around him, and to experience life from the air. Instead he found himself functioning on pure instinct as the plane lurched up and down, one moment plunging straight for the ground, the next nosing upward, threatening to stall and fall over on its back. "Let me down!" he shouted.

Orville and Bill pulled on the ropes and brought the glider safely down onto the sand. Wilbur had done it. He had flown. But he was not intending to risk it again, not until he understood the plane a lot better. For the next two weeks, they went back to testing the craft as a kite, using weights instead of a pilot, noting how it behaved in different wind conditions, and measuring everything: drag, lift, wind speed, and the angle at which the glider kite flew. They even tried turning the glider around, with the elevator in the rear.

In the final week, Wilbur had the confidence to fly again and this time he would try free flight, without the ropes. Altogether, he made about a dozen glides between 200 feet (61 m) and 300 feet (91 m) in length. On October 23, they went home, leaving the glider behind on the dunes. During the winter, it would be destroyed by the savage Atlantic gales—all except for the sateen wing covering. A few days after they left, Mrs. Tate removed the material and made it into dresses for her daughters.

Next July, the brothers were back in Kitty Hawk with a new glider, twice as big as the 1900 model. They made camp at the foot of Kill Devil Hills, a group of huge sand dunes four miles (6.5 km) to the south of Kitty Hawk. They built a shed for the glider, where they could sleep at night and be sheltered from the punishing weather—either the pounding rain or the scorching sun.

With Wilbur at the controls, Bill and Dan Tate let the wind lift the new glider off the top of the dunes.

Then there were the mosquitoes. "The sand and grass and trees and hills and everything were covered with them," Orville wrote to Katharine. "They chewed us right through our underwear and socks. Lumps began swelling all over my body like hen's eggs." They tried everything to protect themselves—blankets, netting, and finally smoking the mosquitoes out by burning old tree stumps.

At first the glider performed poorly, but after making adjustments to the elevator and the camber (the upward curve from the front to the rear of the wings), the brothers started doing better. Their friend Octave Chanute was present for their best glide—390 feet (119 m) in 17 seconds. He was impressed, but the brothers were dissatisfied. The glider's lift was not much better than last year, and the controls seemed worse.

On August 9, when Wilbur tried to turn the glider, he crashed nose-first into the ground, banging his head against a wooden strut.

The accident was not serious, but it added to the brothers' frustration, and they left Kitty Hawk earlier than planned. On the train home, Orville said what both of them were feeling: "Not within a thousand years will man ever fly."

The brothers did not stay depressed for long. Instead they decided to go back to the beginning and think through everything they had done. If size alone hadn't improved their performance, then maybe the secret was the shape of the glider and the wings. To research this, they built a wind tunnel in the workshop. For the next few months, there would be no camping on the dunes and gliding in the open air. Instead they were indoors, testing almost two hundred wing shapes. Every day, they made new discoveries about how the wings of a plane behave in the air. At the end of their research, they had the design of a new glider that was very different from the ones they had made before.

ANALYZE THE TEXT

Text Structure How does the author organize the text on pages 646–647? What clues in the text show this?

In the first three days back at Kitty Hawk, they made more than fifty flights in the 1902 glider. Already they were staying in the air longer than they had before. Orville had begun to fly a little in the previous year, and now he was making half the flights. One day, as he took the plane higher, the glider nosed upward at a dangerous angle. Orville pushed on the elevator, struggling to get the plane level again. To his horror, he found himself slipping backward, tail-first, toward the ground. There was a crash of splintering timber as the tail pounded into the sand.

Orville stepped out of the glider without a scratch. The tail could soon be mended, but it was obvious that there was something wrong with its design. The 1902 glider was their first one to have a tail, which was fixed in a vertical position. The tail was supposed to give the plane more control, but Orville felt it wasn't doing that. He had an idea. What if they put a hinge on the tail, so that the pilot could move it at the same time as he warped the wings to make a turn?

Orville suggested this to Wilbur, then waited for his brother's reaction. He expected an argument, because that was the way the

The 1902 glider was their first one with a fixed tail. After problems during early trials, Orville suggested a movable tail or rudder. With a rudder, they could keep the glider pointed in the proper direction as they rolled into a turn.

brothers worked out their ideas. "Both boys had tempers," Charles Taylor later recalled. "They would shout at one another something terrible. I don't think they really got mad, but they sure got awfully hot." Instead, on this occasion, Wilbur said nothing for a while, then told Orville he agreed about hinging the rudder but he had a better idea. Instead of having a separate control, they should connect the wing-warping controls and the rudder, so the pilot could use the hip cradle to move both at the same time.

That's what they did, and it worked perfectly. They started doing longer glides, and the control problem was solved.

That year, the Wright brothers made almost a thousand flights. On their final day of gliding, they broke their record again with a glide of 622 feet (190 m), lasting 26 seconds. Wilbur and Orville went home happy. They had achieved their first goal, designing a glider that could be controlled in the air. Now they were ready to build a plane with an engine and propellers.

ANALYZE THE TEXT

Conclusions/Generalizations What generalizations can be made about the Wright brothers based on the text evidence on pages 648–649?

Twelve Magic Seconds

On the morning of December 17, 1903, Wilbur and Orville Wright stepped out of their shack and looked around them. Ice had formed in puddles between the sand dunes from the heavy rain overnight, but the sky was now clear. The weather was almost perfect—except for the wind.

The winds were stiff today—thirty knots. The brothers were cautious men. Any other day, they would have waited for calmer conditions, but they had lost enough time already in the two months they'd spent at Kitty Hawk. There had been problems tuning the engine, making it run smoothly, and cranking up the power, and twice they had had to send the propeller shafts back to Dayton for repairs. Soon it would be winter, the weather would be too harsh, and they'd have to get back to the bicycle shop.

They decided to risk it. Today was the day. They were going to attempt to fly their plane.

Orville hoisted a large red flag on the roof of the shack. The flag was a signal to the men of the Kill Devil Life Saving Station, a mile (1.6 km) away, to come and lend a hand. The over 700-pound (318-kg) *Flyer* was too heavy for two men to carry by themselves. And the brothers had another reason for inviting people to join them. If the world was going to believe them, they had to have witnesses.

A short distance from the house, Wilbur and Orville started laying a line of wooden beams. The machine would move along this track until the propellers pushed the wings through the air fast enough to lift the plane off the ground. By the time they'd finished, the lifesaving crew had arrived.

Once the *Flyer* was in position, Wilbur and Orville took hold of the blades of the two propellers and pulled hard to give them a spin. The engine sputtered and coughed into life.

ANALYZE THE TEXT

Personification The author uses the phrase "coughed into life" on this page. What does the phrase mean? Why does the author use personification here?

Wilbur and Orville start their engine by spinning the blades of the two propellers.

Wilbur took aside one of the lifesavers, John Daniels, and showed him the camera placed on a tripod near the ramp. There was a cord attached to it with a rubber ball at the end. When the *Flyer* leaves the ground, Wilbur explained, you squeeze this ball. Daniels looked worried. He had never used a camera before.

The two brothers walked away from the others for a quiet moment. They had spent five years on this project, designing a series of gliders, learning how to control them in the air, and finally, because no one else could make an engine light enough and powerful enough, they had built one themselves in the bicycle workshop.

They had made their first attempt with the Wright *Flyer* three days earlier, on December 14. The track was laid down the side of a hill; then the brothers tossed a coin to decide who would be the pilot. Wilbur won. He climbed into the plane. The *Flyer* rattled down the ramp and lifted off. Wilbur was in the air—but soon he was in trouble. He rose no higher than fifteen feet (4.6 m), then lost height, landing awkwardly with the left wing plowing into the sand. Some might call this a flight, but not the Wrights. A flight for them had to be controlled.

The *Flyer* was soon repaired. It was a mistake, the brothers decided, to take off going downhill. Today they had laid the track on a flat piece of sand.

Now it was Orville's turn to be the pilot. He climbed into the hip cradle on the bottom wing and lay flat on his stomach, settling his hips into the cradle that controlled the wing-warping and rudder, and grasping the lever that controlled the elevator.

"Orville's going to be nervous," Wilbur said to the men watching. "Let's try and cheer him on. Holler and clap."

He turned back to his brother and they clasped hands as if, one of the lifesavers said later, "they weren't sure they'd ever see each other again."

Wilbur took his place at the wing tip as his brother released the wire holding the straining plane in place. The propellers began to move the plane faster and faster along the track.

Wilbur was running next to him, shouting encouragement, ready to let go of the wing.

Then, forty feet (12 m) down the track, the *Flyer* lifted into the air.

Wilbur clicked on his stopwatch.

Orville pulled up on the elevator. The *Flyer* started up at a dangerous angle, about to stall and fall back on its tail. Orville reacted,

At Kill Devil Hills, at 10:35 A.M., December 17, 1903, Orville takes off on the first-ever manned and powered flight. Wilbur, who steadied the plane while it moved down the launching rail, is still half-running. This famous photograph was taken with Orville's camera by John Daniels, one of the lifesaving station crew.

throwing the elevator lever down. Now the *Flyer* was heading for the ground. Another touch on the elevator pulled the plane up again. Then down, and the *Flyer* pancaked into the ground. It was a hard landing, but both the plane and the pilot were in one piece.

Wilbur stopped his watch. The *Flyer* had been in the air for twelve seconds. He turned to John Daniels. "Did you get it?"

He had. His picture of the *Flyer* three feet (.9 m) off the ground, with Orville on board and Wilbur running beside him, is one of the most famous photographs ever taken.

Orville had flown 120 feet (36.5 m). Both of them thought they could do better. At 11:20 A.M., Wilbur made a flight of 175 feet (53 m). Then it was Orville's turn again. He managed 200 feet (61 m). At noon, Wilbur climbed into the pilot's cradle.

For the first 300 feet (91 m), it was like the other flights, with the plane bouncing up and down. Then Wilbur managed to keep it level for another 500 feet (152 m) until a sudden gust of wind caught it, sending it diving toward the ground.

Wilbur stepped out of the cradle, unhurt. He had flown for 59 seconds, traveling 852 feet (260 m).

The brothers made several successful flights at Kitty Hawk before moving their base to Huffman Prairie, near Dayton.

Once again, the seven men started back to the track carrying the plane. Just as they reached the track and set the machine down, the wind rose suddenly and caught the *Flyer*. Everyone jumped for it, John Daniels getting tangled in the wires as the plane rolled over and over. When it finally came to rest, the others rushed up and cut him free, snapping a few more wires and wooden ribs as they did so. He was lifted out uninjured.

The *Flyer* was smashed to pieces—but no matter. The Wrights were already thinking ahead, to their next and even *better* plane.

One of the young men dashed all the way to the post office at Kitty Hawk to deliver the news. For the Wright family it took a while longer, until the telegram arrived at 5:30 that evening. "Success four flights Thursday morning," it read. "All against twenty-one-mile wind started from level with engine power alone, average speed through air thirty-one miles, longest 59 seconds. Inform press. Home Christmas. Orville Wright."

Dig Deeper

How to Analyze the Text

Use these pages to learn about Conclusions and Generalizations, Text Structure, and Personification. Then read "First to Fly" again to apply what you learned.

Conclusions and Generalizations

In "First to Fly," author Peter Busby includes many details about the Wright brothers, but sometimes he does not tell the reader everything. In those cases, readers must draw **conclusions,** or make judgments on their own, based on text evidence. Readers can also make a **generalization** from many details in the text. A generalization is a broad statement based on a range of facts. A generalization is not always true, but it is most of the time.

Look back at pages 652–653 in "First to Fly." Orville and Wilbur Wright take turns piloting the *Flyer*. You can draw the conclusion that each brother wanted a turn at trying to fly the plane. Based on their four successful flights and on the telegram they sent to their family members, what generalization can you make about the Wright brothers' desire to prove themselves?

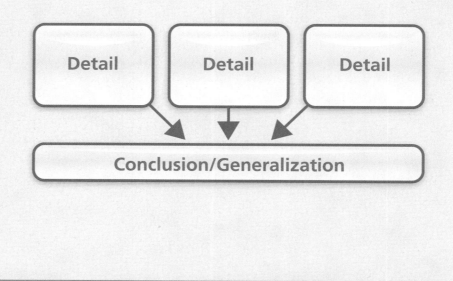

Detail   Detail   Detail

Conclusion/Generalization

COMMON CORE **RI.6.1** cite textual evidence to support analysis of what the text says explicitly as well as inferences drawn; **RI.6.4** determine the meaning of words and phrases, including figurative, connotative, and technical meanings; **RI.6.5** analyze how a sentence, paragraph, chapter, or section fits in the overall structure; **L.6.5a** interpret figures of speech in context

Go Digital

Text Structure

To understand a nonfiction selection, look at its **text structure,** or the way the ideas are organized. An author may **compare and contrast** ideas to make a point. **Description** is a text structure used to explain what something is like. An author may also describe the **sequence** in which events happen. In a science journal, for example, you might use sequence to record minute by minute what you observe as birds fly to a birdfeeder. Analyzing how text is organized helps you figure out how a part of a text fits within the whole.

Personification

In a **figure of speech,** words have meanings other than their dictionary meanings. **Personification** is one figure of speech. When authors use personification, they give human qualities to an object or idea. *The sand bit me on the face as it blew* is an example of personification. Sand can't actually bite, but it can feel like it does if it hits hard against your face. Interpreting personification and other figures of speech helps you picture what the text describes.

Your Turn

RETURN TO THE ESSENTIAL QUESTION

Turn and Talk

Review the selection with a partner to prepare to discuss this question: *How can trial and error lead to new inventions?* As you discuss, pose questions and respond with comments that contribute to the discussion.

Classroom Conversation

Continue your discussion of "First to Fly" by using text evidence to explain your answers to these questions:

1. Why would inventors and others be inspired by the Wright brothers?

2. In what ways did other inventors help the Wrights accomplish their goal?

3. It took three years for the Wrights to progress from testing a glider at Kitty Hawk to flying a manned airplane. What do you think they learned during that time?

FLIGHT PATHS

Design a Feature With a partner, design a diagram or a graph to show the distances the Wright brothers flew at different times during their work at Kitty Hawk. Use a ruler or another measuring device to make sure that the distances are shown in correct proportion to each other. Use the text as your guide. Share your results. Tell how using the text and the graph together helps you better understand the events.

WRITE ABOUT READING

Response The Wright brothers had determination, patience, and the ability to solve problems. Which of these traits do you think was the most important in helping them become the first to fly an airplane? Write a paragraph to express your opinion. Introduce the paragraph with your claim, and then make your argument using reasons and evidence from the selection. End with a concluding statement that summarizes your argument.

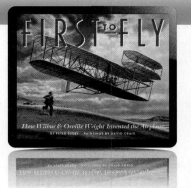

Writing Tip

State your claim at the beginning of your paragraph. Use text evidence to support your argument. Make sure you use pronouns correctly in your paragraph. Consider the case, number, and person when choosing which pronoun to use.

COMMON CORE **RI.6.7** integrate information presented in different media or formats as well as in words; **W.6.9b** apply grade 6 Reading standards to literary nonfiction; **SL.6.1a** come to discussions prepared/explicitly draw on preparation to probe and reflect on ideas under discussion; **SL.6.1c** pose and respond to questions and make comments that contribute to the discussion; **L.6.1a** ensure that pronouns are in the proper case

LITERARY NONFICTION

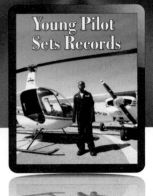

Young Pilot Sets Records

Literary nonfiction, such as this newspaper article, gives factual information by telling a true story.

Narrative nonfiction may include a **chart** that organizes related information about a topic.

COMMON CORE **RI.6.7** integrate information presented in different media or formats as well as in words; **RI.6.10** read and comprehend literary nonfiction

---

TODAY'S

MONDAY, MARCH 16

Young Pilot Sets Records

by Linda Cave

On July 1, 2006, a helicopter pilot named Jonathan Strickland landed his helicopter in Compton, California. Other pilots had done so before him, but this landing was special. It meant a vertical move to the top of an aviation record. Strickland's flight to Canada and back made him, at age fourteen, the youngest African American to fly a helicopter on an international roundtrip.

Jonathan Strickland, fourteen-year-old helicopter and airplane pilot

Jonathan with his flight teacher, Robin Petgrave

A Record-Breaking Flight

Jonathan's flight had begun nine days earlier, on June 22. Because he was too young to fly alone in the United States, his flight teacher, Robin Petgrave, accompanied him. Flying over lush Pacific rainforests and barren fields, Jonathan arrived in British Columbia, where he took tests to fly solo. For many young aviators, flying solo is an elusive goal, calling on instinct and practice. Jonathan's dream was to fly solo in an airplane and in a helicopter on the same day. On June 28, he became the youngest person to do so.

On Jonathan's return flight, rough weather conditions arose. The helicopter lurched at times, but it was not decrepit when it landed in Compton. Jonathan's friends and family greeted him, as did members of the Tuskegee Airmen. This African American squadron of the Army Air Corps endured the frustration of harsh racism at home while becoming one of the most successful fighter groups of World War II.

PEOPLE

Tomorrow's Aviators

Jonathan Strickland was eleven when he began his flight training at Tomorrow's Aeronautical Museum in Compton, California. The museum and its Aviation Explorer Program for teaching young people to fly were founded by Robin Petgrave. In return for their lessons, the students perform community service. Strickland's goals for the future include a lot more flying. He wants to attend the U.S. Air Force Academy, and he hopes to become a test pilot and an airline pilot. "Taking this trip," he said, "gave me the opportunity to see a whole new world and to discover that there is so much more out there for me."

Aviation Explorer pilots Richard Olmos, Diamond Hooper, and Kenny Roy

Tomorrow's Aeronautical Museum Record-Holders

Breean Farfan	Youngest Latina to fly roundtrip across the country	13
Jimmy Haywood	Youngest African American to fly an airplane on an international roundtrip flight	11
Kenny Roy	Youngest African American to fly solo in an airplane	14

Compare Texts

TEXT TO TEXT

Interview Trailblazers Think about what helped Jonathan Strickland and Orville and Wilbur Wright meet their aviation challenges. Write a mock interview in which you ask the three about the hurdles they faced. Have them explain how they overcame their challenges. Use evidence from the selections in your interviews.

TEXT TO SELF

Write About Transportation Planes and other forms of transportation have made travel quicker and easier. Think of a typical day in your life. Write about how you depend on transportation to travel. How do cars, bikes, or buses affect your daily life? Include an illustration with your writing.

TEXT TO WORLD

Make a Timeline The Wright brothers were the first to begin developing what would become a very complicated piece of machinery. How has the airplane evolved over the years? Research and create a timeline of significant events in the development of airplanes. Share your discoveries with the class.

Go Digital

COMMON CORE **RI.6.1** cite textual evidence to support analysis of what the text says explicitly as well as inferences drawn; **W.6.7** conduct short research projects to answer a question, drawing on several sources and refocusing the inquiry when appropriate; **W.6.10** write routinely over extended time frames and shorter time frames

Grammar

Punctuation and Quotations A **direct quotation** gives a speaker's exact words. Set off a direct quotation with beginning and ending **quotation marks.** Use a comma to separate a direct quotation from the rest of a sentence. Capitalize the first word of the quotation; place end punctuation inside the ending quotation mark. Remember, when you write **nonrestrictive elements** (nonessential information), use commas to set them off. Place parentheses or dashes around **parenthetical elements.**

Punctuation and Quotations
"Which one of the Wright brothers, Orville or Wilbur, arrived at Kitty Hawk first?" Rogelio asked his brother Teo.
"Wilbur arrived first," responded Teo. Then he added, "Orville joined him a short time (two weeks) later."
Rogelio asked, "Why did they choose Kitty Hawk—a sandy, windy island—as their test site?"

Try This! **Rewrite each sentence. Use quotation marks, commas, and parentheses or dashes to punctuate the following sentences.**

1. When did Wilbur first fly in the glider asked Loreen.

2. Teo replied Wilbur first flew in the glider in October, 1900.

3. Wilbur got into the glider in the cockpit to get prepared.

4. Bill Tate a friend and Orville Wright hoisted the glider into the air.

Quotation marks let readers know a speaker's exact words. Use the correct placement of quotation marks and end punctuation in quotations. Use commas, parentheses, and dashes correctly to punctuate additional information in nonrestrictive and parenthetical elements.

Incorrect	Correct
"I want to be a pilot, said Margo.	"I want to be a pilot," said Margo.
Raul wondered what kind of aircraft—jets or helicopters, Margo wanted to fly.	Raul wondered what kind of aircraft—jets or helicopters—Margo wanted to fly.
He asked Margo, "What kind of aircraft would you like to fly"?	He asked Margo, "What kind of aircraft would you like to fly?"

Connect Grammar to Writing

As you revise your problem-solution essay, be sure to use commas with nonrestrictive elements. Use parentheses or dashes with parenthetical elements. If you include a direct quotation, use quotation marks, capitalization, and end punctuation correctly.

W.6.1a introduce claim(s) and organize reasons and evidence clearly; W.6.1b support claim(s) with reasons and evidence, using credible sources and demonstrating understanding of the topic or text; W.6.1c use words, phrases, and clauses to clarify relationships; L.6.1e recognize variations from standard English and identify/use strategies to improve expression

COMMON CORE

Argument Writing

☑ **Word Choice** In a **problem-solution essay,** good writers state a problem. Then they state one or more solutions to the problem using claims that are developed with reasons and evidence. They include transition words to clarify the relationships among the claims, reasons, and evidence. They also notice any variations from standard English and make the necessary corrections to their writing.

   Anna wrote a first draft of her problem-solution essay about traffic congestion. Then she revised her draft. She corrected nonstandard usage of words.

Writing Traits Checklist

☑ **Ideas**
Did I include ideas for my argument?

☑ **Organization**
Did I give the problem and then the solution?

☑ **Sentence Fluency**
Did I use transition words to clarify relationships?

☑ **Word Choice**
Did I use correct standard English words?

☑ **Voice**
Did I show interest?

☑ **Conventions**
Did I use correct spelling, grammar, and punctuation?

Revised Draft

My solution is to make a ~~small~~ ^{smart} vehicle that self-adjusts its size according to the number of people ^{traveling} ~~travelin'~~ in it. I call this stylish invention a Trans-Cell. If only one person ^{were} ~~was~~ in the Trans-Cell, it would shrink to a small ,^{cozy} size. This means that the many big ^{gas-guzzlers} ~~cars~~ that now carry only one person would be replaced by ^{superior and} much smaller Trans-Cells.

The Trans-Cell

by Anna Sung

Horns honk. Drivers yell, "Let's go!" Today, traffic congestion frustrates travelers in nearly every city. People are often late or miss important events because they are stuck in traffic. They get angry or impatient as they waste time waiting for traffic to move.

My solution is to make a smart vehicle that self-adjusts its size according to the number of people traveling in it. I call this stylish invention a Trans-Cell. If only one person were in the Trans-Cell, it would shrink to a small, cozy size. This means that the many big gas-guzzlers that now carry only one person would be replaced by superior and much smaller Trans-Cells. As a result, more cars would take up less space.

Another reason why the Trans-Cell would work is that parking would be easier. More cars could fit into parking lots. People wouldn't waste as much time and fuel driving around.

These days, there is a lot of traffic everywhere we go. Using the Trans-Cell, all of us would experience far less congestion and enjoy more pleasant travel.

Reading as a Writer

How does using standard English make your writing clearer? What can you do to recognize any variations in standard English and to improve your writing?

In my final paper, I made sure I used correct standard English. I also used transitions to clarify relationships among the claims, reasons, and evidence.

occupying
confronting
implored
exasperated
contempt
strident
warily
intently
scornfully
subsided

Vocabulary
Reader

Context
Cards

 COMMON CORE L.6.6 acquire and use general academic and domain-specific words and phrases/gather vocabulary knowledge for comprehension or expression

668

Vocabulary in Context

1 occupying

The Danish people needed to be brave when German soldiers invaded and stayed, occupying their nation.

2 confronting

Confronting, or facing, an enemy in battle requires a great deal of courage.

3 implored

During World War II, posters implored, or urged, people to conserve materials and food.

CAN ALL YOU CAN

IT'S A REAL WAR JOB!

4 exasperated

Some people were exasperated with wartime shortages. Others accepted the lack of supplies calmly.

 Go Digital

▶ Study each Context Card.

▶ Discuss one picture. Use a different Vocabulary word from the one on the card.

5 contempt

People who sold scarce items illegally, or on the "black market," were viewed with contempt, or disgust.

don't feed black market greed

6 strident

Dictators might speak to citizens in harsh, strident tones in an effort to intimidate them.

7 warily

During the war, people greeted hopeful news warily, or cautiously. They tried to focus on helping the troops.

ARE YOU DOING ALL YOU CAN?

8 intently

An officer focusing on a battleground often peers intently through a pair of binoculars.

9 scornfully

People who talked about war plans in public were referred to scornfully, with disgust, in World War II posters.

QUIET! LOOSE TALK CAN COST LIVES

10 subsided

When victory came to Europe in World War II, tension subsided and people began to relax.

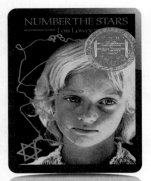

Read and Comprehend

☑ TARGET SKILL

Cause and Effect As you read "Number the Stars," notice how cause-and-effect relationships link episodes in the plot. Remember that a **cause** is why an event happens, and an **effect** is what happens as a result of a cause. Sometimes the effect of one event is the cause of another. Use a graphic organizer like this one to help you record causes and effects as the plot unfolds. Think about how each event fits into the story's overall structure.

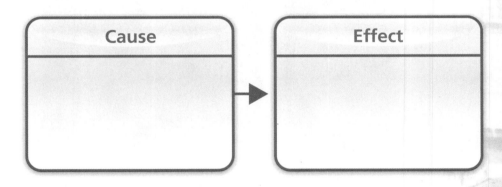

☑ TARGET STRATEGY

Analyze/Evaluate Think carefully about, or **analyze,** text evidence and then **evaluate,** or form an opinion about, what you are reading.

RL.6.1 cite textual evidence to support analysis of what the text says explicitly as well as inferences drawn; **RL.6.3** describe how a story's or drama's plot unfolds and how characters respond or change; **RL.6.5** analyze how a sentence, chapter, scene or stanza fits in the overall structure

PREVIEW THE TOPIC

World War II

In 1939, Germany invaded Poland. As a result of the invasion, France and Great Britain declared war on Germany. Germany then invaded other countries in Europe, including Denmark, prompting many countries around the world to join forces against Germany.

During World War II, Germany's Nazi leader, Adolf Hitler, had Jewish people arrested and sent to prison camps. However, many people worked in secret to keep Jewish people safe from harm. In the historical fiction selection "Number the Stars," you'll read about a brave family who helps Jewish people escape from Nazi-occupied Denmark.

ANCHOR TEXT

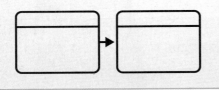

✓ TARGET SKILL

Cause and Effect Identify cause-and-effect relationships in the episodes that make up the plot.

✓ GENRE

Historical fiction is a story set in the past with events that did happen or could have happened. As you read, look for:

▶ actual historical figures
▶ a setting that is a real time and place in the past
▶ details that show the story is set in a real period of history

COMMON CORE **RL.6.3** describe how a story's or drama's plot unfolds and how characters respond or change; **RL.6.4** determine the meaning of words and phrases, including figurative and connotative meanings/ analyze impact of word choice; **RL.6.10** read and comprehend literature; **L.6.5a** interpret figures of speech in context

MEET THE AUTHOR

Lois Lowry

Twice a recipient of the prestigious Newbery Medal for *Number the Stars* and *The Giver*, Lois Lowry has published more than forty novels for young people, including nine narratives about the energetic Anastasia Krupnik—the main character in a series of popular middle-grade novels about an adolescent who deals with everyday predicaments. When she first became an author, Lowry penned books for an adult audience, but she was encouraged by her editor to write for children instead. Her books often present mature themes by using characters and circumstances that younger readers can comprehend and appreciate.

"My books have varied in content and style," says Lowry, "yet it seems that all of them deal, essentially, with the same general theme: the importance of human connections."

Discussions during a week-long vacation to Bermuda with a Danish friend inspired Lowry to write *Number the Stars*, and as Lowry talked with her friend about her childhood, she began to visualize what it was like for her traveling companion during World War II. To continue her investigation for the story that became *Number the Stars*, Lowry eventually journeyed overseas to Denmark where she communicated with other people who experienced the war firsthand; she also visited the Holocaust Museum, which is dedicated to the role Denmark played in the war. Another of Lowry's well-liked books, *Autumn Street*, takes place in the same time period as *Number the Stars*, but the events occur in much different setting: Philadelphia, Pennsylvania.

MEET THE ILLUSTRATOR

James Bentley

James Bentley studied design and illustration at Dawson College in his hometown of Montreal, Quebec, in Canada. Bentley has created artwork for theater posters, advertisements, book covers, and magazines, as well as for private collectors. James Bentley has won a number of awards for his work, including one of his most valued awards—the Joseph Morgan Henninger Best of Show Award, given by the Society of Illustrators of Los Angeles.

Number the Stars

by Lois Lowry
selection illustrated by James Bentley

ESSENTIAL QUESTION

How did the courageous acts of people in the past affect history?

With Nazi soldiers occupying Copenhagen, Denmark, in 1943, Annemarie Johansen travels with her mother and younger sister Kirsti to her Uncle Henrik's house on the Danish coast. Uncle Henrik and Peter Neilsen, the fiancé of Annemarie's older sister, are helping Danish Jews escape in Henrik's boat to safety in Sweden. Among them is the family of Ellen Rosen, Annemarie's best friend. After helping escort a group of escapees to the harbor, Annemarie's mother trips on the way home and breaks her ankle. In the house, she discovers that an important packet was not delivered, and in alarm, Mrs. Johansen directs Annemarie to place the packet at the bottom of a lunch basket and scurry to the harbor before Uncle Henrik departs. On the way, Nazi soldiers stop Annemarie, and they roughly search the contents of the basket.

Annemarie gave an exasperated sigh. "Could I go now, please?" she asked impatiently.

The soldier reached for the apple. He noted its brown spots, and made a face of disgust.

"No meat?" he asked, glancing at the basket and the napkin that lay in its bottom.

Annemarie gave him a withering look. "You know we have no meat," she said insolently. "Your army eats all of Denmark's meat."

Please, please, she implored in her mind. Don't lift the napkin.

The soldier laughed. He dropped the bruised apple on the ground. One of the dogs leaned forward, pulling at his leash, sniffed the apple, and stepped back. But both dogs still looked intently at the basket, their ears alert, their mouths open. Saliva glistened on their smooth pink gums.

"My dogs smell meat," the soldier said.

"They smell squirrels in the woods," Annemarie responded. "You should take them hunting."

The soldier reached forward with the cheese in one hand, as if he were going to return it to the basket. But he didn't. Instead, he pulled out the flowered cotton napkin.

ANALYZE THE TEXT

Figurative Language Annemarie gives the soldier a "withering look." What is the meaning of this phrase? Find another example of figurative language at the top of page 675 and tell what it means.

Annemarie froze.

"Your uncle has a pretty little lunch," the soldier said scornfully, crumpling the napkin around the cheese in his hand. "Like a woman," he added with contempt.

Then his eyes locked on the basket. He handed the cheese and napkin to the soldier beside him.

"What's that? There, in the bottom?" he asked in a different, tenser voice.

What would Kirsti do? Annemarie stamped her foot. Suddenly, to her own surprise, she began to cry. "I don't know!" she said, her voice choked. "My mother's going to be angry that you stopped me and made me late. And you've completely ruined Uncle Henrik's lunch, so now *he'll* be mad at me, too!"

The dogs whined and struggled against the leashes, nosing forward to the basket. One of the other soldiers muttered something in German.

The soldier took out the packet. "Why was this so carefully hidden?" he snapped.

Annemarie wiped her eyes on the sleeve of her sweater. "It wasn't hidden, any more than the napkin was. I don't know what it is." That, she realized, was true. She had no idea what was in the packet.

The soldier tore the paper open while below him, on the ground, the dogs strained and snarled, pulling against their leashes. Their muscles were visible beneath the sleek, short-haired flesh.

He looked inside, then glared at Annemarie. "Stop crying, you idiot girl," he said harshly. "Your stupid mother has sent your uncle a handkerchief. In Germany the women have better things to do. They don't stay at home hemming handkerchiefs for their men."

He gestured with the folded white cloth and gave a short, caustic laugh. "At least she didn't stitch flowers on it."

He flung it to the ground, still half wrapped in the paper, beside the apple. The dogs lunged, sniffed at it eagerly, then subsided, disappointed again.

"Go on," the soldier said. He dropped the cheese and the napkin back into her basket. "Go on to your uncle and tell him the German dogs enjoyed his bread."

All of the soldiers pushed past her. One of them laughed, and they spoke to each other in their own language. In a moment they had disappeared down the path, in the direction from which Annemarie had just come.

Quickly she picked up the apple and the opened packet with the white handkerchief inside. She put them into the basket and ran around the bend toward the harbor, where the morning sky was now bright with early sun and some of the boat engines were starting their strident din.

The *Ingeborg* (EENG uh bawrg) was still there, by the dock, and Uncle Henrik was there, his light hair windblown and bright as he knelt by the nets. Annemarie called to him and he came to the side, his face worried when he recognized her on the dock.

She handed the basket across. "Mama sent your lunch," she said, her voice quavering. "But soldiers stopped me, and they took your bread." She didn't dare to tell him more.

Henrik glanced quickly into the basket. She could see the look of relief on his face, and knew that it was because he saw that the packet was there, even though it was torn open.

"Thank you," he said, and the relief was evident in his voice.

Annemarie looked quickly around the familiar small boat. She could see down the passageway into the empty cabin. There was no sign of the Rosens or the others. Uncle Henrik followed her eyes and her puzzled look.

"All is well," he said softly. "Don't worry. Everything is all right.

"I wasn't sure," he said. "But now"—he eyed the basket in his hands—"because of you, Annemarie, everything is all right.

"You run home now, and tell your mama not to worry. I will see you this evening."

He grinned at her suddenly. "They took my bread, eh?" he said. "I hope they choke on it."

"Poor Blossom!" Uncle Henrik said, laughing, after dinner that evening. "It was bad enough that your mother was going to milk her, after all these years of city life. But Annemarie! To do it for the very first time! I'm surprised Blossom didn't kick you!"

ANALYZE THE TEXT

Understanding Characters How does Annemarie react to being stopped and questioned by the German soldiers? How does her behavior change from the beginning of her encounter with the soldiers to the end of it? What does Annemarie's attitude with the soldiers tell you about her character?

Mama laughed, too. She sat in a comfortable chair that Uncle Henrik had moved from the living room and placed in a corner of the kitchen. Her leg, in a clean white cast to the knee, was on a footstool.

Annemarie didn't mind their laughing. It *had* been funny. When she had arrived back at the farmhouse—she had run along the road to avoid the soldiers who might still be in the woods; now, carrying nothing, she was in no danger—Mama and Kirsti were gone. There was a note, hastily written, from Mama, that the doctor was taking her in his car to the local hospital, that they would be back soon.

But the noise from Blossom, forgotten, unmilked, uncomfortable, in the barn, had sent Annemarie warily out with the milking bucket. She had done her best, trying to ignore Blossom's irritated snorts and tossing head, remembering how Uncle Henrik's hands had worked with a firm, rhythmic, pulling motion. And she had milked.

"I could have done it," Kirsti announced. "You only have to pull and it squirts out. I could do it *easily*."

Annemarie rolled her eyes. I'd like to see you try, she thought.

"Is Ellen coming back?" Kirsti asked, forgetting the cow after a moment. "She said she'd make a dress for my doll."

"Annemarie and I will help you make a dress," Mama told her. "Ellen had to go with her parents. Wasn't that a nice surprise, that the Rosens came last night to get her?"

"She should have waked me up to say goodbye," Kirsti grumbled, spooning some imaginary food into the painted mouth of the doll she had propped in a chair beside her.

"Annemarie," Uncle Henrik said, getting up from the table and pushing back his chair, "if you come with me now to the barn, I'll give you a milking lesson. Wash your hands first."

"Me too," said Kirsti.

"Not you too," Mama said. "Not this time. I need your help here, since I can't walk very well. You'll have to be my nurse."

Kirsti hesitated, deciding whether to argue. Then she said, "I'm going to be a nurse when I grow up. Not a cow milker. So I have to stay here and take care of Mama."

Followed as usual by the kitten, Annemarie walked with Uncle Henrik to the barn through a fine misty rain that had begun to fall. It seemed to her that Blossom shook her head happily when she saw Henrik and knew that she would be in good hands again.

She sat on the stacked hay and watched while he milked. But her mind was not on the milking.

"Uncle Henrik," she asked, "where are the Rosens and the others? I thought you were taking them to Sweden on your boat. But they weren't there."

"They were there," he told her, leaning forward against the cow's broad side. "You shouldn't know this. You remember that I told you it was safer not to know.

"But," he went on, as his hands moved with their sure and practiced motion, "I will tell you just a little, because you were so very brave."

"Brave?" Annemarie asked, surprised. "No, I wasn't. I was very frightened."

"You risked your life."

"But I didn't even think about that! I was only thinking of—"

He interrupted her, smiling. "That's all that *brave* means—not thinking about the dangers. Just thinking about what you must do. Of course you were frightened. I was too, today. But you kept your mind on what you had to do. So did I. Now let me tell you about the Rosens.

"Many of the fishermen have built hidden places in their boats. I have, too. Down underneath. I have only to lift the boards in the right place, and there is room to hide a few people. Peter, and others in the Resistance who work with him, bring them to me, and to the other fishermen as well. There are people who hide them and help them, along the way to Gilleleje."

Annemarie was startled. "Peter is in the Resistance? Of course! I should have known! He brings Mama and Papa the secret newspaper, *De Frie Danske* (dee free DAN skee). And he always seems to be on the move. I should have figured it out myself!"

"He is a very, very brave young man," Uncle Henrik said. "They all are."

Annemarie frowned, remembering the empty boat that morning. "Were the Rosens and others there, then, underneath, when I brought the basket?"

Uncle Henrik nodded.

"I heard nothing," Annemarie said.

"Of course not. They had to be absolutely quiet for many hours. The baby was drugged so that it wouldn't wake and cry."

"Could they hear me when I talked to you?"

"Yes. Your friend Ellen told me, later, that they heard you. And they heard the soldiers who came to search the boat."

Annemarie's eyes widened. "Soldiers came?" she asked. "I thought they went the other way after they stopped me."

"There are many soldiers in Gilleleje and all along the coast. They are searching all the boats now. They know that the Jews are escaping, but they are not sure how, and they rarely find them. The hiding places are carefully concealed, and often we pile dead fish on the deck as well. They hate getting their shiny boots dirtied!"

He turned his head toward her and grinned.

Annemarie remembered the shiny boots confronting her on the dark path.

"Uncle Henrik," she said, "I'm sure you are right, that I shouldn't know everything. But, please, would you tell me about the handkerchief? I knew it was important, the packet, and that's why I ran through the woods to take it to you. But I thought maybe it was a map. How could a handkerchief be important?"

He set the filled pail aside and began to wash the cow's udder with the damp cloth. "Very few people know about this, Annemarie," he said with a serious look. "But the soldiers are so angry about the escaping Jews—and the fact that they can't find them—that they have just started using trained dogs."

"They had dogs! The ones who stopped me on the path!"

Uncle Henrik nodded. "The dogs are trained to sniff about and find where people are hidden. It happened just yesterday on two boats. Those dogs, they go right through dead fish to the human scent.

"We were all very, very worried. We thought it meant the end of the escape to Sweden by boat.

"It was Peter who took the problem to scientists and doctors. Some very fine minds have worked night and day, trying to find a solution.

"And they have created a special drug. I don't know what it is. But it was in the handkerchief. It attracts the dogs, but when they sniff at it, it ruins their sense of smell. Imagine that!"

Annemarie remembered how the dogs had lunged at the handkerchief, smelled it, and then turned away.

"Now, thanks to Peter, we will each have such a handkerchief, each boat captain. When the soldiers board our boats, we will simply pull the handkerchiefs out of our pockets. The Germans will probably think we all have bad colds! The dogs will sniff about, sniff the handkerchiefs we are holding, and then roam the boat and find nothing. They will smell nothing."

"Did they bring dogs to your boat this morning?"

"Yes. Not twenty minutes after you had gone. I was about to pull away from the dock when the soldiers appeared and ordered me to halt. They came aboard, searched, found nothing. By then, of course, I had the handkerchief. If I had not, well—" His voice trailed off, and he didn't finish the sentence. He didn't need to.

If she had not found the packet where Mr. Rosen had dropped it. If she had not run through the woods. If the soldiers had taken the basket. If she had not reached the boat in time. All of the ifs whirled in Annemarie's head.

"They are safe in Sweden now?" she asked. "You're sure?"

Uncle Henrik stood, and patted the cow's head. "I saw them ashore. There were people waiting to take them to shelter. They are quite safe there."

"But what if the Nazis invade Sweden? Will the Rosens have to run away again?"

"That won't happen. For reasons of their own, the Nazis want Sweden to remain free. It is very complicated."

Annemarie's thoughts turned to her friends, hiding under the deck of the *Ingeborg*. "It must have been awful for them, so many hours there," she murmured. "Was it dark in the hiding place?"

"Dark, and cold, and very cramped. And Mrs. Rosen was seasick, even though we were not on the water very long—it is a short distance, as you know. But they are courageous people. And none of that mattered when they stepped ashore. The air was fresh and cool in Sweden; the wind was blowing. The baby was beginning to wake as I said goodbye to them."

"I wonder if I will ever see Ellen again," Annemarie said sadly.

"You will, little one. You saved her life, after all. Someday you will find her again. Someday the war will end," Uncle Henrik said. "All wars do."

"Now then," he added, stretching, "that was quite a milking lesson, was it not?"

ANALYZE THE TEXT

Cause and Effect What would have happened if Annemarie had not delivered the handkerchief to Uncle Henrik in time?

For Further Reading

Numerous well-known books—both historical fiction and nonfiction—have been written about the time period that is depicted by Lois Lowry in *Number the Stars*. One of the most celebrated and classic books from this era is *Anne Frank: The Diary of a Young Girl*, the actual diary of a Dutch Jewish girl, who upon receiving a blank red-and-white checkered diary for her thirteenth birthday, recorded in profound detail her own experiences while in hiding with her family for twenty-five months in Nazi-occupied Amsterdam.

Anne Frank initially wrote the diary entries for herself, filling up the original volume and multiple other notebooks with her memoir; however, after hearing a plea on a Dutch radio broadcast for eyewitness accounts of the war (including letters and diaries), Anne decided that after the war she would publish her diary as a book. Because Anne Frank did not survive World War II, her father, Otto Frank, assumed responsibility for seeing that the diary entries would be published and shared with a large audience.

The diary was not accepted for publication immediately; many publishers rejected the manuscript before it was first printed in Holland in 1947, and later in the United States in 1952. The rest is history: the famous diary has been translated into more than seventy different languages and has become one of the world's most widely read works of literature. In 1955, a play based on Anne Frank's chronicle won the Pulitzer Prize, and a motion picture soon followed.

Anne Frank's diary entries were not the only pieces of prose she produced while hiding in a labyrinth of rooms above her father's office; she also penned several short stories and collected her favorite quotes, an idea that her father gave her. In portions of her diary, Anne Frank reflects on her favorite quotes and references her story-writing, too.

To read more about Anne Frank and her family's harrowing experiences during World War II, look for the famous diary during your next visit to the library or research her history on the Internet. Many websites and museums around the world are dedicated to educating people about the life of Anne Frank and the historical context for her memorable diary.

Dig Deeper

How to Analyze the Text

Use these pages to learn about Cause and Effect, Figurative Language, and Understanding Characters. Then read "Number the Stars" again to apply what you learned.

Cause and Effect

Good readers use **cause-and-effect** relationships to help them understand how a story's plot unfolds. Sometimes authors use words such as *because*, *when*, *then*, and *so* to signal causes and effects, but other times readers have to use text evidence to figure out causes and effects. As you read "Number the Stars," think about the events that make up the plot. For each event, ask yourself, "Why did this happen, and what might happen next because of it? How does this event fit into the overall structure of the story?"

Look back at pages 674–676. The soldiers stop Annemarie to search her lunch basket. What causes and effects lead up to the soldiers' decision to return the basket to Annemarie?

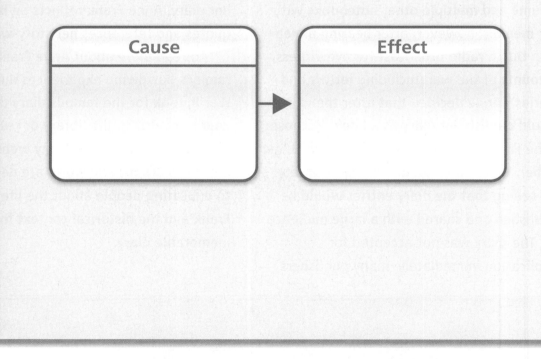

Cause		Effect
	→	

COMMON CORE **RL.6.1** cite textual evidence to support analysis of what the text says explicitly as well as inferences drawn; **RL.6.3** describe how a story's or drama's plot unfolds and how characters respond or change; **RL.6.4** determine the meaning of words and phrases, including figurative and connotative meanings/analyze impact of word choice; **RL.6.5** analyze how a sentence, chapter, scene or stanza fits in the overall structure; **L.6.5a** interpret figures of speech in context

Figurative Language

Authors often use words and phrases in ways that are different from their literal meanings. This **figurative** use of language helps a reader imagine one thing in terms of another. One example of figurative language is the expression *crush our opponent*. It means "to win by a complete defeat." As you reread "Number the Stars," look for places where the author uses figurative language. Use clues in the text to help you figure out the meanings of these words or phrases.

Understanding Characters

Understanding story **characters** can help you better comprehend a story. To understand the characters in "Number the Stars," pay attention to text evidence, such as what characters say and do, how they feel, and what others say or how they feel about them. Use what you learn about Annemarie, Uncle Henrik, and the other story characters to help you understand how they respond to story events and how they change as the plot moves toward a resolution, or conclusion.

Your Turn

RETURN TO THE ESSENTIAL QUESTION

 Review the selection with a partner to prepare to discuss this question: *How did the courageous acts of people in the past affect history?* As you discuss, ask questions of each other and reflect on your ideas.

Classroom Conversation

Continue your discussion of "Number the Stars" by using text evidence to explain your answers to these questions:

1 What do you think Annemarie will do if she is asked to help the Resistance in the future? Why?

2 Based on what you have learned from the story, why do you think the author chose "Number the Stars" as the title?

3 What do you think the author wants you to feel about Uncle Henrik?

CHARACTER MOTIVATION

Discuss Characters' Actions Work with a partner to discuss Annemarie, her mother, and Uncle Henrik in "Number the Stars." Discuss the following: *What risks do these characters take? Why are they willing to take the risks? What would have happened if the characters were not willing to take those kinds of risks?* Use text evidence and inferences about what you have read to answer the questions. Ask questions to clarify your understanding of your partner's answers.

WRITE ABOUT READING

Response Uncle Henrik decides to tell Annemarie why the handkerchief is so special. Write a paragraph to explain whether you agree or disagree with his decision to share this information. Use text evidence from the story to support your argument. Include in your response how story events might have been different if Annemarie had known about the handkerchief before she met the soldiers.

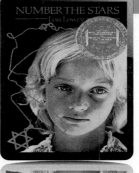

Writing Tip

Begin your paragraph by stating your claim. Support it with evidence from the text. Use key words and phrases, such as *if* and *then*, to signal cause-and-effect relationships.

COMMON CORE **RL.6.1** cite textual evidence to support analysis of what the text says explicitly as well as inferences drawn; **W.6.1a** introduce claim(s) and organize reasons and evidence clearly; **W.6.9a** apply grade 6 Reading Standards to literature; **SL.6.1a** come to discussions prepared/explicitly draw on preparation to probe and reflect on ideas under discussion; **SL.6.1c** pose and respond to questions and make comments that contribute to the discussion; **SL.6.1d** review key ideas expressed and demonstrate understanding of multiple perspectives

OPINION ESSAY

✓ GENRE

An **opinion essay,** such as a book review, gives the author's opinion or point of view about a subject.

✓ TEXT FOCUS

When writing an **argument,** an author introduces claims and then provides reasons to support them.

COMMON CORE **RI.6.8** trace and evaluate the argument and specific claims in a text; **RI.6.10** read and comprehend literary nonfiction

BOOK REVIEW

NUMBER THE STARS

by Carl Wallach

The award-winning novel *Number the Stars,* by Lois Lowry, is a story about danger, bravery, and friendship. It is set in Copenhagen and Gilleleje, Denmark, in 1943, during World War II. With German Nazi troops occupying Denmark, life is hard for Annemarie Johansen and her family.

Life is even harder for the family of Annemarie's friend Ellen, who is Jewish. The Nazis are planning to move the Jews from Denmark to concentration camps. Feeling contempt for the German soldiers, Annemarie's family resolves to help Ellen's family.

In the course of the novel, Annemarie finds her courage by confronting her fears. In a tense scene, she is delivering a mysterious package to her Uncle Henrik when she crosses paths with a group of German soldiers. In harsh voices, they demand to know where Annemarie is going. They search through her possessions and interrogate her. After her panic has subsided, Annemarie responds scornfully. She acts exasperated and begins to cry. Unable to find anything of interest, the soldiers finally move on.

Just as memorable as the exciting action are the characters' relationships. The friendship between Annemarie and Ellen is the heart of this book. It makes personal an amazing event in history: the heroic actions of Danish citizens in smuggling some seven thousand Danish Jews to safety in Sweden.

Number the Stars is one of Lois Lowry's most powerful novels. Lowry has tackled a difficult subject with sensitivity. Readers who enjoy history as well as action will appreciate the historical details and the suspenseful plot. All readers will relate to Annemarie and Ellen's friendship and the moving examples of the strength of the human spirit.

(Left) Danish fishermen ferry Jewish passengers to safety in Sweden during World War II. (Above) Jewish refugees arrive safely in Sweden, October 1943.

An Interview
with Lois Lowry

*What led you to write about the topic of
Denmark during World War II?*

I think every piece of human history has
fascinating individual stories connected to it. I
just happened to have a Danish friend who told
me of her own childhood in Copenhagen during
the Nazi occupation there. With that personal
connection, I was able to research the greater
historical significance of the events in Denmark.
But I tried to tell them on a personal scale, one
child's story.

*What are the challenges and rewards of writing
historical fiction?*

The challenge is to get it right. There had
been some misinformation about the occupation
of Denmark—people are still telling the
(false) story that the king wore a yellow star in
sympathy with the Jews. It didn't happen. I
didn't want to be guilty of repeating myth. So
I read a lot of history, talked to real people who
had been there then, and tried to write the truth.

The reward was making an important story
available and interesting to a young audience.
There are countless children now who know
about the integrity of the Danish people during
that time, and who have been inspired by it.
It's my hope that it has affected the thinking of
young people about issues of prejudice.

Compare Texts

Compare Descriptions Think about the book review you just read of "Number the Stars." Then compare the book review to the story "Number the Stars." How does the author of the book review describe the events in the story? In what ways are these descriptions different from the story? Write your answers. Use evidence from both texts to support your ideas.

Make Lists During World War II, many people were forced to flee their homelands. If you had to start life somewhere else, what aspects of your old life would you miss most? What would you do differently in your new home? Make two lists.

Compare Characters People all over the world perform acts of bravery. The same is true for Annemarie in "Number the Stars" and Matt in "Airborn" (Lesson 12). Compare and contrast the characters' actions. How do their actions contribute to the common theme of bravery in both stories? Use text evidence to support your ideas. Share your ideas with other members of a small group.

COMMON CORE **RL.6.1** cite textual evidence to support analysis of what the text says explicitly as well as inferences drawn; **RL.6.9** compare and contrast texts in different forms or genres on their approaches to themes and topics; **RI.6.9** compare and contrast one author's presentation of events with that of another

Grammar

What Is a Contraction? A **contraction** is a word formed by combining two words and shortening one of them. An **apostrophe** takes the place of the letter or letters left out of the combined word. You can combine personal pronouns with verbs such as *am, is, are, have, had,* and *will* to make contractions such as *I'm.* You can also combine some verbs with the word *not* to make contractions such as *isn't.*

Contractions	
Pronoun Plus Verb	<u>She's</u> my best friend. (She is)
Pronoun Plus Verb	<u>They've</u> gone to the boat already. (They have)
Verb Plus *not*	Annemarie <u>hasn't</u> delivered the packet yet. (has not)
Verb Plus *not*	The soldiers <u>aren't</u> letting her go. (are not)

When you use a contraction with *not*, make sure you are not creating a double negative. Avoid using *ain't,* which looks like a contraction but is usually not accepted as a word.

Try This! **Rewrite each sentence below on another sheet of paper. Replace the words in bold type with a contraction.**

1. **He is** worried about Annemarie.

2. That young girl **was not** acting politely.

3. If she angers the soldiers, **they will** probably arrest her.

4. She **had not** said anything to endanger the Rosen family.

692

A single punctuation error can confuse your reader, so edit your writing carefully. When you write contractions, be sure to set the apostrophe in the correct place.

Incorrect	Correct
There are'nt any papers in the envelope.	There aren't any papers in the envelope.
Its empty except for a handkerchief.	It's empty except for a handkerchief.
The soldier does'nt expect this.	The soldier doesn't expect this.
Hes tossing the handkerchief to the dogs.	He's tossing the handkerchief to the dogs.

 Connect Grammar to Writing

As you edit your persuasive letter, check for contractions and make sure you have written them correctly.

W.6.1b support claim(s) with reasons and evidence, using credible sources and demonstrating understanding of the topic or text; **W.6.1c** use words, phrases, and clauses to clarify relationships; **W.6.1d** establish and maintain a formal style; **W.6.1e** provide a concluding statement or section; **W.6.5** develop and strengthen writing by planning, revising, editing, rewriting, or trying a new approach

COMMON CORE

Argument Writing

✓ **Ideas**   Good writers use more than one approach in their arguments. As you revise your **persuasive letter,** use additional approaches to be more convincing. Use words and phrases to link the different reasons and evidence that support your claim. End with a conclusion.

   John drafted a letter that the king of Denmark might have written to persuade the German government to remove its troops during World War II. Later, he added a third approach to his argument.

Writing Traits Checklist

✓ **Ideas**
Did I use more than one approach in my argument?

✓ **Organization**
Did I introduce my claim and follow it with clear reasons?

✓ **Sentence Fluency**
Did I try combining sentences by changing words to adjectives?

✓ **Word Choice**
Did I use the proper greeting and closing?

✓ **Voice**
Did I maintain a convincing tone?

✓ **Conventions**
Did I use correct spelling, grammar, and punctuation?

Revised Draft

Third, like Germany, Denmark   an independent
~~Denmark, like Germany,~~ is ~~its own~~
                                        with
country. ~~It has~~ the right to govern itself.
Because of this reason, we
~~We~~ simply cannot tolerate uninvited foreign

troops in our midst any longer.

   I'm certain that after you carefully consider

all of my reasons, you will understand that you

must withdraw your troops from my country.

Your country would feel the same way if the

situation were reversed.

                              Sincerely,
                              King of Denmark

Final Copy

Government of Germany:

I urge you to withdraw your troops from Denmark immediately. This withdrawal is in your best interest for three reasons.

The first reason is that you are upsetting the population. The soldiers' practice of searching the Danish citizens on the street frightens them.

The second reason is that you are damaging your reputation. As long as you keep troops in Denmark, your reputation as a bullying nation grows. Surely you must care what the world thinks.

Third, like Germany, Denmark is an independent country with the right to govern itself. Because of this reason, we simply cannot tolerate uninvited foreign troops in our midst any longer.

I'm certain that after you carefully consider all of my reasons, you will understand that you must withdraw your troops from my country. Your country would feel the same way if the situation were reversed.

Sincerely,

King of Denmark

Reading as a Writer

Look for a new approach to strengthen your writing, such as finding common ground. What other approaches might you use to improve your persuasive letter?

I tried a new approach to strengthen my argument. I pointed out the common ground shared by Denmark and Germany.

☑ TARGET VOCABULARY

intention
retorted
motioned
inexplicable
legitimate
hoarding
gnarled
destination
inconsolable
guttural

Vocabulary Reader   Context Cards

COMMON CORE **L.6.6** acquire and use general academic and domain-specific words and phrases/gather vocabulary knowledge for comprehension or expression

696

1 intention
The student's intention, or plan, was to provide details about the heroic women.

2 retorted
Some African Americans held sit-ins in the 1950s. They rarely retorted, or replied sharply, to angry comments.

3 motioned
With a flick of his head, the leader motioned for the others to follow.

4 inexplicable
The idea of slavery is inexplicable, or impossible to understand, for most people today.

Go Digital

► Study each Context Card.

► Use a dictionary to confirm the meanings of these words.

5 legitimate

Martin Luther King, Jr., said that African Americans had legitimate reasons for their dissatisfaction.

6 hoarding

The abolitionists began hoarding large amounts of food in their attics for their hidden visitors.

7 gnarled

The gnarled and twisted, tree stood as a symbol of this harsh climate.

8 destination

The destination, or end point, for some escaped slaves heading North was Canada.

9 inconsolable

At Dr. King's funeral, many people were inconsolable, shedding tears over the nation's great loss.

10 guttural

Some languages include guttural sounds. Speakers produce these sounds from the back of their throats.

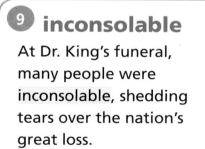

Read and Comprehend

✓ TARGET SKILL

Author's Purpose As you read "Harriet Tubman: Conductor on the Underground Railroad," look for evidence in the text that are clues to the **author's purpose,** or reason for writing (such as to entertain, inform, or persuade). The details will help you infer the author's purpose as well as her viewpoint of, or feelings toward, her subject. Use a graphic organizer like this one to help you.

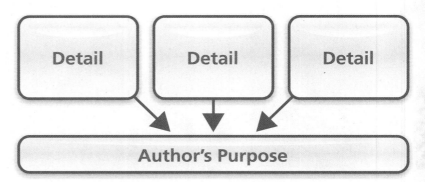

Detail → Detail → Detail → Author's Purpose

✓ TARGET STRATEGY

Question Ask **questions** about the selection before you read, as you read, and after you read. Look for text evidence to help you answer your questions.

COMMON CORE

RI.6.1 cite textual evidence to support analysis of what the text says explicitly as well as inferences drawn; **RI.6.6** determine the author's point of view or purpose and explain how it is conveyed

698

Civil Rights

The United States Constitution guarantees life, liberty, and the pursuit of happiness to Americans. Having freedom has not always guaranteed being treated equally, however, as Harriet Tubman's story illustrates. Many people were often discriminated against; they were singled out and treated unfairly. The Civil Rights Act of 1964 made it a crime to discriminate against people because of their race, color, religion, or gender. The civil rights of all Americans are now guaranteed under law.

In "Harriet Tubman: Conductor on the Underground Railroad," you'll learn about one woman's brave attempts to gain her freedom from slavery in 1849.

ANCHOR TEXT

✅ TARGET SKILL

Author's Purpose Use details in the text to figure out the author's reason for writing and his or her feelings toward a subject.

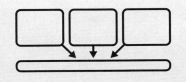

✅ GENRE

Literary nonfiction gives factual information by telling a true story. As you read, look for:

- ▶ elements of nonfiction and fiction
- ▶ information about a topic
- ▶ a story that involves real people and events

RI.6.3 analyze how a key individual, event, or idea is introduced, illustrated, and elaborated; **RI.6.6** determine the author's point of view or purpose and explain how it is conveyed; **RI.6.10** read and comprehend literary nonfiction; **L.6.1e** recognize variations from standard English and identify/use strategies to improve expression

MEET THE AUTHOR

Ann Petry

Ann Petry was born in 1908 above her father's apothecary in Old Saybrook, Connecticut, and matriculated at a college near her home in order to become a pharmacist. She did indeed become a pharmacist, but her life took an unexpected turn. She married, moved to New York City, and soon began an award-winning writing career. Her long list of works is a cornucopia of writing and includes many types of fiction and nonfiction for both young readers and adults.

MEET THE ILLUSTRATOR

London Ladd

London Ladd was a senior in high school when he took his first art class. He had a eureka moment, enjoying art and illustration so much that he abandoned plans to study computers in favor of pursuing a degree in illustration. Ladd's drawing talent and acumen for sharing with others soon led to a collaboration with Christie King Farris, sister of Dr. Martin Luther King, Jr., on the book *March On: The Day My Brother Changed the World*. Ladd, who is a multiracial artist, said that working with the King family was like living out his own dream.

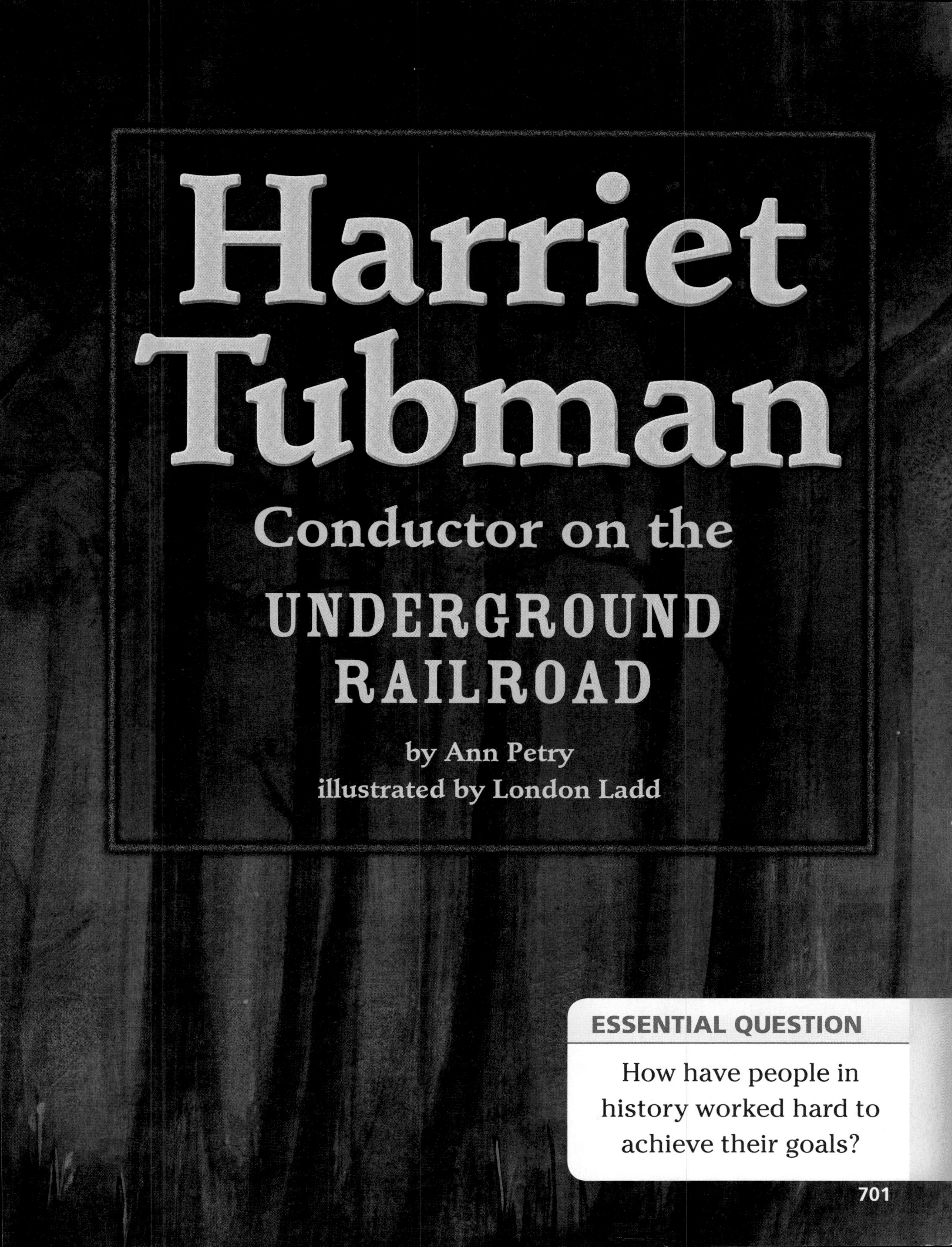

Harriet Tubman

Conductor on the

UNDERGROUND RAILROAD

by Ann Petry

illustrated by London Ladd

ESSENTIAL QUESTION

How have people in
history worked hard to
achieve their goals?

Harriet Tubman was born a slave in eastern Maryland in 1820. Harriet's life with her parents, Ben and Old Rit, was one of hard work and constant fear, including the fear of being sold to another slave owner and sent away forever. The day finally arrived when Harriet had endured enough of this life. She decided to escape to a free northern state, even though her own husband John had vowed he would never let her go.

One day, in 1849, when Harriet was working in the fields, near the edge of the road, a white woman wearing a faded sunbonnet went past, driving a wagon. She stopped the wagon, and watched Harriet for a few minutes. Then she spoke to her, asked her what her name was, and how she had acquired the deep scar on her forehead.

Harriet told her the story of the blow she had received when she was a girl. After that, whenever the woman saw her in the fields, she stopped to talk to her. She told Harriet that she lived on a farm, near Bucktown. Then one day she said, not looking at Harriet, but looking instead at the overseer, far off at the edge of the fields,

"If you ever need any help, Harriet, ever need any help, why you let me know." That same year the young heir to the Brodas estate died. Harriet mentioned the fact of his death to the white woman in the faded sunbonnet, the next time she saw her. She told her of the panic-stricken talk in the quarter, told her that the slaves were afraid that the master, Dr. Thompson, would start selling them. She said that Doc Thompson no longer permitted any of them to hire their time. The woman nodded her head, clucked to the horse, and drove off, murmuring, "If you ever need any help—"

The slaves were right about Dr. Thompson's intention. He began selling slaves almost immediately. Among the first ones sold were two of Harriet Tubman's sisters. They went South with the chain gang on a Saturday.

When Harriet heard of the sale of her sisters, she knew that the time had finally come when she must leave the plantation. She was reluctant to attempt the long trip North alone, not because of John Tubman's threat to betray her, but because she was afraid she might fall asleep somewhere along the way and so would be caught immediately.

She persuaded three of her brothers to go with her. Having made certain that John was asleep, she left the cabin quietly, and met her brothers at the edge of the plantation. They agreed that she was to lead the way, for she was more familiar with the woods than the others. The three men followed her, crashing through the underbrush, frightening themselves, stopping constantly to say, "What was that?" or "Someone's coming."

She thought of Ben and how he had said, "Any old body can go through a woods crashing and mashing things down like a cow." She said sharply, "Can't you boys go quieter? Watch where you're going!"

One of them grumbled, "Can't see in the dark. Ain't got cat's eyes like you."

"You don't need cat's eyes," she retorted. "On a night like this, with all the stars out, it's not black dark. Use your own eyes."

She supposed they were doing the best they could but they moved very slowly. She kept getting so far ahead of them that she had to stop and wait for them to catch up with her, lest they lose their way. Their progress was slow, uncertain. Their feet got tangled in every vine. They tripped over fallen logs, and once one of them fell flat on his face. They jumped, startled, at the most ordinary sounds: the murmur of the wind in the branches of the trees, the twittering of a bird. They kept turning around, looking back.

They had not gone more than a mile when she became aware that they had stopped. She turned and went back to them. She could hear them whispering. One of them called out, "Hat!"

"What's the matter? We haven't got time to keep stopping like this."

"We're going back."

"No," she said firmly. "We've got a good start. If we move fast and move quiet—"

Then all three spoke at once. They said the same thing, over and over, in frantic hurried whispers, all talking at once:

They told her that they had changed their minds. Running away was too dangerous. Someone would surely see them and recognize them. By morning the master would know they had "took off." Then the handbills advertising them would be posted all over Dorchester County. The patterollers would search for them. Even if they were lucky enough to elude the patrol, they could not possibly hide from the bloodhounds. The hounds would be baying after them, snuffing through the swamps and the underbrush, zigzagging through the deepest woods. The bloodhounds would surely find them. And everyone knew what happened to a runaway who was caught and brought back alive.

ANALYZE THE TEXT

Variations of English Where does the author use nonstandard English on page 704? Why does the author use this type of language here? Restate the sentences using formal English.

She argued with them. Didn't they know that if they went back they would be sold, if not tomorrow, then the next day, or the next? Sold South. They had seen the chain gangs. Was that what they wanted? Were they going to be slaves for the rest of their lives? Didn't freedom mean anything to them?

"You're afraid," she said, trying to shame them into action. "Go on back. I'm going North alone."

Instead of being ashamed, they became angry. They shouted at her, telling her that she was a fool and they would make her go back to the plantation with them. Suddenly they surrounded her, three men, her own brothers, jostling her, pushing her along, pinioning her arms behind her. She fought against them, wasting her strength, exhausting herself in a furious struggle.

She was no match for three strong men. She said, panting, "All right. We'll go back. I'll go with you."

She led the way, moving slowly. Her thoughts were bitter. Not one of them was willing to take a small risk in order to be free. It had all seemed so perfect, so simple, to have her brothers go with her, sharing the dangers of the trip together, just as a family should. Now if she ever went North, she would have to go alone.

Two days later, a slave working beside Harriet in the fields motioned to her. She bent toward him, listening. He said the water boy had just brought news to the field hands, and it had been passed from one to the other until it reached him. The news was that Harriet and her brothers had been sold to the Georgia trader, and that they were to be sent South with the chain gang that very night.

Harriet went on working but she knew a moment of panic. She would have to go North alone. She would have to start as soon as it was dark. She could not go with the chain gang. She might die on the way, because of those inexplicable sleeping seizures. But then she—how could she run away? She might fall asleep in plain view along the road.

But even if she fell asleep, she thought, the Lord would take care of her. She murmured a prayer, "Lord, I'm going to hold steady on to You and You've got to see me through."

Afterward, she explained her decision to run the risk of going North alone, in these words: "I had reasoned this out in my mind; there was one of two things I had a *right* to, liberty or death; if I could not have one, I would have the other; for no man should take me alive; I should fight for my liberty as long as my strength lasted, and when the time came for me to go, the Lord would let them take me."

At dusk, when the work in the fields was over, she started toward the Big House. She had to let someone know that she was going North, someone she could trust. She no longer trusted John Tubman and it gave her a lost, lonesome feeling. Her sister Mary worked in the Big House, and she planned to tell Mary that she was going to run away, so someone would know. As she went toward the house, she saw the master, Doc Thompson, riding up the drive on his horse. She turned aside and went toward the quarter. A field hand had no legitimate reason for entering the kitchen of the Big House—and yet—there must be some way she could leave word so that afterward someone would think about it and know that she had left a message.

As she went toward the quarter she began to sing. Dr. Thompson reined in his horse, turned around and looked at her. It was not the beauty of her voice that made him turn and watch her, frowning, it was the words of the song that she was singing, and something defiant in her manner, that disturbed and puzzled him.

When that old chariot comes,
I'm going to leave you,
I'm bound for the promised land,
Friends, I'm going to leave you.

I'm sorry, friends, to leave you,
Farewell! Oh, farewell!
But I'll meet you in the morning,
Farewell! Oh, farewell!

I'll meet you in the morning,
When I reach the promised land;
On the other side of Jordan,
For I'm bound for the promised land.

That night when John Tubman was asleep, and the fire had died down in the cabin, she took the ashcake that had been baked for their breakfast, and a good-sized piece of salt herring, and tied them together in an old bandanna. By hoarding this small stock of food, she could make it last a long time, and with the berries and edible roots she could find in the woods, she wouldn't starve.

She decided that she would take the quilt with her, too. Her hands lingered over it. It felt soft and warm to her touch. Even in the dark, she thought she could tell one color from another, because she knew its pattern and design so well.

Then John stirred in his sleep, and she left the cabin quickly, carrying the quilt carefully folded under her arm.

Once she was off the plantation, she took to the woods, not following the North Star, not even looking for it, going instead toward Bucktown. She needed help. She was going to ask the white woman who had stopped to talk to her so often if she would help her. Perhaps she wouldn't. But she would soon find out.

When she came to the farmhouse where the woman lived, she approached it cautiously, circling around it. It was so quiet. There was no sound at all, not even a dog barking, or the sound of voices. Nothing.

She tapped on the door, gently. A voice said, "Who's there?" She answered, "Harriet, from Dr. Thompson's place."

When the woman opened the door she did not seem at all surprised to see her. She glanced at the little bundle that Harriet was carrying, at the quilt, and invited her in. Then she sat down at the kitchen table, and wrote two names on a slip of paper, and handed the paper to Harriet.

She said that those were the next places where it was safe for Harriet to stop. The first place was a farm where there was a gate with big white posts and round knobs on top of them. The people there would feed her, and when they thought it was safe for her to go on, they would tell her how to get to the next house, or take her there. For these were the first two stops on the Underground Railroad—going North, from the Eastern Shore of Maryland.

Thus Harriet learned that the Underground Railroad that ran straight to the North was not a railroad at all. Neither did it run underground. It was composed of a loosely organized group of people who offered food and shelter, or a place of concealment, to fugitives who had set out on the long road to the North and freedom.

Harriet wanted to pay this woman who had befriended her. But she had no money. She gave her the patchwork quilt, the only beautiful object she had ever owned.

That night she made her way through the woods, crouching in the underbrush whenever she heard the sound of horses' hoofs, staying there until the riders passed. Each time she wondered if they were already hunting for her. It would be so easy to describe her, the deep scar on her forehead like a dent, the old scars on the back of her neck, the husky speaking voice, the lack of height, scarcely five feet tall. The master would say she was wearing rough clothes when she ran away, that she had a bandanna on her head, that she was muscular and strong.

She knew how accurately he would describe her. One of the slaves who could read used to tell the others what it said on those handbills that were nailed up on the trees, along the edge of the roads. It was easy to recognize the handbills that advertised runaways, because there was always a picture in one corner, a picture of a black man, a little running figure with a stick over his shoulder, and a bundle tied on the end of the stick. Whenever she thought of the handbills, she walked faster. Sometimes she stumbled over old grapevines, gnarled and twisted, thick as a man's wrist, or became entangled in the tough, sinewy vine of the honeysuckle. But she kept going.

In the morning, she came to the house where her friend had said she was to stop. She showed the slip of paper that she carried to the woman who answered her knock at the back door of the farmhouse. The woman fed her, and then handed her a broom and told her to sweep the yard.

Harriet hesitated, suddenly suspicious. Then she decided that with a broom in her hand, working in the yard, she would look as though she belonged on the place, certainly no one would suspect that she was a runaway.

That night the woman's husband, a farmer, loaded a wagon with produce. Harriet climbed in. He threw some blankets over her, and the wagon started. It was dark under the blankets, and not exactly comfortable. But Harriet decided that riding was better than walking. She was surprised at her own lack of fear, wondered how it was that she so readily trusted these strangers who might betray her. For all she knew, the man driving the wagon might be taking her straight back to the master.

ANALYZE THE TEXT

Author's Purpose What is the author's purpose for writing this selection? What details in the text show the author's viewpoint of Harriet Tubman?

She thought of those other rides in wagons, when she was a child, the same clop-clop of the horses' feet, creak of the wagon, and the feeling of being lost because she did not know where she was going. She did not know her destination this time either, but she was not alarmed. She thought of John Tubman. By this time he must have told the master that she was gone. Then she thought of the plantation and how the land rolled gently down toward the river, thought of Ben and Old Rit, and that Old Rit would be inconsolable because her favorite daughter was missing. "Lord," she prayed, "I'm going to hold steady onto You. You've got to see me through." Then she went to sleep.

The next morning when the stars were still visible in the sky, the farmer stopped the wagon. Harriet was instantly awake.

He told her to follow the river, to keep following it to reach the next place where people would take her in and feed her. He said that she must travel only at night, and she must stay off the roads because the patrol would be hunting for her. Harriet climbed out of the wagon. "Thank you," she said simply, thinking how amazing it was that there should be white people who were willing to go to such lengths to help a slave get to the North.

When she finally arrived in Pennsylvania, she had traveled roughly ninety miles from Dorchester County. She had slept on the ground outdoors at night. She had been rowed for miles up the Choptank River by a man she had never seen before. She had been concealed in a haycock, and had, at one point, spent a week hidden in a potato hole in a cabin which belonged to a family of free Negroes. She had been hidden in the attic of the home of a Quaker. She had been befriended by stout German farmers, whose guttural speech surprised her and whose well-kept farms astonished her. She had never before seen barns and fences, farmhouses and outbuildings, so carefully painted. The cattle and horses were so clean they looked as though they had been scrubbed.

When she crossed the line into the free state of Pennsylvania, the sun was coming up. She said, "I looked at my hands to see if I was the same person now I was free. There was such a glory over everything, the sun came like gold through the trees, and over the fields, and I felt like I was in heaven."

ANALYZE THE TEXT

Analyze Events How is Harriet Tubman's escape introduced in the text? Give examples of how the author elaborates on the events that led to her escape to Pennsylvania.

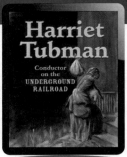

Dig Deeper

How to Analyze the Text

Use these pages to learn about Author's Purpose, Variations of English, and how to Analyze Events. Then read "Harriet Tubman: Conductor on the Underground Railroad" again to apply what you learned.

Author's Purpose

In "Harriet Tubman: Conductor on the Underground Railroad," author Ann Petry includes many details about Harriet Tubman's life, her persistence, and her courage. Through Petry's choice of genre, organization, and words, she reveals her **purpose for writing.** By analyzing these choices, you can also infer the author's viewpoint toward her subject.

Look back at pages 704–706 of the selection. The author tells of Tubman's failed escape attempt with her brothers. What is the author's viewpoint toward Tubman's brothers? How can you tell?

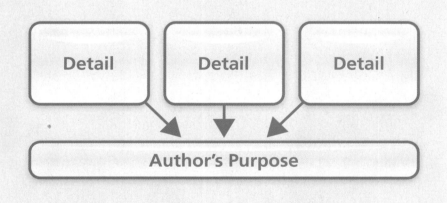

RI.6.3 analyze how a key individual, event, or idea is introduced, illustrated, and elaborated; **RI.6.6** determine the author's point of view or purpose and explain how it is conveyed; **L.6.1e** recognize variations from standard English and identify/use strategies to improve expression

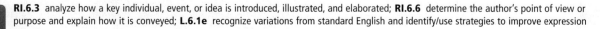

Variations of English

Sometimes authors of historical text include dialogue representing speakers from different times in history. The dialogue may contain words or expressions that are not used in **standard English.** Nonstandard English can contain grammatical errors, such as those in "I haven't never gone nowhere with him." It can also contain words and expressions no longer used, such as "I am beholden to you." Recognizing variations from standard English can help you make improvements in your own writing.

Analyze Events

Literary nonfiction tells a true story about an event or a person. Ann Petry focuses on one event, Harriet Tubman's escape north to freedom. To help readers understand a major event like this, authors often introduce the events leading up to the main one. They also elaborate by including other text evidence to further expand the story. To **analyze an event** in literary nonfiction, look for how and where the event is introduced and how it is elaborated.

A house on the Underground Railroad

Your Turn

Turn and Talk Review the selection with a partner to prepare to discuss this question: *How have people in history worked hard to achieve their goals?* As you discuss, include text evidence when you pose and respond to questions. Make comments and share opinions.

Classroom Conversation

Continue your discussion of the selection by using text evidence to explain your answers to these questions:

1. What do you think Harriet Tubman learned from her experience?

2. Judging from the title "Harriet Tubman: Conductor on the Underground Railroad," what became of Harriet after she reached freedom?

3. Why were people willing to help slaves who sought their freedom? Considering the risks, what did they have to gain?

WHAT DOES IT MEAN?

Summarize the Selection Work with a partner to plan an oral summary of the selection. Make a list of the most important ideas from the selection. Be sure to list events in the correct order. Remember to use only evidence from the text, not personal opinions. Then present your summary orally to another pair of partners.

Harriet Tubman

WRITE ABOUT READING

Response Did Harriet Tubman risk too much? Write a paragraph expressing your argument about Tubman's second attempt to escape to the free North. Introduce the paragraph with your claim. Support your claim with the reasons why you feel as you do and with evidence from the text. End with a concluding statement.

Writing Tip

State your claim at the beginning of your paragraph. Use correct capitalization and punctuation in your writing.

Go Digital

COMMON CORE

RI.6.2 determine a central idea of a text/provide a summary; **W.6.1a** introduce claim(s) and organize reasons and evidence clearly; **W.6.1b** support claim(s) with reasons and evidence, using credible sources and demonstrating understanding of the topic or text; **W.6.9b** apply grade 6 Reading standards to literary nonfiction; **SL.6.1a** come to discussions prepared/explicitly draw on preparation to probe and reflect on ideas under discussion; **SL.6.1c** pose and respond to questions and make comments that contribute to the discussion

Home
of the
Brave

Home of the Brave

What represents bravery to you? Maybe it is a person who has achieved status for helping others. Maybe it is an emotion, like the feeling of pride in overcoming a fear. These two poets each conceive of bravery in a different way. As you read, compare their ideas of bravery with your own. Then use your ideas to write your own poem about bravery.

I, Too

by Langston Hughes

I, too, sing America.

I am the darker brother.
They send me to eat in the kitchen
When company comes,
But I laugh,
And eat well,
And grow strong.

Tomorrow,
I'll sit at the table
When company comes.
Nobody'll dare
Say to me,
"Eat in the kitchen,"
Then.

Besides,
They'll see how beautiful I am
And be ashamed —

I, too, am America.

Who Could Tell?

by Carmen T. Bernier-Grand

¡Híjole!
Who could tell?

Who could tell
that Cesario Estrada Chávez,
the shy American
wearing a checkered shirt,
walking with a cane to ease his back
from the burden of the fields,
could organize so many people
to march for La Causa, The Cause?

Who could tell
that he with a soft pan dulce voice,
hair the color of mesquite,
and downcast, Aztec eyes,
would have the courage to speak up
for the campesinos
to get better pay,
better housing,
better health?

¡Híjole!
Who could tell?

Write a Poem About Bravery

César Chávez (1927–1993) faced prejudice
as a child. His desire for change led to better
conditions for migrant workers. Write a poem
about someone you know who has also shown
bravery. The person might be a distinguished
hero, a friend, or a relative who is inclined to
take on big challenges for a worthy cause.

Compare Texts

TEXT TO TEXT

Compare Presentations Compare "Harriet Tubman: Conductor on the Underground Railroad" to the poetry in "Home of the Brave." Compare how all of the selections tell about bravery. Contrast the selections, based on how the idea of bravery is presented in the true story and in each poem.

TEXT TO SELF

Write About an Experience Harriet Tubman received help from a friend as well as many strangers on her journey to freedom. Write a paragraph about a time when someone helped you, even when you didn't expect it.

TEXT TO WORLD

Give a News Report Think about how the actions of Harriet Tubman and César Chávez continue to have an impact on people today. Then write a news report about a person—from the present day or from history—who has made an impact on your life. Keep in mind your purpose for writing, and organize your report to suit the purpose. Share your report with members of a small group.

Go Digital

COMMON CORE   **RL.6.9** compare and contrast texts in different forms or genres on their approaches to themes and topics; **W.6.4** produce writing in which development, organization, and style are appropriate to task, purpose, and audience; **W.6.10** write routinely over extended time frames and shorter time frames

Grammar

Making Comparisons A **comparative adjective** compares two persons, places, or things. To form the comparative, add *–er* to a short adjective and use *more* before a long adjective. A **superlative adjective** compares more than two persons, places, or things. To form the superlative, add *–est* to a short adjective and use *most* before a long adjective. Add *more* in front of most adverbs to form the **comparative** and *most* to form the **superlative**. The adjectives *good* and *bad* and the adverb *well* have special comparative and superlative forms.

Adjectives and Adverbs	Comparatives	Superlatives
simple (short adjective)	simpler	simplest
powerful (long adjective)	more powerful	most powerful
good (adjective)	better	best
bad (adjective)	worse	worst
joyfully (adverb)	more joyfully	most joyfully
well (adverb)	better	best

Try This! **With a partner, read aloud each sentence below. Identify each comparative adjective, superlative adjective, comparative adverb, and superlative adverb.**

1. Leaving the plantation was Harriet Tubman's bravest act.

2. Harriet was a more determined person than her husband.

3. Who helped Harriet Tubman as she most eagerly sought freedom?

4. Harriet's younger brother discouraged her more vigorously than anyone.

When you compare two persons, things, or actions in your writing, be sure to use the comparative form. When you compare three or more, use the superlative form. When writing forms of *good* and *bad*, use their unique forms.

Incorrect Forms	**Correct Forms**
Ben is the best of the two poets.	Ben is the better of the two poets.
He writes gooder than the other.	He writes better than the other.

 ## Connect Grammar to Writing

Making comparisons can help readers better understand the importance of your claim and the reasons that support it. As you revise your argument next week, make sure you have used comparatives and superlatives correctly.

COMMON CORE

Argument Writing

Reading-Writing Workshop: Prewrite

✓ **Ideas** When you plan an argument, be aware of any objections that your audience might have. Think of convincing responses that will persuade your readers to agree with you.

Orlando wanted to convince readers that cell phones have improved people's lives. As part of his planning on this topic, he explored possible objections and responses to them. Later, he included this information in a persuasion chart to help organize his writing.

Writing Process Checklist

▶ **Prewrite**

✓ Did I choose a position or goal I feel strongly about?

✓ Did I include strong reasons that will appeal to my audience?

✓ Did I give facts and examples to support each reason?

✓ Did I plan how to address possible objections?

✓ Did I arrange my reasons in a persuasive order?

Draft

Revise

Edit

Publish and Share

Exploring a Topic

Possible Objection	My Response
• People annoy others when they talk on the phone.	*Ask* • ~~Tell~~ users to move to another area to talk on the phone.
• Talking on cell phones distracts drivers, causing accidents.	• Cell phone use can be regulated.

726

Persuasion Chart

Topic:

Cell phones have improved people's lives.

Reason: Families need to communicate.

Details: Kids might need permission to go somewhere after school.

Reason: Cell phones are good for emergencies.

Details: Few pay phones are available.

People can call for help right away.

Objection: People who talk on their cell phones annoy others.

Response: Ask users to move to another area to talk.

Objection: Talking on cell phones distracts drivers, causing accidents.

Response: Cell phone use can be regulated.

Reading as a Writer

Which of Orlando's two responses is more convincing? What possible objections and responses can you add to your own chart?

When I planned my argument, I included my own answers to possible objections from readers.

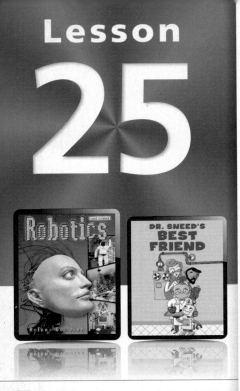

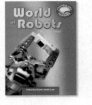 

Vocabulary in Context

1 artificial

A robot does not have a real brain. Its intelligence is artificial, created by humans.

2 interaction

A controller allows the interaction between a player and video game. The game and the player act on each other.

3 sensors

Sensors in devices detect information. If a camera's sensor doesn't detect enough light, it activates a flash.

4 data

A computer can sort through long lists of data, or information, often by converting it into ones and zeros.

Go Digital

▶ Study each Context Card.

▶ Tell a story about two or more pictures, using Vocabulary words of your choice.

5  **ultimate**

The "last word" in technology is always replaced by a model that is the *new* ultimate version.

6 **domestic**

A robot might be programmed to wash dishes or do other domestic chores around the house.

7 **uncanny**

In science fiction books and movies, robots often have uncanny, or strange, powers.

8 **stimulus**

In this robot's motion detector, movement is the stimulus that causes its lights to turn on.

9 **literally**

If a robot took the command "Make the bed" literally, or word for word, it might begin by sawing wood for a frame.

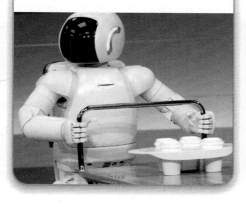

10 **inaccessible**

A robot can dive to an ocean depth that is inaccessible to people. Scuba divers could not go there.

729

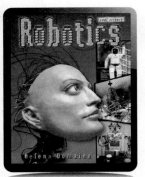

Read and Comprehend

Go Digital

☑ TARGET SKILL

Sequence of Events As you read "Robotics," keep track of the **sequence,** or time order, of events in the history and development of robots. Text evidence, such as dates and signal words such as *first*, *after*, *next*, and *finally* will help you follow the sequence of events. Keeping track of how events are sequenced helps readers understand how each event fits into the overall structure of the text. Use a graphic organizer like this one to help you keep track of events in the text.

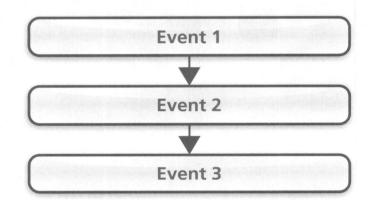

☑ TARGET STRATEGY

Visualize Use text details to **visualize,** or picture in your mind, what you are reading.

RI.6.5 analyze how a sentence, paragraph, chapter, or section fits in the overall structure

Robots

Robotics is the branch of technology that focuses on the many uses of robots. It also focuses on robot design and structure, how robots are built, and how they work. Some robots are machines that do the same tasks that humans do. They can operate like "mechanical people." Others do jobs that are too dangerous or too difficult for humans to do. These robots help humans accomplish tasks that were once thought impossible.

In "Robotics," you'll learn about the history of robots. You'll also learn some amazing things robots can do.

ANCHOR TEXT

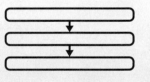

☑ TARGET SKILL

Sequence of Events Identify the time order in which events take place.

☑ GENRE

Informational text gives facts and other information about a topic. As you read, look for:
- ▶ headings that begin sections of related text
- ▶ photographs and captions
- ▶ text structure—the way facts and information are organized

COMMON CORE **RI.6.2** determine a central idea of a text/provide a summary; **RI.6.4** determine the meaning of words and phrases, including figurative, connotative, and technical meanings; **RI.6.5** analyze how a sentence, paragraph, chapter, or section fits in the overall structure; **RI.6.10** read and comprehend literary nonfiction

MEET THE AUTHOR
HELENA DOMAINE

As a young girl, Helena Domaine viewed Fritz Lang's classic 1927 silent movie *Metropolis,* which is a renowned German expressionist science-fiction film starring Alfred Abel, Brigitte Helm, Gustav Frohlich, and Rudolf Klein-Rogge, and she became fascinated by the interaction between the robots and humans. *Metropolis* is set in a futuristic urban dystopia in which wealthy but corrupt intellectuals residing in towers rule over and oppress the throngs of suffering laborers who subsist beneath them. From the catacombs of the city emerges a virtuous woman who ultimately has a malevolent robotic double made of her by a megalomaniac scientist, with her robot double eventually inciting a catastrophic melee between the laborers and intellectuals. By the end of the film, the robot has been destroyed and the apocalypse averted, after which a truce ensues, with the laborers and intellectuals finally beginning to work together. Based on the fascination she had with this scintillating movie and with other characters in science fiction, Helena Domaine became a book author who now writes science fiction and scientific nonfiction, and she remains interested in a variety of topics including popular myths such as the Loch Ness monster, Bigfoot (or "Sasquatch"), the Abominable Snowman, and UFOs.

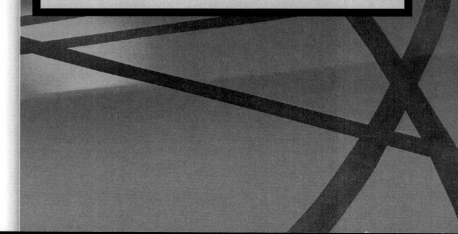

Robotics

by Helena Domaine

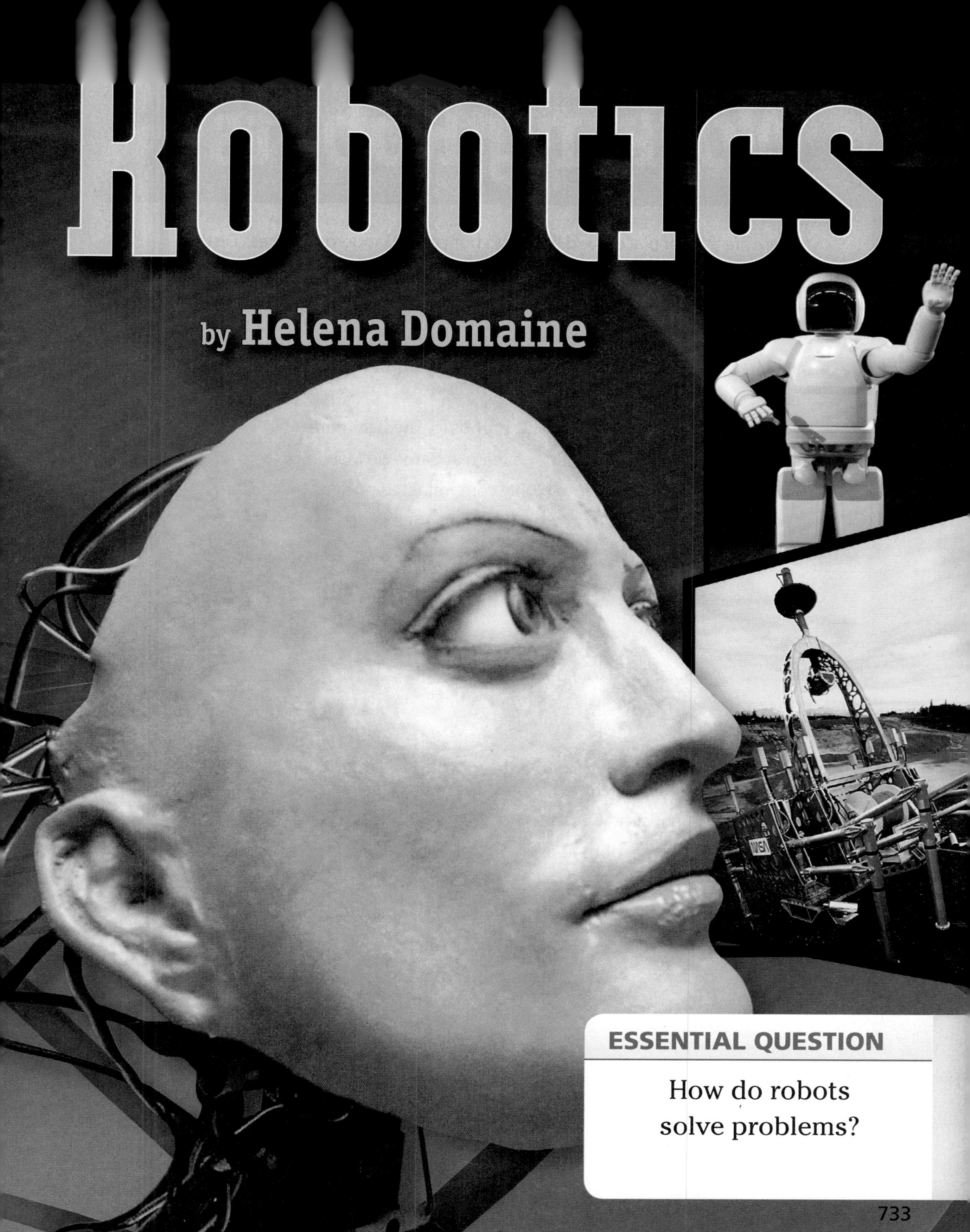

ESSENTIAL QUESTION

How do robots solve problems?

Working Robots

There are a lot of places we'd like to go but can't. Dangerous places. Distant places. Inaccessible places. We can explore these places by sending in robots. These mechanical adventurers have computer brains that don't feel fear or panic. Killer levels of radioactivity? No problem. The black, airless vacuum of space? The crushing pressure of tons of ocean water? Tiny paths through ancient rock? Bring it on, say these brave new robots.

Andros 5, for example, handles live bombs for the Baltimore (Maryland) Police Department. Rosie was built by a team at Carnegie Mellon University in Pennsylvania. It can safely roll into highly contaminated nuclear facilities and wash them down or take them apart. Houdini might be considered Rosie's baby brother. This robot can enter hazardous waste storage tanks to clean them.

You Want Me to Go Where?

In 1994, the National Aeronautics and Space Administration (NASA) teamed up with scientists at Carnegie Mellon University and the Alaska Volcano Observatory. They sent a robot to explore an active volcano. Scientists explore volcanoes to learn how they work and how to read the warning signs of a volcanic eruption. An eight-legged robot named Dante II climbed down into Alaska's Mount Spurr, 90 miles (145 km) west of Anchorage. Dante's job was to explore the crater floor and take gas and soil samples. It was something that no human could have done.

Dante's designers knew the descent would be very tricky. The north wall of the volcano has a 1,000-foot (305-meter) drop. The south wall is steep and covered with rocks. Designers gave Dante servomotors, mechanisms that help Dante's main computer. The servomotors allow Dante to raise and lower each leg as the robot climbs over rocky surfaces. Dante's footpads and legs also have sensors. The sensors keep it from crashing into rocks or falling into holes.

Dante II makes its way beside a river in Alaska.

But even with all this technology, nobody trusted Dante to make its own decisions. Dante was connected to its human team by satellite and the Internet. Its main computer analyzed every step before it allowed the robot to go forward. Eventually Dante reached the floor of the crater, safe and sound.

As Dante gathered samples, the robot's cameras sent a three-dimensional view to the computer screens in front of the scientists at the volcano's rim. And thanks to something called Virtual Environment Vehicle Interface software, the scientists felt as if they were right there in the volcano with Dante.

But a near-perfect robotic adventure ended in a way familiar to anyone who's ever climbed a steep hill. Dante slipped in some loose dirt on the way out of the volcano and could not climb out. The science team had to call in a helicopter to rescue the robot.

ANALYZE THE TEXT

Sequence of Events What steps does the author describe in Dante's adventure? How does this section provide clues about what you will learn in the overall selection?

Unfortunately, no one can fly to Mars to save robots that get into trouble. NASA landed twin Rover robots, Spirit and Opportunity, on Mars in 2004. The robots were sent to explore the planet, collect soil and rock samples, and take pictures. Spirit and Opportunity are all alone on the red planet. They are millions of miles from Earth. And Mars is a far more hostile place than the inside of a volcano. Mars is very cold, averaging −67°F (−55°C). Its strong winds whip red dust across the rocky surface of the planet.

The Rovers' connection to NASA is tricky, too. Communications between the robots and NASA scientists are sent through millions of miles of space. The information travels via computer connections to orbiting spacecraft and antennas on Earth. As the Rovers roll across Mars, any helpful messages from their human teammates on Earth are delayed by several minutes. So the Rovers are designed to make many of their own choices. They are given jobs, but it is up to them to figure out how to get them done. The Rovers also have a "survival instinct" programmed into them. It helps them adapt to unexpected situations.

The Exploration Rovers collect rock and soil samples and take photographs on Mars.

The Incredible Shrinking Bot

Scientists at the California Institute of Technology are working on the designs for a tiny snake-bot to travel through the human gastrointestinal system (the stomach and intestines). As a doctor looks down a patient's throat for swelling or other signs of illness, the snake-bot would look at a patient's insides. A camera and sensors would help the snake-bot gather medical information for doctors. The snake-bot's information would help doctors diagnose disease. It may even help in therapy.

Miniature robots from New Mexico's Sandia Laboratory also explore tight spots.

But without question, the tiniest and most daring medical robots are being designed in Sweden. The Swedish micro-bots are smaller than the hyphen between *micro* and *bots* in this sentence. The micro-bots are made of silicon. The silicon is coated in gold and then covered in polymer (a plastic compound) that can shrink or swell. This allows the pieces of the robot to bend so it can pick things up and move them around.

The Swedish micro-bots are designed to operate in all kinds of fluids. The research team imagines a time in the near future when the micro-bots can be injected into the human bloodstream. Doctors hope the micro-bots will be able to clean up the plaque that causes heart attacks and break through the blood clots that cause strokes. The micro-bots could also remove bacteria. One day they may even fix disease-causing cells.

In the old sci-fi movie *Fantastic Voyage*, five scientists and their submarine, the *Proteus*, were shrunk to microscopic size. They were injected into the bloodstream of a fellow scientist. Their mission was to reach a blood clot in their friend's brain and save his life. What Hollywood imagined as movie fantasy in 1966 is becoming science fact.

Sandia researcher Doug Adkins designed the miniature robots to work in swarms, like insects. They communicate with each other and with a central station.

Artsy Robots

The Sony Corporation's QRIO robot took center stage—literally—in March 2004, when it conducted the Tokyo (Japan) Philharmonic Orchestra. QRIO can perform many tasks. But Sony, a Japanese electronics company, wanted to show off the robot's ability to control its motions. QRIO held a conductor's baton and led the human musicians through Beethoven's Symphony No. 5. Japanese automaker Toyota has also proudly produced a musical robot. The Toyota robot can play "When You Wish Upon a Star" on a trumpet. Toyota says it hopes to soon have an entire robot band ready to belt out tunes.

QRIO was designed to test controlled robotic movement.

Who's Got the Ball?

Robots aren't all work and no play. On May 4, 2003, robots from around the world played soccer in the International RoboCup Federation's American Open. The event was held at Carnegie Mellon University. Hiroaki Kitano established RoboCup in 1997. He hoped that it would lead to the development of robotic soccer players good enough to play against human athletes.

That first 1997 tournament was a little chaotic. The robots had a tough time finding the ball. They struggled to recognize their teammates and figure out which goal they were supposed to aim for. As engineers improved the robots' vision systems, play improved. By the 2001 games, the 8-inch (20-cm)-tall, wheeled robots in the Small League were doing better. They played two ten-minute halves on a field the size of a Ping-Pong table. Their soccer ball was an orange golf ball.

The Sony Corporation sends its Aibo team to the Open. Most RoboCup players are two-legged, but the Aibos are little robotic dogs. The Aibos kick the ball by getting down on their elbows. This position allows them to use both front paws. Play is slow and a bit goofy. The Aibos are, after all, still amateurs.

Aibos, robotic dogs, compete in a RoboCup soccer game.

Bertram, your robot butler, rolls into the living room and says in a flat voice, "Dinner is served." You're slouched down in a corner of the couch. "I'm not hungry, thanks," you answer. Your parents or friends might ask if you feel all right, or if there's anything they can get you. But Bertram has no reaction. He simply rolls back into the kitchen without a word and puts away the uneaten dinner. Bertram has understood your reply, but he can't respond to your tone of voice or your body language. And most people, Allison Bruce discovered, really don't like that about robots.

Bruce is a researcher at the Robotics Institute at Carnegie Mellon University. Bruce is part of the institute's Social Robot program. The program studies ways to improve interaction between humans and robots. In Bruce's experiment, a laptop computer was attached to a robot. The robot stood in the hall of a college classroom building and asked passing students a question. Sometimes the laptop screen would be blank, but sometimes it showed a face with a range of expressions.

Bruce was not really interested in the students' answers to the questions. What she was interested in was the students' willingness to stop and talk to the robot. She found that more students responded to the robot when it had a face.

Like Bruce, others who work with robots have realized that humans prefer robots they can relate to. They have developed robots that can show human emotions, such as anger, happiness, embarrassment, and sadness.

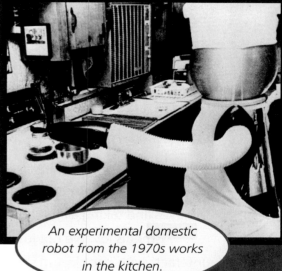

An experimental domestic robot from the 1970s works in the kitchen.

A student pauses to talk with one of the Social Robots at Carnegie Mellon University.

I Feel, Therefore I Am

Kismet the robot was designed and built by Cynthia Breazeal, a researcher at the Massachusetts Institute of Technology's (MIT's) Artificial Intelligence Laboratory. The lab is home to many kinds of interesting robots. But Kismet is not like the others. This robot can display emotion. Kismet's lips can pout or smile. His eyebrows can arch, and his ears can wiggle. A combination of clever computer programming and sophisticated engineering has given Kismet the ability to actually respond to a stimulus in an emotionally recognizable way.

If you say words of praise to Kismet, he will smile. Bright colors also earn a smile. So does his own reflection in a mirror. But raise your voice and scold Kismet, and his lips will sink into a frown. And when Kismet becomes overstimulated by too much noise or movement, he will withdraw, lowering his eyes and taking a kind of robotic time-out.

Kismet is lovable not just because of his blue golf-ball-sized eyes. Kismet interacts with people and shows he has "understood" them through his facial expressions. His success in relating to people may be reflected in the fact that everyone refers to Kismet as "he" instead of "it."

Kismet was developed to interact with people.

His name is David Hanson. In 2003 he showed up at a science conference in Denver, Colorado, carrying a head. The head was backless and bald and bolted to a piece of wood. But it was still pretty. It had high cheekbones, blue eyes, and smooth rubber polymer skin. Hanson set the head down on a table. He plugged it into his laptop computer and tapped a few keys. Everyone stopped to watch what would happen.

Moments later, the head began to move, turning right and left. It smiled, sneered, and frowned. Hanson, a robot scientist at the University of Texas at Dallas, called the head K-bot. K-bot can mimic the major muscles in a human face. It has 24 servomotors under its specially developed skin. Digital cameras in its eyes watch the people who are curiously studying it, and software helps it to imitate what it sees.

David Hanson designed K-bot to express human emotions.

ANALYZE THE TEXT

Domain–Specific Vocabulary
When the author uses a term such as *polymer skin,* she is using language specific to her own field of study. How does the author help you understand this term? What other technical words does the author use? How can you figure out their meanings?

Hanson has built several robotic heads, but he isn't the only one. In Tokyo, Hiroshi Kobayashi's face robots, as he calls them, are also eerily lifelike. So is the head sitting in Fumio Hara's robotics lab at the Science University of Tokyo. Hara's robotic head can scan the face of the person standing in front of it. Then it can compare the face to those in its memory bank. Once the robot identifies which of six emotions the person is expressing, tiny machines under the robot's skin remold its face to mimic what it sees.

Fumio Hara poses with a skeleton of one of his face robots. The face robot's network of wires and pulleys is covered with a flexible skin.

For Hara, heads are just the beginning. His goal is to design a robot that is interactive, friendly, and most of all, familiar. But do we really want a robot that looks just like us? Maybe not.

In the late 1970s, Japanese robot engineer Masahiro Mori did some fascinating research on how human beings interact with robots. Mori discovered that people like friendly-looking mechanical robots. But Mori found that when robots look too much like humans, people stop liking them. Mori called this sudden shift the Uncanny Valley, the place where people begin to feel uncomfortable with humanlike robots.

Engineers have begun building robots that can adapt to their environment. They operate on what are called patterns of behavior.

Most of these robots are quite small and behave a lot like insects. Insects don't really think. They rely on their senses and instincts to find food and survive. Like insects, the little insect-bots have been equipped for sensing their physical environment. But they have not been preprogrammed with any data about their environment. So when they are first turned on, they're brainless.

But the insect-bots' computers are programmed with separate "layers of behavior." The behavior layers help an insect-bot learn about its environment. The more it learns, the more it can do. Once the insect-bot has mastered one layer of behavior, the next higher layer of behavior kicks in. With each layer, the insect-bot gets better at dealing with the world around it.

At MIT, James McLurkin has built robot ants using these layers of behavior. But McLurkin's ant-bots are even more amazing because they are able to signal each other when they find ant-bot "food." In other words, the ant-bots learn how to work together to achieve a shared goal. The ultimate ant-bot, however, is yet to come—one that can communicate with real ants.

A robotic ladybug, developed by Sanyo Electric Company, sits on a leaf.

"I believe," says Hans Moravec, a research professor at Carnegie Mellon, "that robots with human intelligence will be common during the next 50 years." Certainly, the Center for Intelligent Systems (CIS) at Vanderbilt University in Tennessee shows how close we are getting. The CIS has developed a robot called ISAC (for Intelligent Soft Arm Control). ISAC can express emotion and has both short-term and long-term memory. And because this robot's brain has been designed to "think" much like ours, ISAC may soon actually be able to dream.

It seems almost certain that in the future we will share our planet with robots. What we build in the lab will have the potential to become as smart as we are. It may even improve upon its own technology. Will we love these robots or fear them? Time will tell.

ANALYZE THE TEXT

Main Ideas and Details What is the main idea of this selection? What details does the author give to support the main idea?

ISAC was built to help people who have physical handicaps. Improvements focus on learning skills and response to human emotions.

WILL ROBOTS OBEY THE "LAWS"?

In the informational article you just read, author Helena Domaine asks whether the future's highly intelligent robots will be loved by humanity or loathed and feared by us. The answer to this question may hinge upon whether robots can either be designed to regulate their own behavior or somehow restrained from breaking certain basic rules of behavior. Fans of science fiction are already familiar with one proposed set of rules to govern robotic "morals" and keep our robotic servants from becoming our masters.

In 1942, science-fiction patriarch Isaac Asimov, in a short story titled "Runaround," enumerated the Three Laws of Robotics, which were thenceforth integrated into much of Asimov's future fiction involving robots; the Three Laws form an interdependent series and may be paraphrased as follows:

- **First Law of Robotics:** A robot may not cause injury to a human through the robot's actions or allow a human to be injured as a result of the robot's failure to act.

- **Second Law of Robotics:** A robot must obey the edicts or orders of its human rulers, unless such orders would cause the robot to violate the First Law.

- **Third Law of Robotics:** A robot must not allow itself to be eradicated or destroyed, unless its own self-protection would violate the First Law or the Second Law.

Here is a theoretical puzzle for you: Can you imagine any scenario in which the Three Laws of Robotics, if built into a robot's software so that it was forced to follow them, would not ensure the safety of humanity? If robots obeyed Asimov's Laws, could we feel secure with them working, playing, and "living" among us?

Dig Deeper

How to Analyze the Text

Use these pages to learn about Sequence of Events, Domain-Specific Vocabulary, and Main Ideas and Details. Then read "Robotics" again to apply what you learned.

Sequence of Events

Authors of informational texts such as "Robotics" often use **sequence,** or time order, to organize information about a topic. Dates and signal words such as *first*, *after*, *next*, and *finally* help readers figure out the order in which events occur. Paying attention to the overall sequence of events allows you to figure out where a single event or a group of events fits within the sequence.

Look back at page 738 in "Robotics." The author explains the sequence of events in the RoboCup Open, which began in 1997. What happened from 1997 to 2003 that shows how the robots' soccer competition changed and improved through the years?

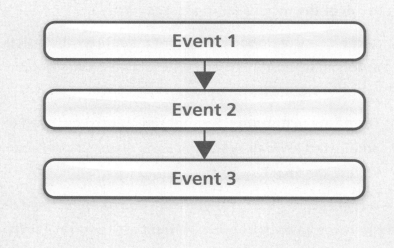

Event 1

↓

Event 2

↓

Event 3

Go Digital

Domain-Specific Vocabulary

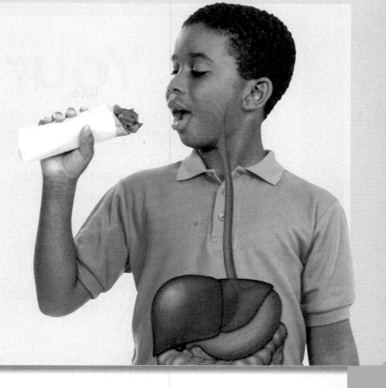

Authors of informational text often use words and phrases specific to one domain, or field of study. This **vocabulary** can include words only used in the field, such as *micro-bot*. It can also include familiar words with **technical meanings,** such as *stroke*. Look back at page 737 for words used in medicine, such as *diagnose* and *bloodstream*. As you read informational text, look for clues that help you figure out the meaning of domain-specific vocabulary.

Main Ideas and Details

The **main idea** of a selection is the **central idea,** or most important idea. It tells what the selection is mainly about. **Details** support the main idea by giving facts and other text evidence. Look back at "First to Fly" in Lesson 22. The main idea of the selection is that the Wright brothers invented the first airplane. Many details support this main idea by telling about the brothers' work with gliders, their building of the airplane, and their first flights. Identifying the main idea of a selection and the details that support it helps you better understand the selection.

Your Turn

RETURN TO THE ESSENTIAL QUESTION

Turn and Talk

Review the selection with a partner to prepare to discuss this question: *How do robots solve problems?* As you discuss, use text evidence to review and explain your key ideas, asking questions to clarify your partner's responses.

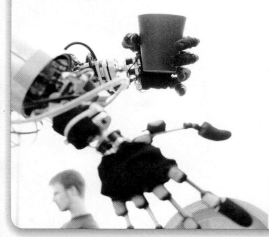

Classroom Conversation

Continue your discussion of "Robotics" by explaining your answers to these questions using text evidence:

1 The author suggests that robotics "may even improve upon its own technology." What does she mean by this statement?

2 In what ways are Dante and the NASA twin Rovers alike and different?

3 What might the author's purpose have been in choosing the headings in the selection?

WHAT DOES IT MEAN?

Use Reference Sources Choose three of these words from the selection: *contaminated, hazardous, descent, compound, behavior*. Find each word in the selection. Then look up each word in a print or digital dictionary. Write a new sentence for each word that gives a clue to its meaning. Share your sentences with a partner.

WRITE ABOUT READING

Response Do you think the current widespread use of robots to do work for people is a change for the better? Why or why not? Write a paragraph that presents and explains your argument. Introduce the paragraph with your claim, and use your own knowledge as well as text evidence to support it. End with a conclusion that summarizes your opinion.

Writing Tip

As you write, make sure you use commas to set off nonrestrictive information from the rest of a sentence. Use dashes or parentheses to set off parenthetical information.

COMMON CORE **RI.6.1** cite textual evidence to support analysis of what the text says explicitly as well as inferences drawn; **W.6.1a** introduce claim(s) and organize reasons and evidence clearly; **W.6.9b** apply grade 6 Reading standards to literary nonfiction; **SL.6.1c** pose and respond to questions and make comments that contribute to the discussion; **L.6.2a** use punctuation to set off nonrestrictive/parenthetical elements; **L.6.4c** consult reference materials, both print and digital, to find pronunciation and determine or clarify meaning or part of speech

PLAY

A **play** tells a story through the words and actions of its characters. It is meant to be performed for an audience.

Stage directions in a play identify a time or place, describe a setting, or tell about a character's feelings or actions.

COMMON CORE
RL.6.5 analyze how a sentence, chapter, scene, or stanza fits in the overall structure; **RL.6.10** read and comprehend literature

DR. SNEED'S BEST FRIEND

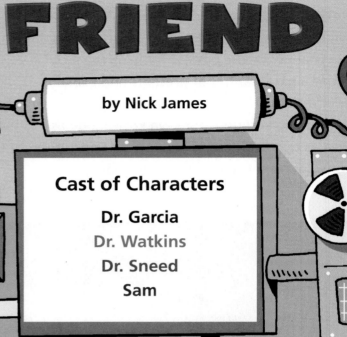

by Nick James

Cast of Characters

Dr. Garcia
Dr. Watkins
Dr. Sneed
Sam

Scene 1

(It is Monday morning at a robotics laboratory. Two scientists enter to find Dr. Sneed, hard at work.)

Dr. Garcia: *(looking around)* Wow, Sneed, it looks as if you've been working all weekend.

Dr. Watkins: Yes, I thought the data for our new project wasn't due yet.

Dr. Sneed: *(nervously)* Well, actually, ah, I've been working on a top-secret project that requires my undivided attention. I didn't even have time to eat breakfast.

Dr. Garcia: Top-secret? Hmm. Interesting. Care to share any information about it?

Dr. Sneed: Impossible. All I can say is that it's about artificial intelligence.

Dr. Watkins: Well, that's what we all do. Come on, Sneed, you can trust us.

Dr. Sneed: (*pacing*) Fine, if you must know, the project concerns the use of sensors in a domestic setting.

Dr. Garcia: I have an uncanny feeling there is a lot more to it than that—but I've got work to do. Now, good day, gentlemen.

Scene 2

(*Later that morning, a small robot knocks and enters, carrying an apple and a glass of milk.*)

Dr. Watkins: (*to the robot*) Hello, little dude. Can I help you?

Sam: (*in a flat, mechanical voice*) No, I do not require any help.

Dr. Sneed: (*rushing over to the robot*) Sam, what are you doing here?

Sam: I am delivering your apple and glass of milk, Dr. Sneed. A healthy snack!

Dr. Sneed: (*in an embarrassed whisper*) Sam, you were programmed to come here at noon. It's only nine o'clock.

Sam: I am sorry, Dr. Sneed. A stimulus in my motherboard overrode my internal clock.

Dr. Garcia: What's he talking about?

Sam: You did not eat breakfast, Dr. Sneed. I sensed that your stomach was growling.

Dr. Garcia: Well, Dr. Sneed, I see you've achieved a new interaction between human and machine.

Dr. Watkins: Yes, I always thought this kind of friendship from a robot was impossible. I suppose this is your top-secret project?

(*Dr. Sneed nods, embarrassed. He takes a big bite of the apple.*)

Sam: Goodbye, Dr. Sneed. (*He turns around and rolls toward the door.*)

Dr. Sneed: Hold on a second, Sam.

Sam: A second is not an object that I can hold, Dr. Sneed.

Dr. Sneed: I didn't mean it literally, Sam. Please go to my office and get two more apples for Dr. Garcia and Dr. Watkins.

Sam: A healthy snack. I will be right back.

(*Sam exits, stiffly. Dr. Watkins and Dr. Garcia stare at Dr. Sneed.*)

Dr. Garcia: You spent all weekend programming a robot to bring you food? What a waste of time!

Dr. Sneed: (*shrugging*) That's a matter of opinion. Besides, tomorrow he's making me macaroni and cheese. (*He smiles.*) It's my favorite.

SAM

Compare Texts

Evaluate Robot Tasks The robots in "Robotics" and in "Dr. Sneed's Best Friend" perform a variety of tasks. Which tasks do you think are most worthy of the time, effort, and resources required to develop a robot? Which are least worthy? Think about all the robot tasks you have read about, and then list them from most to least important. Use text evidence to support your ideas.

Write a Scene Choose one of the robots mentioned in "Robotics." Write a short play scene in which the robot helps you do a typical activity in your life, whether for school, work, or fun.

My Robot
A Play

Use Robot Resources Choose a kind of robot that interests you, such as a robot used in school competitions, a robot from a movie, or a robot used to work in space. Use print and online sources to find out more about that kind of robot.

 RL.6.1 cite textual evidence to support analysis of what the text says explicitly as well as inferences drawn; **RI.6.1** cite textual evidence to support analysis of what the text says explicitly as well as inferences drawn; **W.6.8** gather information from print and digital sources/assess credibility of sources/quote or paraphrase data and conclusions of others/provide bibliographic information

Grammar

 Go Digital

What Are the Mechanics of Writing? *Mechanics* refers to the correct use of **capitalization** and **punctuation.** You have learned to capitalize proper nouns and proper adjectives. You have learned how to punctuate declarative, interrogative, imperative, and exclamatory sentences, too.

Declarative Sentence	proper noun period A robot named Dante II will descend into a volcano.
Interrogative Sentence	proper adjective question mark Which Alaskan volcano will it explore?
Imperative Sentence	period Let me see the viewing screen.
Exclamatory Sentence	exclamation point What strength that robot has!

An **interjection** is a word or words that show feeling. If it stands alone, follow it with an exclamation point. If it begins a sentence, set it off with a comma.

exclamation point

         Wow! The robot is walking on red-hot rock!

comma

         Hey, its sensors have detected toxic fumes!

Try This!

Write the sentences below on another sheet of paper. Use correct capitalization and end punctuation. Place the correct punctuation after the interjection.

1. Look at this photo of the martian landscape

2. Did a robot take that photo while on mars

3. Oh What a breathtaking photo it is

4. I want to attend the california institute of technology

Your readers will have an easier time reading and understanding what you write if you use correct capitalization and punctuation.

Incorrect Capitalization and Punctuation	Correct Capitalization and Punctuation
will a robot be aboard the next american space vehicle. Hey here is an article about an upcoming flight to mars, According to the article, the passengers will be robots Give it a quick read, and then return it to me?	Will a robot be aboard the next American space vehicle? Hey, here is an article about an upcoming flight to Mars. According to the article, the passengers will be robots! Give it a quick read, and then return it to me.

Connect Grammar to Writing

As you revise your argument, correct any errors in capitalization or punctuation that you find.

W.6.1a introduce claim(s) and organize reasons and evidence clearly; **W.6.1b** support claim(s) with reasons and evidence, using credible sources and demonstrating understanding of the topic or text; **W.6.1c** use words, phrases, and clauses to clarify relationships; **W.6.1d** establish and maintain a formal style; **L.6.3b** maintain consistency in style and tone

Argument Writing

Reading-Writing Workshop: Revise

✔ **Word Choice**   When writing a strong **argument,** good writers state a **claim,** or an opinion they want to express. To argue their claim, they include **reasons** supported by **evidence.** The evidence may take the form of facts, details, examples, and believable sources. As you revise your argument, be sure you have used strong, specific words in order to convince readers. Also check for transition words, phrases, and clauses that clarify relationships between the claim and its reasons.

Orlando wrote a first draft of his argument about cell phones. Then he revised his draft. He replaced a vague word with a strong word to make his claim clearer and his reason stronger.

Writing Process Checklist

Prewrite

Draft

▶ **Revise**

✔ **Did I state my claim clearly?**

✔ **Did I order my reasons according to importance?**

✔ **Did I maintain a formal style and consistent tone?**

✔ **Did I clarify relationships between my claim and its reasons?**

✔ **Did I end with a conclusion?**

Edit

Publish and Share

Revised Draft

For one thing, cell phones are ~~a good~~ the perfect

tool for families to use to share important

information quickly. For example, i ~~If~~ parents will be late

picking up their children, cell phones can help.

Likewise, i ~~If~~ children want permission to go

somewhere, they can call or text on a cell

phone. Whenever there is a change of plans,

cell phones can help.

Cell Phones Are Beneficial

by Orlando Reyes

On a typical day, look around you. How many people are talking or texting on cell phones? Today, cell phones are widely used by both adults and kids. Cell phones are an invention that has changed people's lives for the better.

For one thing, cell phones are the perfect tool for families to use to share important information quickly. For example, if parents will be late picking up their children, cell phones can help. Likewise, if children want permission to go somewhere, they can call or text on a cell phone. Whenever there is a change of plans, cell phones can help.

A recent TV news report told of a family of five who got separated at the mall and couldn't find each other. They did not have cell phones with them. Once mall security helped them out using a cell phone, the family got together. Using cell phones can resolve problems quickly. Families benefit from having cell phones because family members can all stay connected.

Reading as a Writer

Which words did Orlando replace in his draft to make his argument stronger? What can you add to make your reasons clearer and stronger?

In my final paper, I made sure my claim was supported with reasons. I also added transition words to clarify the relationship between my claim and reasons. I made sure my essay had a conclusion.

Test POWER

Read the passages "Bessie Coleman, Aviator" and "Remembering Bessie." As you read, stop and answer each question using text evidence.

Bessie Coleman, Aviator

Bessie Coleman was a daring and determined young woman. Born to a poor family in Texas on January 26, 1892, she grew up at a time when few opportunities were open to African Americans or to women. Bessie was not quite twelve years old in December of 1903 when Wilbur and Orville Wright made the first airplane flight. After that historic event, many people became enchanted with the idea of flying. In the early years of aviation, however, only white men and a very few white women became licensed pilots.

As a young girl, Bessie worked alongside her mother picking cotton and doing people's laundry to help support the family. She attended a one-room schoolhouse from first grade through eighth grade and would read aloud to her family in the evenings. It is reported that she often vowed to her mother that she intended to amount to something.

> **1** What does the phrase *amount to something* mean?

After she finished school, Bessie worked and saved her money until she had enough to continue her education. At the age of 18, she left home to attend college in Oklahoma. After one year there, however, her money ran out, and she returned home. She worked for several years doing laundry, and then moved to Chicago, Illinois, in 1915.

In Chicago, Bessie lived for a time with her older brothers, who had served in France during World War I. Her brother John often teased her by telling her that French women had careers and could even fly airplanes. Bessie had read about aviation and watched short films about it. Now she set an ambitious goal for herself. She was determined to become a pilot!

Bessie applied to flight schools all over the United States, but none would accept her. The publisher of an important African American newspaper in Chicago was a friend of Bessie's. He suggested that she go to flight school in France. Bessie kept working and saving her money, and she also went to night school to learn to speak French.

RI.6.2 determine a central idea of a text/provide a summary; **RI.6.3** analyze how a key individual, event, or idea is introduced, illustrated, and elaborated; **RI.6.4** determine the meaning of words and phrases, including figurative, connotative, and technical meanings; **RI.6.9** compare and contrast one author's presentation of events with that of another

In November of 1920, Bessie traveled to France to attend a famous flight school, the Caudon Brothers' School of Aviation. The course usually required ten months to complete, but it took Bessie only seven months. On June 15, 1921, Bessie Coleman received her international pilot's license from the Fédération Aéronautique Internationale. The international federation had been founded in 1905 to advance the science and sport of flying. On that day in 1921, Bessie Coleman became the first African American woman in the world to be licensed as a pilot. She also became the first licensed African American pilot in the United States, male or female.

Bessie's dream was to return to the United States and earn enough as a pilot to establish her own flight school. In 1922, she told news reporters in New York that she hoped to become a leader in introducing African Americans to the new technology of flight. Because she was both African American and a woman, however, her opportunities were limited. She would once again have to work hard to achieve her goal.

To earn money, Bessie became a barnstormer. Barnstormers were pilots who traveled around the country putting on air shows. Bessie had learned to perform daring stunts, such as tailspins, barrel rolls, and loop-the-loops. In a tailspin, the plane spirals rapidly toward the ground. In a barrel roll, the plane spins around in the air, turning upside down and right side up again. To do a loop-the-loop, the plane flies straight up, turns over, and zooms down; then it turns straight up again, completing a loop in the sky.

Bessie's first air show was held in New York on September 3, 1922. It was reported that approximately 3,000 people came to see her thrilling performance. After that, Bessie traveled around the country performing in air shows, making speeches, and teaching people to fly.

Bessie Coleman did not live to fulfill her dream of founding a flight school. On April 30, 1926, she was riding in the passenger seat of her plane with her mechanic at the controls. Bessie planned to parachute out of the plane as part of her air show the next day. She was leaning out of the cockpit to look for good landing spots and not wearing a seat belt. The plane suddenly went into a dive and turned over, throwing Bessie out of the plane. It was a sad and sudden end to a life of courage and determination.

2 What is the central idea of this passage? Summarize the passage briefly, without including personal opinions or judgments.

Remembering Bessie

It was on June 19, 1925, when Mama took my brother George and me to see an air show. We had never heard of such a thing, but Mama explained that an air show is an exhibition where pilots fly airplanes and do all kinds of amazing tricks. It was held at an auto racetrack in Houston, where we lived. The place had even been given a fancy new name, the Houston Aerial Transport Field.

I could hardly believe it when Mama told us that the star pilot was a woman! George said he downright refused to believe any such nonsense, but Mama said he would see for himself, and he did. The pilot's name was Bessie Coleman, and besides being a woman, she was also African American, just like us. Mama said that going to see Bessie Coleman was a perfect way to celebrate June 19, or Juneteenth, as we called it. Every year, we celebrated the emancipation of African Americans in Texas, which had happened on June 19, 1865, sixty years ago that very day.

So off we went to the air show, and we had another surprise before the show even began. Many white people had come to see Bessie Coleman fly, too, right there at the same field where we were. That was something that didn't happen often back in 1925.

Once the show got underway, though, we stopped thinking about anything. We just stared at the sky in wonder. Bessie Coleman flew that plane upside down and spinning around. She dived and swooped and zoomed and looped so that I was sure at any moment the plane would break apart or fall out of the sky. What a thrilling and astounding day! I knew then that I wanted to grow up to be just like Bessie Coleman.

> **3** What details or examples does the author include to show why she admired Bessie Coleman?

I was heartsick the following year when I learned that Bessie Coleman had died. I knew that her wonderful courageous spirit would live on, though. It would live on in girls like me who would grow up as I did to follow in Bessie's footsteps, spread our wings, and fly. Years later, on the day I received my pilot's license, I said a silent thank you to my heroine and role model, the great Bessie Coleman.

> **4** How are these two passages alike, and how are they different? Use details from the passages to support your response.

This glossary contains meanings and pronunciations for some of the words in this book. The Full Pronunciation Key shows how to pronounce each consonant and vowel in a special spelling. At the bottom of the glossary pages is a shortened form of the full key.

Full Pronunciation Key

Consonant Sounds

b	**bib**, ca**bb**age	m	a**m**, **m**an, du**mb**	y	**y**es, **y**olk, on**i**on
ch	**ch**ur**ch**, sti**tch**	n	**n**o, sudd**en**	z	ro**s**e, si**z**e, **x**ylophone, **z**ebra
d	**d**ee**d**, mail**ed**, pu**dd**le	ng	thi**ng**, i**nk**	zh	gara**g**e, plea**s**ure, vi**s**ion
f	**f**ast, **f**i**f**e, o**ff**, **ph**rase, rou**gh**	p	**p**o**p**, ha**pp**y		
		r	**r**oar, **rh**yme		
g	**g**a**g**, **g**et, fin**g**er	s	mi**ss**, **s**au**c**e, **sc**ene, **s**ee		
h	**h**at, **wh**o	sh	di**sh**, **sh**ip, **s**ugar, ti**ss**ue		
hw	**wh**ich, **wh**ere	t	**t**igh**t**, stop**p**ed		
j	**j**u**dg**e, **g**em	th	ba**th**, **th**in		
k	**c**at, **k**i**ck**, s**ch**ool	*th*	ba**the**, **th**is		
kw	**ch**oir, **qu**ick	v	ca**v**e, val**v**e, **v**ine		
l	**l**id, need**l**e, ta**ll**	w	**w**ith, **w**olf		

Vowel Sounds

ă	p**a**t, l**au**gh	oi	b**oy**, n**oi**se, **oi**l	ŭ	c**u**t, fl**oo**d, r**ou**gh, s**o**me
ā	**a**pe, **ai**d, p**ay**	ou	c**ow**, **ou**t	û	c**ir**cle, f**ur**, h**ear**d, t**er**m, t**ur**n, **ur**ge, w**or**d
â	**ai**r, c**a**re, w**ea**r	o͝o	f**u**ll, b**oo**k, w**o**lf		
ä	f**a**ther, k**oa**la, y**a**rd	o͞o	b**oo**t, r**u**de, fr**ui**t, fl**ew**	yo͞o	c**u**re
ĕ	p**e**t, pl**ea**sure, **a**ny			yo͞o	**a**buse, **u**se
ē	b**e**, b**ee**, **ea**sy, pian**o**			ə	**a**go, sil**e**nt, penc**i**l, lem**o**n, circ**u**s
ĭ	**i**f, p**i**t, b**u**sy				
ī	r**i**de, b**y**, p**ie**, h**igh**				
î	d**ea**r, d**ee**r, f**ie**rce, m**e**re				
ŏ	s**o**ck, p**o**t				
ō	g**o**, r**ow**, t**oe**, th**ough**				
ô	**a**ll, c**augh**t, f**o**r, p**aw**				

Stress Marks

Primary Stress ´: bi•ol•o•gy [bī **ŏl**´ ə jē]
Secondary Stress ´: bi•o•log•i•cal [bī´ ə **lŏj**´ ĭ kəl]

Pronunciation key and definitions © 2003 by Houghton Mifflin Company. Adapted and reprinted by permission from *The American Heritage Children's Dictionary*.

A

a·ban·don (ə **băn´** dən) v. To leave and not intend to return: *Derek will **abandon** his old car at the junkyard and buy a new one.*

a·brupt (ə **brŭpt´**) adj. Unexpected; sudden: *The television show came to an **abrupt** end when the thunderstorm caused the TV to lose its signal.*

a·bun·dance (ə **bŭn´** dəns) n. A great amount or quantity; a plentiful supply: *The heavy spring rains gave us an **abundance** of water for the summer.*

abundance

ac·cus·tomed (ə **kŭs´** təmd) adj. Used to; in the habit of: *Farmers are **accustomed** to working long days.*

af·firm (ə **fûrm´**) v. To give approval or validity to; confirm: *The appeals court **affirmed** the lower court's ruling.*

aim (ām) n. Purpose; goal: *My **aim** is to be a writer when I grow up.*

al·le·vi·ate (ə **lē´** vē āt) v. To relieve or make less: *The heavy rains should **alleviate** the threat of more forest fires.*

al·ter (ôl´ tər) v. To change or make different: *We **altered** our plans for the weekend after checking the weather.*

am·ble (ăm´ bəl) v. To walk or move along at a slow pace: *The horses **ambled** out of the corral.*

an·ces·tral (ăn **sĕs´** trəl) adj. Of, relating to, or inherited from an ancestor or ancestors: *Every living thing has an **ancestral** trait.*

a·non·y·mous (ə **nŏn´** ə məs) adj. Nameless or unnamed: *The prize was awarded by a panel of **anonymous** judges.*

ap·peal (ə **pēl´**) v. To be attractive or interesting: *That game is very **appealing** to me.*

ap·pro·pri·ate (ə **prō´** prē ĭt) adj. Suitable, as for a particular occasion; proper: *White shorts are **appropriate** for playing tennis.*

apt·ly (ăpt´ lē) adv. In a way that is exactly suitable; appropriately: *The boa constrictor, **aptly** named Squeeze, rested comfortably, awaiting his next meal.*

ar·chae·ol·o·gist (är´ kē ŏl´ ə jĭst) n. A person who is an expert in archaeology: ***Archaeologists** use different tools to study cultures from the past.*

a·rise (ə **rīz´**) v. To come into being; appear: *We took advantage of opportunities as they **arose**.*

ar·ray (ə **rā´**) n. An impressively large number or group: *The cast for the play shows an impressive **array** of talents.*

ă r**a**t / ā p**a**y / â c**a**re / ä f**a**ther / ĕ p**e**t / ē b**e** / ĭ p**i**t / ī p**ie** / î f**ie**rce / ŏ p**o**t / ō g**o** / ô p**a**w, f**o**r / oi **oi**l / o͝o b**oo**k

ar•ti•fi•cial (är´ tə **fish**´ əl) *adj.*
1. Made by humans rather than occurring in nature. **2.** Not genuine or natural: *The flowers on the tables are made to look real, but they are* **artificial.**

art•is•try (är´ tĭ strē) *n.*
1. Artistic quality or workmanship. **2.** Artistic ability: *Visitors to the museum observed the* **artistry** *of different paintings.*

as•cent (ə **sĕnt**´) *n.* The act of moving, going, or growing upward: *The climbers planned their* **ascent** *of the peak for a clear day so they could enjoy the views from the top.*

as•pect (**ăs**´ pĕkt) *n.* The way in which something can be viewed by the mind; an element or facet: *In prescribing a treatment, the doctor considered every* **aspect** *of the patient´s history.*

bit•ter (**bĭt**´ ər) *adj.* **1.** Showing or proceeding from strong dislike or animosity: *The soldiers fought* **bitterly** *to win the war.* **2.** Resulting from grief, anguish, or disappointment: *Fans wept* **bitterly** *when the team lost the final match.*

bland (blănd) *adj.* Lacking distinctive character; dull; flat: *The politician´s* **bland** *speech did not present any interesting ideas.*

blurt (blûrt) *v.* To say something suddenly without thinking: *The teacher accidentally* **blurted** *out the answer to the test question.*

brain•wash (**brān**´ wŏsh´) *v.* To persuade (a person) by intense means, such as repeated suggestions, to adopt a belief or behave in a certain way: *The TV commercials* **brainwashed** *me into buying the junk food.*

brainwash
Brainwash is a literal translation of a Chinese word meaning "to wash the brain." It first came into English as a military term during the Korean War.

B

bar•ren (**băr**´ ən) *adj.*
1. Lacking plants or crops: *The drought left our farm with* **barren** *fields.* **2.** Empty; bare: *The volunteers worked to help make the neighborhood streets* **barren** *of litter and other trash.*

be•rate (bĭ **rāt**´) *v.* To scold severely; upbraid: *No one should* **berate** *a friend for something that isn´t the friend´s fault.*

C

ca•reen (kə **rēn**´) *v.* To lurch or swerve while in motion: *As it moved down the icy road, the car was* **careening** *out of control.*

ce•re•mo•ny (**sĕr**´ ə mō nē) *n.*; **ceremonial** *adj.* A formal act or series of acts performed in honor of an event or special occasion: *The graduating students walked down the aisle in a* **ceremonial** *procession.*

barren

ōō b**oo**t / ou **ou**t / ŭ c**u**t / û f**u**r / hw **wh**ich / th **th**in / *th* **th**is / zh vi**si**on / ə **a**go, sil**e**nt, penc**i**l, lem**o**n, circ**u**s

clam•or (**klăm´** ər) *n.* A loud, continuous, and usually confused noise: *A **clamor** arose from the crowd as the rock star emerged onstage.*

clus•tered (**klŭs´** tərd) *adj.* Gathered in groups: ***Clustered** around the fire, they held out their hands to get warm.*

coax (kōks) *v.* To persuade or try to persuade by gently urging: *The trainer **coaxed** the lion into the cage.*

col•lab•o•rate (kə **lăb´** ə rāt´) *v.* To work with another or others on a project: *When people **collaborate** on a project, they work together.*

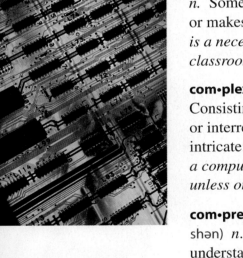

complex

com•ple•ment (**kŏm´** plə mənt) *n.* Something that completes or makes perfect: *Homework is a necessary **complement** to classroom study.*

com•plex (kəm **plĕks´**) *adj.* Consisting of many connected or interrelated parts or factors; intricate: *The **complex** wiring of a computer is hard to understand unless one is an expert.*

com•pre•hen•sion (kŏm´ prĭ **hĕn´** shən) *n.* **1.** The act or fact of understanding. **2.** The ability to understand something: *The tutor helped him improve his **comprehension** in English class through writing and reading lessons.*

com•pro•mise (**kŏm´** prə mīz´) *n.* A settlement of differences between opposing sides in which each side gives up some claims and agrees to some demands of the other: *By agreeing to share the cost, our neighbors reached a **compromise** over rebuilding the fence.*

con•cept (**kŏn´** sĕpt´) *n.* A general idea or understanding, especially one based on known facts or observation: *The **concept** that all matter is made up of atoms is well accepted.*

con•di•tion (kən **dĭsh´** ən) *n.* **1.** A state of being or existence. **2.** The existing circumstances: *Paul bundled up in his coat and hat before going out into the harsh **conditions** of the winter weather.*

con•front (kən **frŭnt´**) *v.* To come face to face with, especially in opposition: *He did not have an easy time **confronting** his fear of flying, but once he sat down in the airplane he started to relax.*

con•se•quence (**kŏn´** sĭ kwĕns´) *n.* Something that follows from an action or condition; an effect; a result: *Having a large vocabulary was one of the **consequences** of so much reading.*

ă rat / ā **pay** / â **care** / ä f**ather** / ĕ **pet** / ē be / ĭ **pit** / ī **pie** / î **fie**rce / ŏ **pot** / ō **go** /
ô **paw, for** / oi **oil** / o͝o b**oo**k

con•tempt (kən tĕmpt´) *n.* A feeling that a person or thing is inferior or worthless: *The two lawyers looked at each other with* **contempt** *in the courtroom because each thought the other's argument was worthless.*

con•test (kən tĕst´) *v.* To dispute; challenge: *Because the parking ticket had been given unfairly, he* **contested** *it in court.*

cor•re•spond (kôr´ ĭ spŏnd´) *v.* To be very similar: *The eyelids* **correspond** *to the shutter of a camera.*

cred•it (krĕd´ ĭt) *n.* Recognition or approval for an act, ability, or quality: *The two authors share* **credit** *for the book's success.*

cul•mi•nation (kŭl´ mə nā´ shən) *n.* The highest point or degree, often just before the end; climax: *The* **culmination** *of the celebration was a huge display of fireworks.*

cul•prit (kŭl´ prĭt) *n.* A person or thing guilty of a fault or crime: *The* **culprit** *who took the basketball net should put it back.*

cul•tur•al (kŭl´ chər əl) *adj.* Of or relating to the arts, beliefs, customs, institutions, and all other products of human work and thought at a particular time and place: *Paris is the* **cultural** *center of France.*

D

da•ta (dā´ tə) *pl. n.* Information, usually in numerical form, suitable for processing by computer: *His job is to compile lists of information and input the* **data** *into a computer to be sorted.*

de•com•po•si•tion (dē kŏm pə zĭsh´ ən) *n.* The act or process of rotting or decaying: *Microbes caused the* **decomposition** *of dead plants on the forest floor.*

de•crep•it (dĭ krĕp´ ĭt) *adj.* Weakened, worn-out, or broken down because of old age or long use: *Tony's motorcycle grew* **decrepit** *over the years, so he could no longer use it.*

de•duce (dĭ do͞os´) *v.* To reach (a conclusion) by reasoning, especially from a general principle: *The engineers* **deduced** *from the laws of physics that the new airplane would fly.*

de•fy (dĭ fī´) *v.* To oppose or resist openly or boldly: *There is no good reason to* **defy** *school rules on the field trip.*

de•pict (dĭ pĭkt´) *v.* To represent in or as if in a painting or words: *The artist* **depicted** *his subject in an accurate way, rather than create an abstract portrait.*

de•prive (dĭ prīv´) *v.* To prevent from having or enjoying; deny: *Heavy snow* **deprived** *the deer of food.*

culprit
The word *culprit* is from Norman French, the language of English law courts from 1066 to 1362. In court, the prosecutor would say of the defendant, "Guilty (*culpable*); ready (*prit*) to proceed." The court clerk abbreviated the phrase as *cul. prit*, and the term came to indicate the defendant.

---

o͞o **boo**t / ou **ou**t / ŭ **cu**t / û **fu**r / hw **wh**ich / th **th**in / *th* **th**is / zh vi**si**on / ə **a**go, sil**e**nt, penc**il**, lem**o**n, circ**u**s

domestic

dormant
The word *dormant* means to "lie asleep, or as if asleep." It comes from the Latin word *dormire*, meaning "sleep." Two related words are *dormitory*, "a room or building designed as sleeping quarters for a number of people," and *dormer*, from a French word meaning "sleeping room." Since sleeping rooms were usually on the top floor of a house, *dormer* gradually came to refer to a gable or window projecting from a sloping roof.

des·ti·na·tion (dĕs′ tə nā′shən) *n.* A place to which someone is going or to which something is sent: *The girl was walking, and her destination was school.*

des·ti·ny (dĕs′ tə nē) *n.* The fortune, fate, or lot of a person or thing that is considered to be unavoidable: *Because Karen loved animals, she believed that growing up to be a veterinarian was her destiny.*

de·tached (dĭ tăcht′) *adj.* Marked by absence of emotional involvement: *She tried to ignore her emotions and keep a detached view of the problem.*

dig·ni·fied (dĭg′ nə fīd′) *adj.* Worthy of esteem or respect: *The volunteers helped clean the park in a dignified and polite manner.*

dis·close (dĭs klōz′) *v.* To make known (something previously kept secret): *The child promised not to disclose where the gifts were hidden.*

dis·tinct (dĭ stĭngkt′) *adj.* Different from all others; separate: *Everybody in the talent show had a distinct talent.*

dis·tin·guish (dĭ stĭng′gwĭsh) *v.* To recognize as being different; tell apart: *Counting their legs is one way to distinguish spiders from ants.*

di·vine (dĭ vīn′) *adj.* Of, from, or like God or a god; being in the worship or service of God: *Ancient civilizations often relied on divine advice to help them make decisions.*

dole·ful (dōl′ fəl) *adj.* Filled with or expressing grief; mournful: *The cat's doleful cry in the rain was pitiful.*

do·mes·tic (də mĕs′ tĭk) *adj.* Of or relating to the family or household: *Gathering in the living room to watch a movie together is one example of a domestic activity for families.*

dor·mant (dôr′ mənt) *adj.* **1.** In an inactive state in which growth and development stop for a time. **2.** Not active but capable of renewed activity: *When the wind stilled, the windmill sat dormant.*

du·ra·ble (do͝or′ ə bəl) *adj.* Capable of withstanding wear and tear; sturdy: *Denim is a durable fabric used for work clothes.*

E

ed·i·to·ri·al (ĕd′ ĭ tôr′ ē əl) *adj.* Of or relating to making (written material) ready for publication by correcting, revising, or marking directions for a printer: *The editorial department made numerous corrections to early drafts of the textbook.*

ă **rat** / ā **pay** / â **care** / ä **father** / ĕ **pet** / ē **be** / ĭ **pit** / ī **pie** / î **fierce** / ŏ **pot** / ō **go** / ô **paw, for** / oi **oil** / o͝o **book**

e·lab·o·rate (ĭ lăb´ə rĭt) *adj.* Having many details or parts: *The Great Wall of China was an* **elaborate** *building project.*

el·e·gant (ĕl´ĭ gənt) *adj.* Marked by or showing refinement, grace, and beauty in appearance or behavior: *The dancers moved in an* **elegant** *waltz across the stage.*

e·lu·sive (ĭ lōō´ sĭv) or (ĭ lōō´ zĭv) *adj.* **1.** Tending to escape: *The* **elusive** *wren kept flying away from our bird feeder.* **2.** Difficult to define or describe: *The idea seemed* **elusive** *when she tried to write it down on paper. It was hard for her to grasp.*

em·bod·y (ĕm bŏd´ ē) *v.* **1.** To give a bodily form to. **2.** To make part of a system or whole: *The team leaders* **embodied** *the spirit of teamwork.*

em·brace (ĕm brās´) *v.* To take up willingly or eagerly: *We knew that the mayor would* **embrace** *our idea to clean up the community center playground.*

e·merge (ĭ mûrj´) *v.* To come into existence, arise; to become known for or as: *Both women and men would* **emerge** *as strong voices for change during the civil rights era.*

em·ploy (ĕm plŏĭ´) *v.* To put to use or service: *In order to finish the project, the girl* **employed** *a strategy of working on it for one hour each night.*

em·u·late (ĕm´ yə lāt´) *v.* To strive to equal or excel, especially through imitation: *My mentor was an experienced pianist whose style I tried to* **emulate.**

en·gulf (ĕn gŭlf´) *v.* To swallow up or overwhelm by or as if by overflowing and enclosing: *The residents feared the floodwaters would* **engulf** *the land near the river.*

e·qua·tion (ĭ kwā´ zhən) *n.* A mathematical statement asserting that two expressions are equal: *The math teacher wrote several* **equations** *on the blackboard for the students to learn.*

e·quiv·a·lent (ĭ kwĭv´ ə lənt) *adj.* Equal, as in value, meaning, or force: *The wish of a king is* **equivalent** *to a command.*

e·rect (ĭ rĕkt´) *v.* To build; construct: *Six volunteers* **erected** *the heavy tent before we set up the rest of our camp.*

e·ven·tu·al (ĭ vĕn´ chōō əl) *adj.;* **eventually** *adv.* Occurring at an unspecified future time; at last: *He did not worry about his missing keys because he knew that he would find them* **eventually.**

ex·as·per·ate (ĭg zăs´ pə rāt´) *v.* To make angry or impatient; irritate greatly: *The dog's constant barking* **exasperated** *the neighbors.*

equation

ōō b**oo**t / ou **ou**t / ŭ c**u**t / û f**u**r / hw **wh**ich / th **th**in / th **th**is / zh vi**s**ion / ə **a**go, sil**e**nt, penc**i**l, lem**o**n, circ**u**s

flair

In the Middle Ages, the French used the word *flair* to mean "odor or scent." The modern English meaning of "showiness" or "a special aptitude" may come from a hound's special ability to track a scent.

frayed

ex·ca·vate (ĕk´ skə vāt´) *v.* **1.** To make a hole in; hollow out. **2.** To remove by digging or scooping out: *Luisa decided to* **excavate** *the soil in her backyard before beginning her garden.*

ex·hil·a·rate (ĭg zĭl´ ə rāt´) *v.* To cause to feel happy: *The young man felt a burst of* **exhilaration** *after helping to rebuild an abandoned house in his community.*

ex·panse (ĭk spăns´) *n.* A wide and open extent, as of surface, land, or sky: *Gazing out at the vast* **expanse** *of desert, the explorer wondered if he would be able to cross it.*

ex·plode (ĭk splōd´) *v.* To burst forth: *We* **exploded** *with shouts and laughter during the show.*

F

fal·ter (fôl´ tər) *v.* **1.** To lose confidence or purpose; hesitate: *As the work became more difficult, she knew her determination would* **falter**. **2.** To move haltingly: *I might* **falter** *on this slippery path.*

fa·nat·ic (fə năt´ ĭk) *n.* A person who is excessively or unreasonably devoted to a cause or belief: *The football* **fanatic** *covered his walls with posters of his favorite players.*

flair (flâr) *n.* Distinctive elegance or style: *The dancer had a certain* **flair** *that set her apart from everyone else.*

flare (flâr) *v.* To burn with a sudden or unsteady flame: *The candles* **flared** *briefly.*

forge (fôrj) *v.* To give form or shape to, especially by means of careful effort: *Common goals can be used to* **forge** *a new friendship.*

frag·ment (frăg´ mənt) *n.* A piece or part broken off from a whole: *I dropped the plate, and it shattered into* **fragments**.

frail (frāl) *adj.* Physically weak; not robust: *The* **frail** *child was at constant risk of getting injured.*

fray·ed (frād) *adj.* Worn away or tattered along the edges: *Because the cuffs of his jeans dragged on the ground as he walked, they quickly became worn and* **frayed**.

frig·id (frĭj´ ĭd) *adj.* Extremely cold: *The house was* **frigid** *because they never turned on the heat.*

frus·trate (frŭs´ trāt) *v.*; **frustration** *n.* **1.** To prevent from accomplishing something. **2.** To bring to nothing: *The long wait at the airport brought* **frustration** *to many of the travelers, who were anxious to get to their destinations.*

ă rat / ā pay / â care / ä father / ĕ pet / ē be / ĭ pit / ī pie / î fierce / ŏ pot / ō go / ô paw, for / oi oil / o͞o book

fun·da·men·tal (fŭn´ də měn´ təl) *adj.* Of, relating to, or forming a foundation; elemental; basic; primary: *A fundamental knowledge of mathematics should be part of every student´s education.*

fu·ry (fyoor´ ē) *n.* **1.** Violent anger; rage: *The batter threw his hat down in fury after striking out.* **2.** Violent and uncontrolled action: *The blizzard's fury caused roadways to be shut down to prevent car accidents.*

G

gen·u·ine·ly (jěn´ yoo ĭn lē) *adv.* Not falsely; truly or purely: *Oliver is not exaggerating; he genuinely believes every word of the book.*

gi·gan·tic (jī gǎn´ tĭk) *adj.* Being like a giant in size, strength, or power: *Some of the dinosaurs were gigantic creatures.*

gloat (glōt) *v.* To feel or express great, often spiteful pleasure: *Because she would gloat after each victory, the runner was disliked by her opponents.*

gnarled (närld) *adj.* Thick, twisted, and full of knots: *The orchard was full of gnarled old apple and peach trees.*

grim·ly (grĭm´ lē) *adv.* Unrelentingly; rigidly: *Despite his injury, the runner was grimly determined to finish the marathon.*

gut·tur·al (gŭt´ ə rəl) *adj.* Throaty; low; unpleasant: *The nervous watchdog let out a guttural sound.*

H

harsh (härsh) *adj.* **1.** Unpleasant; rough. **2.** Extremely severe: *The rainstorm´s harsh downpours and severe winds caused flooding in the city.*

haz·ard (hāz´ ərd) *n.* Something that may cause injury or harm: *A pile of oily rags can be a fire hazard.*

her·i·tage (hěr´ ĭ tĭj) *n.* Something passed down from preceding generations; a tradition: *Our country has a great heritage of folk music.*

hoard (hôrd) *v.* To save and store away, often secretly or greedily: *The townspeople accused the miser of hoarding all the firewood.*

hov·er (hŭv´ ər) *v.* To stay floating, suspended, or fluttering in the air: *The hummingbirds were hovering over the flowers in our backyard.*

I

im·mac·u·late·ly (ĭ măk´ yə lĭt lē) *adv.* In a way that is perfectly clean: *The operating room was cleaned immaculately between procedures.*

hover

---

oo b**oo**t / ou **ou**t / ŭ c**u**t / û f**u**r / hw **wh**ich / th **th**in / *th* **th**is / zh vi**si**on / ə **a**go, sil**e**nt, penc**i**l, lem**o**n, circ**u**s

im·pair (ĭm pâr´) v. To weaken in strength, quality, or quantity: *Fatigue **impaired** their judgment.*

im·pend (ĭm pĕnd´) v. To be about to occur: *Her retirement is **impending**, so she may not be with the company next year.*

im·plore (ĭm plôr´) v. **1.** To appeal to (a person) earnestly or anxiously. **2.** To plead or beg: *The kids **implored** their mother to buy them several new toys at the mall.*

im·pres·sive (ĭm prĕs´ ĭv) adj. Making a strong, lasting impression: *A cathedral is often a very **impressive** building.*

im·print (ĭm´ prĭnt) n. A marked influence or effect; an impression: *The Mayan **imprints** on the wall showed signs of early civilization.*

in·ac·ces·si·ble (ĭn ăk sĕs´ ə bəl) adj. Not accessible; unable to approach: *The toys on the shelf were **inaccessible** to the little girl because they were too high for her to reach.*

in·con·sol·a·ble (ĭn kən sō´ lə bəl) adj. Not able to be consoled or helped with grief, loss, or trouble: *The crying child with the broken toy seemed **inconsolable**.*

in·ex·plic·a·ble (ĭn ĕk splĭk´ ə bəl) adj. Not able to be explained: *The theft of jewelry from the locked safe remains **inexplicable** to this day.*

in·no·va·tion (ĭn´ ə vā´ shən) n. Something newly introduced: *Automatic transmission was a major **innovation** in automobiles.*

in·stinct (ĭn´ stĭngkt´) n. A natural talent or ability: *Parents usually have a natural **instinct** to protect their offspring.*

in·tense (ĭn tĕns´) adj. Existing in an extreme degree; very strong: *The wall was painted an **intense** blue; it overwhelmed every other color in the room.*

in·ten·tion (ĭn tĕn´ shən) n. An aim, purpose, or plan: *It is not my **intention** to fool you.*

in·tent·ly (ĭn tĕnt´ lē) adv. In a way that shows concentration or firm purpose: *The girl searched her room **intently**, determined to find the missing book.*

in·ter·act (ĭn´ tər ăkt´) v.; **interaction** n. To act on or affect each other: *Tennis is an example of an **interaction** between two or more people.*

in·trig·uing (ĭn trēg´ ĭng) adj. Catching the interest or arousing the curiosity of: *The witnesses' comments about a flashing light were **intriguing**.*

J

jeop·ard·y (jĕp´ ər dē) n. Risk of loss or injury; danger: *He would be in **jeopardy** of getting hurt if he didn't wear his helmet while riding his bike.*

ă rat / ā pay / â care / ä father / ĕ pet / ē be / ĭ pit / ī pie / î fierce / ŏ pot / ō go / ô paw, for / oi oil / o͞o book

jos•tle (jŏs´ əl) *v.* To push and come into rough contact with while moving; bump: *The couple was* **jostled** *as they attempted to move across the crowded dance floor.*

L

lab•y•rinth (lăb´ ə rĭnth´) *n.* **1.** A maze. **2.** Something complicated or confusing in design or construction: *The inside of the cave was built to look like a* **labyrinth** *of secret pathways.*

le•git•i•mate (lə jĭt´ ə mĭt) *adj.* Having rights or being legal under the law: *The ring proved that the prince was the* **legitimate** *heir to the throne.*

like•li•hood (līk´ lē hŏŏd´) *n.* The chance of a thing happening; probability: *The* **likelihood** *of snow is very remote in July.*

lin•ger (lĭng´ gər) *v.* To be slow in leaving: *The children* **lingered** *in the toy shop until closing.*

lit•er•al•ly (lĭt´ ər ə lē) *adv.* Really; actually: **Literally** *millions of lives were saved by the vaccine.*

lit•er•ar•y (lĭt´ ər ĕr´ ē) *adj.* Of or relating to writers or the writing profession: *The* **literary** *magazine published short stories, poems, and book reviews.*

loom (lōōm) *v.* To come into view, often with a threatening appearance: *We turn a corner and, suddenly, the dark castle* **looms** *before us.*

lore (lôr) *n.* The accumulated facts, traditions, or beliefs about something: *Achilles is a famous godlike warrior in Greek* **lore.**

lu•nar (lōō´ nər) *adj.* Of or relating to the moon: *The* **lunar** *mission was designed to send people to the moon.*

lurch (lûrch) *v.* To move suddenly and unsteadily; stagger: *The bumper cars* **lurched** *forward at the amusement park, steered by excited drivers of all ages.*

lush (lŭsh) *adj.* Having or covered in thick plant growth: *The homeowner worked hard to maintain a* **lush** *green lawn.*

lus•trous (lŭs´ trəs) *adj.* Having luster; shining; gleaming: *Nancy wore a* **lustrous** *gown to her aunt's wedding.*

lux•ur•i•ous (lŭg zhŏŏr´ ē əs) or (lŭk shŏŏr´ ē əs) *adj.* **1.** Fond of luxury. **2.** Costly; extravagant: *The* **luxurious** *apartment building she lived in offered an outdoor swimming pool, a garage, and a tennis court.*

jostle
This word comes from the word *joust*, a sport that was popular in medieval times. In these contests, each mounted knight attempted to knock his opponent off of his horse using a weapon such as a lance.

lush

ōō b**oo**t / ou **ou**t / ŭ c**u**t / û f**u**r / hw **wh**ich / th **th**in / *th* **th**is / zh vi**s**ion / ə **a**go, sil**e**nt, penc**i**l, lem**o**n, circ**u**s

G11

M

ma·jes·tic (mə **jĕs´** tĭk) *adj.* Having or showing majesty: *The king and queen lived in a* **majestic** *palace surrounded by waterfalls and trees.*

man·u·script (**măn´** yə skrĭpt´) *n.* The form of a book, paper, or article as it is submitted for publication in print: *The author sent the* **manuscript** *to the publisher after completing it.*

mas·sive (**măs´** ĭv) *adj.* **1.** Bulky, heavy, and solid. **2.** Unusually large or impressive: *The sea animals at the aquarium are housed in* **massive** *tanks that give them enough room to move around.*

maze (māz) *n.* A complicated and often confusing network of pathways: *The mouse worked his way through the* **maze** *to get to the piece of cheese at the finish.*

mea·ger (**mē´** gər) *adj.* Lacking in quantity or richness; very little: *There was only a* **meager** *amount of popcorn left at the theater, so some people were not able to buy any for the movie.*

men·tor (**mĕn´** tôr) *n.* A wise and trusted advisor: *Katherine serves as a* **mentor** *to a number of the younger students in her school.*

mi·rac·u·lous (mĭ **răk´** yə ləs) *adj.* Having the nature of a person, thing, or event that causes great admiration, awe, or wonder: *In one* **miraculous** *year, Albert Einstein revolutionized the way we think about physics.*

miss·ion (**mĭsh´** ən) *n.* A group of people sent to carry out an assignment: *My parents joined an international rescue* **mission.**

mo·tion (**mō´** shən) *v.* To signal or direct by a motion, such as a wave of the hand: *The police officer* **motioned** *to the driver to proceed.*

mo·tive (**mō´** tĭv) *n.* An emotion or need that causes a person to act in a certain way: *Our* **motive** *in writing the book was to make people aware of the issue.*

mute (myo͞ot) *v.* To muffle or soften the sound of: *The additional insulation* **muted** *the sound of the people living next door.*

myth·i·cal (**mĭth´** ĭ kəl) *adj.* **1.** Of or existing only in myths. **2.** Imaginary: *The new science fiction movie takes place in a* **mythical** *town.*

maze

N

ne·go·ti·a·tion (nĭ **gō´** shē ā´ shən) *n.* A discussion with another in order to reach an agreement: *The renters and the landlord began* **negotiations** *over a new contract.*

ă rat / ā **p**ay / â **c**are / ä **f**ather / ĕ **p**et / ē **b**e / ĭ **p**it / ī **p**ie / î **fie**rce / ŏ **p**ot / ō **g**o / ô **p**aw, **fo**r / oi **oi**l / o͞o **b**ook

O

ob•serve (əb zŭrv´) *v.* To see and pay attention to; watch: *Did you* **observe** *that bird's behavior on the ledge?*

oc•cu•py (ŏk´ yə pī´) *v.* To seize possession of and maintain control over by force: *The soldiers patrolled the streets day and night, observing and* **occupying** *the land they had seized.*

op•tion (ŏp´ shən) *n.* The act of choosing; choice: *The flight attendant offered each passenger the* **option** *of chicken or beef.*

op•u•lent (ŏp´ yə lənt) *adj.* **1.** Having or showing great wealth; rich. **2.** Abundant; plentiful: *The queen's* **opulent** *outfits always included jewelry, fancy hats, and expensive shoes.*

or•a•cle (ôr´ ə kəl) *n.* A shrine in ancient Greece for the worship and consultation of a god who revealed knowledge or revealed the future: *In ancient civilization, people depended on* **oracles** *to tell about the future.*

or•nate•ly (ôr nāt´ lē) *adv.* Elaborately or excessively decorated: *The last float in the parade was an* **ornately** *painted pirate ship.*

out•ly•ing (ŏut´ lī´ ĭng) *adj.* Lying outside the limits or boundaries of a certain area: *Kent visits his grandfather, who lives in an* **outlying** *suburb several miles from the city.*

P

pain•stak•ing (pān´stā kĭng) *adj.* Taking pains; showing great care and effort: *Stitching the fifty stars onto the flag was a* **painstaking** *task.*

par•al•lel (păr´ ə lĕl´) *adj.* Matching feature for feature; corresponding: *The two companies are similar and have* **parallel** *business plans.*

par•tic•i•pant (pär tĭs´ ə pənt) *n.* A person who joins with others in doing something or taking part: *All of the* **participants** *in the card game received ten cards from the deck.*

per•il•ous (pĕr´ ə ləs) *adj.* Full of danger; hazardous: *The spy was sent off on a perilous mission, during which her life would be in grave danger.*

per•me•ate (pûr´ mē āt´) *v.* To spread or flow throughout: *The smell of baking cookies* **permeated** *the house.*

phe•nom•e•nal (fĭ nŏm´ ə nəl) *adj.* Extraordinary; outstanding: *Jon has a* **phenomenal** *memory and remembers almost everything he has read.*

---

 o͞o b**oo**t / ou **ou**t / ŭ c**u**t / û f**u**r / hw **wh**ich / th **th**in / *th* **th**is / zh vi**s**ion / ə **a**go, sil**e**nt, penc**i**l, lem**o**n, circ**u**s

pho•ny (**fō´** nē) *adj.* Not genuine; fake: *This is a **phony** diamond!*

poise (poĭz) *v.* To balance or hold in equilibrium: *The statue was poised on the pedestal.*

pon•der (**pŏn´** dər) *v.* To think about carefully; consider: *I **pondered** the meaning of my dream.*

pre•cede (prĭ **sēd´**) *v.* To come, exist, or occur before in time, order, position, or rank: *The host´s introduction will **precede** the awards ceremony.*

pre•dom•i•nant (prĭ **dŏm´** ə nənt) *adj.* Greater than all others in strength, authority, or importance; dominant: *The team is **predominantly** made up of players from Guilford; there are only two players from other towns.*

pres•sure (**prĕsh´** ər) *v.* To force, as by influencing or persuading: *The lineman broke through, **pressuring** the quarterback and forcing him to throw the ball away.*

pre•sum•a•bly (prĭ **zōō´** mə blē) *adv.* In a way that can be taken for granted; by reasonable assumption: ***Presumably,** he missed the train since we did not see him on the platform.*

prime (prīm) *v.* To make ready; prepare: *She described the questions he might be asked in order to **prime** the celebrity for the interview.*

prin•ci•ple (**prĭn´** sə pəl) *n.* A statement or set of statements describing natural phenomena or mechanical processes: *Scientific **principles** help us understand how the world works.*

pro•claim (prə **klām´**) *v.* To announce publicly; declare: *The mayor **proclaimed** a holiday.*

pro•sper•i•ty (prŏ **spĕr´** ĭ tē) *n.* The condition of being successful, especially in money matters: *When the weather is good and soil conditions are right, farmers can enjoy times of great **prosperity.***

pub•lish•ing (**pŭb´** lĭsh ĭng) *adj.* Related to preparing and issuing something, such as a book, for public distribution, or sale: *The **publishing** company produced novels, textbooks, and notebooks.*

pur•suit (pər **sōōt´**) *n.* The act or an instance of pursuing or chasing: *The cat ran quickly in **pursuit** of the mouse that fled.*

R

ran•dom (**răn´** dəm) *adj.* Having no specific pattern, purpose, or objective: *Although the numbers appeared to be **random,** there was a hidden pattern to them.*

rash (răsh) *adj.* Too bold or hasty; reckless: *The driver made a **rash** decision to run the red traffic light.*

pressure
The word root *press-* in English words and the English word *press* itself come from the past participle *pressus* of the Latin verb *premere*, "to squeeze, press." Thus, we have the noun *pressure* from the Latin noun meaning "a squeezing, as of the juice from grapes or of the oil from olives." We also have the verbs *compress*, "to squeeze together"; *depress*, "to squeeze down"; *express*, "to extract by pressure, expel, force"; and *impress*, "to press on or against, drive in, imprint."

ă rat / ā pay / â care / ä father / ĕ pet / ē be / ĭ pit / ī pie / î fierce / ŏ pot / ō go / ô paw, for / oi oil / ŏŏ book

rau•cous (rô′ kəs) *adj.* Wild; disorderly: *The* **raucous** *crowd made everyone on the stage feel nervous.*

re•cep•tion (rĭ sĕp′ shən) *n.* **1.** A social gathering, especially one honoring or introducing someone: *The wedding* **reception** *took place in the hotel's ballroom.* **2.** A welcome, greeting, or acceptance: *The newcomer was given a friendly* **reception.**

rec•re•a•tion (rĕk′ rē ā′ shən) *n.*; **recreational** *adj.* Refreshment of one's mind or body after work through some activity: *Reading a book is a great* **recreational** *activity.*

rel•ish (rĕl′ ĭsh) *v.* To take pleasure in; enjoy: *As Andrea happily arose from bed, she was* **relishing** *the idea of going to the beach at dawn.*

re•luc•tant (rĭ lŭk′ tənt) *adj.* Unwilling; averse: *Because they were having such a good time, the couple was* **reluctant** *to leave the party.*

re•pet•i•tive (rĭ pĕt′ ət ĭv) *adj.* Characterized by saying or stating again: *The speaker then listed the same, tiresome complaints in a* **repetitive** *and boring manner.*

rep•li•ca (rĕp′ lĭ kə) *n.* **1.** A copy or reproduction of a work of art, especially one made by an original artist. **2.** A copy or reproduction, especially one smaller than the original: *Sean's toy airplanes are* **replicas** *of real airplanes.*

re•serve (rĭ zûrv′) *adj.* Kept back or saved for future use or a special purpose: *The family kept a* **reserve** *supply of food in case of emergencies.*

re•tain (rĭ tān′) *v.* To keep possession of; continue to have: *The new premier* **retains** *his post as minister of finance.*

re•tort (rĭ tôrt′) *v.* To reply; to answer back sharply: *After hearing about the theft, the accused man* **retorted** *that he knew nothing about it.*

re•vi•sion (rĭ vĭzh′ ən) *n.* Changes or modifications made after reconsidering: *After the* **revisions** *had been made, the story was much more enjoyable to read.*

rig•id (rĭj′ ĭd) *adj.* Not changing shape or bending; stiff; inflexible: *The* **rigid** *iron frame provided the building with a solid structure.*

ru•di•men•ta•ry (roo′ də mĕn′ tə rē) *adj.* Of or relating to the basic principles or facts; elementary: *Before taking the class, he had only a* **rudimentary** *knowledge of economics.*

replica

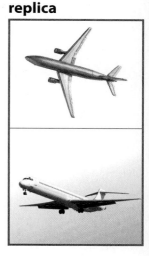

---

oo b**oo**t / ou **ou**t / ŭ c**u**t / û f**u**r / hw **wh**ich / th **th**in / *th* **th**is / zh vi**si**on / ə **a**go, sil**e**nt, penc**i**l, lem**o**n, circ**u**s

ruth•less (rōoth´ lĭs) *adj.*
Showing no pity; cruel: *The
robbers were* **ruthless.**

S

sac•ri•fice (săk´ rə fis´) *v.* To
give up one thing for another
considered to be of greater value:
The brave soldier **sacrificed** *his
own life to save his comrades.*

sa•ga (sä´ gə) *n.* **1.** A long
adventure story written during
the Middle Ages that deals with
historical or legendary heroes,
families, deeds, and events. **2.**
A modern story that resembles a
saga: *Troy's comic book series is
a fictional* **saga** *about war in the
seventeenth century.*

sal•vage (săl´ vĭj) *v.* To save
endangered property from loss:
The brothers hoped to **salvage**
*their parents' old home because
they did not want it to be torn
down.* — *n.* Goods or property
saved from destruction.

sa•vor (sā´ vər) *v.* To taste or
smell, especially with pleasure:
The hungry family planned to
savor *each morsel of the feast.*

scholastic

scho•las•tic (skə lăs´ tĭk) *adj.*
Of or relating to schools or
education; academic: *The student
was very proud of her* **scholastic**
*achievement and studied hard in
order to maintain it.*

scorn•ful (skôrn´ fəl) *adj.*;
scornfully *adv.* Full of or
expressing scorn or contempt:
*In a serious competition, people
often speak* **scornfully** *about
their opponents to challenge them
or express their dislike.*

scrounge (skrŏŭnj) *v.* To obtain
by rummaging or searching: *She
was running late for school so
she* **scrounged** *together an outfit
as quickly as she could.*

sen•sor (sĕn´ sər) or (sĕn´ sôr)
n. A device that responds to a
particular type of change in its
condition or environment: *The*
sensors *in the porch lamp cause
the lamp to light up every time
someone steps onto the porch.*

show•down (shō´ doun) *n.* An
event, especially a confrontation,
that forces an issue to a
conclusion: *Superman readied
himself for the* **showdown** *with
his archenemy, Lex Luthor.*

shriv•eled (shrĭv´ əld) *adj.*
Shrunken or wrinkled: *Because
they did not receive water, the
plants in the desert became*
shriveled *and died.*

skep•ti•cal (skĕp´ tĭ kəl) *adj.* Of,
relating to, or characterized by a
doubting or questioning attitude:
*As she listened to her friend's
tall tale, a* **skeptical** *expression
formed on her face.*

smol•der (smōl´ dər) *v.* To
burn slowly with smoke and no
flame: *An underground fire might*
smolder *for days before erupting.*

ă rat / ā **pay** / â **care** / ä **father** / ĕ **pet** / ē **be** / ĭ **pit** / ī **pie** / î **fierce** / ŏ **pot** / ō **go** /
ô **paw, for** / oi **oil** / ŏŏ **book**

som•ber (sŏm′ bər) *adj.* Dark; gloomy: *The heavy thunderstorm made the neighborhood look gray and* **somber.**

so•phis•ti•cat•ed (sə fis′ tĭ kā′ tĭd) *adj.* Elaborate, complex, or complicated: *The highly* **sophisticated** *technology was understood by only a few people in the world.*

sparse•ly (spärs′ lē) *adv.* In a way that is not dense or crowded: *The* **sparsely** *vegetated tundra of the Arctic has few plants.*

spec•i•men (spĕs′ ə mən) *n.* A sample, as of blood, tissue, or urine, used for analysis: *The doctor collected* **specimens** *of blood from each of the subjects in the research study.*

spite•ful (spīt′ fəl) *adj.* Filled with, caused by, or showing spite; cruel: *The best friends were sorry that they had shared* **spiteful** *words with each other during an argument.*

sta•ble (stā′ bəl) *adj.* **1.** Not likely to change, change position, or change condition; firm: *Our house has a* **stable** *foundation.* **2.** Not likely to be affected or overthrown: *After years of civil war, the country was finally able to establish a* **stable** *government.* **3.** Firm or steady, as in purpose or character: *His friends knew they could always rely on him because he was so* **stable.** **4.** Mentally or emotionally sound; sane or rational: *Because of the professor's erratic behavior,* *some of his students wondered if he was* **stable.** **5.** Not known to decay; existing for an indefinitely long time, as an atomic particle: *Plutonium is not a* **stable** *element, and the energy from its decay can be used in nuclear reactors.*

stead•fast (stĕd′ făst′) *adj.* **1.** Not moving; fixed; steady. **2.** Firmly loyal or constant; faithful: *The runner stayed* **steadfast** *in his effort to win the race.*

sti•fling (stī′ flĭng) *adj.* Smothering; lacking oxygen: *When the logs in the fireplace started roaring, the living room became* **stifling.**

stim•u•lus (stĭm′ yə ləs) *n.* Something causing or regarded as causing a response: *Many hope the road repairs will be a* **stimulus** *to the state's economy.*

stri•dent (strīd′ ənt) *adj.* Loud; harsh: *In the locker room, the coach talked to his players in a firm,* **strident** *tone to show that he was upset with the way they had played.*

sub•ject (səb jĕkt′) *v.* To cause to undergo: *The workers were* **subjected** *to the harsh rules of the workplace.*

sub•mit (səb mĭt′) *v.* To put forward for someone else's consideration, judgment, or approval: *I* **submitted** *my outline to the teacher.*

sparsely

stable
Stable comes from an old French word related to the Latin word meaning "to stand." Something that is stable stands firm.

ōō b**oo**t / ou **ou**t / ŭ c**u**t / û f**u**r / hw **wh**ich / th **th**in / *th* **th**is / zh vi**si**on / ə **a**go, sil**e**nt, penc**i**l, lem**o**n, circ**u**s

sub•side (səb **sīd´**) *v.* To become less agitated or active: *The shouting between the two teams* **subsided** *when they came to an agreement over when to use the soccer field.*

sup•ple (**sŭp´** əl) *adj.* Easily bent or folded: *The wallet was made of* **supple** *leather, so it opened and closed easily.*

sup•por•tive (sə **pôrt´** ĭv) *adj.* Giving support, sympathy, or encouragement: *My friends were* **supportive** *when I told them about my goals for this year.*

swiv•el (**swĭv´** əl) *v.* To turn or rotate on or as if on a pivot: *The child* **swiveled** *on his stool while sitting at the counter.*

swivel

T

taut (tôt) *adj.* Pulled or drawn tight: *The sails were* **taut** *with wind as the ship entered the harbor.*

teem (tēm) *v.* To be full of things; swarm or abound: *The pond water was* **teeming** *with microbes.*

tem•per•a•ment (**tĕm´** prə mənt) or (**tĕm´** pər ə mənt) *n.* The manner of thinking, behaving, or reacting in a way that is characteristic of a specific person: *The two best friends share different* **temperaments** *simply because they are different people.*

ten•den•cy (**tĕn´** dən sē) *n.* A characteristic likelihood: *Linen has a* **tendency** *to wrinkle.*

ten•sion (**tĕn´** shən) *n.* Unfriendliness or hostility between persons or groups: *The* **tension** *in the room kept building until finally an argument erupted.*

tor•rent (**tôr´** ənt) *n.* A swift flowing stream: *Every spring, the* **torrent** *flows down the mountain as the snow melts.*

trans•mis•sion (trăns **mĭsh´** ən) *n.* Something, such as a message, that is sent from one person, place, or thing to another: *The codebreaker deciphered each of the* **transmissions** *as it was intercepted.*

tre•mor (**trĕm´** ər) *n.* A shaking or vibrating movement, as of the earth: *The volcano's explosion could be felt through the* **tremors** *in the ground.*

tu•mult (**tōō´** mŭlt´) *n.* A disorderly commotion or disturbance: *The fire in the theater created a* **tumult** *as everyone scrambled to get outside as quickly as possible.*

U

ul•ti•mate (**ŭl´** tə mĭt) *adj.* The greatest extreme; the maximum: *The new camera model has more features than others, which makes it an* **ultimate** *leader in picture technology.*

ă rat / ā pay / â care / ä father / ĕ pet / ē be / ĭ pit / ī pie / î fierce / ŏ pot / ō go / ô paw, for / oi oil / ōō book

un·af·fect·ed (ŭn´ ə fĕk´ tĭd) *adj.* Not changed, modified, or affected: *The dinner party went as planned. It was* **unaffected** *by the people who showed up late.*

un·can·ny (ŭn kăn´ ē) *adj.* Arousing wonder and fear, as if supernatural: *The computer-generated characters in the fantasy film had* **uncanny** *personalities that matched their supernatural abilities.*

un·der·state·ment (ŭn´ dər stāt´ mənt) *n.* Lack of emphasis in expression, especially for rhetorical effect: *He often uses* **understatement**, *as in saying "not bad" to mean "very good."*

un·du·late (ŭn´ jə lāt´) *v.* To move in waves or with a smooth, wavy motion: *The fields of wheat were* **undulating** *in the breeze.*

un·earth (ŭn ûrth´) *v.* **1.** To bring up out of the earth; dig up. **2.** To bring to public notice; uncover: *Research scientists* **unearthed** *Mayan artifacts.*

un·pre·dict·a·bil·i·ty (ŭn´ prĭ dĭk´ tə bĭl´ ĭ tē) *n.* The quality of being difficult to foretell or foresee: *Forming a plan to defend this team is difficult due to its* **unpredictability.**

un·ra·vel (ŭn răv´ əl) *v.* **1.** To be separated, as thread: *The kite string* **unravels** *as the kite flies away.* **2.** To separate, as a problem or mystery: *Every day the author* **unravels** *a new clue in his detective novel.*

un·re·lent·ing (ŭn´ rĭ lĕnt´ ĭng) *adj.* Not softening or yielding; not letting up: *The hurricane's winds pounded the walls with* **unrelenting** *force.*

ur·gent (ûr´ jənt) *adj.* Calling for immediate action or attention; pressing: *The* **urgent** *situation demanded immediate action.*

V

veer (vîr) *v.* To turn aside from a course, direction, or purpose; swerve: *The plane* **veered** *east to avoid the oncoming storm.*

ven·ture (vĕn´ chər) *v.* To brave the dangers of: *The sailor was brave enough to* **venture** *the high seas in a light boat.*

ver·ti·cal (vûr´ tĭ kəl) *adj.* Being or situated at right angles to the horizon; upright: *Most apartment buildings in New York City are tall and* **vertical**, *built this way to accommodate the many people who live there.*

void (void) *n.* An empty space; a vacuum: *The shuttle raced through the* **void** *of outer space.*

W

war·y (wâr´ ē) *adj.*; **warily** *adv.* On guard; watchful: *The lifeguard stood near the pool, looking* **warily** *at the swimmers to make sure they stayed safe in the water.*

understatement

The prefix *under-* has essentially the same meaning as the preposition *under.* For example, in words such as *underbelly, undercurrent, underlie,* and *undershirt, under-* denotes a position beneath or below. *Under-* also frequently conveys incompleteness or falling below a certain standard. Some examples are *undercharge, underdeveloped, underestimate,* and *underfeed.* Note that in this sense, words beginning with *under-* often have counterparts beginning with *over-: overcharge, overestimate, overstate.*

ōō b**oo**t / ou **ou**t / ŭ c**u**t / û f**u**r / hw **wh**ich / th **th**in / *th* **th**is / zh vi**si**on / ə **a**go, sil**e**nt, penc**i**l, lem**o**n, circ**u**s

wel•fare (wĕl´fâr´) *n.* Health, happiness, and good fortune; well-being: *The government should promote the general* **welfare.**

wry (rī) *adj.* **1.** Twisted in an expression of displeasure or regret: *Tom shook his head with a* **wry** *half-smile when his dog dropped the torn newspaper in his lap.* **2.** Funny in an understated or ironic way; dry: *Because she had a* **wry** *sense of humor, it took her friends a few moments to realize she was joking.*

zany

Z

zan•y (zā´nē) *adj.* Comical in an absurd or ridiculous way; like a clown: *My aunt's* **zany** *antics made everyone at the party laugh.*

ă **r**a**t** / ā **pay** / â **c**a**re** / ä **f**a**ther** / ĕ **p**e**t** / ē **be** / ĭ **p**i**t** / ī **pie** / î **fie**rce / ŏ **p**o**t** / ō g**o** / ô **p**a**w, fo**r / oi **oil** / ŏŏ b**oo**k

Acknowledgments

"The ACES Phone" by Jeanne DuPrau. Text copyright © 2005 by Jeanne DuPrau. Reprinted by permission of the author.

Airborn by Kenneth Oppel. Text copyright © 2004 by Kenneth Oppel. All rights reserved. Reprinted by permission of HarperCollins Publishers and the author.

All Alone in the Universe by Lynne Rae Perkins. Text and illustrations copyright © 1999 by Lynne Rae Perkins. Reprinted by permission of HarperCollins Publishers.

Adapted from *Any Small Goodness: A Novel of the Barrio* by Tony Johnston. Text copyright © 2001 by Roger D. Johnston and Susan T. Johnston as Trustees of the Johnston Family Trust. All rights reserved. Reprinted by permission of Blue Sky Press/Scholastic, Inc.

Bodies from the Ash: Life and Death in Ancient Pompeii by James M. Deem. Text copyright © 2005 by James M. Deem. All rights reserved. Reprinted by permission of Houghton Mifflin Harcourt Publishing Company.

The Boy Who Saved Baseball by John Ritter. Copyright © 2003 by John H. Ritter. Reprinted by permission of Philomel Books, a division of Penguin Young Readers Group, a member of Penguin Group (USA) Inc., 345 Hudson Street, New York, NY 10014, and Curtis Brown, Ltd. All rights reserved.

Children of the Midnight Sun: Young Native Voices of Alaska by Tricia Brown, photography by Roy Corral. Text copyright © 1998 by Tricia Brown. Photographs copyright © 1998 by Roy Corral. Reprinted by permission of Alaska Northwest Books, an imprint of Graphic Arts Center Publishing Company.

"Do Knot Enter" from *Math Trek: Adventures in the Math Zone* by Ivars Peterson and Nancy Henderson. Copyright © 2000 by Ivars Peterson and Nancy Henderson. Reprinted by permission of John Wiley & Sons, Inc.

The Emperor's Silent Army: Terracotta Warriors of Ancient China by Jane O'Connor. Copyright © 2002 by Jane O'Connor. Reprinted by permission of Viking Penguin, A Division of Penguin Young Readers Group, a Member of Penguin Group (USA) Inc., 345 Hudson Street, New York, NY 10014. All rights reserved.

"Eleven" from *Woman Hollering Creek* by Sandra Cisneros. Text copyright © 1991 by Sandra Cisneros. Published by Vintage Books, a division of Random House, Inc., and originally in hardcover by Random House, Inc. Reprinted by permission by Susan Bergholz Literary Services, New York, NY and Lamy, NM. All rights reserved.

First to Fly: How Wilbur and Orville Wright Invented the Airplane by Peter Busby, paintings by David Craig. Text, design, and compilation copyright © 2002 by Madison Press Books. Paintings copyright © 2002 by David Craig. Reprinted by permission of Madison Press Books. Cover illustartion from *Freedom Walkers: The Story of the Montgomery Bus Boycott* by Russell Freedman. Reprinted by permission of Holiday House.

Excerpt from *The Great Fire* by Jim Murphy. Copyright © 1995 by Jim Murphy. Reprinted by permission of Scholastic Inc. SCHOLASTIC'S Material shall not be published, retransmitted, broadcast, downloaded, modified or adapted (rewritten), manipulated, reproduced or otherwise distributed and/or exploited in anyway without the prior written authorization of Scholastic Inc.

Excerpt from *Harriet Tubman: Conductor of the Underground Railroad"* by Ann Petry. Copyright © 1955 by Ann Petry, renewed 1983. Reprinted by the permission of Russell & Volkening as agents for the author.

The Hero and the Minotaur by Robert Byrd. Copyright © 2005 by Robert Byrd. Reprinted by permission of Dutton Children's Books, a Division of Penguin Young Readers Group, a Member of Penguin Group (USA) Inc., 345 Hudson Street, New York, NY 10014. All rights reserved.

"I, Too" from *The Dream Keeper and Other Poems* by Langston Hughes. Text copyright © 1994 by the Estate of Langston Hughes. Reprinted by permission of Alfred A. Knopf, a division of Random House, Inc. and Harold Ober Associates Incorporated.

Kensuke's Kingdom by Michael Morpurgo. Copyright © 1999 by Michael Morpurgo. Reprinted by permission of Scholastic, Inc. and Adams Literary.

Knots in My Yo-yo String by Jerry Spinelli. Copyright © 1998 by Jerry Spinelli. Cover photograph copyright © 1998 by Penny Gentieu. Map copyright © 1998 by Jenny Pavlovitz. Reprinted by permission of Alfred A. Knopf, a division of Random House Children's Books, a division of Random House, Inc.

"Lesson in Fire" by Linda Noel from *The Dirt is Red Here: Art and Poetry from Native California*, edited by Margaret Dubin. Text copyright © 2002 by Linda Noel. Reprinted by permission of Linda Noel.

"A Mighty Fine Fella" from *Nathaniel Talking* by Eloise Greenfield. Text copyright © 1988 by Eloise Greenfield. Reprinted by permission of the author.

"The Myers Family" from *Pass It Down: Five Picture-Book Families Make Their Mark*. Copyright © 2007 by Leonard S. Marcus. All rights reserved. Reprinted by permission of Walker & Company and Sterling Lord Literistic, Inc.

Number the Stars by Lois Lowry. Copyright © 1989 by Lois Lowry. Reprinted by permission of Houghton Mifflin Harcourt Publishing Company.

Onward: A Photobiography of African-American Explorer Matthew Henson by Dolores Johnson. Copyright © 2006 National Geographic Society. All rights reserved. Reprinted by permission of the National Geographic Society.

"The Princess Who Became a King" from *African Princess: The Amazing Lives of Africa's Royal Women* by Joyce Hansen. Text copyright © 2004 by Joyce Hansen. Painting copyright © 2004 by Laurie McGaw. Reprinted by permission of Hyperion Books for Children.

"Quitter" from *A Suitcase of Seaweed and Other Poems* by Janet S. Wong. Copyright © 1996 by Janet S. Wong. Reprinted by permission of Margaret K. McElderry Books, an imprint of Simon & Schuster Children's Publishing Division, and the author.

The Real Vikings: Craftsmen, Traders, and Fearsome Raiders by Melvin Berger and Gilda Berger. Copyright © 2003 by Melvin Berger. Reprinted by permission of The National Geographic Society.

Robotics by Helena Domaine. Copyright © 2006 by Helena Domaine. All rights reserved. Reprinted by permission of Lerner Publications Company, a division of Lerner Publishing Group, Inc.

"Science Friction" by David Lubar from *Tripping Over the Lunch Lady and Other Stories* edited by Nancy Mercado. Copyright © 2004 by David Lubar. Reprinted by permission of Dial Books for Young Readers, a Division of Penguin Young Readers Group, a Member of Penguin Group (USA) Inc., 345 Hudson Street, New York, NY 10014. All rights reserved.

Credits

Photo Credits

Placement Key: (r) right, (l) left, (c) center, (t) top, (b) bottom, (bg) background

Illustration